Clinical
Supervision

Clinical Supervision

A COMPETENCY-BASED APPROACH

Carol A. Falender and Edward P. Shafranske

American Psychological Association
Washington, DC

First printing April 2004
Second printing January 2005
Third printing January 2006
Fourth printing June 2006
Fifth printing April 2007
Sixth printing April 2008
Seventh printing February 2009

Published by
American Psychological Association
750 First Street, NE
Washington, DC 20002
www.apa.org

To order
APA Order Department
P.O. Box 92984
Washington, DC 20090-2984
Tel: (800) 374-2721
Direct: (202) 336-5510
Fax: (202) 336-5502
TDD/TTY: (202) 336-6123
Online: www.apa.org/books/
E-mail: order@apa.org

In the U.K., Europe, Africa, and the Middle East, copies may be ordered from
American Psychological Association
3 Henrietta Street
Covent Garden, London
WC2E 8LU England

Typeset in Goudy by World Composition Services, Inc., Sterling, VA

Printer: Edwards Brothers, Inc., Ann Arbor, MI
Cover Designer: Naylor Design, Washington, DC
Technical/Production Editor: Dan Brachtesende

The opinions and statements published are the responsibility of the authors, and such opinions and statements do not necessarily represent the policies of the American Psychological Association.

Library of Congress Cataloging-in-Publication Data

Falender, Carol A.
    Clinical supervision : a competency-based approach / Carol A. Falender and Edward P. Shafranske.—1st ed.
        p. cm.
    Includes bibliographical references and index.
    ISBN 1-59147-119-2
    1. Clinical psychologists—Supervision of.   I. Shafranske, Edward P.   II. Title.

RC467.7.F354 2004
362.2'0425'0683—dc22   2003023166

British Library Cataloguing-in-Publication Data
A CIP record is available from the British Library.

Printed in the United States of America

To our spouses and children, Martin Zohn and sons, David and Daniel,
and Kathy Shafranske and daughters, Kristen and Karen,
for their endless support and patience, and to the supervisors, students,
trainees, and interns who have challenged and inspired us.

CONTENTS

ACKNOWLEDGMENTS

We want to acknowledge and express our appreciation to the many professionals in the American Psychological Association (APA) Books Department who contributed to the development and production of this text. First, we want to thank Lansing Hays, our acquisitions editor, who provided encouragement throughout the early development of the manuscript. With his support, we were able to include many tools, which supervisors may use in the evaluation of the competencies discussed in the book. Development editors have the challenging task of collaborating with authors in refining and improving a manuscript. We are grateful to Ed Meidenbauer for his thoughtful review of the original manuscript and clearly stated recommendations, which brought improvement and never compromised the integrity of our work. We wish to also express our appreciation to the external and internal reviewers who provided useful feedback, which was incorporated into the text. We are grateful as well to Daniel Brachtesende, our production editor, who closely refined our prose and worked collaboratively with us in preparing the manuscript for publication. We also want to acknowledge the contributions of Anne Woodworth, who considered our recommendations regarding the design of the cover and to the other staff at APA Books who supported the publication of the book. We want to also acknowledge Gary VandenBos and Julia Frank-McNeil for their dedication and leadership. They have assembled a publishing team that supports the APA's mission by publishing thought-provoking books relevant in the professional practice of psychology. We also want to express our appreciation to the authors and publishers of the tools, exhibits, and figures contained in this book, which were published with their permission. Although too numerous to name personally, we want to acknowledge our colleagues, professors, supervisors, and supervisees who have influenced our development and in so many ways have contributed to the ideas put forth in this book.

Clinical
Supervision

1

THE PRACTICE OF CLINICAL SUPERVISION

Supervised practice is the cornerstone in the education and training of a psychologist (ASPPB Task Force on Supervision Guidelines, 1998; Russell & Petrie, 1994, p. 27). It provides the experiential foundation for the psychologist's knowledge, skills, and values to be consolidated and applied. As an integral facet of such experience, clinical supervision serves two essential and interrelated functions: to ensure the integrity of clinical services provided to the client and to develop competence in the supervisee. We define supervision as follows:

> Supervision is a distinct professional activity in which education and training aimed at developing science-informed practice are facilitated through a collaborative interpersonal process. It involves observation, evaluation, feedback, the facilitation of supervisee self-assessment, and the acquisition of knowledge and skills by instruction, modeling, and mutual problem solving. In addition, by building on the recognition of the strengths and talents of the supervisee, supervision encourages self-efficacy. Supervision ensures that clinical consultation is conducted in a competent manner in which ethical standards, legal prescriptions, and professional practices are used to promote and protect the welfare of the client, the profession, and society at large.

In our view, effective supervision builds on three interrelated pillars: the supervisory relationship, inquiry, and educational praxis. Each pillar

3

relies on and contributes to the others through a synergistic confluence, either enhancing or compromising the supervisory process. The supervisory relationship provides the foundation for the development of an alliance in which the individual and shared responsibilities in the supervision of clinical practice will be fulfilled. We suggest that the supervisory alliance is, to a great extent, the result of the nature and quality of the relationship that is formed between the supervisor and supervisee. Inquiry refers to all the processes that facilitate critical understanding of the therapeutic process as well as foster in the supervisee greater awareness of his or her professional and personal contributions to it. Educational praxis provides multiple learning strategies, including instruction, observation, and role playing, tailored to enhance the supervisee's knowledge and to develop his or her technical skills. These pillars represent the assemblage of a number of professional competencies as well interpersonal skills, personal strengths, and values.

Each pillar requires skillful attention to establish a supervisory process in which the highest quality care and welfare of clients are assured and clinical training objectives are met. These responsibilities are extremely important and can be fulfilled only with a foundation of competent supervisory practice. As a distinct professional activity, supervision incorporates many personal and professional competencies that require further articulation, understanding, and development through professional training.

This book presents a competency-based approach to supervision that emphasizes the use of science-informed theory and practice. Without minimizing the complexity of supervision or ignoring the present scientific standing of the field, we posit that the practice of supervision involves identifiable competencies, which can be learned and in turn promote the supervisee's clinical competence through the integration and application of specific knowledge, skills, attitudes, and values. Furthermore, we present four superordinate values that we believe to be integral to supervision and clinical practice: integrity-in-relationship, ethical values-based practice, appreciation of diversity, and science-informed practice. Finally, we advocate for an approach to supervision that recognizes the personal strengths supervisees bring to their education and clinical training and, drawing on principles derived from positive psychology, informs the learning process and leads to increased competence and self-efficacy.

In this chapter, we discuss competence and the intended outcomes of supervision. We then review the approaches to the practice of supervision and present an overview of the competency-based approach, including the four superordinate values that inform the process. We conclude with a discussion of the structure of the book.

COMPETENCE

On the basis of Epstein and Hundert (2002), we define competence to be "the habitual and judicious use of communication, knowledge, technical skills, clinical reasoning, emotions, values, and reflection in daily practice for the benefit of the individual and the community being served" (p. 226). Further, we consider competence to be the state of sufficiency relative to the specific performance or training requirements within the given setting in which such abilities are exercised. Competence therefore is not an absolute, nor does it involve a narrow set of professional behaviors; rather, competence reflects *sufficiency of a broad spectrum of personal and professional abilities relative to a given requirement.* Roe (2002) distinguished between input-model approaches to professional competency, which define the educational curricula necessary for one to become a psychologist, and the output-model approaches, or approaches that emphasize the particular roles and functions a psychologist should be able to perform. Although Kitchener (2000) concluded that "it may be easier to require psychologists [and trainees] to be competent than it is to define what competence means [and] competence is sometimes easier to identify in its absence than it is to specify what a proficient level of practical or scientific expertise involves" (pp. 154–155), we suggest that specific competencies can be identified, evaluated, and developed. From the output-model perspective, these competencies consist of unique assemblages of discrete clinical abilities that incorporate the specific knowledge, skills, values, emotions, etc., required to perform the specific professional activity (e.g., psychological assessment, family therapy, and cognitive-behavioral therapy). Because the competencies required involve distinct assemblages of abilities, they require supervision and training relating to the input model, which directs attention to the development of specific skills. As will be presented in the chapters that follow, supervision practices attuned to the unique constituents required to perform a specific clinical activity can be used to heighten awareness and to build competence.

In clinical training, the assessment of competence refers to the sufficiency or coincidence of an individual's abilities in relation to an externally defined training requirement. Although both the student and the licensed practitioner are duty bound to practice competently, the measure of competence for a graduate student is not the same as that for a licensed practitioner or for an expert. In competency-based supervision, explicit measurable standards of competence are established relative to the training requirements within a developmental trajectory. For example, the initial standard of competence in psychological assessment for a first-year graduate student might be established as the ability to administer a test in compliance with the instructions and to score the instrument accurately. Later in the training rotation, the definition of competence will be expanded to include the ability to interpret test scores in light of the research literature; later still, the production of a concise, well-written report will be the measure of competence. Through the use of this competency-based perspective, accurate assessments of performance can be obtained with a high degree of specificity and reliability. Rather than providing a global assessment of competence, formative and summative evaluations focus on the applications of specific knowledge, skills, and values, which lead to targeted development that will have been articulated in the training agreement or contract.

OUTCOMES OF SUPERVISION

In general terms, supervision monitors and ensures competency in client care and contributes to the education and training of a psychologist. The most important task of the supervisor is to monitor the supervisee's conduct to ensure that appropriate and ethical professional practices are implemented leading to the best possible clinical outcome for the client. Quality assurance is the primary ethical responsibility of the supervisor and supersedes educative, training, and evaluative functions. Supervision provides the structure and framework for learning how to apply knowledge, theory, and clinical procedures to solve human problems. Such experience complements academic and research training, transfers applied knowledge and skills, and establishes competencies in science-informed clinical practice. Socialization to the profession goes hand in hand with the development of clinical competence. Supervision provides a relationship in which professional values, commitments, and identity are formed and career goals are formulated. In addition to enhancing clinical competence, intermediate outcomes include increases in role assimilation, self-assessment, and self-efficacy as trainees advance through the practicum, internship, and fellowship training that lead to licensure. Ultimately, the outcome of supervision is to support the entire process of professional development that leads to competency as a psychologist and to enable the supervisee to assume the role of a colleague who contributes to the community and to the field.

Formative and summative feedback is provided to the supervisee and to those responsible for monitoring the supervisee's professional development, through the formal structure of the training agreement or contract and associated evaluative procedures. The supervisor formally evaluates and verifies the supervisee's competence and readiness to assume the next level of training or professional development. The assessment and gatekeeper functions are important aspects of supervision and constitute the supervisor's responsibilities to the supervisee, the education and training institutions, the profession, and ultimately the public. A further outcome associated with the evaluative function is the supervisor's consultation with academic programs and others involved in the education and training of psychologists, whereby the supervisor provides feedback which ensure that adequate preparation is being provided to beginning practitioners of psychology to meet present and future psychological service needs.

Supervision also provides tacit training in the practice of supervision itself. One inevitable outcome of supervision is that a supervisee's experiences form the basis for his or her own future conduct of supervision. Supervision is integral not only to clinical training, but also to the whole developmental and professional trajectory. The sum of one's experiences in supervision influences the development of attitudes and skills that will support meaningful self-assessment and contributes to lifelong increases in competence. We turn now to the approaches that inform the process of clinical supervision.

APPROACHES TO SUPERVISION

A review of the literature finds a gradual acknowledgment of supervision as a distinct competence, and although systematic approaches (J. M. Bernard & Goodyear, 1998; Falender et al., in press; Watkins, 1997b) have been proposed, there are probably as many approaches to supervision as there are supervisors. Some approaches may focus on the interaction, "a quintessential interpersonal interaction with the general goal that one person, the supervisor, meets with another, the supervisee, in an effort to make the latter more effective in helping people" (Hess, 1980a, p. 25), whereas others emphasize the development of technical skills through "an interpersonally focused, one-to-one relationship in which one person is designated to facilitate the development of the therapeutic competence in the other person" (Loganbill, Hardy, & Delworth, 1982, p. 4). Some approaches are client focused, didactic, and aimed at better understanding the client (Dewald, 1987), whereas others stress multiple roles, considering supervision to be a form of management in which teaching within the context of a relationship enhances competence (Peterson, Peterson, Abrams, & Stricker, 1997, p. 377). Furthermore, despite the availability of theory and knowledge, we find that many, if not most, supervisors practice without the benefit of education, training, or supervision (ASPPB Task Force on Supervision Guidelines, 1998; Scott, Ingram, Vitanza, & Smith, 2000). Without such experience, it is likely that supervisors' behaviors are based on implicit models of supervision, culled from their experiences as a supervisee, from their identifications with past supervisors, or from skills derived from psychotherapy or teaching. Although such informal "training" is inherently limited and subject to many potential inadequacies, it has been the usual avenue for training in supervision throughout the history of applied psychology (Tipton, 1996).

Originally, academically trained psychologists obtained supervised experience through placement in hospitals and mental health clinics as interns. The clinical staff was assigned the responsibility for training the interns and relied on their expertise as psychotherapists for this task. The practice of supervision drew liberally from clinical theories and adopted psychotherapy-based methods. This approach to supervision was based in part on the unexamined assumption that clinical knowledge and skills are readily transferable to the supervisory situation and, as such, afford sufficient preparation to oversee cases and to provide training. Early supervisory practice emphasized the authority of the supervisor, and the master–apprentice model of the supervisory relationship was thereby initiated (Binder & Strupp, 1997b, p. 44). Initially, didactic consultation was directed to the dynamics of the patient's behavior; however, with the publication of Ekstein and Wallerstein's *The Teaching and Learning of Psychotherapy* (1958), attention shifted in both content and process to the psychology of the supervisee. Supervision became primarily an experiential, rather than didactic, process in which the resistances, anxieties, and learning problems of the supervisee were brought into focus (Frawley-O'Dea & Sarnat, 2001, p. 34). With this development, supervision offered different emphases; attention was primarily directed either to the dynamics of the patient or to the dynamics of the supervisee and was conducted in either a didactic or a process-oriented manner.

During this stage in the development of supervision practice, personal experience of having been supervised remained the primary resource through which novice supervisors learned and conducted supervision. Without the benefit of an alternative pedagogical perspective, what had seemed to be sufficient training was perpetuated, including the errors inherent in previous supervisory practices (E. L. Worthington, 1987). Although such an approach accomplished the task of transferring professional practices from one generation of clinicians to the next, the distinctive nature of the tasks and processes was obscured; as a consequence, the need for specialized training in supervision went unrecognized.

With the evolution of professional psychology from a field with fewer than 7,500 members in 1950 to a field consisting of almost 84,000 members 50 years later (American Psychological Association [APA], 2002d), advances obtained through psychotherapy research and the investigation of process and outcome dimensions (Bergin & Garfield, 1994) led to initiatives to establish evidence-based practice (Chambless & Hollon, 1998; Clinical Treatment and Services Research Workgroup, 1998; Task Force on Promotion and Dissemination of Psychological Procedures, 1995). Complementing the increased focus on the requirement to empirically demonstrate efficacy, attention, particularly within counseling psychology, turned to clinical training, and a burgeoning literature focusing on the process and outcomes of supervision began to emerge. Over the past 20 years, a number of models of supervision have been introduced that are intended to better describe and scientifically investigate the supervision process and to improve the quality of training.

Like J. M. Bernard and Goodyear (1998, p. 16), we have found it useful to classify approaches to supervision according to whether they are extensions of psychotherapy theory or are developed specifically for supervision; we refer to the latter category as process-based approaches. In light of their contributions to our understanding of the process of supervision, we include discussion of developmental models (Loganbill et al., 1982; Stoltenberg & McNeill, 1997; Stoltenberg, McNeill, & Delworth, 1998; see also Watkins, 1995b); however, we view these approaches to be primarily descriptive rather than prescriptive.

Psychotherapy-Based Approaches

Supervision originally incorporated clinical approaches and techniques. This approach continues to inform practice in which supervision models have been developed for each of the major theoretical orientations, including psychodynamic (Binder & Strupp, 1997b; Dewald, 1987, 1997; Ekstein & Wallerstein, 1972; Frawley-O'Dea & Sarnat, 2001; Rock, 1997), cognitive and cognitive–behavioral (Friedberg & Taylor, 1994; Fruzzetti, Waltz, & Linehan, 1997; Liese & Beck, 1997; Milne & James, 2000; Perris, 1994; Rosenbaum & Ronen, 1998; Woods & Ellis, 1997), client centered and existential–humanistic (Mahrer & Boulet, 1997; Patterson, 1997; Sterling & Bugental, 1993), intersubjective (Bob, 1999), and systemic and family systems (Breunlin, Rampage, & Eovaldi, 1995; Liddle, Becker, & Diamond, 1997; Liddle, Breunlin, & Schwartz, 1988; Storm, Todd, Sprenkle, & Morgan, 2001). Psychotherapy-based approaches are incorporated into the supervisory process in a number of ways. Inevitably, theoretical orientation informs the observation and selection of clinical data for discussion in supervision as well as the meanings and relevance of those data. For example, observable cognitions and behaviors are of primary consideration for cognitive–behavioral therapists, whereas affective reactions and subjective experiences of the therapist are of likely interest to psychodynamic clinicians (Frawley-O'Dea & Sarnat, 2001; Liese & Beck, 1997; Rock, 1997). Also, the skills associated with the use of specific, theory-based interventions will necessarily shape the focus of training within supervision. To illustrate, Woods and Ellis (1997), writing from a rational–emotive behavioral-therapy perspective, encourage their supervisees to acquire skills in being "active-directive persuasive teachers of REBT theory and practice . . . [and] to often monitor and dispute their own irrationalities . . . to serve as reasonably good role models" (p. 112). Systemic supervisors consider the roles and functions of the entire system in assessing clinical and supervisory processes and relationships, whereas the narrative approach, which is intersubjective, focuses on the dialogue that explores the constructed realities of client, supervisee, and supervisor (Bob, 1999). Furthermore, practices that have been identified as helpful in the treatment setting are adapted for use in supervision. For example, cognitive–behavioral therapy techniques (e.g., agenda setting, homework, and capsule summaries) are directly applied in supervision for that orientation (Liese & Beck, 1997, p. 121).

Incorporation of perspectives and techniques drawn from models of psychotherapy may be inevitable, as clinical orientation substantively contributes to the supervisor's worldview and directly influences beliefs about how learning best occurs (J. M. Bernard & Goodyear, 1998, p. 18). One advantage of psychotherapy-based approaches is that clinical techniques used in the therapeutic process may be demonstrated and modeled within the dynamics of the supervisory relationship, and a seamless consistency of conceptualization may thereby occur. However, these approaches may prove to be the Scylla and Charybdis in supervisory practice. Although clinical techniques may at first glance seem to offer effective heuristics for learning and consistency in focus, such approaches, if solely applied, are limited in their ability to address the multiple responsibilities involved in supervision. The aims of supervision are not equivalent to those of psychotherapy, and therefore the approaches and learning strategies used in supervision must be specifically tailored to accomplish the goals of clinical oversight and clinical training.

Developmental Approaches

Developmental models of supervision (Loganbill et al., 1982; Sansbury, 1982; Stoltenberg et al., 1998) are metatheoretical (Watkins, 1995b) and readily applicable to varying theoretical persuasions. Each presents a developmental sequence in which the novice therapist progresses through stages to become a seasoned or master therapist. In some of the models, stages have been identified such as stagnation, confusion, and integration (Loganbill et al.); excitement and anticipatory anxiety; dependency and identification; exuberance and taking charge; and identity and independence (Friedman & Kaslow, 1986). Models have also been proposed that emphasize skill-based progression (Grater, 1985), emotional characteristics (Friedman & Kaslow, 1986), or a combination (Hogan, 1964) thereof, including attention to awareness, motivation, and autonomy of the developing trainee (Stoltenberg et al., 1998). The integrated developmental model (IDM), originally developed by Stoltenberg (1981) and Stoltenberg and Delworth (1987) and refined by Stoltenberg et al., is the most comprehensive model available today and is summarized in Exhibit 1.1. This model considers the trainee's cognitive and affective awareness of the client, motivation relating to perceived efforts, enthusiasm, and investment across time, as well as the client's autonomy, individuation, and independence. It proposes a sequence of development from increasing autonomy to shifting of awareness from self to client and finally to independent functioning. As the supervisee progresses, the behavior of the supervisor is adjusted to correspond to the appropriate developmental level. Specific supervisory behavior is spelled out in Exhibit 1.1 and more thoroughly in Stoltenberg et al. The Supervisee Levels Questionnaire (McNeill, Stoltenberg, & Romans, 1992) has been proposed to assess the developmental stage of the trainee. A developmental trajectory does exist; however, in light of the unique strengths and competencies that supervisees, including novices, bring to training, a priori assumptions applied to individual supervisees are not particularly helpful. We present a simple sketch, based on supervisory experiences, of some of the components of a broadly conceived developmental approach. As it is derived from nonsystematic and personal observation, its tenets require empirical investigation to establish its validity and further testing to propose its utility.

In addition, developmental theories have been proposed for the supervisor (Stoltenberg et al., 1998; Watkins, 1993; see Table 1.1, this chap.), internship director (Lamb, Anderson, Rapp, Rathnow, & Sesan, 1986; Lamb, Roehlke, & Butler, 1986), and intern and postdoctoral fellow (Kaslow & Deering, 1994; Kaslow & Rice, 1985; Lamb, Baker, Jennings, & Yarris, 1982; Lipovsky, 1988). The theories of supervisor development share many of the characteristics of the supervisee developmental models: They are metatheoretical, sequential, and progress to a fixed endpoint. Supervisor developmental models have been articulated by Stoltenberg at al. (1998), Watkins (1993), Rodenhauser (1994), and Hess (1986, 1987b). Watkins (1993) described the primary issues that supervisors confront across the developmental process: competency–incompetency (the degree to which one feels competent to perform as a supervisor), autonomy–dependency (the degree of independence with which one performs), identity–identity diffusion (the degree of identification versus confusion with one's supervisory role), and self-awareness–unawareness (one's degree of awareness concerning the role and process of supervision). To progress, supervisors must establish favorable ratios within the continuums of these issues. The novice supervisor experiences "role shock," or the phenomenon of feeling like an imposter as a supervisor. The progression moves through recovery and transition with enhanced identity formation to role consolidation and eventual mastery. Although his results are not empirically supported, Watkins (1993) predicted that higher stage supervisors would show higher levels of identity and skill and be more competent, self-aware, and autonomous; more facilitative in supervisee growth; perceived more favorably by supervisees; and more

EXHIBIT 1.1
Stoltenberg, McNeill, and Delworth's Theory

Characteristics of levels of supervisee development. (Development is domain specific and will occur at different times and rates across the eight domains addressed in the book.)

Level-1 Supervisee

- exhibits high anxiety
- exhibits high motivation
- is dependent on the supervisor
- focuses predominantly on the self, particularly on performance of technique or following of guidelines
- is fearful of evaluation

Supervisor of Level-1 Supervisee

- should be supportive and prescriptive
- should provide structure and positive feedback
- should use minimal direct confrontation
- should have the supervisee work with only mildly distressed clients
- should institute observation and role-play
- should put theory on the back burner to emphasize and encourage conceptualization, skill acquisition and development, self-monitoring of skill development, and attention to the client response to therapeutic intervention
- Level-2 supervisees can be excellent Level-1 supervisors.

Methods to Foster Transition from Level 1 to Level 2

- encourage increased autonomy
- begin reduction in structure
- encourage new techniques rather than familiar ones only
- foster focus on the client and his or her reactions and process

Level-2 Supervisee

- is going through "trial and tribulation" period
- experiences dependency–autonomy conflicts
- has fluctuating confidence and motivation levels
- shifts focus to the client, with increased empathy
- links mood to success with clients
- has an increased understanding of own limitations
- uses therapeutic self in interventions
- demonstrates uneven theoretical and conceptual integration
- is sensitive and anxious about evaluation

Supervisor of Level-2 Supervisee

- balances the fostering of autonomy with support and structure
- desires to increase autonomy and confidence within realistic boundaries of competence
- introduces and considers countertransference
- deals with self, defensiveness, transference, affect, and the supervisory relationship
- articulates theory and conceptual frames
- challenges and uses catalytic interventions, stirring up and increasing awareness
- helps the supervisee identify and understand his or her strengths and weaknesses
- accepts deidealization of him- or herself
- monitors use of videotapes and direct observation
- promotes multiple theoretical conceptualizations of the same

(continued)

EXHIBIT 1.1
Stoltenberg, McNeill, and Delworth's Theory (*continued*)

Level-3 Supervisee

- exudes an attitude of "calm after the storm"
- exhibits stable motivation
- is secure with autonomy
- focuses on the client, process, and self
- has professional identity at the core of his or her treatment
- is not disabled by remaining doubts
- accepts own strengths and weaknesses
- exhibits high empathy and understanding
- uses the therapeutic self in interventions
- integrates client information, personal responses, theoretical information, and empirical information
- may find it a challenge to be flexible in approach
- has accurate empathy that is tempered by objectivity and processing of reactions, feelings, and thoughts
- has a high level of insight into personal strengths and weaknesses
- addresses areas of weakness with increased confidence and nondefensiveness

Supervisor of Level-3 Supervisees

- carefully assesses consistency in performance areas across domains
- works towards integration across domains
- continues careful monitoring
- emphasizes autonomy and growth
- avoids creating an intrusive and overly structured supervisory environment
- creates a supportive supervisory environment
- engages in confrontation
- devotes attention to parallel process, countertransference, and the supervisor–supervisee relationship
- focuses on leading the supervisee to make personal self-discoveries
- interacts with empathy and in a nonjudgmental manner, with encouragement of experimentation and exploration
- provides advice concerning professional development and job searches as needed

Methods to Foster Transition from Level 2 to Level 3

- encourage movement towards stable motivation across domains
- foster flexibility to autonomously move conceptually and behaviorally across domains
- encourage creation of a solid professional identity
- encourage development of a personalized understanding across domains
- encourage assessment of the impact of personal events on professional life

Summarized from Stoltenberg, McNeill, and Delworth (1998).

effective in dealing with transference and countertransference, boundary issues, and conflict in the supervisory relationship.

We believe that the novice supervisor has significant entry-role insecurity, which may be manifested in rigidity; a crisis orientation; the personalization of trainee performance, errors, and feedback; or flip-flopping between being unforgiving, enthusiastic, and oversupervising. As the supervisor gains experience, his or her confidence grows and his or her personal identity as a supervisor is consolidated. He or she begins to take appropriate responsibility

TABLE 1.1
Theories of Supervisor Development

Hess (1986)	Stage 1 Beginning: movement from supervisee to supervisor; lack of awareness of issues; sensitivity to feedback; self-consciousness; focus on teaching	Stage 2 Exploration: feelings of greater confidence; greater effectiveness; stronger ability to evaluate work; may be too intrusive or restrictive in roles employed	Stage 3 confirmation of supervisory identity; strong sense of identity, excitement about involvement; less work and more relationship; increased focus on learning agenda	
Stoltenberg, McNeil, & Delworth (1998)	Level 1 Strong expert roles; reliance on recent supervisors as models; high anxiety; preference for a structured-feedback format	Level 2 Still high levels of confusion and conflict; fluctuating motivation; overfocus on supervisee or loss of focus in general; temptation to provide therapy to trainees; continuation of search for comfort areas	Level 3 Stable and consistent motivation	Level 4 Assumption of role of integrated master supervisor
Watkins (1993) supervisor complexity model	Stage 1 Role Shock: experience of "imposter phenomenon"; awareness of weaknesses; lack of identity as supervisor; feeling of being overwhelmed; sensitivity to feedback; may withdraw or "attack" supervisees	Stage 2 Recovery and Transition: first steps are taken towards supervisory identity formation; strengths are recognized; confidence increases; identity begins to form; a more realistic appraisal of self is developed	Stage 3 Role Consolidation: increased confidence; more realistic appraisals of skills; more completely developed sense of identity; transference and countertransference are identified	Stage 4 Role Mastery: consistent, coherent, well-integrated identity; sense of reality and calmness about work; comfortableness with mistakes
Rodenhauser (1997)	Stage I Unconscious identification with or unconscious emulation of one's former supervisor	Stage II Conceptualization: A personal search for concepts	Stage III Incorporation: Learning that supervision is a relationship	Stage IV Consolidation of knowledge into a predictable, workable instructional model
Littrell, Lee-Borden, & Lorenz (1979)	Stage I Establishment and definition of supervisory relationship; supervisory role is used to facilitate goal setting	Stage II Supervisor takes responsibility for structuring and managing the supervision sessions; roles are teacher and counselor	Stage III Responsibility for structure of supervision shifts to trainee; self-evaluation is encouraged; supervisor acts as a consultant	Stage IV Trainee operates independently

and to develop a normative sense of trainee development and predictability in some supervisory patterns. As the supervisor continues to consolidate his or her experience and identity, a greater sense of security is manifested in the supervisor's openness and eagerness to learn and receive input from supervisees and his or her increased empathy, enthusiasm, and synthesis of all aspects of theory, science-based practice, values, and experience. We believe that there is no final phase of supervisor development: Even the most senior supervisor, in performing as a mentor and leader, is fostering the innovation and development of others and is continuing to evolve and develop him- or herself.

Developmental models that focus on multicultural counseling competence and multicultural supervision (Carney & Kahn, 1984; D'Andrea & Daniels, 1997; Leong & Wagner, 1994), racial consciousness identity (as described in chap. 6, this volume; Helms, 1990; Sabnani, Ponterotto, & Borodovsky, 1991) and specific clinical skills such as psychodiagnostics (Finkelstein & Tuckman, 1997) have also been proposed. These models reflect the importance of tailoring training to insure diversity competence.

Developmental approaches potentially contribute to the establishment of congruence in expectations and roles in supervision and encourage supervisory behavior appropriate to the needs of the supervisee. Although developmental approaches are heuristically appealing and convey "experiential validity" (Sansbury, 1982), empirical support for them has not been obtained. The research literature, when reviewed as a whole (Ellis & Ladany, 1997; Stoltenberg, McNeill, & Crethar, 1994; Watkins, 1995b), identifies only a small proportion of the studies completed that met criteria for methodological inclusion. The shortcomings, including very small sample size, redundant supervisor ratings, total reliance on self-reports, statistical irregularities, and insufficient research models (Ellis & Ladany, 1997; Ellis, Ladany, Krengel, & Schult, 1996), have led to a veritable methodological morass. Ellis and Ladany (1997) reported that "the overall quality of research during the past 15 years was substandard" (p. 492) and concluded that developmental "theories and the central premises of these remain untested" (p. 493). They suggested that the process of supervision is more complex than connoted in the current models and that perhaps other aspects of trainee experience or personality have a similar or greater impact than that of supervision.

In addition to the failure to conclusively establish empirical support, a number of practical considerations limit the utility of developmental approaches in the clinical setting. Homogeneity is not present within or across training levels, and often disciplines are combined without consideration to differences in orientation to training, experience, and supervision (e.g., clinical psychology and counseling psychology students and interns at all levels of training, psychiatric residents, social work trainees, and marriage and family trainees). Further, aspects important to clinical practice, such as integration of empirical research in treatment planning; the use of metaphor, process, nonverbal communication, and the development of assessment strategies; and the use of culture or diversity as a framework for conceptualization (M. T. Brown & Landrum-Brown, 1995; Wisnia & Falender, 1999), are typically not included as factors in developmental models. Subtle, yet salient, aspects of the supervision process, such as responses to accurate self-report, distortions, and client–therapist demands, are not reflected directly in existing developmental models.

Research suggests, however, that certain supervisor behaviors appear to be related to the developmental level. Stone (1980) found that more experienced supervisors generated more planning statements concerning the supervisee, which is consistent with Watkins' (1995b) view that supervisor planning and conceptual behavior may vary as a function of supervisee developmental level. Marikis, Russell, and Dell (1985) found experienced supervisors to be more verbal, more self-disclosing, and to provide more direct instruction in counseling skills. E. L. Worthington (1984a) found only one significant difference between pre- and post-PhD supervisors: Experienced supervisors used humor more frequently in the supervision process. However, in a later study he found that more experienced supervisors were also less likely to project negative personal attributes onto supervisees who were experiencing difficulty and were more likely to attribute the problems to situational variables that can be affected (E. L. Worthington, 1984b). It is valuable to examine the finding that, in contrast to the more simplistic, idiosyncratic conceptualizations generated by novices, experienced counselors produced parsimonious, highly complex, domain-specific schemas (Mayfield, Kardash, & Kivlighan, 1999). Novices attended to superficial detail, whereas experienced clinicians observed abstract and therapeutically relevant dimensions (Kivlighan & Quigley, 1991). McCarthy et al. (1994) found few differences by years of experience or degree, and Rodolfa at al. (1998) found no significant difference in supervisory styles and practices, based on time of licensure. According to Ellis and Dell (1986), the act of supervising does not increase proficiency in supervision; improvement occurs through specific training and perhaps increased cognitive complexity. However, these observations are drawn from just a few studies, and have rarely been replicated; when they have been replicated, it has often been with methodological shortcomings.

Perhaps the most salient finding is that almost no theory or empirical investigation has addressed the impact of supervision on the development of the trainee and consequently on client outcome or satisfaction (Holloway & Neufeldt, 1995), although the implicit assumption is that there is a strong positive relationship. Watkins (1995b) reiterated E. L. Worthington's (1987) summary of the missing link of clinical efficacy: "There is still virtually no attention given to client change, sophisticated influence strategies, or theoretical match-mismatch problems" (Watkins, 1995b, p. 668). However, Goodyear and Guzzardo (2000) countered this conclusion, suggesting that the positive relationship between supervision and client outcomes can be inferred by combining the knowledge that specific supervision processes affect trainee–client working alliances (Patton & Kivlighan, 1997) and that working alliances between clients and therapists are associated with therapeutic outcomes (Horvath & Symonds, 1991). Although they need refinement to better address the complexities in supervision, these approaches hold the potential to articulate both the general and idiosyncratic impacts of professional development on therapy outcome.

Process-Based Approaches

Process-based approaches, sometimes referred to as social role supervision models (J. M. Bernard & Goodyear, 1998), were developed to provide descriptions of the component roles, tasks, and processes within supervision and as a means to uniformly classify events occurring in supervision. These approaches aim to provide reliable and valid procedures for studying the supervision process and for assessing outcomes, particularly as related to the congruence between trainee and supervisor tasks and expectations. Other process models, such as an ecological–behavioral model (Kratochwill, Lepage, & McGivern, 1997), microcounseling (Daniels, Rigazio-Digilio, & Ivey, 1997), and the experiential learning model (Milne & James, 2002), offer specific training procedures to enhance competence. Although a comprehensive review of these models is not attempted here, approaches developed by J. M. Bernard (1997) and Holloway (1995, 1997) are presented to illustrate their contributions to our understanding of the supervision process.

The Discrimination Model

J. M. Bernard (1997, p. 310) developed the discrimination model to provide "the simplest of maps" to supervisors-in-training so that they could conceptualize their interventions. Three focus areas were identified: *process* (or intervention skills), which includes all behaviors that distinguish counseling as a purposeful therapeutic interpersonal activity; *conceptualization skills*, which includes the trainee's ability to make some sense of the information that the client is presenting and to consider a response; and *personalization skills*, which includes all of the features of the trainee as an individual that contribute to the therapeutic process, such as personality and culture (cf. Bernard, 1997, pp. 310–311). Lanning (1986) proposed a fourth category, *professional behavior*, although Bernard (1997, p. 311) responded that this dimension can be subsumed into the original model. The second part of the discrimination model presents three general roles that the supervisor might assume in responding to the trainee: the teacher role (the supervisor takes on the responsibility for determining what is required for the trainee to become more competent), the counselor role (the supervisor facilitates exploration in addressing the interpersonal or intrapersonal reality of the trainee), and the consultant role (the supervisee serves as a resource, "but encourages the trainee to trust his or her own thoughts, insights, and feelings about the work with the client" [J. M. Bernard, 1997, p. 312]). This model is explicitly designed to address the training aspects of supervision (J. M. Bernard & Goodyear, 1998, p. 30) and provides a means to identify preferred supervisory roles and to evaluate the degree of congruence between the supervisee's needs and the supervisor's responses. An instance of incongruence would be found, for example, when a trainee needs help in case conceptualization and the supervisor assumes the teacher role and provides a diagnosis rather than facilitating a process of conceptualization. Empirical research has not established the adequacy of the model; however, its simplicity and straightforward approach provide a useful tool by which supervisor roles may be conceptualized in relation to supervisee needs (Ellis & Ladany, 1997, p. 467).

Systems Approach to Supervision

Holloway (1995) applied "the principles of a systems approach that emphasize a learning alliance between the supervisor and supervisee based on the multiple interlinking factors in the relationship of supervision" (p. 6). She identified seven interrelated factors that contribute to the process and outcome of supervision. The core factor in the supervisory process is the supervision relationship, which involves "the interpersonal structure, i.e., dimensions of power and involvement, phases of the relationship, i.e., relational development specific to the participants, and the supervisory contract, i.e., the establishment of a set of expectations for tasks and functions of supervision" (p. 42). All of the other factors—that is, the client, supervisor, trainee, institution, and the functions and tasks of supervision—interact dynamically and influence the supervision relationship. Through the Systems Approach to Supervision (SAS) analysis of supervision session transcripts and through the use of recall interviews, Holloway demonstrated how each factor influences the others and provided additional support for the view of supervision as a "shared interactional phenomenon" (p. 117). Emphasis is placed on the mutuality of the interaction and the importance of the participants' shared meaning of a supervision interaction (p. 118). Similar to the discrimination model, the SAS approach provides a means to closely evaluate the interactions that influence the supervision relationship and its effectiveness in building competence. In contrast with developmental approaches, which assume levels of competence, the SAS approach focuses on the unique needs of the supervisee as negotiated within the relationship between supervisor and supervisee.

The Usefulness of Process-Based Models

These process-based models provide conceptual tools for understanding the interrelated forces that contribute to the process of supervision and, to the extent that they are successful in identifying discrete components, furnish models on which empirical research can be conducted. Psychotherapy-based and process-based models articulate the processes by which supervision aims to accomplish the development of clinical competence. The interpersonal and contextual complexity observed in the supervisory process further supports the claim that supervision involves a unique praxis and therefore requires competencies that are not automatically developed through experience as a clinician, professor, or researcher.

Present Status of Supervision Practice

Supervision is now recognized as a distinct clinical practice. Although the requirement of supervised experience was established early in the training guidelines (APA Committee on Training in Clinical Psychology, 1947, 1965a, 1965b; Hoch, Ross, & Winder, 1966; Lloyd & Newbrough, 1966; Raimy, 1950), it was not until the 1990s that supervision was formally identified as a competency (Association for Counselor Education and Supervision, 1995; APA Committee on Accreditation, 2002; Dye & Borders, 1990; Holloway, 1995, pp. 104–106; Peterson et al., 1997), and it has only been within the past 20 years that a substantive literature began to emerge. For example, only 32 citations prior to 1980 were found by using "supervision" as the keyword in a literature search of PsycINFO (APA, 2002c), as opposed to 1,279 citations for literature in the most recent decade.

Despite the many advances in supervision theory, research, and practice (J. M. Bernard & Goodyear, 1998; Hess, 1987b; Holloway, 1995; Watkins, 1997b); the acknowledgment of supervision as a distinct competency; and the increased awareness of issues involving professional responsibility and liability (APA, 2002e; ASPPB, Task Force on Supervision Guidelines, 1998; Saccuzzo, 2002), supervision often appears to be practiced today with what seems to be insufficient education and training. Although clinical supervision is one of the professional activities often performed by psychologists (e.g., 38.3% of full-time academic faculty who were members of APA Division 12 [Tyler, Sloan, & King, 2000] and 48% of the members of APA Division 29 [Norcross, Hedges, & Castle, 2002] regularly provide supervision), most psychologists have not received formal training and supervision in supervision (Scott, Ingram, Vitanza, & Smith, 2000). Consistent with these findings, Rodolfa et al. (1998) reported that their sample of supervisors had received minimal supervisory training in their doctoral programs (42%) and in internship (25%) settings. Following its review of the field, the ASPPB Task Force on Supervision Guidelines (1998) concluded the following:

> Given the critical role of supervision in the protection of the public and in the training and practice of psychologists, it is surprising that organized psychology has failed to establish graduate level training in supervision or training standards for supervisors (e.g., qualifications, content of supervision, evaluation). Few supervisors have had formal courses on supervision, and most rely on their own experience as a supervisee. In addition, the complexity of the supervisory process as well as the reality that supervision itself serves multiple purposes prevents simplistic guidelines. (pp. 1–2)

A paradox appears to exist: The increased recognition of the salience of supervision in professional practice has not been accompanied by a concerted effort to train or support supervisors (cf. Milne & James, 2002, p. 56). Clearly, more opportunities, if not mandated requirements, for education and supervised training appear to be necessary to ensure competence in the practice of clinical supervision. This objective is imperative to safeguard the welfare of clients and ensure the quality of the clinical services they receive, and, simultaneously, to respond to the training requirements of the next generation of clinicians. We suggest that a competency-based approach to supervision provides a viable model to accomplish this charge and to advance efficacy established through sound scientific investigation.

A COMPETENCY-BASED APPROACH TO CLINICAL SUPERVISION

All approaches to supervision are intended to develop competence. A competency-based approach, however provides an explicit framework and method to initiate, develop, implement, and evaluate the processes and outcomes of supervision. Such an approach, consistent with innovations in competency-based education, places emphasis on the ability to apply knowledge and skills in the real world and uses performance outcomes as criteria for evaluating both learners and training programs (U.S. Department of Education, National Center for Education Statistics, 2002; Urch, 1975; R. A. Voorhees, 2001b). This focus is in step with the increased emphasis on explicit procedures of accountability in health care, including evidence-based protocols, and complements training initiatives in problem-based assessment recently undertaken by the Accreditation Council for Graduate Medical Education (Accreditation Council for Graduate Medical Education, 2000) and the American Board of Medical Specialties (cited in Leach, 2002).

Competency-based training programs in psychology have been developed; however, they do not appear to have been widely adopted or sufficiently evaluated. Fantuzzo (1984) developed the MASTERY method, and Fantuzzo and Moon (1984); Fantuzzo, Sisemore, and Spradlin (1983); Sumerall, Lopez, and Oehlert (2000); Kratochwill and Bergan (1978); Kratochwill, Van Someren, and Sheridan (1989); and Stratford (1994) developed competency-based training protocols for psychological assessment, interview skills, and generalist clinical psychology training. For some clinical supervisors, a competency-based approach to supervision might at first glance appear to be nothing new, as clinical training has always been about the development of competencies; however, the explicit use of processes derived from competency-based models may be instructive and, for many training programs, will be novel. In the following sections, we present the theory and procedures for developing a competency-based approach to supervision and describe the superordinate values we believe should inform the supervision process.

Procedures in Competency-Based Supervision

The conceptual learning model provides the foundation of our competency-based approach. Figure 1.1 illustrates the interrelationships

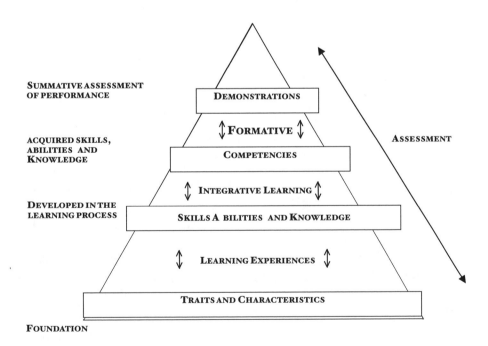

Figure 1.1. A conceptual learning model. U.S. Department of Education, 2002, adapted. In the public domain.

ween three domains in the developmental trajectory in which knowledge, lls, and values are developed, assembled into competencies, and then assessed through demonstrations. The first rung of the ladder depicts the personal traits, values, and interpersonal competencies upon which the foundation of clinical expertise is developed. Next, graduate education (including other life experiences; e.g., employment, volunteer service, etc.) contributes to the acquisition of knowledge, skills, and values that inaugurate socialization to the profession. Clinical training then provides the integrative learning experiences in which skills, abilities, knowledge, and values[1] interact to form learning bundles and, with practice under supervision, become clinical competencies (cf. R. A. Voorhees, 2001a, p. 9). Evaluation includes both formative feedback and summative assessments. Formative evaluations are collaborative and continuous during the integrative learning phase and reinforce the value of consistent self-assessment and external feedback. When the supervisor and supervisee concur that the competency has been sufficiently developed, a formal summative performance evaluation may be obtained. Competencies are formally evaluated on the basis of readiness rather than on a predetermined schedule; collaboration and self-assessment are emphasized throughout the training phase. Competency, as previously discussed, is defined as sufficiency relative to an external standard, and it is assumed that competence can always be enhanced. In clinical training, clear external standards are set, which assist the supervisor and supervisee in developing appropriate learning activities, performance objectives, and processes of assessment.

Establishing Supervision Goals and Objectives

The use of an explicit competency-based approach prepares the supervisor and the supervisee to be deliberate about the learning goals and objectives and to establish the processes by which these goals and objectives may be achieved. Central to the task is identification of the knowledge, skills, and values that will be bundled and integrated as part of the path toward competence. The first step in implementing a competency-based approach is the identification of the competencies or the input that will be the focus of the training experience. The selection process is not conducted in isolation; the faculty considers the clinical service requirements of the setting and reviews the literature in the field to ensure that the competencies are relevant to contemporary clinical practice. As per the philosophy of competency-based education, the competencies should directly relate to real-world job requirements. Once selected, the requisite knowledge, skills,

---

[1]We have added the term "values" to the model originally developed by R. S. Voorhees (R. S. Voorhees, 2001a) in light of the values-based nature of psychological practice.

and values that are assembled to form the competency are identified and become the initial focus of supervision. For example, in an intake interview, listening skills, knowledge of diagnostic systems, risk assessment, diversity awareness, and interpersonal skills are required, among other skills, and command the focus of attention. The identification of the constituents of a competency, through disassembly of the competency into definable and potentially measurable units (cf. Bers, 2001, p. 29), helps the supervisee and supervisor to attend to specific performance requirements. For example, a number of skills are required to conduct an intake interview effectively; some supervisees excel at establishing initial rapport, whereas others demonstrate good use of diagnostic-focused questioning, and so forth. By breaking down a competency into components, precise feedback and learning strategies can be used to reinforce areas of strength and develop skills or to impart knowledge that is lacking. Observable behaviors as well as self-assessment and self-report procedures are developed to encourage formative evaluation.

Although training objectives are identified for the rotation or program as a whole, we recommend individual assessment and collaborative goal setting in supervision. By design, competency-based approaches emphasize the development of individual competencies rather than assigning goals to trainees on the basis of assumed developmental levels. This emphasis is in keeping with our experience that significant variance exists between competencies attained by an individual trainee as well as between members of a particular training class. Skill acquisition is not, in our view, a homogenous process, but rather is usually heterogeneous and discontinuous. Competency-based procedures target individual competencies, allowing supervisors to tailor training to individual needs. The training objectives, learning processes, and modes of assessment are among the aspects included in the development of a formal supervision contract (see chap. 3, this volume). Congruence between supervision and training goals builds the supervisory relationship and establishes a clear focus for inquiry and for learning processes to be initiated.

Case Management and the Learning Process in Supervision

Following the identification of competencies and setting of goals and expectations, supervisees begin providing clinical services, drawing on their prior education, clinical training, and on-site instruction (including didactic presentations, demonstrations, live observation, and practice exercises). The supervision of the supervisee's clinical work begins as well and is aimed at ensuring client care and fostering learning. The supervisor assists the supervisee to become observant and to reflect on the therapeutic interaction, his or her contributions to it, and his or her subjective experience of the session. This step progresses to collaborative inquiry, in which the supervisor and supervisee describe their observations and discuss what occurred, including the nature of the interaction, the theory or literature that informed the therapist's perspective, and alternative approaches. Effective supervision facilitates a nondefensive inquiry into the clinical process and encourages self-reflective assessment not only through judicious questioning, but also primarily through modeling inquiry as a process of exploration through which insight can be gained rather than as an exercise in criticism. Throughout this process, supervisors must be mindful of their oversight responsibilities to ensure quality care. Supervisors determine the sufficiency of the supervisee's abilities with respect to the needs of the client. Some supervisors may find that they can rely on the trainee to facilitate an effective therapeutic process, whereas others may need to be more highly directive to ensure appropriate management of the case.

Central to a competency-based approach is the identification of learning processes that lead to the development of measurable competencies. Drawing on Kolb's (1984) model of experiential learning, Milne and James (2002) developed a clinical supervision approach that, in our opinion, complements our competency-based approach. In their model, the acquisition of skills and understanding is accomplished "through a combination of four modes of reflection, conceptualization, planning and practical experience, within a structured learning environment" (Milne & James, 2002, p. 57). Learners act and reflect, becoming more aware of their actions and of the knowledge base or conceptualizations that might guide them, and thereby grasp the implications of their actions, which in turn inform future actions through planning. The object is for the supervisee to actively participate in a learning cycle that includes experiencing, reflecting, conceptualizing, planning, and experimenting. This cycle is located at the core of a circumplex of clinical training and supervision experiences and reflects the constituents of experiential learning (see Figure 1.2). The supervisor assists the learner "to go round the experiential learning cycle" (p. 57) by using an array of educational methods, such as didactic teaching, role-playing, and modeling. The supervisor encourages the learner to engage in behaviors through the balanced use of interventions (see Table 1.2).

The learning cycle begins with the supervisee's experience of providing the clinical service and is assisted in the supervisee's reflecting on the experience, which leads to an understanding of what happened in the clinical session and planning for what needs to happen in the next session. Experimentation then follows as the supervisee performs new behaviors or applies new understanding within the subsequent session. The entire cycle may be completed in one supervision session, but is usually accomplished over time; the phases of experiencing, reflecting, and conceptualizing may be repeated before planning and experimenting are implemented. Through an iterative process, the cycle promotes learning as specific skills, knowledge,

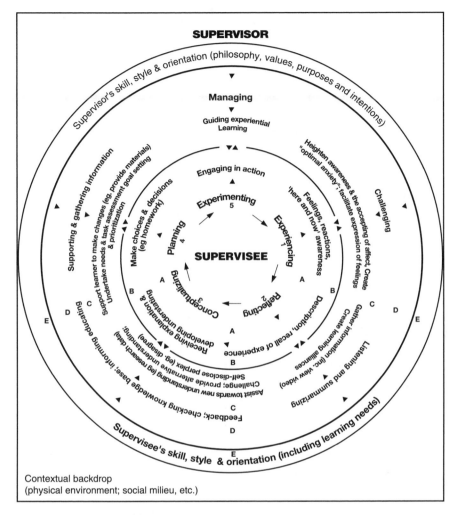

Figure 1.2. Experiential learning model of effective supervision. From "The Observed Impact of Training on Competence in Clinical Supervision," by D. L. Milne and I. A. James, 2002, *British Journal of Clinical Psychology, 41*, pp. 55–72. Copyright 2002 by the British Psychological Society. Reprinted with permission.

and values are identified in respect to the clinical task and gradually assembled to form competencies.

This model also provides a means for the supervisor's competence in facilitating the cycle to be assessed, through evaluation of the extent to which the interventions are balanced and the degree to which the learner engages in experiential learning through the use of the Teacher's PETS, a procedure to code behaviors (Milne, James, Keegan, & Dudley, 2002). For example, a supervisor who used only interventions of listening and supporting

TABLE 1.2

Supervisor and Learner Behaviors Coded by the Process Evaluation of Teaching and Supervision (PETS) Observable Instrument

Supervisor	Behavior
1. Managing	Organizing and managing the flow of the session—e.g., "I would like to cover X today," "Let's move on now," and "Anything you would like to talk about today?"
2. Listening	Engaging in active listening and observing, silently paying attention, and understanding that listening is neither verbal nor nonverbal feedback
3. Supporting	Using verbal and nonverbal *nonspecific* reassurance, agreeing, encouraging (e.g., "That's right," "Fine," "Good," and "Well done"), nodding, smiling, laughing, and expressing empathy, warmth, and genuineness
4. Summarizing	Summarizing information to clarify links and understanding (e.g., "Let me see if I got that right. . ." and "So what you've done was. . .")
5. Giving feedback	Providing *specific* verbal or written feedback, positive or negative, that is intended to weaken or strengthen aspects of the learner's behavior, thoughts, or feelings (e.g., "The way you set the agenda was very good," "You let him go on a tangent there," "That was an excellent behavioral experiment", and "You could have strengthened this with an experiment")
6. Gathering information	Asking for information and facts, not testing knowledge, and defining the trainee's problem (e.g., "How old is she?," "Was that his first episode?," and "What did you do then?")
7. Checking theoretical knowledge base	Explicitly monitoring, checking, or evaluating competence and asking for an opinion (e.g., "What would you do here?", "What does Beck suggest about. . .?", and "What kind of homework task would you set here?")
8. Challenging	Getting the learner to rethink or reason his or her view—similar to checking the knowledge base, but causes the learner to rethink his or her current perspective (e.g., "How else could you have done this?" and "What would have been a better way to. . .?")
9. Informing or educating	Providing abstract (not personal) data to the learner, transmitting information (e.g., facts and figures, theories, formulations, ideas, and methods), using a didactic approach (e.g., traditional teaching), issuing a directive that indicates what the learner should do to achieve goals, and using a convergent emphasis (e.g., "Generally, what you do here is. . .," "There have been trials to treat panic in one session," and "The way to approach this situation is. . .")

10.	Guiding experiential learning: modeling, role-play, and other	Leading practical learning activities in which one learner actively develops competence (e.g., modeling or demonstrating correct performance, using role-play exercises, implementing learning tasks, and assigning behavioral exercises)
11.	Self-disclosing	Leader referring to self to reveal something new about self, such as experience, limitations, and goals (e.g., "I have always found these cases difficult to handle," "I would like to improve myself in . . .," and "I myself find it very hard to. . .")
12.	Disagreeing	Emitting verbal or nonverbal direct negative reaction that is *nonspecific* to the learner's opinion or grasp of facts (e.g., shaking head or making verbal corrections)
13.	Using video observation	Watching a video of a therapy session, generally a case example from trainees
14.	Other	Experiencing difficulty in deciding on a suitable category from the aforementioned; nonobservable behaviors; other behaviors; off-task behavior (e.g., social chat, jokes, paperwork, and setting up equipment)

would be poorly evaluated, particularly if these behaviors did not prompt the learner to fully participate in each of the experiential learning activities. This model provides a means to assess the efficacy of a training protocol in experiential learning that classifies supervisor competence into measurable behaviors. Other methods or models can be used in advancing a competency-based approach to supervision as well. The important elements concern the precise identification of competencies and procedures to enhance their development.

Formative and Summative Evaluations

Evaluation is an important responsibility in supervision and supports case management, quality client care, and the learning process. Formative evaluations are continuous and use both formal and informal procedures, including ongoing inquiry and critique focusing on the supervisee's effectiveness in performing clinical services. Instruments and observation procedures may be used to provide reliable, valid, and useful feedback to supervisees. Formative evaluations also include consideration of the supervisee's ability to reflect on the therapeutic process, his or her contributions to it, and his or her level of competence. Summative evaluation constitutes a more formal process, ensuring the supervisor's accountability to the supervisee, the academic and clinical training programs, and the profession and ultimately safeguarding the public. Summative evaluations typically involve ratings of performance that are culled over time and represent the supervisee's sufficiency in a given competency and describe the extent to which the training objectives were met. Such evaluations are usually conducted at the midpoint and at the end of the rotation, serve as the formal evaluation, and become part of the training record. Because a competency-based approach emphasizes clear objectives throughout the training process and identifies the requisite knowledge, skills, and values that are assembled in particular competencies, a high correspondence can be obtained between training goals, training activities, and assessment procedures.

In addition, we suggest that evaluation be enhanced by providing comprehensive feedback that includes descriptions of the supervisee's strengths as well as shortcomings. Professional development builds on a foundation of personal strengths and values. Although clinical training is explicitly not intended nor is suited to evince development at that level, professional training and practice are certainly influenced by the signature strengths and values a trainee possesses. Seligman (2002) recently identified 24 strengths, many of which may have particular relevance to the applied practice of psychology and to clinical training. For example, curiosity, love of learning, open-mindedness, perseverance, honesty, and fairness are strengths that we believe to influence the process of clinical education and the development of competence. We suggest that, when providing feedback and assisting trainees to reflect on their contributions to the clinical process, one pays attention to the strengths and values that the trainees bring to the clinical and training setting.

In our view, equally essential to evaluations performed by the supervisor is the development of self-assessment capacities in the supervisee. Reflective self-assessment complements the scientific attitude of evaluating all of the factors that influence the clinical process. Schön (1983, 1987, 1995; see also Bevan, 1991) described clinicians' cultivation of the ability for "reflection-in-action," in which multiple, spontaneously available sources of information, including personal sources, contribute to an understanding of the therapeutic process and the clinicians' contributions to it. We encourage reflexivity whereby supervisees consider how they have obtained their knowledge. Such exploration leads to the development of metacognition, in which awareness is gained into the processes by which understanding is constructed, both in session and in supervision. This awareness allows for a critical examination of biases and tendencies in approach, which may occlude other sources of knowledge or practices. In addition, reflection should be directed to the values and the personal strengths that the supervisee brings to the process as well as to the personal meanings that clinical experiences are engendering. Hoshmand (1994) suggested the following:

> Reflection can be facilitated in supervision by allowing the supervisee to think aloud and pose his or her own questions. For example, in reviewing a taped session of therapeutic practice, the supervisee can be encouraged to identify critical choice points when decisions on action alternatives were in question. By reflecting on one's own rationale for the chosen action, evaluating its fit with the needs of the context and its impact on the interaction, and considering possible alternatives with the benefit of hindsight, one can use the process to build a repertoire of contextualized thought and action sequences. Reflective self-questioning can also help us to critique implicit assumptions and identify reasoning biases in practice (Arnoult & Anderson, 1988) . . . . In a reflexive orientation to knowledge, reflection serves as a form of self-observation and self-monitoring. It is an important part of a personalized approach to knowledge that includes the self in understanding (Hamacek, 1985). Thus, the development of reflective habits of mind goes hand in hand with holistic teaching and learning that focus on the total person (p. 182; see also Hoshman & Polkinghorne, 1992; Neufeldt, Karno, & Nelson, 1996).

Through practice of this method of inquiry, supervisees become more aware of their contributions to the therapeutic process, encouraging reflection-in-action and facilitating self-monitoring and disciplined and thoughtful practice.

Through the application of a competency-based approach, supervisors and supervisees identify training goals and objectives that encourage the development of specific competencies, including the capacity for self-assessment and reflection. They collaboratively work to reflect, understand, plan, and experiment through experiences within the clinical and supervisory settings. The supervisor uses a number of skills that facilitate learning processes and ensure the welfare of the client.

Superordinate Values in the Applied Practice of Psychology

Of the many influences that inform supervision, we have selected four superordinate values—integrity-in-relationship, ethical values-based practice, appreciation of diversity, and science-informed practice—that we believe to be integral to clinical competence and to psychology as a human science. We suggest that these values influence every aspect of the supervisory process and as such require faithful attention.

Integrity-in-Relationship

The importance of the counselor–client relationship to the therapeutic process and to its outcome is unquestionable, and the supervisor–supervisee relationship is likely just as crucial (J. M. Bernard & Goodyear, 1998; Bordin, 1983; Ellis & Ladany, 1997; Holloway, 1995; Ladany, 2002; see chap. 2, this volume). It is only in the setting of a strong working alliance that the inevitable personal and professional challenges associated with clinical training will be disclosed and supportively addressed. Therefore, we place particular emphasis on the responsibility to advance and to maintain the integrity of the relationship.

Integrity refers to a state of completeness as well as moral incorruptibility. The association between these elemental meanings can be illustrated in the supervisory relationship. Any corruption in the relationship—for example, by boundary violations or inattention to professional responsibilities—compromises the integrity of the relationship and results in supervision that is lacking. Similarly, if the supervisor and the supervisee do not actively commit to the complete use of supervision (i.e., to consider all of the factors that contribute to clinical work), then the process will be corrupted and little may actually be accomplished. Integrity contributes to the development of a supervisory alliance, which is collaborative, trusting, and supportive, through which the responsibilities to the client and to the supervisee will be fulfilled.

Ethical Values-Based Practice

Rather than being a values-free, "objective" science, psychology is very much a human enterprise in which faith commitments and values shape methods of inquiry and clinical practice. The aspiration that psychologists will perform lives of service "to improve the condition of individuals, organizations, and society" (APA, 2002a, Preamble) is consistent with the values of psychology as a profession (Sinclair, Simon, & Pettifor, 1996) and reflects organized psychology's long-standing commitment to human welfare, both in its contributions to knowledge and in direct service to persons (APA, 2002a).

Supervisors play an important role in modeling professional values, principles, and ethics, and supervision provides a setting in which awareness of the values informing one's commitment to the profession is to be encouraged. Further, such inquiry highlights the values-based nature of psychological practice—for example, that the acts of encouraging hope in the face of despair or challenging a client to further self-responsibility are moral acts as well as technical interventions.

It is through their experiences in clinical training that students of psychology will discover—or, rather, construct—the meaning that entering this profession has for them. The commitment of most trainees to the field will be strengthened, and they will be grateful to be able to have an opportunity to talk about their values. We are not suggesting that supervisors go down the slippery slope of providing psychotherapy or counseling in supervision; rather, we are saying that the exploration of values is relevant to training in the profession. We are mindful that values influence all human decision making and that part of the modeling in professional training is that our own values perspectives, like that of our clients, deserve articulation. Finally, supervision emphasizes and demonstrates that ethics and competence are yoked together, as two sides of the same coin: Ethics demands competence, and competence requires ethical practice. Supervision leads to the awareness that values are woven into the fabric of knowledge and that clinical practice in every instance involves the application of ethics.

Appreciation of Diversity

Appreciation of diversity, in all of its forms, is an expression of the profession's respect for people's rights and dignity (APA 2002a, Principle E). The American Psychological Association puts this concept in unequivocal terms:

> Psychologists respect the dignity and worth of all people, and the rights of individuals to privacy, confidentiality, and self-determination. Psychologists are aware that special safeguards may be necessary to protect the rights and welfare of persons or communities whose vulnerabilities

impair autonomous decision making. Psychologists are aware of and respect cultural, individual, and role differences, including those based on age, gender, gender identity, race, ethnicity, culture, national origin, religion, sexual orientation, disability, language, and socioeconomic status, and consider these factors when working with members of such groups. Psychologists try to eliminate the effect on their work of biases based on those factors, and they do not knowingly participate in or condone activities of others based upon such prejudices (APA, 2002a, Principle E).

At first glance, this principle might appear to be readily achievable; however, as with most principles, it is easier to put into words than it is to accomplish. The development of an appreciation for diversity is a psychologically challenging task, if it is taken seriously. The task, in its most radical sense, involves a deconstruction of the "inescapable framework" of beliefs, assumptions, and morality that provides the implicit scaffolding of our sense of reality and identity (C. Taylor, 1989). Deconstruction involves "demystifying a text, tearing it apart to reveal its internal, arbitrary hierarchies and its presuppositions" (Rosenau, 1992, p. 120). For our purposes, this task means that we assume an antiobjectivist stance to the assumptions that we tacitly hold about human nature. We contend that identity is socially constructed and privileged by the happenstance of the culture into which one is born and affiliates. When we come upon difference, we recognize the difference as being inherent to the other party (e.g., "they are different") rather than appreciate that it is our internal construction of difference. Gadamer (1962/1976) offers, "In the last analysis *all* understanding is self understanding" (emphasis in original; p. 55). With this postmodern sensitivity, we attempt to appreciate diversity by first recognizing that "all people are 'multicultural beings,' that all interactions are cross-cultural, and that all of our life experiences are perceived and shaped from within our own cultural perspectives" (APA, 2002b).

In the clinical setting, appreciation for diversity is integral in the quest to understand the experience of the other, to gain insight into the inherent limitations and cultural biases in our perceptions, to develop awareness and respect for cultural and individual differences, and to accurately assess the appropriate use of psychological assessment and intervention procedures. A major responsibility and challenge in supervision is to actively support the development of diversity competence and to ensure that culturally appropriate practices inform applied clinical service (see chap. 6, this volume; APA, 2000b). Our definition of diversity competency draws on many of the others provided in the literature. We believe that diversity competency includes the incorporation of self-awareness by both supervisor and supervisee and is an interactive process of the parties involved in the clinical session and in supervision, incorporating all of their diversity factors. It entails awareness, knowledge, and appreciation of the interactions among the client's, supervisee's, and supervisor's assumptions, values, biases, expectations, and worldviews, integrating and practicing appropriate, relevant, and sensitive assessment and intervention strategies and skills and taking into account the larger milieu of organization, society, and sociopolitical variables.

The development of cultural and diversity competency is particularly timely in light of how the United States is "becoming more racially and ethnically diverse, increasing the urgency for culturally responsive practices and services" (APA, 2002b). As the U.S. Surgeon General recommends, "To be effective, the diagnosis and treatment of mental illness must be tailored to all characteristics that shape a person's image and identity. The consequences of not understanding these influences can be profoundly deleterious" (U.S. Department of Health and Human Services, 1999).

Science-Informed Practice

Whether one conceives of a psychologist as a scientist–practitioner (Academy of Psychological Clinical Science, 2002; Raimy, 1950), practitioner–scholar (Peterson et al., 1997), clinical scientist (Belar & Perry, 1992), local clinical scientist (Stricker & Trierweiler, 1995), or scientific practitioner (Peterson, 2000), there is consensus that one of the defining characteristics of the profession is the integration of science with practice. The relationship between science and practice is not one of opposition; rather, "together they equally contribute to excellence in clinical training in professional psychology" (APA, Committee on Accreditation, 2000e, p. 3). In our view, science-informed practice constitutes a superordinate value, and one of the primary goals of supervision is to provide practical experience in learning how to meaningfully integrate science and practice in the provision of clinical services. We agree with the following from Holloway and Wolleat (1994):

> because the goal of clinical supervision is to connect science and practice, supervision is among the most complex of all activities associated with the practice of psychology. The competent clinical supervisor must embrace not only the domain of psychological science, but also the domains of client service and trainee development. The competent supervisor must not only comprehend how these various knowledge bases are connected, but also apply them to an individual case (p. 30).

Supervisors, as clinical educators, stand at the forefront of this task. They teach and demonstrate how knowledge and practices derived from science are systematically applied in professional consultation. By modeling the use of such practices in case consultation and supervision, by actively using the scientific literature (see, e.g., Kanfer, 1990), and by initiating, participating or supporting applied research projects within the clinic setting (Borkovec, Echemendia, Ragusea, & Ruiz, 2001), supervisors affirm the importance of science-informed practice. More salient, perhaps, they instill "the questioning attitude of the scientist" (Shakow, 1976, p. 554) whereby skills in observation, critical thinking, and hypothesis testing are incorporated into one's understanding of the therapeutic process.

THE STRUCTURE OF THE BOOK

Supervision aims to assist trainees in developing a number of competencies, attitudes, and values that support science-informed practice, safeguard client welfare, and instill a commitment to professional ethics and service. In the following chapters, we critically examine the theoretical and empirical literature and present a competency-based model of clinical supervision. In advocating for a science-informed approach to supervision and clinical practice, we base our recommendations on the existing empirical evidence. We identify inconsistencies in the research literature and point out issues that require further investigation.

The chapters in this volume are organized around topics we consider to be foundational to supervision practice: effective practices in supervision, technical competence, personal factors, the therapeutic and supervisory alliance, diversity competence, ethical and legal responsibilities and case management, and evaluation. We conclude with a discussion of the existing challenges and opportunities that must be addressed to advance the practice of clinical supervision. Although these topics are divided into separate chapters for organizational purposes, we believe that, in practice, they are highly interrelated. For example, ethics cannot be considered without incorporating diversity competence, and the therapeutic and supervisory alliance cannot be understood without paying attention to personal factors.

Throughout the text, we emphasize the interaction between competencies enacted within supervision and within the clinical setting. It is our view that there is likely a correspondence between the use of a competency within the supervisory relationship—for example, diversity competence or attending to strains in the supervisory alliance—and the development and use of that competency by the trainee in the clinical arena. We present examples from both supervision and clinical practice to illustrate the importance of the competency in both settings. We use the terms "*trainee*" and "*supervisee*" interchangeably, as synonymous terms, and consider the principles espoused in the book to be applicable to the entire range of clinical training settings, from first-year field placement externships and practica through internship and postgraduate fellowships.

Although this volume is written primarily for the field of professional psychology, the competency-based model that is presented could readily be applied to any of the allied mental health professions, psychiatry, social work, counseling, and so forth. No intellectual work is constructed in a vacuum; rather, such work draws on the contributions of others. The work presented in this volume builds on the existing foundation of scholarship in the field, enlivened by our own personal experiences as supervisors, educators, clinicians, and supervisees. As you read further, we suggest that you stop along the way and consider the literature and our recommendations in light of your own experiences in supervision. In so doing, you may gain a deeper appreciation for what was gained and missed in the past and what can be provided to others in the future.

2

WHAT MAKES FOR
GOOD SUPERVISION?

Research on the "best" and "worst" supervisors is useful in understanding what factors contribute to high-quality supervision and acts as the framework for defining dimensions of competence in the chapters that follow. In this chapter, existent research is reviewed to define the particular constellation of characteristics that distinguish a good therapist from a good supervisor, to describe a "good" supervisor, and to determine the factors that contribute to supervisee's perceptions of effective (and ineffective) clinical supervision. A summary of research on qualities associated with excellent supervision and with lousy supervision is presented, followed by a description of the factors involved in provision of high-quality supervision, including conflict resolution, disclosure, mentoring, culture, gender, and format. The last section of the chapter details how an understanding of the qualities of best and worst supervisors contributes to practice and the development of specific competencies for best supervision. The material presented in this section is particularly relevant because "about one half of a professional psychologist's formal training involves learning through supervision" (Bent, Schindler, & Dobbins, 1991, p. 124).

It has been suggested that the same personal characteristics of the "ideal psychotherapist" may apply to the "ideal supervisor" (Carifio & Hess, 1987). These characteristics included empathy, respect, genuineness, concreteness, and self-disclosure as well as self-knowledge, tolerance, and superior ability (Raimy, 1950). However, McCarthy, DeBell, Kanuha, and McLeod (1988) viewed the idea of equating the most effective supervisor with a master counselor as a myth. In addition to the lack of empirical support for equating the two, McCarthy et al. pointed out that the ideal supervisor clearly separates supervision from psychotherapy and does not provide counseling as part of supervision (Carifio & Hess, 1987), thus using a different skill set with different outcome goals. However, it is important to note that the best supervisors use therapeutic qualities such as empathy and genuineness in the process of supervision (Stout, 1987).

Many of the studies of best and worst supervision have been fraught with the types of methodological flaws prevalent in research on development of the supervisee (Ellis & Ladany, 1997). Researchers are concerned that the entire self-report methodology underlying best and worst studies is flawed in that effective supervision may not be the most satisfying or pleasurable at the time (Ladany, Ellis, & Friedlander, 1999), and that variables of liking may influence reporting. Thus, we lack significant empirical data to support results, and our conclusions must be tentative at best. However, there does appear to be some consensus on the constituent areas comprising good supervision described throughout this chapter. These areas are supported by individual research studies and several reviews in which the categories were inferred (Henderson, Cawyer, & Watkins, 1999; Neufeldt, Beutler, & Banchero, 1997; Worthen & McNeil, 1996). Two consensually important aspects of supervision are the supportive relationship and the working alliance.

RESEARCH ON HIGH-QUALITY SUPERVISION

Supportive Relationship

Studies of the best or most effective supervisor have provided us with a profile of a high-quality supervisory relationship (Henderson, Cawyer, & Watkins, 1999; Worthen & McNeill, 1996), the establishment of which is determined to be a central aspect of supervisory competency. This finding is not surprising in light of Ekstein and Wallerstein's (1958) description of the art of psychotherapy as transmitted through the relationship with the supervisor and Ellis and Ladany's (1997) conclusion from their comprehensive methodological review that "the quality of the supervisory relationship is paramount to successful supervision" (p. 495). Many of the characteristics of the supervisory relationship are parallel to factors previously defined as significant in the therapeutic alliance (Stein & Lambert, 1995). A high-quality supervisory relationship entails a combination of facilitating attitudes, behaviors, and practices. Facilitating attitudes and behaviors consist of supervisor empathy with and understanding of the difficult struggles and self-analysis through which the supervisee must go. Facilitation also refers to the creation of a sense of teamwork between supervisor and supervisee (Henderson, Cawyer, & Watkins, 1999). Facilitating behaviors include empathy (Carifio & Hess, 1987; Nerdrum & Ronnestad, 2002; Worthen & McNeil, 1996); warmth and understanding (Hutt, Scott, & King, 1983; Martin, Goodyear & Newton, 1987); a sense of validation or affirmation (Wulf & Nelson, 2000); acceptance (Hutt et al., 1983); approachability and attentiveness (Henderson et al., 1999); respect for personal integrity, autonomy (Henderson et al., 1999; Hutt et al., 1983), and strengths (Heppner & Roehlke, 1984); and a nonjudgmental stance. Highly valued supervisors are flexible, genuine (Carifio & Hess, 1987; Nelson, 1978), interested, experienced, and currently conducting therapy regularly themselves. They have a sense of humor and use it in their supervision (E. L. Worthington, 1984a).

Also valued was competence in facilitating learning (Henderson et al., 1999), including knowledge and experience relevant to the supervisee, and an open-minded approach to allow for maximal autonomy of the supervisee. Specific components include specialized expertise (Allen, Szollos, & Williams, 1986; McCarthy et al., 1994); skill (Hutt et al., 1983); theoretical, technical, and conceptual knowledge (Watkins, 1995b); and significant skill at analyzing events of therapy (Henderson et al., 1999). Practices that facilitate learning include encouragement of exploration and experimentation (Worthen & McNeill, 1996); encouragement of supervisee disclosures of actions, feelings, attitudes, and conflicts (Hutt et al., 1983; McCarthy et al., 1994); understanding of personal supervisee characteristics and the dynamics of the supervisory relationship (Gandolfo & Brown, 1987); and knowing when to self-disclose to normalize a trainee's experience (Worthen & McNeill, 1996).

Nelson (1978) concluded that interest in supervision appears to override experience and knowledge as an essential component. High-quality supervision has been distinguished by duration of experience (quality is associated with duration and frequency of contact) and occurring after a less favorable supervisory experience (Allen et al., 1986).

Evaluation practices have been highly valued as a component of good supervision. Evaluation refers to a predesignated procedure for providing regular feedback structured around agreed-on goals. Specific components include constructive criticism balanced with encouragement, regular feedback (Henderson et al., 1999), articulation of shared expectations and mutual goals for the supervision and relationship (Leddick & Dye, 1987), and constructive confrontation (Gandolfo & Brown, 1987; Henderson et al., 1999; C. D. Miller & Oetting, 1966).

Use of theoretical grounding or working within a cohesive theory (Allen et al., 1986) and a shared theoretical framework (Kennard, Stewart,

& Gluck, 1987; Putney, Worthington, & McCullough, 1992) were valued supervision skills. These skills refer to significant theoretical under-pinnings—and agreement on these factors—as a basis for supervision. Congruent theories or supervisors and supervisees who shared a theoretical orientation were associated with greater client improvement (Steinhelber, Patterson, Cliffe, & LeGoullon, 1984).

Putney et al. (1992) reported that theoretical orientation may affect the supervisor–supervisee relationship in that cognitive–behavioral supervisors were perceived to assume a consultant role and to focus on skills and strategies more than did humanistic, psychodynamic, or existential supervisors. Humanistic, psychodynamic, and existential supervisors were perceived as using a relationship model with a focus on conceptualization.

Supervisory emphasis on personal growth was valued more than a technical-skills orientation (Allen et al., 1986). The best supervisors cultivated in supervisees a sense of accomplishment, imagination, respect, inner harmony, and wisdom (P. D. Guest & Beutler, 1988). Supervisees preferred an emphasis on learning personally relevant "artistic" aspects of psychotherapy (Allen et al., 1986).

Although supervisees and supervisors may not agree on what factors make for the best supervision, there is consensus that the amount and quality of supervision constitute one of the top criteria that differentiate first-choice internship sites from others (Stedman, Neff, Donahoe, Kopel, et al., 1995). In terms of differences in perception, Rotholz and Werk (1984) reported that supervisees much preferred autonomy-giving behaviors, whereas supervisors favored cognitive-structuring behaviors. Supervisors perceived best supervision to be based on feedback to the student, whereas supervisees valued being directly taught in a supportive, facilitative relationship (E. L. Worthington & Roehlke, 1979). Supervisees' expectations of the supervisory relationship may have been lower in some instances than their perceptions of the actual relationship. Supervisees experienced significantly higher levels of empathic understanding, unconditional regard, and total relationship than they had expected from their supervisors (J. C. Hansen, 1965).

Working Alliance

A strong working alliance has also been associated with greater satisfaction with supervision (Ladany et al., 1999), and thus the ability to establish this should be considered a supervisory competency. The working alliance consists of a bond or relationship, agreement on goals, and agreement on tasks (Bordin, 1994). Supervisory pairs with a strong emotional bond, including trust, respect, and caring, experienced less role conflict and role ambiguity. This finding implies that such pairs work through and resolve conflicts more readily (Ladany & Friedlander, 1995). Greater self-disclosure by the supervisor was associated with a stronger supervisory working alliance (Ladany & Lehrman-Waterman, 1999). Goodyear and Bernard (1998) cited Patton and Kivlighan's (1997) study relating the quality of the working alliance between supervisor and supervisee and adherence to the intended treatment model to the supervisor's final evaluation of the supervisee.

There have been several efforts to describe supervision stylistically. Lochner and Melchert (1997; 32% response rate) added the dimensions of cognitive style and manner of conceptualization of psychotherapy or theoretical orientation. They found that whether the ideal supervisor should be task oriented (an approach typically associated with a novice trainee) or warm, supportive, and friendly depended on the supervisee's theoretical orientation. Those interns who reported their theoretical orientation as behavioral tended to prefer task-oriented supervisors, whereas interns with a psychodynamic or humanistic theoretical orientation preferred supervisors who were warm, supportive, and friendly.

Although they concluded that supervisory style is multidimensional, encompassing parts of all styles, Friedlander and Ward (1984) differentiated three metastyle categories. The first, "attractive," consists of components connoting positive and supportive: friendly, warm, trusting, open, and flexible. The second, "interpersonally sensitive," includes an amalgam of perceptive and intuitive, including invested, committed, reflective, creative, and resourceful. The third, "task oriented," includes descriptors depicting a goal-oriented, didactic, and prescriptive focus that is thorough, evaluative, practical, and concrete. Cognitive–behavioral supervisors had higher task-oriented ratings, whereas psychodynamic and humanistic supervisors were rated as being more interpersonally sensitive and less task directed. It was predicted that these styles would be correlated with other stylistic variables, including self-disclosure (Ladany & Lehrman-Waterman, 1999).

Cherniss and Equatios (1977) described the best supervision styles as insight oriented, with the supervisor asking questions designed to activate the supervisee to solve problems independently, and feelings oriented, with the supervisor encouraging the supervisee to question and deal with emotional responses to the clinical process. The didactic–consultative style, with the supervisor offering advice, suggestions, and interpretations concerning client dynamics and clinical technique, was the most prevalent style used in the community mental health settings studied, as well as what supervisees preferred. The laissez-faire approach was negatively associated with satisfaction, and the authoritative supervisory style was not correlated with satisfaction. Cherniss and Equatios (1977) concluded that the ideal supervisor combines multiple styles, with much higher frequencies of the insight-oriented, feelings-oriented, and didactic–consultative styles.

The Developmental Model in Quality Supervision

The developmental model has direct relevance to what constitutes the "best" supervisor. According to developmental models, the novice trainee most highly values directive, didactic, technical-skills-based training with a high degree of structure, whereas the advanced trainee prefers supervision involving issues of countertransference, theory-anchored conceptualizations with multiple levels, and emphasis on personal and professional development. "Lousy supervisors" were not sensitive to developmental levels or the developing skills of their supervisees (Magnuson, Wilcoxon, & Norem, 2000).

SUPERVISEES WHOM SUPERVISORS PREFER

Because supervision is a two-way process, variables related to the supervisee contribute significantly to good supervision. Although most research has concerned supervisors from the point of view of the supervisee, several studies have addressed characteristics of the supervisee that supervisors rate as effective or desirable and that thus significantly contribute to supervisory success. Especially because response to and effective use of supervision are typically part of the evaluation component resulting in unstated expectations being evaluated, it is important to articulate that the behaviors are comprising effective response to and use of supervision. This definition of supervisee role is referred to as role induction and is a significant component in orienting the supervisee to the process of supervision (Vespia, Heckman-Stone, & Delworth, 2002). A list of characteristics defining supervisees who use supervision well was developed, and ratings were collected from supervisees and supervisors. Beginning supervisees rated "asks for help when appropriate" as highest, whereas advanced supervisees ranked "demonstrates a willingness to grow" highest. For interns, the highest ranked item was "actively participates in supervision sessions." In contrast, the highest ranked item for supervisors was "implements supervisor's directives when client welfare is of concern to supervisor." Vespia et al. highlighted items from nonempirical post hoc analyses in which there were differences in ratings between supervisors and supervisees. Supervisor ratings were lower than those of supervisees for items on inviting feedback and demonstrating awareness of personal dynamics. Similarly, Henderson et al. (1999) reported that only supervisees, not supervisors, rated evaluation as contributing to effective supervision. Vespia et al.'s Supervisor Utilization Rating Form shows promise in articulating supervisee behaviors effective for supervision and in highlighting differences in perceptions of supervisees and supervisors as a function of the developmental level of each.

Kauderer and Herron (1990) reported that supervisors viewed most positively less dependent, assertive trainees who actively participated in the process and limited their self-exploration, thus respecting the boundary differentiating supervision from therapy. However, Kauderer and Herron's sample size was very small, and the duration in which the study was conducted was short.

Factors that supervisors have identified as contributing to effective supervision include trainees' ability to integrate what they have learned in class with conceptualization and therapy, ability to be aware of their own emotional response to clients as the response happens, and ability to use their own response in the therapy. Trainee abilities to form relationships with clients, peers, and supervisors; be flexible; and adhere to ethical codes and standards are all viewed by supervisors as supervisee-related factors contributing to effective supervision (Henderson et al., 1999). From supervisee ratings, Efstation, Patton, and Kardash (1990) identified rapport and client focus as significant factors in the supervisory relationship. Supervisors identified client focus, rapport, and identification (with the supervisor).

Wong and Wong (2002) expressed concern that supervisors may be focusing too much on their own need for support and praise from supervisees. They cited such statements as "supervisee admired my approach in therapy," "did his best to follow my directions," and "trusted in me and never questioned me" (p. 8), as behaviors viewed by supervisors as positive and cautioned against the creation of submissive, obedient trainees.

DIFFERENCES ACROSS DISCIPLINES

Although congruence exists in best and worst supervisors across disciplines, there are several interesting findings specific to one discipline or modality. For example, in training medical residents, the most highly valued supervisors (a) allowed the resident to develop the story of his or her client experience (Shanfield, Matthews, & Hetherly, 1993); (b) provided guidance about highly charged clinical dilemmas (Shanfield, Hetherly, & Matthews, 2001), acknowledged personal concerns (Shanfield et al., 2001); and (c) were empathic towards the supervisee (Shanfield, Mohl, Matthews, & Hetherly, 1992).

In family therapy supervision, Liddle, Davidson, and Barrett (1988) described criteria for which supervisor competence is correlated with trainee satisfaction. In addition to the already discussed relationship, conceptualization, and feedback skills, they placed value on the supervisor as a role model and on a supervisor who can provide guidance that enables supervisee autonomy, a supervisory structure that includes readings or tape analysis, assistance in adapting models to the individual, supervision to fit the trainee's skills and experience, training in self-assessment of strengths and weaknesses, case consultation, and supervisory flexibility.

EMPIRICALLY SUPPORTED RESULTS

In a methodological review of some of the studies cited, Ellis and Ladany (1997) concluded that there is empirical support for differentiation of extreme qualities of supervision (best and worst); the potential importance of goal setting in supervision; the different perception of supervision by supervisors and supervisees, and the existence of differences between actual and ideal supervision. However, overall, the quality of research during the past 15 years has been substandard (Ellis & Ladany, 1997).

Most of the research is based on reports of supervisees and has no link to treatment efficacy or other variables that one would expect to be positively affected by excellent supervision. As Holloway and Carroll (1996) concluded, "Losing that perspective (impact of clinical supervision on the client outcome) is a bit like viewing parenthood solely for the enrichment of the parents" (p. 54). Attention has not been directed to the difference between supervisee satisfaction and supervisee effectiveness. As Goodyear and Bernard (1998) stated in an analogy to customer satisfaction with a donut factory, "To ask trainees about whether they were satisfied with supervision or their supervisor gives minimal information about the 'nutritional' value of their experience" (p. 10). It may be that satisfaction taps into liking, pleasantness, relationship, or other variables but perhaps not to effectiveness with clients or growth as a supervisee. Goodyear and Bernard concluded that data indicate that if a supervisor likes a supervisee, the supervisor is more likely to give the supervisee a positive evaluation. It would also seem that if the supervisor likes the supervisee, the supervisee will often like the supervisor as well. Supervisees also tend to give higher satisfaction ratings to supervisors they like.

WORST SUPERVISORS

Styles Potentially Leading to Problematic Interactions

Problematic supervision can have a significant negative impact on the supervisory process and ultimately on the supervisee. Kadushin (1968) described interactional patterns or "games" prototypic of problematic supervision. Each was an interactive phenomenon in which maladaptive patterns were established, akin to a dance in which supervisee behavior elicited inappropriate supervisor behavior. These patterns resulted in boundary crossings. In one example, the supervisee flattered the supervisor by praising the supervisor's brilliant insights. The supervisor then found it difficult or impossible to supervise or give corrective feedback because of the emotional blackmail and the gratification of being viewed as omniscient. In another example, the supervisee gradually redefined the supervisory relationship by urging the supervisor to go out for coffee or lunch with him or her, transforming the relationship into one of friendship rather than supervision. Another supervisee alluded to areas of knowledge unknown to the supervisor (literature or theories), thereby changing the power differential and leading to collusion or to the supervisor's covering up ignorance. Yet another supervisee alluded to personal or professional experiences (such as substance use, rearing children, or public service work), which placed him or her in an expert position compared with the supervisor. One supervisee plied the supervisor with such extensive lists of questions during the supervisory hour that supervision was deflected from any case discussion or interaction. In another example, the supervisee cast the supervisor as a capable, knowing parent and was dependent on him or her for advice and guidance. In a different game, the supervisee scrupulously followed the supervisor's suggestions and input and then reported that they did not work. The supervisor ended up defending his or her position and was accordingly placed in a position of disadvantage, and supervision was derailed. Another supervisee expressed confusion over contradictory input from several supervisors. The supervisor then adopted a defensive stance, protecting his or her position against competing supervisors. In another game, the supervisee flagellated him- or herself about all the perceived mistakes he or she had made. The supervisor found it necessary to support, reassure, and praise the supervisee and thus avoided discussion of the "errors" themselves, as they elicited such angst in the supervisee. In another example, the supervisee raised personal problems and invited the "wise" supervisor to help solve them. The supervisor was tempted to help and, if he or she had done so, might have actually crossed the boundary into treatment. In yet another example, the supervisee disagreed with the supervisor, and the supervisor redefined the interaction as a supervisee psychological defense. One supervisee posed questions to the supervisor, who then simply responded with other questions. In a supervisor-initiated example, the supervisor redefines supervisee questions or disagreement as resistance.

Each of these examples pinpoints potential pitfalls and vulnerabilities in the supervisory relationship and its boundaries. Kadushin (1968) outlined the losses to the supervisor of playing these games. However, ultimately, dealing with the games as process issues provided potential for an all-around win. A valuable exercise is to address each of these patterns in the context of a supervisor–supervisee seminar and deal with them intellectually. Then, when they arise in the supervisory context, they can be labeled and dealt with directly. Identification and confrontation are very effective tools with both supervisee and supervisor.

Worst Supervisors Across Disciplines

Studies of "worst" supervisors did not necessarily identify opposite characteristics as those attributed to the "best" supervisors. Instead, each end of the spectrum possessed its own characteristics (Hutt et al., 1983). Magnuson et al. (2000) described overarching principles of "lousy supervision," a category described by E. L. Worthington (1987). Principles included unbalanced supervision, which does not represent all elements of the supervision experience or focuses on detail to the exclusion of larger themes; developmentally inappropriate supervision, which is not sensitive to the individual developmental needs of the trainee, intolerant of differences or not allowing the trainee to have separate views or styles from the supervisor; poor modeling of professional and personal attributes, which occurs when supervisors are untrained or poorly prepared to supervise and are professionally apathetic, lazy, or uncommitted to the profession. Lousy supervision included problems in the organizational–administrative, technical–cognitive, and relational–affective spheres. In the organizational–administrative sphere, neither expectations nor standards of accountability were clear, and supervisee needs were not assessed. In the technical–cognitive sphere, the supervisor was viewed as unskilled as a clinician and supervisor and unreliable as a professional resource. In the relational–affective sphere, the supervisor did not provide a safe environment, gave too little or too much affirming and corrective feedback, was insensitive to the trainee's developmental needs, and imposed a personal agenda, avoiding issues that arose between supervisor and supervisee. It would appear that a number of these categories violate part of Principle A in the *Ethical Principles of Psychologists and Code of Conduct* to "do no harm" (American Psychological Association, 2002a, p. 3). Although this is a preliminary analysis, it provides direction for the converse: excellent-quality supervision.

Instances of worst supervisors cited by others include supervisors who were lacking in effective teaching strategies and role modeling and supervisors who were disinterested or inept. Although we know that trainees viewed these supervisors as "worst," we do not know what evaluation each supervisor would ascribe to him- or herself. Worst supervisors were unavailable or lacked time for supervision, disagreed theoretically or conceptually with supervisees, were too nondirective or vague, had personality conflicts with supervisees, spent too much time on administrative issues, lacked expertise, or discussed their own work too much (McCarthy et al., 1994). They canceled or interrupted supervision sessions or seemed distracted (Chung, Baskin, & Case, 1998) and were preoccupied with and spent considerable supervisory time discussing their personal problems (Allen et al, 1986; Ladany & Walker, 2003). Worst supervisors were also authoritarian, encouraging conformity and punishing divergence from the "party line." Both laissez-faire and authoritarian supervision styles were linked to low trainee satisfaction (Cherniss & Equatios, 1977).

Worst supervisors emphasized the shortcomings of the trainee and were inflexible and intolerant (Watkins, 1997c). They demeaned the supervisee (Allen et al., 1986), were indirect or avoidant, or did not foster individuation (Wulf & Nelson, 2000). The most significant aspect of "worst" supervision experiences was relationship: Rather than feeling that the supervisor trusted him or her, the supervisee reported feeling mistrusted. The trainee then began to expect criticism rather than support. Cyclically, the supervisor did not identify conflicts and take responsibility for exploring them, indicating supervisory insensitivity (Hutt et al., 1983). "Worst" supervisors were defensive and uninterested in training to improve supervisory skills (Watkins, 1997c).

Analysis of Negative Supervision

Several researchers have analyzed patterns or events pivotal to ineffectual or bad supervision. Nelson and Friedlander (2001) analyzed supervisory experiences that supervisees felt had had detrimental effects on their training. They categorized the experiences into initiation of the relationship, impasse characteristics, and contributing factors. In initiation of the relationship, deleterious factors included supervisors who were remote and uncommitted to the training relationship or too busy. Impasse characteristics included the occurrence of power struggles or role conflicts precipitated by situations in which the supervisee was perceived to have greater status by virtue of age, experience, or knowledge. Also present in this category were role (boundary) conflicts including supervisors attempting to be friends with the supervisee, to confide in the supervisee, or to use the supervisee as a sounding board. Other cases involved misunderstandings based on differences in worldviews of gender or culture. The other contributing factors included supervisees being made privy to internecine quarrels within the agency or setting.

Negative supervision may be identified through specific negative events. Ramos-Sanchez et al. (2002) found that 21.4% of their sample of predoctoral interns and practicum students reported they had had a negative event in supervision (28% response rate). Those who reported negative experiences had weaker supervisory alliances and lower levels of satisfaction with that supervisor. Some of the negative events involved harsh criticism and judgmental attitudes. In exploration of what types of "counterproductive events" occur in supervision, Gray, Ladany, Walker, and Ancis (2001) described the supervisor's dismissing the supervisee's conceptualizations in favor of the supervisor's, inappropriate self-disclosure, being unprepared for supervision, misunderstanding the supervisee, or focusing on negative instances rather than areas of improvement. Supervisees reported having negative thoughts during the counterproductive event about themselves, the supervisor, or the supervisory relationship. Although the supervisees wished that the event had been recognized or acknowledged directly and then processed (and, in some instances, that they had taken the initiative to do so), there was a sense of lack of safety in doing so. To these categories, Veach (2001) added supervisory failure to address supervisee poor performance as a category of "counterproductive events."

Other researchers have studied critical incidents (Ellis, 1991a) or major turning points within the supervisory process with respect to relationship, competence, emotional awareness, or autonomy. Consequences of these incidents included the supervisee deferring to the supervisor, adopting a guarded or hypervigilant stance, censoring or limiting expression, becoming disengaged, proactively thinking of ways to facilitate better supervision (Gray et al., 2001), or spuriously complying with what the supervisor indicated (Moskowitz & Rupert, 1983). Spurious compliance refers to pretending to do what the supervisor suggested, and then perhaps distorting process notes or concealing difficulties in performance.

Ultimately, in some instances, the counterproductive supervisory event had a negative impact on the client. Negative events were found most frequently in the interpersonal relationships and style, in specific supervisory tasks, and in the fulfillment of supervisory responsibilities. Problematic supervision is discussed further in chapter 8.

FACTORS INVOLVED IN HIGH-QUALITY SUPERVISION

Conflict Resolution

In a study addressing sources of conflict in supervision, Moskowitz and Rupert (1983) provided insight into what effective supervisors did to handle conflict, in light of the fact that 38% of their sample reported a major conflict with a supervisor. Conflicts over style of supervision (direction and support) were more readily resolved successfully, whereas solutions to conflict over theoretical orientation or therapeutic approach were more difficult to formulate and substantially less successful. Most difficult to resolve, and most frequently reported, were conflicts involving personality issues. There was strong indication that trainees preferred supervisors to take the lead in identification and discussion of conflict situations. Eighty-six percent of the 158 participants preferred that the supervisor identify and initiate discussion of the conflict situation, compared with the 13.9% who preferred that the supervisor identify the problem and wait for the trainee to initiate discussion. Forty of 52 practicum students indicated they had initiated a discussion with supervisors. The discussion led to some improvement in the supervisory situation in over half of the 40 cases. For the small group of trainees who had discussions that did not lead to improvement, the supervisor did not change his or her behavior in the way the student had desired, or the supervisor felt that the trainee's personal problem was the crux of the conflict.

Key elements in effective supervision were that supervisors identified problems and initiated discussion of them. Simply identifying the problem and waiting for the supervisee to initiate discussion was substantially less desirable. A significant issue was how the supervisor responded to complaints, the trainee's raising issues of conflict, or negative feedback by the supervisee. Trainees often raise the issue that when they attempted to complain, discuss conflict, or provide negative feedback, the supervisor became confrontational, defensive, accusatory, or outright angry. It is critical for supervisors to respond nondefensively to supervisees' negative feedback or highlighting of areas of disagreement. Practicing nondefensive response would be an excellent role-play activity for supervisory seminars or support groups.

Disclosure With Supervisors

The competency of establishing a good supervisory alliance, with trust and communication, is essential to effective supervision. Ladany and Walker (2003) suggested that supervisory disclosures directly influence the emotional-bond component of the supervisory alliance by communicating trust. Secondarily, disclosures by the supervisor may model and encourage supervisee self-disclosure. Ladany, Hill, Corbett, and Nutt (1996) reported an average of eight nondisclosures to the supervisors in their study and that the issues involved were of moderate importance. Most often, nondisclosures concerned negative reactions to supervisors, personal issues, evaluation concerns, clinical mistakes, or general clinical observations. Ninety percent of those surveyed had experienced a negative reaction to a supervisor that they did not disclose. Nondisclosures occurred because the trainee viewed the information as unimportant, too personal, involving feelings that were too negative or feared that the supervisory alliance was not strong. Yourman and Farber (1996) also reported that 39.8% of their sample (35.2% response rate) failed to inform supervisors of their perceived clinical errors at a moderate to high frequency. Further, 30% never or only infrequently disclosed to the supervisor when they thought he or she was wrong. Nearly 50% of the sample reported that they told the supervisor what he or she wanted to hear, and 59% reported that they never or only infrequently felt comfortable disclosing negative feelings toward their supervisor. The only protective factors enhancing disclosure were discussion of countertransference and supervisee satisfaction.

Ninety one percent of trainees polled in one study reported at least one self-disclosure having been made by their supervisor (21% return rate). Most frequent categories were personal issues, neutral counseling experiences, and counseling struggles (Ladany & Lehrman-Waterman, 1999). Seventy three percent of supervisors made at least one personal self-disclosure. Ladany and Lehrman-Waterman (1999) reflect on the time lost to supervision, placing needs over supervisee, and risk for role reversal. In contrast, self-disclosures relating to supervisors' emotional reactions to clients, their own counseling struggles and successes, personal feedback on the supervisory relationship, general professional experiences, and didactic mentoring providing vicarious experiences, all appeared to be facilitative. There may be differing perceptions regarding supervisory events affecting disclosures. Although their study had a very small sample and had other methodological issues, Reichelt and Skjerve (2002) reported only low to moderate correspondence in how supervisors and supervisees perceived supervisory events. In the case of low correspondence, there was a relationship to supervisor didactic style, a hidden agenda, strong opinions, and avoidance of discussion of the trainee's emotional reactions in client discussion. In contrast, a trainee-centered approach, a direct style, and exploration of trainee thoughts and ideas were associated with a high correspondence of supervisor and supervisee perceptions. Further exploration is necessary to identify competencies associated with conflict prevention, resolution, and disclosures to understand the facilitating factors.

Supervisors also had significant rates of nondisclosures to supervisees: Ninety-eight percent of the supervisors in the Ladany and Melincoff's (1999) study reported that they have withheld information from their trainees. Most often (in 74% of the cases), the information withheld was the supervisor's negative reaction to the supervisee's professional performance or therapy, and it was not disclosed because of a perceived developmental process into which the behavior fit or because the supervisor felt that the trainee was not ready for the particular feedback. Supervisors also sometimes chose to address the issue less directly and more generally. The second most frequent type of case (67%) was that supervisors did not disclose personal issues relating to their own life, an appropriate boundary definition. Negative reactions to the trainee's performance accounted for 56% of nondisclosures; trainee personal issues, 37%; negative self-efficacy of the supervisor, 32%; dynamics of the training site, 27%; the supervisor's clinical and professional issues, 22%; trainee appearance, 18%; positive reactions to the trainee's counseling and professional performance, 11%; attraction to the trainee, 10%; reactions to the trainee's clients, 4%; and experiences as a supervisor with other trainees, 4%. It is noteworthy that supervisors did not disclose both negative and positive impressions. More evaluative feedback would be beneficial to the trainee. Culture is a significant factor in issues of self-disclosure. Constantine and Kwan (2003) described considerations for client–therapist dyads that are applicable to the supervisor–supervisee–client triad. They proposed considerations of "inescapable" (p. 584) self-disclosures such as skin color and inadvertent self-disclosures such as those that occur through transference–countertransference to guide deliberate therapist self-disclosure. Awareness and assessment of client (and supervisee) response to the first two categories should then guide subsequent deliberate self-disclosures.

Mentoring

A component of trainee socialization that has been highly rated by those who experience it is mentoring. Johnson (2002) draws from multiple definitions to describe the mentor as someone who "provides the protégé with knowledge, advice, challenge, counsel and support in the protégé's pursuit of becoming a full member of a particular profession" (p. 88). The mentor serves as a teacher, adviser, and role model, typically without have received any training or supervision in the process. Mentoring is distinguished from supervision by virtue of its volitional quality (i.e., it is typically sought out by the protégé), lack of an evaluative or legal component associated with supervision, and longer duration. However, some supervisors do become mentors to their supervisees. Koocher (2002) encourages us to call recipients of mentoring "mentor's charges" rather than protégés to avoid masculinization of the concept. Mentor's charges advance more rapidly in their careers and report enhanced professional-identify development and career satisfaction. Interestingly, fewer clinical psychology students (53%) have been mentored than those in other areas of psychology (73%; Johnson, Koch, Fallow, & Huwe, 2000) and PsyDs are less likely than PhDs to be mentored (Clark, Harden, & Johnson, 2000). Mentoring occurs frequently in business executive programs.

Increased interest in abusive (Tepper, 2000), dysfunctional (Johnson & Huwe, 2002), and negative (Eby, McManus, Simon, & Russell, 2000) supervision practices has drawn attention to the darker side of mentoring, which had previously received scant attention. Because, like the supervisor, the mentor holds greater power, there is potential for abuse relating to the unbalance in the mentor–charge relationship. A dysfunctional relationship is defined as unproductive or is characterized primarily as conflictual, resulting in distress of one or both members. Results can be exploitation, sabotage, or tyranny. Because of the multiple roles mentoring brings to a relationship, it is critical to devote attention to its ethical considerations (Johnson & Nelson, 1999). There is some consensus that potential mentors require more preparation, training, and support and that value be attached to the function of mentoring. For example, in academic settings, minority faculty were reported to be excessively in demand as mentors by all students, but were given no credit for that function and still needed to complete committee and research responsibilities and quotas (Dickinson & Johnson, 2000). Johnson and Huwe (2002) suggest preventative strategies for dysfunction, including creation of a culture of mentoring, assessment of new faculty hires as potential mentors, using mentorship skills as a criterion when hiring new faculty members, mentor training, mentor monitoring, providing rewards for faculty members who are mentors, and creation of a clear structure for addressing dysfunction.

Culture

The role of culture in "best" and "worst" supervision has been sorely neglected. One exception is a pilot study to explore critical incidents in supervision, conducted with 18 racial–ethnic minority students who had completed their APA-approved internship in a university counseling center (Fukuyama, 1994a). When both supervisors and supervisees were asked to offer positive and negative incidents and to describe organizational or environmental conditions that contributed to their professional development, a number of categories emerged. Supervisees preferred openness and support, as well as not being stereotyped. Supervisees valued supervisors demonstrating belief in their clinical work with difficult clients, most especially when cultural issues were presented; supervisees valued culturally-specific supervision that addressed cultural implications both for supervisees and for clients; and opportunities for multicultural experience through which they may enhance their expertise. The few negative incidents reported ($N = 4$) included lack of supervisor awareness of cultural-specific norms (e.g., interpreting culturally consistent behavior as countertransference), use of expressions offensive to the supervisee, and questioning of supervisee interpretation of client behavior as culturally relevant when the supervisee and client shared same cultural heritage.

In a study of supervisor and supervisee perceptions of cultural factors, McRoy, Freeman, Logan, & Blackmon (1986) described cross-cultural barriers to supervisory relationships, including language barriers, prejudice or bigotry, lack of knowledge of cultural differences, student defensiveness, and differences in opinions, background, and life experiences. Twenty-eight percent of the reporting field supervisors and 16 percent of the trainees indicated they had experienced an actual problem in these areas.

It is strongly advised that cultural and diversity issues be addressed in supervision. This is a competency area for supervision and is relevant for supervisees from ethnic or racial minority groups (McNeill, Hom, & Perez, 1995) as well as for supervisees and supervisors from *any* ethnic or racial group and their clients (Wisnia & Falender, 1999). Supervision should be guided by an attitude of discovery, exploration, and critical thinking, rather than political correctness (Stone, 1997). Competency includes respect and a strong knowledge base in multicultural psychology. It may be that flexibility is an antidote to stereotyping: Stereotypes are lacking in flexibility (Abreu, 2001), and thus flexibility might relate to a cognitive frame of openness. It has been suggested that acts of discrimination and racism may occur covertly, either accidentally or intentionally, as a result of ignorance and misunderstanding (McNeill et al.). Recognition of the Eurocentric influence on theory, intervention, (McNeill et al.) and the general lens with which we approach culture needs to be acknowledged. Constantine (1997) reported that 30% of predoctoral interns and 70% of supervisors in her sample had never completed a multicultural or cross-cultural counseling course. As J. M. Bernard (1994) suggested, a minimum requirement for supervision is being as multiculturally competent as one's supervisees. A more complete discussion of these issues is provided in chapter 6.

Gender

Allen et al. (1986) reported gender differences on several dimensions, but the overall quality of supervision was unrelated to the supervisor's gender. Differences include less encouragement of the assumption of power in female trainees (Nelson & Holloway, 1990), female relational focus versus male client focus (Sells, Goodyear, Lichtenberg, & Polkinghorne, 1997), and, in general, are affected by gender stereotypes within supervision (J. M. Bernard & Goodyear, 1998). Feminist supervisors informally described unconditional positive regard combined with intellectual and personal challenge as best (Porter & Vasquez, 1997).

In terms of preferred characteristics from male supervisees, the "best" supervisors placed heavy emphasis on evaluation and peer observation. Male supervisees also found technical aspects of supervision more salient. For females, the absence of sexist attitudes and practices was rated as optimal (Allen, et al., 1986). To male supervisees, the "worst" supervisors were those for whom one had to compete with other supervisees for attention. Also rated worst were supervisors who did not teach practical skills and did not encourage exploration of new psychotherapeutic strategies (Allen et al., 1986). For female supervisees, the "worst" supervisors used sexist language, emphasized traditional sex role stereotypes, subtly devalued the supervisee on the basis of sex, or violated personal privacy. Feminist working-group members described worst supervisors as overdirecting or requiring conformity; pathologizing supervisee conflicts, worries, or problems; and promoting sexist or racist interpretations (Porter & Vasquez, 1997).

PREFERRED SUPERVISORY FORMATS

In a compilation of previous research on preferred supervisory formats for family therapy, Goodyear and Nelson (1997) contrasted supervisor and trainee reports of effectiveness. In the review, the most highly rated forms of supervision were "supervisor and trainee review videotapes of therapy sessions" and "live supervision using phone call-ins to direct the trainee". Both trainees and supervisors rated these forms as 1st and 2nd choices. There was some divergence with respect to the 3rd choice, with supervisors rating "trainee participation on a treatment team behind the one-way mirror" and trainees rating "supervisor conducts co-therapy with trainee" and "trainees' participate on treatment team behind one-way mirror." "Live supervision using a mid-session break to consult with trainee" was ranked 4th by supervisors and 5th by trainees. The most frequently used form of supervision for trainees and supervisors was "individual case consultation," which accounted for in excess of 85% of the responses by both trainees and supervisors. Individual case consultation was rated as the 14th most favored format by supervisors and the 10th most favored format by trainees (out of 17 possible rankings), confirming McCarthy et al.'s (1988) "myth" that individual supervision was the best. Group supervision was the second most frequently used modality and was ranked 5th by supervisors and 9th by trainees. The techniques most frequently used by supervisees, "use of specific readings related to a specific case" and "supervisor demonstrates specific therapy skills for supervisee," were not highly ranked by trainees or by supervisors (rankings of 12th to 17th). The lowest ranked forms of supervision were reviewing written verbatim transcripts with supervisees, "live supervision using an earphone to direct supervisee" (especially low ranked by trainees), and "family sculpting," or having families form actual spatial body placements to represent relationships in family therapy.

It is interesting to contrast these findings with Nelson (1978), in which videotaping and supervisor observation were the methods most preferred for acquiring information regarding trainee's therapy sessions, but trainees observing supervisors performing therapy and supervisors acting as a cotherapist to trainees were more highly ranked as methods of teaching therapy techniques. Training-program directors rated cotherapy as being the strongest method for supervision, followed by live supervision, videotape review, audiotape review, and self-report only (Romans, Boswell, Carlozzi, & Ferguson, 1995). Supervisees reported that they preferred less emphasis on discussion and more on demonstration by supervisor or videotape and on observation across their graduate training (Gonsalvez, Oades, & Freestone, 2002). Milne and Oliver (2000) found that while all their participants made use of individual supervision (100%), there was interest in the more flexible formats of group supervision (used by 43% of participants) and cotherapy

(29%). However, resistance to change, the possibility of neglecting weaker trainees, and the extra coordination and time required were given as reasons that alternative forms of supervision were not implemented.

There was a discrepancy between the most commonly used forms of supervision and the forms of supervision that were most highly ranked by trainees and supervisors. It appeared that the expediency of individual-case consultation won out over other, more highly valued forms, even though the latter were viewed by training directors as an effective mode of supervision (Romans et al., 1995). However, this result may have occured because this area has been so infrequently studied and the results have not been linked to treatment (client) outcomes. Should it be shown that trainees who receive review of videos of the sessions achieve substantially higher treatment compliance, attendance, and resolution of problem behavior, it is likely that videotaping would occur more frequently. This trend may be strengthened by Ellis, Krengel, and Beck's (2002) findings that, contrary to popular belief, supervisor observation behind a one-way mirror, audio taping, and videotaping do not elicit significant deleterious counselor anxiety and performance. It is also significant that the Association for Counselor Education and Supervision's (1995) "Ethical Guidelines for Counseling Supervisors" (not adopted by APA) define audiotaping and videotaping of sessions as a standard of care. The highest level of client protection, best vicarious learning, and possibility of taking on more difficult clients were all maximized through live supervision. Video review and live supervision both allowed for immediate feedback, access to actual trainee and client verbal and nonverbal behaviors, and potential for supervision intervention and treatment intervention (Goodyear & Nelson, 1997).

Intricacies of videotape supervision were delineated by Breunlin, Karrer, McGuire, and Cimmarusti (1988). Six guidelines were provided to attenuate affective and cognitive processes and provide optimum supervision in this modality. These guidelines include focusing by setting supervision goals related to trainee development; relating the internal process across contexts so that feelings may be ventilated soon after the session, in the context of the goals; selecting tape segments that focus on remedial performance or approaches that the trainee is capable of changing; using comments to compare observations of the session with the established goals, refining goals moderately; and maintaining a moderate level of arousal (a midpoint between relaxation and stress). These practices allow enough stimulation to activate supervisees, but not so much stress as to overwhelm them.

Although group supervision is conducted by 65% of surveyed predoctoral internship sites (51% return rate) with 73% of the sites spending some time in group processes (Riva & Cornish, 1995), it is not a predominant format for supervision even though its merits have been lauded (Marcus & King, 2003). For example, the emotional learning component enhanced by the informal camaraderie are potential benefits (Marcus & King, 2003). There may be less comfort in providing it, as very little attention has been devoted to the methodology of group supervision as being distinct from individual supervision (J. M. Bernard & Goodyear, 1998) or to the components that make it most successful. In a single-subject case study, group cohesion and receipt of guidance in their individual counseling work were aspects of a positive group-supervision experience (Werstlein & Borders, 1997). Riva and Cornish (1995) suggested exploration of therapeutic factors, leadership style, and group cohesion as potential correlates of successful supervision. Benefits of the group format include economy of time, money, and expertise; less dependence on the supervisor; provision for trainees' self-evaluation relative to their peers; multiple perspectives on each client and exposure to more clients; modeling of the giving of feedback to promote growth; ability of the supervisor to observe the trainee in a different context; and facilitation of risk-taking and action techniques (J. M. Bernard & Goodyear, 1998). The group may provide a reflective space, a mirror, and a secure base for the beginning trainee (Scanlon, 2002). However, Enyedy et al. (2003) described processes hindering group supervision, including between-member problems, problems with supervisors, supervisee anxiety or other negative affects, logistical constraints, and poor group time management. Facilitating group supervision entails facilitating positive aspects of group interaction and feedback rather than overweighing negative features, addressing diversity issues that may affect the process, providing structure to the group (in process and time), and normalizing anxiety. Given that group supervision is such a highly rated format, it warrants more systematic exploration.

WHAT DOES AN UNDERSTANDING OF "BEST" AND "WORST" SUPERVISORS CONTRIBUTE TO ACTUAL PRACTICE OF SUPERVISION?

We suggest that the highest quality of supervision occurs in the context where there are multiple levels of support for each level of supervisor, even the most experienced; where there is an atmosphere of benevolence, nurturance, hope, and optimism; and where a sense of humor is maintained. The supervision is strength based and embedded within a competency-based curriculum that is modified depending on the needs of the training group and individuals within it. There is a constant input and influx of new models, information, interventions, and the most current thinking in the field. Attention is devoted to professionalism, including ethics, legal considerations, and modeling of the roles of psychologists and other mental health professionals.

One of the major findings is the importance of the supervisory relationship:

- Bidirectional trust, respect, and facilitation were hallmarks of a strong supervisory relationship.
- Committing enthusiasm and energy to supervision was critical.
- The amount of time devoted, the sanctity of the time commitment, sensitivity to the supervisee's developmental needs, encouragement of autonomy, and disclosure of discomfort were also highly valued qualities of the "best" supervisors.
- In the "best" supervisory relationship, there was comfort in disclosure of perceived errors, by either member of the supervisory dyad. However, the responsibility for identifying discomfort or conflict lies with the supervisor.
- Confrontation is a desirable component, as are clarity of expectations, regular feedback, and evaluation mechanisms.
- How the supervisor responds to complaints, the trainee's raising issues of conflict, or negative feedback from supervisee to supervisor is very critical in the supervisory relationship. Trainees often raise the issue that, during training sessions, they find the supervisor confrontive, defensive, accusatory, or outright angry. It is critical for supervisors to respond nondefensively to supervisees' negative feedback or highlighting of areas of disagreement.
- Pernicious and harmful supervision appear to be more prevalent than previously suspected (Ellis, 2001; Nelson & Friedlander, 2001; Gray et al., 2001). Ellis purposes teaching supervisees their rights and responsibilities so that they are more likely to appropriately confront supervisors or attempt to seek help from training directors or others.
- The use of videotaping of sessions or live supervision greatly enhances supervisory effectiveness and general accountability. Videoing role-play of supervisory vignettes is also recommended.
- If, after reading the section on "worst" supervisors, one identifies with the characteristics or has been told by supervisees that some of them apply to oneself, the individual needs to examine his or her attitudes toward supervision, experience, and level of supervisory training:
  - Veach's (2001) framework is useful in assessing the problem: Is lack of knowledge, lack of skills, motivational issues, personal impairment, transference–countertransference issues, cultural difference, or administrative constraints at the heart of the difficulty?

- It would be important to get some consultation or supervision on supervisory style.
- Veach (2001) advocated that peer-group supervision be mandated for supervisors, as well as training in conflict resolution.
- In addition, there needs to be time allotted administratively for the development of strong alliances and for appropriate supervision (Nelson, Gray, Friedlander, Ladany, & Walker, 2001).

Competencies

We now provide competencies inferred from the literature on "best" supervision. They are not empirically supported. The competencies are as follows:

- Capacity to enhance trainee self-confidence through support, appropriate autonomy, and encouragement
- Capacity to model strong working alliances and develop strong supervisory alliances with the supervisee
- Ability to dispense feedback, give constructive criticism, and provide formative and summative evaluation
- Knowledge of multiple formats of supervision and skill in each of these formats.
- Adaptability and flexibility
- Excellent communication of case conceptualization, with strong theoretical underpinnings
- Ability to maintain equilibrium and, as appropriate, a sense of humor, even in the face of crises
- Ability to identify and bring up potential conflict situations or areas of discomfort with the supervisee
- Openness to self-evaluation and to evaluation by supervisees and peers

3

BUILDING TECHNICAL COMPETENCE

Competencies and core content associated with their development have been central issues in psychology for decades, both in determining psychology curricula and in defining standards for licensure and practice. Approaches to definition include the *input model*, which focuses on the educational curricula needed to produce a competent psychologist, and the *output model*, which outlines the roles or activities a competent psychologist should be able to perform to practice independently (Roe, 2002). Competence in supervision is essential to both input and output models and is a mechanism ensuring that each occur. In this section, we consider the dimensions of input- and output-model competence of both the psychologist and the supervisor. We also discuss the history of the definition of the competent psychologist, how other fields approach competency, assessment of competency, the competent psychology trainee, the competent psychology supervisor, and the process of becoming such a supervisor. Understanding competencies is a critical part of constructing a training program and is a component part of the development of supervision contracts and assessment and evaluation procedures.

THE COMPETENT PSYCHOLOGIST: HISTORY AND CURRENT CONCEPTIONS

Competence as a psychologist has been defined in terms of "learned ability to adequately perform a task, duty or role" (Roe, 2002, p. 195), with the caveat that it relates to particular work in specific settings and that it involves integration of knowledge, skills, and values. To this, Kaslow (2002) adds the necessity of achievement of a standard accepted by the field. In addition, there are metacompetencies, or abilities to judge one's own level of acquisition and use of competencies (Kaslow, 2002), and subcompetencies. Subcompetencies refer to functions that integrate knowledge, skills, and attitudes (e.g., administering tests or conducting group therapy). Competence is a necessary, but not sufficient, condition for performance. Other personal (e.g., motivation and energy) and situational (e.g., social support, management, and availability of tools) factors play a critical role in whether competence translates into performance (Roe, 2002).

We first turn to the input model. In his critical history of psychology's movement toward a competency-based curriculum, Weiss (1991) described that, as early as the Boulder conference in 1949, it was assumed that the training of clinical psychologists would have a common core, leaving room for significant individuality to be displayed by the universities. Summarizing conclusions of the NCSPP 1989–1990 conference, Weiss stated, "(a) the core competency areas should be the organizing principle for curriculum construction, and (b) a content-based core curriculum should not be an end in itself" (p. 21).

The idea of evaluating competence in psychology training and curricula dates back to the 1973 Vail conference (Weiss, 1991) and was articulated in the Mission Bay resolutions as well. The resolutions resulted in a framework of superordinate characteristics that describe a competent psychologist and are consistent with the output model. Polite and Bourg (1991) described the resolutions that the Mission Bay conference proposed. Relationship competency, or establishing and maintaining a therapeutic relationship, was described as foundational and as the prerequisite for all other competencies in psychology, across theoretical orientations. Other components of professional competence provided descriptors of knowledge, skills, and attitudes that were later defined as the pillars of competence (Roe, 2002). The knowledge included knowledge of self and others and expert knowledge of relevant data in one or more areas of psychology. The skills articulated were communicating empathy, engaging others, setting others at ease, establishing rapport, and communicating a sense of respect. The attitudes encompassed intellectual curiosity, flexibility, scientific skepticism, open-mindedness, psychological health, belief that change can occur, appreciation of diversity, integrity and honesty; and capacity for empathy, respect for others, personal relatedness, and self-awareness (resolution reported by Polite & Bourg, 1991, from Mission Bay Conference Resolutions for Professional Psychology Programs, 1987).

The integration of these concepts into training is reflected in the revised guidelines for professional psychology training published by the

American Psychological Association (APA) in 1996 and later amended, which provide a mechanism for implementation of competency-based evaluation and program design, bridging the input and output models (APA, 2002e). "Domain B: Program Philosophy, Objectives and Training Plan" of APA's *Guidelines and Principles for Accreditation of Programs in Professional Psychology* (2002e) states the following:

> The program specifies education and training objectives in terms of the competencies expected of its graduates. Those competencies must be consistent with (1) the program's philosophy and training model; and (b) the substantive area(s) of professional psychology for which the program prepares its interns for the entry level of practice. (p. 12)

Domain B also says that

> [i]n achieving its objectives, the program requires that all interns demonstrate an intermediate to advanced level of professional psychological skills, abilities, proficiencies, competencies, and knowledge in the areas of: (a) Theories and methods of assessment and diagnosis and effective intervention (including empirically supported treatments); (b) Theories and/or methods of consultation, evaluation, and supervision; (c) Strategies of scholarly inquiry; and (d) Issues of cultural and individual diversity that are relevant to all of the above. (APA, 2002e, p. 13)

In Domain B, competencies are defined in terms of specific skills and areas of knowledge. Each program is expected to tailor competencies corresponding to an intermediate to advanced level expected of its graduates. In light of the finding that empirically supported interventions were not predominant in training (a finding supported by Hays et al., 2002)—or, as Barlow (1981) had stated years before, that clinical research has minimal, if any, influence on clinical practice. An agenda was to increase the research and empirical side of training. Site visitors focus on methods of assessing competence and assuring that criteria for successful program completion are defined and met, with procedures in place for trainees who are not meeting the criteria. Whether there is a set of "core competencies" defining a psychology curriculum or whether competencies can be idiosyncratic and syntonic with a particular articulated program remains at issue (Benjamin, 2001). The fear that competency assessment will lead to the similar development of all trainees or to all trainees reaching identical end points was expressed by those who opposed competency-based instruction (Weiss, 1991).

Using competence as a standard, psychologists moved from normative to criterion-based conceptualizations and assessment. Multiple definitions of competency have emerged. On the output side are designation of a particular, agreed-on skill set (as in Domain B); defined sets of higher order capabilities or characteristics; consistent levels of performance; and criterion-reference. On the input side is analysis of tasks into sequential increments.

Professional competency has been described as "a complex, multidimensional construct that includes both applied skills and psychological fitness" (Procidano, Busch-Rossnagel, Reznikoof, & Geisinger, 1995, p. 426). A pragmatic approach to competence was proposed by Shaw and Dodson (1988). They described a competent psychologist as a psychologist who manifests (a) use of a theoretical or conceptual frame to direct therapy, (b) memory of the client's central issues, (c) skillful use of intervention techniques to promote desired change in behavior or to set the stage for conditions of change, and (d) knowledge of when to apply (or not to apply) these interventions. We add (e) knowledge of self and role of the self and (f) knowledge of the role of culture, ethnicity, gender, and variables of diversity of the self, client (family), and community in the interaction.

We now move on to specific competency domains. In summarizing areas of competence, Gould and Bradley (2001) added unnamed interpersonal skills and multicultural competencies to theoretical knowledge and skills in therapy-related behaviors. The National Council of Schools and Programs in Professional Psychology (Peterson et al., 1991) defined six competency areas, which were expanded on by Sumerall et al. (2000), who advocated a developmental process for the assessment of competency, with "competency at one stage remains dependent on competency at preceding stages" (p. 12). The development and maintenance of effective working relationships is the first component of this process. Assessment, intervention, and use of advanced clinical skills follow, as do research, knowledge of a systematic model of inquiry involving problem identification, acquisition, organization, and interpretation of information relating to psychological phenomena. Next are education or facilitation to enhance growth of knowledge, skills, and attitudes in the learner (client, student, or other), and management of activities that direct, organize, or control services that psychologists and others offer to the public, including supervision.

Ethics, including knowledge and execution of problem-solving strategies addressing conflicts related to moral values, ethics, and law, is another core competency. A basic competency in this area is the development of appropriate attitudes toward the understanding of concepts such as individual differences, cultural diversity, and professional development. The developmental concept espoused by Sumerall et al. (2000), congruent with the developmental model, is important because not all competencies are established at the same time. The definition of competencies required by an adequate, but not expert, practitioner, potentially supplies a common language for discussing effectiveness and around which the culture of a program may be organized (Stratford, 1994).

Rather than articulating particular competencies necessary for a psychologist, exit criteria from a training sequence may be defined. Robiner, Fuhrman, and Ristvedt (1993) described the exit criteria proposed by the

Joint Council on Professional Education in Psychology, which include effective interpersonal functioning and ability to make sound professional judgments, self-assessment of personal strengths and limitations, and the need for continued supervision, consultation, and education. Also proposed are the ability to extend and expand basic assessment and intervention techniques to meet the needs of diverse settings, problems, and populations; the ability to apply ethical and legal principles to practice; and, ultimately, the development of a primary professional identity as a psychologist with adequate self-awareness to choose appropriate advanced training (Stigall et al., 1990, cited by Robiner et al., 1993, p. 5). This approach is an admirable effort that requires only operationalization for measurement.

In an approach to an output model of competency specific to particular defined areas of task analysis, competency has been described as MASTERY (Fantuzzo, 1984), an acronym that stands for *mastering* knowledge, *assessing* skill competency, *setting* minimal competency standards, *training* to competency, *evaluating* understanding of relevant legal and ethical principles, *reviewing* skill level, and *yielding* to continuing education. The MASTERY algorithm has been used successfully in child-intelligence testing administration. The content of the task needs to be clearly defined, as do specific competencies, making it relatively easy to identify and assess skill sets and rendering this approach comparable to some of the medical and allied medical skill and task analyses and potentially applicable to that for higher level competencies.

MEDICAL, DENTAL, AND ALLIED HEALTH PROFESSIONALS' APPROACHES

Members of other disciplines, sometimes with the assistance of psychologists, have developed definitions and assessments of competency that are sometimes more sophisticated than those used within psychology training settings. Examples of such fields include business management (McClelland, 1998), medicine (Epstein & Hundert, 2002; Neufeld, 1985), nursing (Brady et al., 2001), dentistry (McCann, Babler, & Cohen, 1998), and allied health professions (American Society for Healthcare Education and Training, 1994), all of which contain examples of studies and implementations of competency evaluations of performance. Many of these professions use combinations of competency measures for accreditation and licensure, and most focus on the output model.

In medicine, significant attention is devoted to the physician's cognitive process, including clinical reasoning, clinical judgment, problem-solving, and critical incidents (asking candidates to identify, from their own experience, incidents that had a positive or negative effect on the quality of patient care; Norman, 1985) in addition to the gradated sequences of skills. A physicians' definition of competence is "the habitual and judicious use of communication, knowledge, technical skills, clinical reasoning, emotions, values, and reflection in daily practice for the benefit of the individual and the community being served" (Epstein & Hundert, 2002, p. 2).

In dentistry, competencies are classified into the domains of professionalism, assessment of the patient and his or her oral environment, establishment and maintenance of a healthy oral environment, restoration, health promotion, and practice administration. Aspects of practice beyond the technical essentials of dentistry are included. Psychology has not included practice management, dealing with HMOs and insurance companies, or other, more applied aspects, including supervision, as part of its competencies. It would be useful for psychologists to consider the example set by dentistry in this regard. Self-assessment is an intrinsic part of evaluation, as it is viewed as a tool to enhance feelings of competence, and the use of self-assessment in the evaluation process is intended in part to instill it as a lifelong practice (McCann et al., 1998). Another valuable schema is that the performance to be evaluated is to closely resemble the competency as it is performed in practice. Following this dictum, psychology certification could use procedures like those suggested by McNamara (1975) in concept evaluation and simulation to test working conceptual strategies. Peer review is another evaluation device for skill assessment.

An approach proposed by psychiatrists that seeks to describe the overriding competency set identifies attributes of the supervisee that "facilitate the process of learning psychotherapy" (Rodenhauser, Rudisill, & Painter, 1989, p. 370). The attributes are divided into basic personal qualities of supervisees in general (e.g., openness, reliability, and integrity), of supervisees as facilitators of relationships with supervisors (e.g., interest, motivation, willingness to take initiative, enthusiasm, and eagerness), of supervisees as facilitators of relationships with patients (e.g., interpersonal curiosity, flexibility, and empathy), of supervisees as facilitators of content or theory learning (e.g., intellectual openness, intellectual curiosity, and capacity for conceptual abstraction), and of supervisees as facilitators of process or skills learning (e.g., minimal defensiveness, receptivity to feedback, and tolerance for ambiguity; Rodenhauser et al., pp. 370–371).

MEASUREMENT AND METHODOLOGIES OF COMPETENCY ASSESSMENT

Regardless of the conceptualization of competency, as Sumerall et al. (2000) conclude, "While there are different models that one may use, in order to establish competency one must identify the core competency being assessed, develop a tool for assessing the core competency, and develop a plan to train to achieve that core competency" (p. 14). Roe (2002) suggested construction of a competence profile for the individual, containing competences, subcompetences, knowledge, skills, attitudes, abilities, and personality traits. In this profile, competences are the higher level integrated types of work, required, whereas knowledge, skills, and attitudes refer to more elemental, basic components.

Assessment of competence has been described as "a moving target with an elusive criterion" (Robiner et al., 1993, p. 5). Development of competency-based curricula is even more difficult because of the tendency to de-emphasize evaluation and psychodiagnostics in psychology training (Falender, 2000), areas identified as primary deficits of internship applicants (Lopez, Oehlert, & Moberly, 1996). Measurability, operationalization, quantification, and validity are components that could reduce the elusive quality of competency assessment.

Medicine provides us with a considerable number of ways to analyze competencies. Reflective and philosophical approaches are considered the oldest and are valued especially for their insights into problem-solving and prerequisite abilities. However, they are difficult to reconcile with more systematic research and formal approaches to competency or skill analysis. In task-analysis approaches, the conventional methods of defining competence, consensus is plagued by problems of sampling to ensure inclusion of a representative group of experts. Critical-incident approaches have been used successfully in medical clinical examinations, but do not directly lead to adequate practice, as they focus on only the very poor or very exemplary. Procedural logs also do not address competence of behavior; they simply note behavior that has occurred (Norman, 1985).

There are a number of properties necessary to the measurement of clinical competence, including face validity; comprehensiveness or content validity; reliability, concurrent, predictive, and construct validity, economic and time feasibility, and a match with the purpose of the measurement (Neufeld, 1985). It is preferable to use multiple modalities rather than just one technique or modality to enhance validity. Techniques vary in terms of the subjectivity of the individual being assessed and of the evaluator, depending on the content and specificity of the competencies rated (Sumerall et al., 2000). For example, critiques of portfolios describe the time required and lack of reliability of scoring or evaluation of each unique piece. Reasonable reliability has been established on ratings of work samples, especially if the supervisor and supervisee shared similar theoretical orientations (Dienst & Armstrong, 1988).

Competency of the trainee has been approached from the perspective of analysis of current "outstanding" trainees. Peterson and Bry (1980) studied dimensions of professional competence by having psychology faculty assign characteristics to individuals they thought of as outstanding (in competence) and those they thought of as mediocre or poor within their training program. For the outstanding group, they obtained lists of adjectives from which they derived four common factors: responsibility, interpersonal warmth, intellectual acuity, and a set of qualities acquired through experience (self-assurance, technical skill, self-sufficiency, maturity and dedication). Warmth figured strongly in general competence ratings among supervisors who were not behaviorally oriented, highlighting the interaction of theory and perceived competence.

The role of personal attributes and their association with positive change are often neglected in descriptions of components of competence (Herman, 1993). Personal attributes include the ability to establish a therapeutic bond, which appears to be related to therapist's skill at communication of empathy, concern, and a sense of humor. Shaw and Dodson (1988) stated that the incoming trainee must possess certain personal traits to facilitate his or her development as a therapist. The ideal trainee is an empathic, caring, sensitive, and bright individual who then learns the specific competencies defined. Most training programs are skills oriented, with emphasis on the personal aspects relegated to the trainee-selection process. Although screening for personal attributes is reported to occur in doctoral programs, generally it is intuitive rather than competency based, based on interviews, letters of recommendation, or personal statements (Procidano et al., 1995).

Approaches to competency assessment in psychology can be contrasted with those used in business management. In the latter field, executives from a broad range of disciplines were evaluated by setting the criteria for success and then assessing their competencies with respect to the criteria (McClelland, 1998). Interviewees were presented with three positive and three negative episodes and were told to respond with what they said, thought, felt, and did in each instance. The behavior of each executive was analyzed to distinguish between those who are outstanding in their skills and those who are average. Competencies that distinguish these two groups were then identified. Competencies identified that distinguish outstanding performers included achievement orientation, analytic thinking, conceptual thinking, flexibility, impact and influence, initiative, and self-confidence. Each executive did not necessarily apply each competency in all situations. The organizational climate and occupational group dictated variation in competencies of the outstanding executives. This approach provides a framework to identify competencies that supercede specific skill sets.

Moore (1984) described competencies for insurance office employees used for self-evaluation and for supervisory evaluation both before and after training. The competencies were problem solving and decision making, adaptability to change, time-management capabilities, planning and organizing, creative contributions, self-management, troubleshooting, interpersonal effectiveness, interpersonal communications, job knowledge, quality of work, and quantity of work. Scores were used to enhance training and to monitor those who scored poorly.

These examples provide working models of approaches to defining qualitative competency variables that might be definitive. However, sets of such variables would differ for different tasks, and one cannot directly generalize from management to psychology practice.

Analyzing reports of the representation and emphasis of defined competencies in graduate curricula, Morrison, O'Connor, and Williams (1991) found high emphasis on dynamics of therapeutic relationships, ethics in relationships, and interviewing, and slightly lower emphasis on culture-sensitive approaches. They also found high emphasis on intelligence testing, objective personality assessment, and child assessment. A very low emphasis was placed on techniques of supervision and administrative issues, and a medium emphasis on legal, ethical, and professional standards of practice. Thus, training does not always reflect what has been defined as aspirational competencies.

COMPETENCY OF THE PSYCHOLOGY TRAINEE

We are concerned with measuring the competency of the supervisee in two core contexts: (a) the skills the trainee possesses on entering the training sequence and (b) the skills deemed essential for successful completion of the training program. The first step is to define the competencies in both contexts—that is, to define what the trainee should know on entering the training sequence and what he or she needs to be able to do on completion of the training. The second step is to develop a methodology to measure the competencies. Then the curriculum must be altered to teach the competencies to be measured (McCann et al., 1998). However, training staffs have found development of competency-based evaluation extremely difficult and time consuming. One approach requires breaking down the training sequence into series of competency statements as objectives and then analyzing the component parts of those objectives. In the case of manualized treatments, competence is defined in terms of adherence or conformity to the precise steps and procedures included in the manual (Lambert & Ogles, 1997).

One approach to analyzing competencies has been to assess particular component parts. It is extremely important to determine the skills and competencies defining the adequately functioning supervisee. Supervisee competencies and goals vary as a function of developmental level. For example, first-year practicum trainees may have skill levels and corresponding goals that are concrete and specific, related to conceptualization of the client's problem, the treatment plan for the problem, and goals for the client (Talen & Schindler, 1993). In fact, establishment of goals can serve as a basis for a secure foundation for the supervisee–supervisor relationship and can facilitate the evaluation process (see chap. 8, this volume). Competencies may be profession specific or setting specific. For example, assessment as a competency itself would apply to psychology trainees in general, but types of assessment competencies required (e.g., neuropsychology, personality, or developmental) would depend on the setting.

A methodology for the integration of competency into the curriculum consists of (a) a ratings form with pretraining, midtraining, and posttraining, evaluations of each defined competency in a self-report and a supervisor report; (b) a training contract that lays out a formulation of all the component parts of the required training sequence, articulating specific aspects of all requirements and expectations for the training sequence with quantifiable descriptors; (c) a graduate school report of competencies and areas for which the trainee needs improvement; (d) a supervisory plan focused on the identified competencies for which the trainee needs additional experience; (e) a formal evaluation of each of the competency components in an integrated format at a minimum of three or four points during the training year, culminating in the summative evaluation; and (f) a formative evaluation referring to particular highlighted competencies or areas as well as general areas that arise in supervision. The summative evaluation focused on completion of criteria of completion.

The initial assessment of the trainee may be conducted through a rating scale, completed by the trainee (self-assessment) and then by the supervisor. In the self-assessment, the trainee rates him- or herself on a variety of modalities, experiences, and competencies that correspond to those considered essential to the program in which the training occurs. Skill at self-assessment is an important competency for both supervisees and supervisors as movement toward enhanced self-awareness. An example of the pre-training assessment for a child, adolescent, or family internship is presented in Exhibit 3.1. Alternatively, the evaluation form to be used during the training year may be completed as a pre-training assessment prior to the beginning of the training. Then, as stated previously, the second step of this process is to develop a supervision contract or agreement in which specific areas are identified for progress and the expectations of the training site are clearly articulated.

Each item with a "2" or "3" rating is prioritized into a supervisory plan, with a specific methodology for enhancing skills for that item. Within each specific area, supervisors and supervisees must develop a more refined set of competencies. It is desirable to assess each trainee in each area of relevant experience, including proposed interventions to be used and areas of expertise. To assess the developmental level of the trainee, a multiphase process

EXHIBIT 3.1
Competency Rating Form Trainee Self-Rating

Ratings: 1   I am competent   *Plan:*   a. Supervision
        2   I need improvement or   b. Video/Audio Tape
           assistance   and Review
        3   I have had no experience   c. Case Presentation
                                             d. Other (specify)

Demonstrates Competency   *Self-Rating:*
in the following technical
skills:

Theoretical and Practice Orientations: Specify models:	Start 9/	6 months 3/	Final 8/	Comments/ Methodology
Psychodynamic				
Cognitive Behavioral				
Family Systems				
Solution-focused				
Crisis Model				
Other (Specify)				
Specific Play Therapy				
Temporal Orientation:				
Brief Treatment				
Extended Treatment				
Modality:				
Group				
Individual				
Family				
Client Populations: Developmental Considerations:				
Infant				
Preschool				
Elementary school-latency				
Middle school				
High School-Adolescents				
Transitional Youth				
Other				
Client Populations: Diversity Considerations:				
Culture				
Ethnicity				
Gender				
Sexual Orientation				

(continued)

EXHIBIT 3.1
Competency Rating Form Trainee Self-Rating (*continued*)

Ratings: 1   I am competent   Plan: a. Supervision
         2   I need improvement or   b. Video/Audio Tape
             assistance   and Review
         3   I have had no experience   c. Case Presentation
                                                 d. Other (specify)

Demonstrates Competency in the following technical skills: *Self-Rating:*

Theoretical and Practice Orientations: Specify models:	Start 9/	6 months 3/	Final 8/	Comments/ Methodology
Client Populations: Diversity Considerations: (continued)				
Disability				
Deaf/Hard of Hearing				
Other (specify)				
Psychodiagnostics/ Assessment:				
List all measures to be used in training year in personality, intellectual, neuropsychology and education and rate each on separate piece of paper				
Additional Clinical Skills:				
Consultation (specify):				
Program Evaluation				
Case Management				
Other				
Therapeutic/Team Skills:				
Teamwork				
Therapeutic Alliance				
Data Gathering				
Diagnostic-Analytic				
Co-Therapy				
Other				

Supervisor Comments:

The form may be modified with additional columns for supervisors to rate each of these areas of the trainee at each time period as well, either agreeing or not with the trainee self-assessment.

Note that this form is program-specific and can be modified to fit the specifics of an individual program.

EXHIBIT 3.2
Sample Assessment of Child, Family, and Supervision Experience

Child experience

- Children—ages and developmental levels
- Valence of relating to children
- Child development research exposure
- Developmental continua, milestones, and course of development
- Specialization with one level (e.g., adolescence)
- Comfort with children of varying or certain ages
- Ease in communicating with children or adolescents
- Maintenance of objectivity in work with children or adolescents
- Internalized knowledge of development (e.g., what is developmentally appropriate; what is discrepant)
- Attitude towards change in children (theoretical model and implementation)
- Use of play (models, theories, cases)
- Comfort with cultural and gender variables in interaction
- Exposure to presenting problems of a wide range
- Reaction to new situations (e.g., presenting problems; child behavior)

Family experience

- Own personal experience within a family
- Exposure to family-therapy training theories (be specific)
- Particular model expertise
- Observation (live) of clinical experience
- Integration of child into family conceptualization (experience and specific evidence of such conceptual integration)
- Ease in relating to various family members

Supervision experience

- Positive, negative, or mixed
- Identification of at least one positive role model
- Live
- Use of audio- or videotape; frequency of taping
- Comfort in supervision
- Attitude towards supervision process
- Attitude towards supervisor
- Theoretical model(s) used
- Gender or diversity factors of previous supervisors

is used. Performance levels of trainees are ascertained on a wide range of tasks. The program may develop self- and supervisory rating scales, with each clinical task broken into as many component parts as the trainees and training team can develop. One may use a Likert rating scale, usually with three points.

We superimpose on this model a conceptualization of the population to be served. If it is families, for example, we must take into account a whole dimension of theoretical and pragmatic knowledge, comfort, ease, and experience associated with that constellation. (See Exhibit 3.2 for a sample assessment of child, family, and associated supervision experiences.)

In addition, there is the question of skill overlay. For example, the supervisee may be highly trained in play therapy and in family therapy, but not in family therapy with young children in the family constellation.

SUPERVISORY GOALS

Whether in the context of a remediation plan or in the course of ongoing supervision, the supervisor should have a supervision plan, relating to the assessed competencies, developmental level of the trainee, and designated goals, linked to the supervisory contract. In the case of remediation, the supervisee will have been identified through previous assessments or write-ups to have a specific area of deficit. The plan would be centered around specific experiences to address that area. To develop such a plan, observable goals are identified, with action steps to reach the goals. For example, if increasing competence with preschool-age children with behavioral disorders was the goal, a series of steps could be developed, such as coleading a preschool group, being assigned a family with a child that age and presenting problems, and reading appropriate literature and treatment manuals on interventions for that population. If the supervisor and trainee focused on instances of identification of emotional expression in the session, the supervisor might review tapes of sessions with the trainee and assist in identifying emotions that went unrecognized during the course of the session. An action plan would then be developed in which the supervisor would assist the trainee in identifying his or her own feeling states in the session and then focus as well on identifying those of the client. Ways to recognize evidence that the goal has been reached would be articulated in the plan.

COMPETENCY OF THE PSYCHOLOGY SUPERVISOR

Unfortunately, although our pedagogy devotes substantial effort in the form of graduate training, practicum, internship, postdoctoral work, and supervised experience to provide psychologists with basic competence, there has been remarkable neglect of the development process and evaluation of supervisor competence (Association of State and Provincial Psychology Boards, Task Force on Supervision Guidelines, 1998). It has been assumed that any adequate clinician can be an adequate supervisor, that one learns supervision skills from one's own supervisors, and that one can simply learn by doing. However, these alternatives have been discounted, and as a result supervision training is "in need of a systematic, guiding ethos and should not be allowed to languish in its current state of benign neglect" (Watkins, 1992, p. 147). A study of supervision training in graduate curricula (Scott et al., 2000) revealed wide variability in the availability of supervision training. A didactic course in supervision was reported to be offered (but not necessarily required) in 85% of the graduate counseling programs surveyed, but only 34% of the clinical programs (48% return rate). Seventy-nine percent of counseling programs offered supervision practicum, whereas only 34% of clinical programs did so. Finally, in programs in which supervision was taught, respondents in clinical psychology programs were more likely to report a dearth of formal or informal methods of supervision proficiency evaluation than were counseling students (Scott et al.). At the internship level, didactic seminars were offered in 39% of the programs. Among those programs not offering training in supervision (94 out of the 209 surveys returned), the reason cited was that schedules were too heavy or there was no appropriate population to supervise (Scott et al.). McCarthy et al. (1988) summarized that it is a myth that individuals do not need training in order to supervise.

Becoming a supervisor requires a significant transition from being a clinician. The technical competency required for being a supervisor is multifaceted, as it encompasses skills in multiple clinical areas, and depth in several of these areas. These skills include general experience in supervision; education and skills in the diversity components of the population of the trainee and the client; competence in a whole domain of supervision skills, including trainee assessment, educational planning and intervention, laws and ethics, and evaluation; and facility in establishing the supervisory relationship or alliance. Many of these skills are not systematically incorporated in graduate or internship training. As a result, licensure in psychology is not synonymous with competency in supervision, even though in many states it is the requirement for beginning supervision.

Cobia and Boes (2000) outlined a few requirements of supervisory competence:

- to be competent in the areas of the supervisee's practice;
- to limit supervision to those areas in which one has had sufficient training, supervised experience, or both; and
- not to provide supervision in areas in which one is not entitled to practice.

Nelson et al. (2001) defined two fundamental measurable supervision competencies: the ability to establish strong alliances with supervisees and the ability to manage interpersonal conflicts in supervision.

At the Competencies Conference sponsored by the Association of Psychology Postdoctoral and Internship Centers (APPIC, 2002), the workgroup on supervision proposed the following supraordinate factors of supervision competency: recognition that attaining supervision competencies is a lifelong, cumulative developmental process with proficiency levels beyond mere competence; attention to all forms of diversity; attention to legal and ethical issues influenced by professional and personal factors such as values, beliefs, biases, and conflicts; and necessity of peer assessment and self-assessment across all levels of development (Falender et al., in press).

The ACES Standards for Counseling Supervisors defined 11 core characteristics of effective supervisors that provide structure for conceptualizing supervisory competency (Association for Counselor Education and Supervision, 1990). The core characteristics are being an effective counselor first; demonstrating particular traits and characteristics; and being knowledgeable about legal and ethical considerations, the supervisory relationship, methods and techniques of supervision, the developmental process, case conceptualization, assessment and evaluation, record keeping and report writing, evaluation, and supervision research.

The benefit of this outline of traits, knowledge, and competencies is the specificity of description. One could transform this outline into a ratings form that can be individualized to particular settings for assessment of supervisory competence. However, we would encourage the addition of some more interactive criteria into the ratings so that the form is reflective of the reciprocal process of the evolution of training.

Recall that from the developmental perspective, the beginning trainee may be self-absorbed, and the process is one of movement toward attending to the client and his or her milieu. Relevant to the developmental perspective is the controversy over whether supervision should be taught during graduate training, internship, or should be reserved for postdoctoral training. Proponents emphasize the necessity for didactic training, which logically places supervision in the graduate curriculum. They also contend that there is greater understanding and empathy between trainees of similar age, as the trainees have shared similar recent experiences, making the more advanced graduate student an ideal supervisor. Opponents argue that to supervise novices, one must have considerably consolidated clinical skills and general competencies (multicultural, legal and ethical, etc.), as effective supervision requires substantial levels of planning, conceptualization, maturity, and lowered anxiety. Stoltenberg, McNeill, and Delworth (1998) advocated the training of Level 2 supervisors to supervise Level 1 therapists. They say, "While the struggling Level 2 supervisor is a difficult match for any supervisee, the best assignment is with a Level 1 therapist, as this individual tends to elicit a protective, nurturing stance that results in more consistent behavior by the supervisor" (Stoltenberg, McNeill, & Delworth, p. 163). They cautioned that a therapist cannot supervise in an area in which he or she is just learning clinically, saying it would be "analogous to a Little League baseball player's coaching in the major leagues" (p. 159). We suggest that the complexity of supervision of a novice therapist is great.

SELF-ASSESSMENT

The half-life of the knowledge of a psychology doctorate is only 10 to 12 years (Dubin, 1972). That is, half of what one learned in graduate school becomes obsolete within 12 years, making ongoing assessment of one's competence and continuing education obligatory. However, the ease of learning new areas in graduate school is not replicated in the world beyond one's doctoral education. Ultimately, once a psychologist is licensed, much of the assessment of his or her competency is self-assessment (Shaw & Dodson, 1988). That is, the practitioner or supervisor makes judgments regarding his or her own areas of competency and performance. Unfortunately, we have received little preparation to judge ourselves. Belar et al. (2001) described a model for self-assessment that a practitioner can use to gauge his or her readiness to begin new forms of practice. It contains a template that is specific to delivery of services to patients with medical–surgical problems but that could be adapted to other areas as well. The steps in Belar et al.'s model include organizing a sequential set of competencies with reference to current research; consulting with relevant professional peers, colleagues, or other professionals; identifying a mentor; identifying a stepwise progression of experiential components; and creating a peer-learning group around the particular area.

The model introduced by Belar et al. (2001) is excellent for instilling principles of self-evaluation in supervisees. Belar et al. advocate implementation of structured sequential learning experiences to assist professionals in expanding their scope of practice and building on existing competencies. They urge integration of continuing education into a systematic, planned sequence designed to cement competencies rather than engaging in random single continuing-education courses.

Borders and Leddick (1987) developed a self-assessment of supervision-related knowledge and skills (see Appendix G). Specific items in teaching style that relate to the trainee, the conducting of clinical sessions, consulting, and the application of research skills to clinical practice and evaluation are clearly spelled out. In their Competencies of Supervisors scale, subscales for conceptualization and knowledge of therapy skills and supervision, program management, intervention skills, and interactional skills as a supervisor are articulated. The scale may be used as a self-evaluation for supervisors or as an evaluation to be completed by supervisees.

It is important to differentiate self-assessment, a more global approach, from self-monitoring. Self-assessment refers to a more global judgment based on previous experience and education, whereas self-monitoring is an ongoing process noted by management consultants to be a significant factor in competence. Cone (2001) described two actions that define self-monitoring:

identifying a behavior and recording its occurrence. This technique is viewed as very useful for intervention targeting particular specific behaviors but problematic as an assessment technique (Cone, 2001) because it typically focuses on only a particular, very finite behavior. Self-monitoring can be useful as a first step in determining parameters and areas to address in a self-assessment plan.

ASSESSING COMPETENCY OF THE SUPERVISOR

Although supervisor competency is not usually formally assessed in training situations (Sumerall et al., 2000), it is desirable and assumed to exist. Very few programs conduct formal assessments apart from agency-administered annual employee evaluations linked to salary changes or from feedback given by trainees on their perceptions of the supervision or the training experience.

TRANSITION FROM CLINICIAN TO SUPERVISOR

The transition to the supervisory role and the complexity of the competencies of that role require special attention. The transition from therapist to supervisor has been a neglected area. There are two models that address this progression: that of Cormier and Bernard (1982) and that of Borders (1992). Cormier and Bernard (1982) applied the Discrimination Model (J. M. Bernard, 1997) to this progression. They urged the identification of baseline supervisory behaviors, or idiosyncratic ways of observing, processing, and communicating. Several particular roles of the supervisor could be favored over others in the process of becoming a supervisor. They recommended that the roles of teacher, consultant, and counselor be monitored, as excesses in any of these roles would result in anomalous supervision.

Borders (1992) described the cognitive shift that is required to transition from clinician to supervisor. In doing so, she described a number of possible stances of varying effectiveness. First is the view of the supervisee as a surrogate for the supervisor–clinician. In this mode, the supervisor is performing as a clinician, making thorough, copious notes about the client while reviewing tapes, generating hypotheses about dynamics, and devising plans for working with the client. The emphasis is on the client, to the exclusion of the supervisee's reactions or questions, resulting in the supervisee feeling disempowered and overwhelmed, not understanding the directives of the supervisor, as they are not grounded in conceptualization or theory.

The second stance is that of the supervisee as the client. The supervisor focuses on the supervisees' personal issues, assuming that the supervisee's dynamics are the sole reason for shortcomings in performance. A supervisor's inadequate assessment leads to his or her not differentiating what skills the supervisee actually has, as opposed to skills the supervisee may be afraid of or unsure of using.

The third position, and the goal in the progression, is to be a supervisor who thinks of supervisees as learners and him- or herself as an educator. This perspective involves strategizing to help the supervisee be more effective with the client, with priority given to learning the supervisee's needs and meeting those needs. In this mode, the supervisor and supervisee take a proactive stance within a discovery learning process, but keep client welfare tantamount in their consideration. We posit a higher level of supervisor development in which the supervisor is coordinator of a bidirectional process in which he or she influences and is influenced by supervisee behavior. This process is similar to the narrative-supervision process described by Bob (1999) in which supervision is a dialogue that explores the constructed realities of client, supervisee, and supervisor.

To effectively progress as a supervisor, Borders (1992) proposes review of session videotapes, advance planning of supervisory sessions, use of supervisory case notes to link goals to events and successful execution, live observation and supervision, Interpersonal Process Recall (Kagan & Kagan, 1997), peer review, and modeling of effective supervision.

Training Models

Several models have been proposed for training supervisors (J. M. Bernard & Goodyear, 1998; Borders et al., 1991; Getz, 1999; Powell, Leyden, & Osborne, 1990). The types of training programs include skill-development, personal-growth, and integration programs. In skill-development programs, the supervisor enhances the supervisee's conceptual and other skills through teaching and helping the supervisee approach the task of helping the client. In the personal-growth model, emphasis is on enhancing insight, perspective, and sensitivity of the supervisee through focusing on the supervisee's personal responses to the client. The integration model aids in integration of skills and personal awareness in relating to the client (Hart as cited in Getz, 1999). J. M. Bernard and Goodyear (1998) advocated both didactic and experiential training components.

Models of supervision have proposed primary supervisory roles of teacher; counselor; consultant (Ellis & Dell, 1986); facilitator; administrator (J. M. Bernard & Goodyear, 1998); and monitor–evaluator, instructor–advisor, model, supporter–sharer, and consultant (Holloway, 1999). Taibbi (1995) described a progression from supervisor as teacher, guide, gatekeeper, and then consultant. Carroll (1999) suggests seven elements of supervisory roles or tasks: the relationship task, the teaching/learning task, the counseling task, the monitoring task, the evaluation task, the consultation task, and the administrative task. A combination of the conceptions of Holloway and Carroll provides us with a comprehensive view. Supervision is a multilevel, multirole model, encompassing each of the previously mentioned dimensions except therapist or counselor. A model that combines Holloway and Carroll's conceptions would entail the following elements of the supervisory role: creating a forum of reflection (consulting); mentoring (modeling, supporting, and sharing); building an apprenticeship (monitoring, evaluating, and advising); connecting supervision to education; weaving a tapestry of theory and intervention (instructing); incorporating awareness of developmental models of supervision; enhancing awareness of the social role models of supervision as revolving around the roles and tasks in which supervisor and supervisee involve themselves (modeling); and integrating diversity, context, and legal and ethical considerations.

J. M. Bernard and Goodyear (1998) provided an outline for Bernard's structured workshop in supervision. She uses a variety of meta- and experiential activities to train novices in supervision. In the laboratory, she has the trainees observe videos of client therapy sessions and play the role of supervisor, taking notes to give to their "supervisee," who is conducting the therapy session, and organizing the content of the supervisory hour. She categorized the activities into the following groups, using J. M. Bernard's (1997) discrimination model: foci of intervention, conceptualization, and personalization with the supervisor acting as teacher, counselor, or consultant. By superimposing a developmental framework on their supervision plans, Bernard focuses on the aptness of their proposed interventions. Next the supervisors-in-training role-play dyads in which one member is the observed trainee from the previous session and the other is the supervisor. Then the members reverse roles for another situation, audiotaping all supervision sessions for review. The training progresses through six more sessions. The Discrimination Model, Interpersonal Process Recall (IPR), Microtraining, live supervision, evaluation, and ethical and legal issues are the topics of the sessions. Innovative use of video, vignettes, and role-play punctuates the training. This outline appears to be an exceptional introduction to models and pivotal issues in supervision.

Borders et al. (1991) proposed a curriculum centered on themes of self-awareness, theoretical and conceptual knowledge, and skills and techniques. Seven curricular areas were identified: models; supervisee development; methods and techniques; the supervisory relationship; ethical, legal, and professional regulatory issues; evaluation; and administrative skills. The inclusion of self-awareness is a significant strength of this proposed curriculum, as it gives the beginning supervisor a chance to fully integrate his or her existing practices and beliefs into the curriculum described. The curriculum also integrates the developmental process of becoming a supervisor, including dealing with anxiety and personal issues. However, the curriculum only indirectly approaches cultural and diversity competency. A complete outline of the curriculum is presented in Borders et al.'s (1991) article. However, the model is very complex (Russell & Petrie, 1994).

Powell et al. (1990) suggested a different approach. Through task analysis, they developed a core curriculum that addresses process issues in negotiation with supervisees, through use of a "win–win" paradigm, giving and receiving feedback, assessing trainee work, and dealing with difficult issues within supervision, including establishment of trust, boundaries, interpersonal issues, and unsatisfactory work. Although this approach is very different from that of Borders et al. (1991), there is substantial overlap between the two.

Another approach involves supervision, usually group, of beginning supervisors by a seasoned therapist. In this approach, the supervisor-in-training presents material, eventually videotaped, on the supervisory session with the supervisee. The process of the supervision focuses on the juxtaposition of knowledge of the supervisor-in-training's level of development with that of the supervisee and on helping the supervisor-in-training to progress in confidence, flexibility, and anxiety reduction.

An alternative approach is training novice supervisors by conducting group supervision. An analysis of recurrent factors arising for novice supervisors in group supervision (Ellis & Douce, 1994) revealed supervisor anxiety, difficulty in intervention choice, dynamics of group cohesion (competition vs. support), responsibility (tension between client welfare and supervisee growth), parallel process, power struggles, individual differences, and sexual attraction. Each of these factors is highlighted in terms of the personal contribution of the supervisor to the process, a valuable lesson for the novice.

A manualized approach to supervision by Neufeldt (1999a, 1999b) provides a structure for the novice supervisor to approach practicum students. It balances the psychoemotional components of support with challenge to develop supervisee reflective inquiry with week-by-week examples of supervisory interaction and development.

Supervisors functioning within manualized treatment protocols may include manualized supervision as well (Henggeler & Schoenwald, 1998). This articulated approach may be highly beneficial for enhancing therapist and supervisor compliance with the particular treatment protocol. Henggeler, Schoenwald, Liao, Letourneau, and Edwards (2002) studied whether aspects of their multisystemic therapy quality-assurance system contributed to treatment fidelity by focusing on "supervisory practices which are assumed to be the most proximal and significant contribution to therapist adherence"

(p. 156). They found supervisor expertise in empirically supported treatment was positively associated with collaboration of the therapist and family.

In the context of personal factors, countertransference, the supervisory alliance, and ruptures to this alliance, the progression of becoming a supervisor is exceedingly complex. The supervisor of novice supervisors has a multilevel task of interfacing interactions between client and trainee–therapist, trainee–therapist and supervisor-in-training, and supervisor-in-training and supervisor, and of elaborating on the layers of process and content with the overlays of integrity-in-relationship, ethical values-based practice, and appreciation of diversity. Formative and ultimately summative evaluation must be interwoven into these responsibilities as well. Although there are numerous approaches to assist supervisors in their development, we are hopeful that more attention and research will be devoted to this pivotal area.

Competencies

- Vision to establish competencies corresponding to the setting and agenda of the training
- Technical skills to define and articulate component parts of tasks and responsibilities within the training sequence
- Ability to interweave established competencies with goals and assessed skills of trainees

4

ADDRESSING PERSONAL FACTORS
IN SUPERVISION

It is commonly acknowledged that clinicians draw on both personal and professional sources in their conduct of psychological treatment and that the values they derive from these sources "become so intertwined that it is virtually impossible to differentiate among them" (Beutler, Machado, & Neufeldt, 1994, p. 244). It is therefore essential for clinicians to develop an understanding of all the influences, from conscious beliefs and culturally embedded values to unresolved conflicts at the margin of awareness, that contribute to clinical practice. One aim of supervision is therefore to assist the supervisee to become increasingly mindful that the process of psychotherapy is a value-laden enterprise and that both personal values and beliefs about human nature are infused in the theories and techniques that guide the therapeutic process. Supervision practice itself is equally subject to personal influence, and supervisors must develop awareness of the beliefs, values, and dispositions that inevitably influence their conduct. This chapter broadly discusses the appearance of personal influence and values in the therapeutic and supervisory relationships; contemporary considerations of countertransference, including enactment and parallel process; and approaches to the supervisory aspects of personal factors and self-disclosure.

VALUES AND PSYCHOTHERAPY

The assumption that the provision of psychological treatment, particularly psychotherapy, is value neutral is no longer tenable. The postmodern critique leads to the awareness that all perceptions, conceptions, and actions are constructed within culturally derived spheres of meaning. Perception and knowledge are not so much outcomes of objective observation, but rather are the culturally embedded constructions of meaning (Lyotard, 1984; Rorty, 1991; Rosenau, 1992). Clinical theories necessarily include perspectives on human nature, and some suggest that they "are modern forms of religious thinking in so far as they attempt to answer our insecurities, give us generalized images of the world, and form the attitudes we should take toward the value of life, the nature of death, and the grounds for morality" (Browning, 1987, p. 120; see also Jones, 1994). Our efforts to understand and help other human beings are a function of our entire web of belief, in which our beliefs qua clinical psychologists cannot be firmly separated from all our other beliefs (cf. O'Donohue, 1989, p. 1466; see also Jones, 1994). This caveat to the assumption of neutrality is particular important because psychotherapy may be seen as a process of behavior change that necessarily involves the reordering of beliefs and values within an implicit moral framework (Prilleltensky, 1997). Psychotherapists enter the assumptive worlds of their clients and attempt, through implicit and explicit persuasion, to produce changes in the ways in which clients view themselves, the world in which they live, and the behaviors that they enact (Frank & Frank, 1961/1991; London, 1964). Therapeutic action often, if not always, involves a conversion of values in which the orienting system of the psychotherapist shapes the client's meanings and behaviors (Kelly, 1990). Beyond the sway of contemporary philosophical and theoretical inquiry, empirical evidence supports the proposition that personal as well as professional values influence the conduct of psychological treatment (Beutler, 1981; Tjeltveit, 1986) and may contribute significantly to its effectiveness (Beutler, 1979). Clinicians and supervisors therefore need to take into consideration the role of personal influence in their practices.

COUNTERTRANSFERENCE

Countertransference is the term that has been broadly applied to the personal reactions of the psychotherapist, which potentially influence the treatment. Beginning with Freud (1912), concern has been consistently raised about the exercise of undue personal influence on the client, and the effect of the clinician's subjectivity on the therapeutic process. Sources of such influence include transference reactions (Freud, 1910), projections of the client (Heimann, 1950), identifications with the client and others (Racker, 1953), products of the intersubjective nature of the relationship between the client and the psychotherapist (Natterson, 1991), and, in sum, all of the personal beliefs and values of the therapist. From this comprehensive perspective, we suggest that therapists do not possess the means of understanding their clients beyond their own emotionally colored perceptions and responses to their clients, many of which are outside of their immediate awareness (cf. Ogden, 1988, p. 22). These perceptions and responses play a crucial role in the therapeutic process either by providing subjective clinical data that enable the therapist to better understand the client and process or by hindering the process because of the limitations imposed by the clinician's unresolved resistances and complexes (Freud, 1910, p. 145).

Although countertransference was viewed as a source of considerable difficulty, an assumption was fostered that the psychotherapist could be educated to subordinate personal reactions through the process of clinical training, together with psychotherapy, and would therefore be able to assume a therapeutically useful stance of objectivity and to provide technical neutrality. Other forms of psychotherapy, particularly existential–humanistic and experiential approaches, emphasized the positive role that a clinician's genuineness, authentic self-expression, and disciplined self-disclosure could make to facilitate a therapeutic process (Bugental, 1965; Mahrer, 1996; Rogers, 1951; Schneider, Bugental, & Pierson, 2001). Despite significant differences in clinical theory and approach, each variant of psychotherapy has recognized the potential dangers associated with a therapist's acting out of personal reactions and the necessity for developing awareness and discipline in addressing countertransference.

Contemporary clinical scholarship incorporating a postmodern epistemologic stance (e.g., Neimeyer & Mahoney, 1995; Stolorow, Atwood, & Orange, 2002) has called into question the notion of neutrality and value-free objectivity. Indeed, countertransference may be an inevitable feature of any human engagement, including the applied practice of psychology. We find that the clinician's or supervisor's understanding of clients or supervisees, respectively, is always *perspectival*—that is, bears the inescapable influence of personal interests, commitments, and the cultures out of which personal meaning is constructed (Fischer, 1998; Gergen, 1994; Giorgi, 1970; Polkinghorne, 1988; C. Taylor, 1989). Nevertheless, some advocate that attitudinal neutrality (Poland, 1984) can be attained whereby respect for the client's "essential otherness" (p. 285), open-mindedness (Franklin, 1990), and rights to hold autonomous personal beliefs and values are unique clinical features (Shapiro, 1984). Others point to the "irreducible subjectivity" (Renik, 1993) of the clinician, consider personal influence to be at the "heart of technique" (Renik, 1996, p. 496), and describe the therapeutic interaction to be mutually coconstructed (Gill, 1994; Hoffman, 1983, 1991) and intersubjective (Atwood & Stolorow, 1984).

Our view of the role of personal factors in therapeutic and supervisory relationships is in keeping with Dunn's (1995) view of intersubjectivity: "[T]he very formation of the therapeutic [and supervisory] process is derived from an inexplicably intertwined mixture of the *clinical [and supervisory]* participants' subjective reactions to one another. Knowledge of the patient's [*and supervisee's*] psychology is considered contextual and idiosyncratic to the particular clinical [*supervisory*] interaction" (p. 723, emphasis in original). Beyond our ongoing acknowledgment and interest in the intersubjective nature of the therapeutic and supervisory relationships, we recognize that there are particular instances in which countertransference, in the forms of enactments and parallel processes, poses particular challenges and threaten the viability of the therapeutic and supervisory working alliances.

Enactments occur in which both parties participate in a complementary fashion, often reflecting a convergence of their individual psychological conflicts (Chused, 1991; Hirsch, 1998; Jacobs, 1986; Johan, 1992; McLaughlin, 1987, 1991; Roughton, 1993). They are by definition coconstructed and serve both individual and shared motivations of the client and clinician, supervisee and supervisor. Such instances provide opportunities, by virtue of the in vivo nature involved, to gain insight into the problematic ways in which the client or supervisee (as well as the therapist or supervisor) consciously and unconsciously organizes relationships; indeed, "perhaps some form of enactment is a necessary precursor to insight" (Tyson & Renik, 1986, p. 706). Both parties are not only drawn into enactments, but also initiate and coconstruct the enactments through their own subjective influences. Countertransference enactments, in light of the intersubjective nature of the interaction, are far more common and perhaps even inevitable. The therapeutic and supervisory goals are not the elimination of countertransference, an impossible objective even if valued, but rather to bring countertransference into the service of these professional relationships.

Countertransference enactments can also simultaneously occur within the supervisory and therapeutic relationships in the form of a parallel process. Parallel process was originally conceptualized to be the result of the therapist unconsciously identifying with an aspect of the client and then enacting the client's dynamics with the supervisor (Arlow, 1963). From relational and intersubjective perspectives, "it is suggested that a parallel process can begin with the patient, supervisee, or supervisor; involve the other dyadic partner first in an intradyadic relational pattern; then, 'carried' by the analyst/ supervisee, influence the second dyad to enact a related transference–countertransference matrix" (Frawley-O'Dea & Sarnat, 2001, p. 172). No matter the nature of their origins, parallel processes hold the potential to sweep all of the participants into a counterproductive cycle of enactments, straining both the therapeutic and supervisory alliances. Supervisors and supervisees therefore need to be mindful of the expression of transference–countertransference dynamics within the interpersonal exchanges and actions occurring within the clinical and supervisory relationships.

In the case of parallel process, countertransference enactments, within the treatment or supervision relationship, that are not identified may result in ruptures in the therapeutic or supervisory alliance or may unwittingly produce iatrogenic effects through the perpetuation of maladaptive patterns of interpersonal relating. Although few empirical studies exist, Gelso and Hayes's review of the literature (2001) suggests that acting under the sway of countertransference is harmful and that management of countertransference is necessary. Additional support for this conclusion is found in a recent empirical study of the effects of countertransference on distal outcome. Hayes et al. (1997) found that countertransference was not successfully managed in those cases assessed to have poor or moderate outcomes, "so that the adverse effect on treatment results is proportionate to the amount of [countertransference] exhibited" (p. 145). These findings, although limited by the paucity of empirical research, suggest that countertransference, if not managed, has deleterious effects on treatment. Certainly, boundary violations and egregious acts of professional misconduct and malfeasance (e.g., sexual misconduct) illustrate the dangers inherent in mismanagement of personal factors and countertransference (see chap. 7, this volume).

Supervision provides a context for examining the nature of these subjective influences and facilitates a process in which the supervisee may obtain insight into their subjective reactions as well as develop skills to usefully bring countertransference into the service of the treatment. Similarly, supervision in general and timely consultation by supervisors in particular provide a means to examine personal influences affecting the supervisory relationship and, particularly in situations in which the supervisory alliance is compromised, may assist in addressing misalliances and reestablishing a working relationship. These aims are *aspirational* and are offered with the caveat that neither the supervisee nor the supervisor will ever arrive at complete awareness and understanding of the multiple sources and expressions of personal influence. Because of the potential harm in unrecognized countertransference reactions, particularly in relationships in which a power discrepancy exists, competence in addressing the personal, subjective contributions to the clinical and supervisory processes is tantamount.

ADDRESSING COUNTERTRANSFERENCE IN SUPERVISION

Countertransference can be viewed globally to include all personal reactions or, from a more narrow technical perspective, to be the responses of the clinician or supervisor emanating from unconscious transferences and psychological conflicts and needs, which may subvert professional practice. Supervisors and supervisees alike may experience conflicts concerning feelings of attraction, sexual interest, rivalry, jealousy, or a lack of interest, connection, or concern. The identification of blind spots or of repeated interactions of boundary violations and interpersonal or affective disengagement or overinvestment points to the deleterious influences of countertransference. Misunderstanding may arise in the conjunction of appropriate empathy, interest, warmth, and attraction with displaced countertransference love or in response to other personal needs or characterological conflicts (Celenza, 1995). Further, personal reactions may suggest veiled prejudices and biases reflecting misinformed assumptions and, at times, covert or overt bigotry with respect to diversity—attitudes counter to the ethics of the profession. Similar processes exist in both clinical and supervisory relationships and require the supervisor to be equally self-reflective and mindful of the subtle, yet influential, role of personal factors in the practice of supervision, as well as in the supervisee's clinical work. Although the following discussion focuses primarily on the supervision of clinical work, the given approaches are readily available to supervisors conducting peer supervision and consultation as well as in facilitating self-reflection and self-monitoring of countertransference.

Addressing countertransference is one of the central tasks of supervision and appears to be appreciated as such by supervisees. Yourman and Farber (1996) reported that discussion of countertransference was positively associated with supervisee satisfaction and found that "the more frequently a supervisor discussed countertransference, the less [was] the tendency toward supervisee nondisclosure" (pp. 571–572). Within the theoretical and empirical literature, a number of psychological and technical competencies appear to be elemental to the ability to manage countertransference effectively. Gelso and Hayes (2001) identified interrelated self-insight, self-integration, empathy, conceptualizing ability, and the ability to manage anxiety to be factors essential to the management of countertransference. These factors appear to be associated with ratings of excellence in therapists (VanWagoner, Gelso, Hayes, & Diemer, 1991), were negatively related to supervisees' displays of countertransference behaviors (Friedman & Gelso, 2000), and in an initial study were reported to be positively associated with clinician and supervisor ratings of outcome (Gelso, Latts, Gomez, & Fassinger, 2002). Supervision may be particularly well suited to increasing supervisees' conceptualizing abilities and to providing an encouraging environment to refine interpersonal competencies of insight, empathy, and the containment of anxiety.

Inquiry into the supervisee's subjective reactions is often initiated following supervisees' reports of being frustrated, bored, distracted, confused, or irritated; when departures from the supervisee's usual clinical conduct and disruptions of therapeutic frame have occurred; or when the treatment appears to be going nowhere, resulting in minimal behavior change on the part of the client or in threats to the treatment alliance. Supervision assists novice therapists in developing management strategies to minimize interferences stemming from countertransference (E. N. Williams, Judge, Hill, & Hoffman, 1997; E. N. Williams, Polster, Grizzard, Rockenbaugh, & Judge, 2003). Supervisors bring countertransference into consideration when observing therapist behaviors that appear to be counterproductive, inconsistent with the treatment goals, or suggestive of defensiveness or disengagement on the part of the trainee. Supervisors have the advantage of observing from a position outside of the immediate intersubjective field and may note aspects of the process occluded from the therapist's awareness.

Exploration of countertransference is best accomplished on the foundation of a well-established supervisory alliance in which consideration of personal values and factors has been routinely encouraged and modeled. The examination of personal beliefs and attitudes in the context of countertransference complements efforts in the development of diversity competence (see chap. 6, this volume). In such a setting, the presence of countertransference reactions, which potentially compromise the treatment, can be examined in the context of other personal and professional influences. In addition to encouraging self-reflection, interventions addressing countertransference involve expanding the inquiry to elucidate associations and affective and behavioral reactions through the use of focusing techniques. Supervisor self-disclosure may be used to model and encourage forthrightness as well as "normalize" the process of working with countertransference reactions. The use of video observation can be used to identify particular sequences of interaction in which unusual shifts in the supervisee's demeanor, behavior, and affects occur. The supervision should be directed to assess the impact of the countertransference on the therapeutic alliance. In particular, in instances where a strain or rupture in the alliance has occurred, training and supervision in the use of metacommunication (see chap. 5, this volume) are recommended (Safran & Muran, 2000a, 2000b, 2000c).

Of utmost importance in addressing countertransference is the maintenance of the boundary between supervision and psychotherapy. Appropriate to supervision, inquiry directs attention to the interactions and processes specific to the supervised case, and, although personal issues of the supervisee, may surface, such material is considered in light of the case. On the other hand, encouraging exploration of personal conflicts in supervision compromises the integrity of the supervisory alliance and is of service to neither the client nor the supervisee. In instances where countertransference is significantly compromising the supervisee's professional development, a recommendation for consultation is appropriate. Referral to a clinician provides an additional means to ensure appropriate management in which personal issues are addressed in private psychotherapy with a clinician not associated with the training program and through which the effects of countertransference on the course of treatment and the therapeutic alliance are removed.

SELF-DISCLOSURE

Of the many ways in which personal influence is expressed, self-disclosure is the most overt form and requires particular supervisory attention. Disclosure by therapists is inevitable within the therapeutic discourse. In supervision, self-disclosure explicitly serves the functions of socialization and instruction and is integral to modeling and empathic support as reactions and illustrations from one's clinical work are shared. Through the ordinary course of professional practice, clinicians and supervisors unwittingly, as well as at times intentionally, reveal their personal selves. In the selection of the content to which they attend, the observations they make, the interventions they offer, and the manner in which they conduct themselves, therapists and supervisors implicitly convey their personally held attitudes, values, and commitments. Such self-disclosures are broadly defined as "statements that reveal something personal about therapists" (Hill & Knox, 2001, p. 413). Explicit self-disclosures are important events in the therapeutic and supervisory processes and may support or compromise the treatment. Distinctions should be made between the intentional use of self-disclosure for therapeutic or pedagogic benefit and unintentional disclosures, which usually are expressions of countertransference. In either instance, explicit self-disclosure is a matter to be considered in supervision.

Intentional Self-Disclosure

The empirical literature, although somewhat limited in scope, suggests therapist self-disclosure to be infrequent. Hill and Knox (2001) reported that approximately 3.5% of the interventions across a number of studies were found to involve self-disclosure (p. 414). The reasons for such disclosure include the aims of increasing perceived similarity, modeling appropriate behavior, fostering the therapeutic alliance, normalizing clients' experiences, offering alternative ways of thinking and acting, and responding to clients' requests for disclosure (Hill & Knox, 2001, p. 414; see also Stricker, 1990). In light of clinical theory, humanistic psychologists were more likely than psychoanalytic therapists to engage in self-disclosure. The findings of analogue research with nonclients and the few existing naturalistic studies of psychotherapy suggest that therapist self-disclosure is often perceived to be beneficial. One exploratory clinical study found client ratings of therapist helpfulness and levels of client involvement in the therapy process to be positively associated with therapist self-disclosure (Hill et al., 1988); reassuring self-disclosures were later identified to be more helpful than challenging self-disclosures (Hill, Mahalik, & Thompson, 1989).

The intentional use of self-disclosure may reflect the value of genuineness as found in existential–humanistic therapies, as a technical intervention in strategic therapy, or as an integral way of participating within relational psychoanalytic treatments. In these instances, therapist self-disclosures serve particular functions, including providing feedback, and are offered in service of the therapeutic process and relationship. Self-disclosure as a feature of metacommunication provides a form of self-explanation that establishes "an atmosphere of absolute candor" (Renik, 1995, p. 493) and prompts clinicians to reveal their processes of knowing as well as what is known (S. Gerson, 1996, p. 642). Cooper (1998), in advocating a judicious use of self-disclosure, goes further by stating, "There are times when we need to think aloud with the patient" (p. 152). Such commentary can hardly be considered impersonal or objective, as such disclosures reveal the means by which clinicians organize their experiences of their clients. However, countertransference may be revealed in the process of metacommunication, particularly when clinicians explicitly describe the aspects of the interaction that they identified as particularly salient, and discuss the ideas that informed their understanding. Interpretations, observations, and even expressions of empathy may in fact reveal as much about the therapist as they do the about client. Hoffman (1983) concluded that the client serves as the interpreter of the therapist's experience and further commented that, "[a]lthough countertransference confessions are usually ill-advised, there are times when a degree of personal, self-revealing expressiveness is not only inescapable but desirable [, and] . . . there are times when the only choices available . . . are a variety of emotionally expressive responses" (p. 418; see also Aron, 1991).

Bridges (2001) reflecting the reappraisal of intentional self-disclosure, advised therapists to "remain patient focused, rely upon the patient's resources and expertise, model emotional honesty and share their view of the clinical situation at hand" (p. 23). Hill and Knox (2001), following their review of the empirical literature, recommended the following therapeutic practice guidelines:

1. Therapists should generally disclose infrequently.
2. The most appropriate topic for therapist self-disclosure involves professional background, whereas the least appropriate topics include sexual practices and beliefs.

3. Therapists generally use disclosures to validate reality, normalize client experiences, model appropriate behavior, strengthen the therapeutic alliance, or offer alternative ways to think or act.

4. Therapists should generally avoid using disclosures that are chiefly for their own needs, that remove the focus from the client, that interfere with the flow of the session, that burden or confuse the client, that are intrusive, that blur the boundaries, or that overstimulate the client.

5. Therapist self-disclosure in response to client self-disclosure seems to be particularly effective in eliciting client disclosure.

6. Therapists should observe carefully how clients respond to therapist disclosures, ask about client reactions, and use the information to conceptualize the clients and decide how to intervene next.

7. It may be especially important for therapists to disclose with clients who have difficulty forming relationships in the therapeutic setting.

This discussion finds that a degree of self-disclosure will naturally occur through the clinical process, particularly in metacommunication. Intentional self-disclosure may be appropriate and beneficial in specific clinical situations, although therapists must take into account that "crossing the threshold of anonymity" may powerfully affect clients (Hill & Knox, 2001, p. 416). Bachelor and Horvath (1999), in discussing the therapeutic relationship, concluded that "therapist self-disclosure likely contributes to the quality of the relationship for some clients, but may be less productive with others" (p. 143). Gabbard (2001) averred that "[s]elf-disclosure of countertransference may be useful in some situations, but the sharing of some feelings will overwhelm patients and burden them in a way that may be destructive to the therapeutic process" (p. 983). Therefore, the clinical use of intentional self-disclosure requires thoughtful and judicious application. Significant clinical experience may also be required to provide a foundation on which self-disclosure may be introduced as a technical intervention. For novice clinicians, "thinking aloud" and the use of explicit self-disclosure are not recommended without the close monitoring and recommendation of the supervisor. In most instances, the issue of self-disclosure will become relevant to supervision when the supervisee has already disclosed. Attention should be placed on the clinical theory that informed the self-disclosure, the pressures within both the dyad and the therapist, and the effects of the disclosure on the therapeutic process, and the involvement of countertransference should be considered. The intentional use of self-disclosure by the clinician to influence the client to the benefit of the personal aims of the therapist reflects a significant breach of the therapeutic alliance and of professional ethics. Such behavior calls into question the appropriateness of the supervisee for professional training.

In monitoring their own use of personal influence, supervisors need to be aware of the impact that their self-disclosures have on the supervisory process. Of particular note is whether self-disclosure by the supervisor prompts the supervisee to engage in learning behaviors. Self-disclosure is useful to the extent that it builds and maintains the supervisory alliance and prompts active participation in the learning cycle (see chap. 1, this volume). Self-disclosure that does not support such a process is counterproductive, gratuitous, and may reflect countertransference needs (e.g., to be admired), or it may simply reflect inadequate training in supervision.

Unintentional Self-Disclosure

Nondeliberate self-disclosure reflects the role of countertransference in the treatment and supervisory processes and may take the form of disclosing personal facts, background, attitudes, and reactions to the client or supervisee or of providing opinions and advice concerning relationships and situations in which the client or supervisee is involved. The phenomenology of unintentional self-disclosure reflects the "felt sense" of departing from appropriate practice and discomfort regarding the intrusion of personal influence. The therapist or supervisor may experience confusion, anxiety, or shame following the disclosure. In other instances, the therapist or supervisor may be completely unaware of the disclosure, and the occurrence may become known only through the reactions of others or by review of the session within the process of supervision or consultation. In either case, it is useful to approach such self-disclosures as useful data. In supervision, it is important to avoid critical or shame-inducing feedback. Unintentional disclosures provide opportunities to understand the countertransference pressures within the relationship and to mitigate undue influence. In addition to unintentional disclosures, unexpected exposures of the personal life of the therapist or supervisor may occur (B. Gerson, 1996; Gold & Nemiah, 1993; Ulman, 2001). These exposures occur through discussion of unavoidable and obvious circumstances (e.g., pregnancy, unexpected illness, and miscarriage); through public exposure (e.g., lectures, publications, and awards), and through the client's or supervisor's gaining information informally (e.g., overhearing a reference to the clinician while in the waiting room). These exposures are not technically disclosures, because the clinician or supervisor neither intentionally nor unintentionally, under the pressure of countertransference, directly self-revealed. Nevertheless, these experiences affect the therapeutic or supervisory relationship and should be processed within supervision. Supervision can be very beneficial in helping the supervisee determine what to disclose, as well as how to address boundary setting. The intent is neither to burden the client emotionally nor to disengage from the client under the presumption of anonymity. Discussion of this issue early in one's training is particularly useful in light of the inevitability of facing such circumstances later on in one's professional career.

In light of the fact that education and training involve self-disclosure, supervisors have a challenging task in assessing the nature of their self-disclosures. The issue then becomes one of determining the purposes of the self-disclosures and their effects. Whether a disclosure is intentional or unintentional, the impact of self-disclosure on the supervisor alliance, and ultimately on case oversight and training, requires assessment.

COMPETENCIES IN ADDRESSING PERSONAL FACTORS IN SUPERVISION

As we have surveyed, personal influences are abundant and accompany every technical intervention and facet of training. In many respects, it is difficult, if not impossible, to discern the precise origins of our clinical understanding and interventions and to discriminate between personal and professional sources. Our interventions, whether in clinical consultation or supervision, are to be guided by science and yet are influenced by our humanity. Supervision therefore requires adroit attention to the confluence of the personal and professional factors that shape the therapeutic and supervisory discourses. The potential for misalliance based on countertransference influences exists in both relationships. In light of the importance of maintaining integrity-in-relationship, we place particular emphasis on the responsibility of the supervisor to be equally self-reflective and mindful of the subtle, yet influential, role of personal factors in the practice of supervision as well as in the supervisee's clinical work.

Supervisors are influenced by countertransference reactions to their supervisees in a manner similar to the way in which therapists are influenced by countertransference reactions to their clients (Teitelbaum, 1990). In light of the asymmetry in power and status in the supervisory relationship, the potential for abuse of countertransference by the supervisor is great. Although limited empirical research has been conducted, Ladany, Constantine, Miller, Erikson, and Muse-Burke (2000) published the findings of a qualitative investigation of supervisor countertransference that is salient to this discussion. Among the findings, the sources of supervisor countertransference included the intern's personal style, the supervisor's unresolved personal issues, interactions between the intern and the supervisory environment, problematic client–intern interactions, intern–supervisor interactions, and interactions between the supervisor and the supervisory environment (Ladany et al., 2000, pp. 106–108). The supervisor experiencing a range of emotions and included situations of parall

As in clinical work, commitment to self-reflection and the supervision and consultation may enable the supervisor to bec of conflicts that are negatively affecting the development and maintenance of the supervisory working alliance. A number of competencies are involved in addressing personal factors in supervision. These are included at the end of the chapter.

Attention to the impact of personal factors, including countertransference, within the supervisory and clinical relationships is integral to the competent practice of supervision. Failure to attend to countertransference reactions or undue personal influence may result in the perversion of the supervisory process, threatening the integrity of the relationship and compromising the supervisor's ability to provide oversight of the clinical work and effective training. We suggest that supervisees or supervisors who are unable or unwilling to explore their personal contributions or who remain blind to the enactments in which they participate may be unsuitable for clinical training in psychotherapy or for providing clinical supervision.

Competencies

- An understanding of the value-based nature of clinical and supervisory practices
- An understanding of the theoretical and empirical literature concerning countertransference and its appearance in clinical and supervisory practices
- Interpersonal and professional skills that contribute to the establishment and maintenance of a working supervisory alliance, including integrity, sensitivity to diversity, empathy, warmth, clinical competence, maintenance of professional boundaries, and management of countertransference
- Supervision behaviors that foster self-insight, self-integration, anxiety management, empathy, and conceptualization abilities in the supervisee, including providing information and theory on countertransference; observing and listening for the appearance of personal influence and countertransference and attending to these occurrences in a direct, nonpunitive, and uncritical manner as phenomena to be examined; engaging in open-ended inquiry; providing feedback; engaging in self-disclosure, and engaging in modeling response to in-session countertransference
- Monitoring the supervisory alliance and supervisor countertransference, obtaining peer supervision and consultation as appropriate

5

ALLIANCE IN THERAPEUTIC AND SUPERVISORY RELATIONSHIPS

The therapeutic alliance has repeatedly been demonstrated to be essential to the psychotherapeutic process and is considered to be equally salient in the supervisory relationship. This chapter presents an overview of the empirical research on alliances, a discussion of the alliance construct, and an approach and technique to address alliance strain and ruptures in both therapeutic and supervisory relationships.

Meta-analyses of empirical research conducted over the past 25 years have found the therapeutic relationship and the alliance that forms within that relationship to be robust variables associated with treatment outcome (Bachelor & Horvath, 1999; Horvath, 1994, 2000, 2001; Horvath & Symonds, 1991; Lambert, 1982; Lambert & Barley, 2001; Lambert & Bergin, 1994; Luborsky, 1994; Martin, Garske, & Davis, 2000). Horvath (2001) conducted a metaanalysis of 90 independent clinical investigations and concluded, "Two decades of empirical research have consistently linked the quality of the alliance between therapist and client with therapy outcome. The magnitude of this relation appears to be independent of the type of therapy and whether outcome is assessed from the perspective of the therapist, client, or observer" (p. 365; see also Beutler et al., 1994, and Binder & Strupp, 1997a). Although critics point out that the variance estimates are modest—for example, Martin et al. (p. 27) placed their most liberal estimate at 7% (see also Beutler & Harwood, 2002; Stevens, Hynan, &

Allen, 2000)—there is a common-sense appeal, based on clinical experience, to the proposition that the quality of the therapeutic relationship significantly influences treatment outcome and should be a focus of training (American Psychological Association, Division 29 Task Force on Empirically Supported Therapy Relationships, 2002, p. 5).

Bordin (1979), expanding on psychoanalytic contributions of Sterba (1934), Zetzel (1956), and Greenson (1967), together with Rogers' (1957) identification of the necessary and sufficient conditions for personality change, proposed that the therapeutic alliance is an ongoing creation of the client and the clinician and concerns three interrelated features: *change goals and tasks, bonding,* and *strain.* The alliance forms as a result of the client and therapist working together on change goals and therapeutic tasks and via bonding or partner compatibility, which "grows out of their experience of association in a shared activity [and] is likely to be expressed and felt in terms of liking, trusting, respect for each other, and a sense of common commitment and shared understanding in the activity" (Bordin, 1994, p. 16). Strain refers to a significant deviation in the patient's commitment to the working alliance. Bordin (1979) suggested that the kinds of problems that brought the patient to therapy will become manifest in the treatment relationship and will become a necessary focus of the therapeutic work. Strains that occur during the formation of the initial alliance suggest more significant difficulties in forming relationships, whereas strains that emerge after the alliance has been formed reflect the self-defeating propensities of the patient being repeated within the therapeutic relationship. Strains and ruptures in the alliance are seen as normative in the therapeutic process and provide opportunities for change. "The 'work of the alliance' becomes the rebuilding of the damaged alliance and thus the acquisition of new ideas about self and relationships (Bordin, 1976, 1989)" (Horvath, 1994).

Safran and Muran (1998) suggested that a broadened conceptualization of the therapeutic alliance is particularly useful, as it "highlights that at a fundamental level, the patient's ability to trust, hope, and have faith in the therapist's ability to help always plays a central role in the change process" (p. 7). They commented on four implications that are relevant to our consideration of supervision and will serve as a close to our introduction of the therapeutic alliance:

- This conceptualization of the therapeutic alliance highlights the interdependence of relational and technical factors in psychotherapy. It suggests that the meaning of any technical factor can be understood only in the interpersonal context in which it is applied.
- The foregoing condition provides a rational framework for guiding the therapist's interventions in a flexible fashion.

- Ruptures in the therapeutic alliance are the key to understanding the patient's representational world.
- Understanding patients as being diverse in capacity and variable in experiencing highlights the importance of the negotiation between patient and therapist about the tasks and goals of therapy. (cf. pp. 8–9)

The factors that influence the development of the therapeutic alliance similarly affect the formation of the supervisory working alliance. Bordin (1983) described the supervisory version of the model, which is based on establishment of mutually determined goals (e.g., mastering specific skills, enlarging one's understanding of clients, and maintaining standards of service) and the means to achieve them. As with the therapeutic relationship, an emotional bond and alliance will form through the process of working collaboratively toward achievement of the goals. Relational qualities are seen by supervisees as important to the supervisory relationship and, in our view, are particularly salient when addressing factors that are by definition personal to the supervisee (see chap. 3, this volume). Highly rated supervisor qualities include empathy, a nonjudgmental stance, impartment of a sense of validation or affirmation, an attitude of acceptance, provision of encouragement to explore and experiment, integrity, provision of autonomy, warmth, and an understanding nature. Ladany (2002) reported that a strong supervisory working alliance seems to play a significant role in the supervision process and outcome, such as when training in multicultural competence or addressing trainee self-disclosure and non-disclosure; however, "the alliance in supervision also seems to be the one thing that supervisors, particularly beginning or untrained supervisors, are most apt to forget about or not consider" (p. 15). The development of the working supervisory alliance is a central pillar in our model and is supported by the superordinate values, including integrity-in-relationship. We turn now to supervisory approaches to addressing alliance strains and ruptures in both the therapeutic and supervisory relationship.

ADDRESSING ALLIANCE ISSUES IN SUPERVISION

Alliance, as a transtheoretical or pantheoretical concept, is integral to the outcome of psychological treatment (Safran, 1993b). It is "part of a broader set of attitudes, values, expectations, sentiments, and interpersonal interaction patterns that constitute the 'therapeutic' process. Patient and therapist personality variables, as well as therapist techniques and skills (or the lack of them), contribute to this process like tributaries contribute to the main body of a river" (Binder & Strupp, 1997a, p. 121). Alliance is thus a major focus of supervision, particularly with respect to personal factors, which are posited to play a central role in its development.

Although the formation and the maintenance of the therapeutic and supervisory alliances are coconstructed, the clinician and supervisor, respectively, bear primary responsibility in facilitating their development. Personal factors as well as professional training make up the therapist's and supervisor's contributions to the formation of the alliance. Personal qualities of genuineness, reliability, warmth, and the capacity for empathy and emotional engagement support the development of the bond (Rogers, 1957). Supervisors must attend not only to technical skills but also to enhancing the interpersonal, signature strengths of the supervisee as well as attending to the personal qualities that they bring to the supervisory relationship. Personal values and attitudes derived from sociocultural or other personal influences may delimit one's ability to understand and to empathically attune to the other's experiences and worldview. Misattunement, whether based on sociocultural insensitivity or other personal factors, may cause clients or supervisees to experience the therapist or supervisor, respectively, as *not* being understanding and helpful—factors that are associated with positive outcomes. This condition is one of the reasons that building diversity competence and attention to personal factors is fundamental to training. We turn now to a focused discussion on supervisory approaches to assist supervisees in addressing alliance strains and ruptures in their clinical work.

Negative reactions to clients, as compared with other forms of personal response or countertransference, pose a particular challenge, especially when encountered early in treatment. Such experiences, although potentially providing an important source of information about the client, the therapeutic relationship, or the supervisee's attitudes, endanger the development of an adequate working alliance. The sources of these negative reactions may originate in personality variables of the client and clinician (Sexton, Hembre, & Kvarme, 1996) or may emerge as the result of misattunements within the interaction. Clients with hostile–dominant personalities have been found to be less likely to form positive alliances, whereas a personality factors such as histrionic, narcissistic, antisocial, and paranoid features were found to be negatively related to Total Alliance as measured on the Working Alliance Inventory (Muran, Segal, Samstag, & Crawford, 1994). This finding is in keeping with the clinical literature, indicating the difficulties clinicians face in facilitating the development of an initial therapeutic alliance and managing countertransference, including negative responses, when working with clients in the borderline–narcissistic spectrum (Gabbard et al., 1988; Gabbard & Wilkinson, 1994). Although negative reactions on the part of the therapist are expected and understandable, failure to adequately contain them and to respond appropriately may lead to alliance ruptures and precipitous terminations of treatment. Novice clinicians in particular must be provided with safety and understanding within the supervisory relationship to help them explore their responses and to learn the skills of managing rather than acting out their personal reactions.

A more vexing challenge for the supervisor occurs when a supervisee appears to initiate and reinforce negative patterns of interaction with seemingly little cognizance of personal involvement. Beyond the limitations that can accompany inexperience or inadequate training, these interactions may reflect more general relational or personality tendencies. In light of the ethical responsibilities to the client, the supervisor must more actively focus attention on the therapist's in-session behaviors, in an attempt to stave off a therapeutic crisis. Although at times explicit instruction is required, we have found that reorienting the supervisee to take a stance of inquiry, to decenter, and to step back from a defensive mode of reacting is sufficient to interrupt the cycle of misattunements. These episodes may be understood to result from the novice clinician's maladaptive response to a situation of interpersonal anxiety, danger, and loss of control. As the novice therapist feels increased anxiety and incompetence, maladaptive behavioral repertoires derived from personal influences override professional training. In the face of mounting anxiety and self-criticism, the supervisee may resort to becoming increasingly controlling, subtly critical, or disengaged from the client. Negative personal attributes, such as those identified by Ackerman and Hilsenroth (2001; rigid, uncertain, exploitive, critical, distant, tense, aloof, or distracted), may influence the therapist's interventions, covertly reinforcing hostile patterns of interaction. Further, such tendencies may lead the therapist to engage in negative countertransference enactments, and jeopardize the treatment. Rather than offering flexible responses to the client, the therapist may respond by becoming authoritarian and rigid in his or her application of technique. In such circumstances, clinical interventions are used in the service of self-protection and may express aggression toward the client.

Supervisees can be helped by focusing attention to (a) the states of mind and attributions that are being stimulated within the clinical interaction, (b) the mental states they are attempting to ward off, (c) the interventions applied and their effects on the interaction, and (d) alternative behaviors. Further focused inquiry is required for the supervisee to gain insight into the negative countertransference enactments and to obtain a modicum of containment with which the threats to the therapeutic alliance may be addressed. With insight and empathic understanding, the supervisee may be able to offer a countermove that involves more responsive and appropriate interventions and is sufficient to quell the turbulence of the misalliance. With the diminution of the therapeutic crisis, the therapist may then begin the work in supervision of clarifying the nature of the enactment, understanding his or her personal involvement, and learning how to address the rupture in the therapeutic alliance.

No matter the root cause of the misalliance in the therapeutic relationship, the ensuing countertransference and negative reactions must be addressed in supervision. An appropriate and reality-based tone for this examination can be obtained by keeping in mind the rigors of psychotherapeutic work and the unique strains placed on the novice clinician, whose sense of self and budding confidence as a psychologist are on the line in every session. Supervision needs to provide a safe place for the exploration of the personal responses to the psychological demands placed on the psychotherapist, taking into account that negative reactions come with the clinical territory.

Addressing Ruptures in the Alliance

The development and maintenance of the therapeutic alliance is critical to the success of the treatment; indeed, it is one of the most urgent tasks in the beginning of treatment. Horvath (2001) found that "[i]f a good alliance is not developed by the fifth session, then the likelihood of successful treatment outcome is significantly diminished. A corollary of this proposition is that a misjudgment of the status of the alliance can endanger the treatment outcome" (p. 171). Treatment not only proceeds on the foundation of a strong alliance, but also is advanced through the successful resolution of subsequent alliance disruptions, which, as per Bordin's theory, appear to contribute to a client's progress. Strains within the alliance are seen as natural phenomena within the treatment process (Bachelor & Salame, 2000; Bordin, 1994; Safran & Muran, 2000a, 2000b, 2000c).

The multiple roles of clinician, educator, and evaluator become evident when supervisors address ruptures in the therapeutic alliance. Supervisors must act to ensure the welfare of the client and safeguard the treatment process; provide understanding, mentoring, counsel, and instruction to the supervisee; and evaluate the supervisee's ability to implement the recommendations offered and to learn from the experience. Crises in therapeutic relationships inevitably evoke a host of personal responses in novice clinicians, as they may be at a loss as to what to do to effectively address negative reactions and deleterious processes. These circumstances are situations in which personal rather than professional factors are apt to shape the interaction. Theoretical and empirical research conducted by Safran (1993a, 1993b), Safran & Muran (1994, 1995, 1996, 1998, 2000a, 2000b, 2002c), and others (Bordin, 1979, 1994; Horvath, 2000, 2001; Safran, Muran, Samstag, & Stevens, 2001) have contributed significantly to our understanding of the therapeutic alliance, the causes of ruptures in the alliance processes, and procedures that bring about the repair of alliance ruptures.

We start with the premise that threats to the alliance are common rather than rare occurrences and are the products of complex interpersonal interactions that involve the individual subjectivities of both participants. Early in treatment, differences in expectations of treatment may forestall the emergence of a nascent alliance. At times, patterns of hostile interactions develop rapidly in which therapists actively, though unwittingly, contribute to escalations that threaten the alliance and imperil the treatment. Novice clinicians are at particular risk of enjoining these enactments, in light of their understandable performance anxiety, inexperience, and interpersonal discomfort in assuming a new professional role. In addition, personal limitations derived from early and pervasive patterns of interpersonal relating may prompt defense-inspired behaviors in response to the provocations of the client, further exacerbating the negative process. Supervisees may be both personally and professionally unprepared to deal effectively with the emotionally charged and damaging interactions. Safran and Muran (2000b, 2000c) provided a clinical model that supervisors may use in training supervisees to manage alliance ruptures as well as directly in addressing ruptures in the supervisory alliance.

Identifying the Causes of Ruptures in the Alliance

Ruptures and impasses result from conflicts in two major categories: (a) tasks and goals of treatment and (b) problems in the bond dimension of the relationship based on the conceptualization of Bordin (1979; Hill, Nutt-Williams, Heaton, Thompson, & Rhodes, 1996; Safran & Muran, 2000b). There is some evidence that these categories reflect two independent factors (agreement–confidence and relationship) that covary in contribution to the alliance (Andrusyna, Tang, DeRubeis, & Luborsky, 2001). In both circumstances, disagreements, misunderstanding, and confusion negatively affect the development of a collaborative, empathic relationship. Strain may be created in light of the procedures of the treatment; for example, active, directive approaches are more likely to induce ruptures stemming from clients feeling that they are being controlled (cf. Safran & Muran, 2000a), or in experiential therapies, clients may have difficulty turning inward to represent their experience in new ways or may question the usefulness of such an activity (Watson & Greenberg, 2000, p. 175).

Misattunements may arise when differences in beliefs and values lead to misunderstandings. A therapist may ignore or inadvertently devalue matters of importance to the client or be insensitive to culturally anchored experiences, traditions, moral perspectives, and beliefs. In other instances, intense transference–countertransference enactments may be triggered based on personal factors. Both client and therapist may begin to feel at odds with each other and may mutually be in a state of "not being understood," which may lead to negative attributions about the other and thereby undermine the therapeutic alliance. These states of mind raise anxiety and distrust and for some clients (and clinicians) trigger immediate hostility. The associated cognitions and affects then prompt personality-based defensive and aggressive responses. These responses may range from detachment and disinterested compliance to manifest expressions of distrust and hostility. Differences in expectations about treatment rapidly become conflicts in the bond, and conversely, breaches of trust and empathy foreclose meaningful participation in the tasks of therapy. A coconstructed cycle of misattunements becomes established, and the alliance deteriorates.

Although supervisees generally are comfortable disclosing to their supervisors negative feelings toward clients (Yourman & Farber, 1996), many may feel embarrassed or afraid of their supervisors' reactions when reporting breaches in the alliance. Further, they may not perceive or know how to address the tenuous quality of the therapeutic alliance. Supervisors can be helpful by (a) collaborating with the supervisee to identify the initial sources and nature of the conflict or misattunement, (b) processing negative countertransference reactions, and (c) providing support and clinical direction to initiate resolution. Initial supervisory interventions aim to assist the therapist in shifting from a position of negative countertransference to a posture that allows a degree of objectivity. The supervisory alliance provides a context to begin the process of "disembedding from the relational configuration [of the therapy relationship]" (Safran & Muran, 2000b, p. 108) and encourages reflection on the events and meanings being mutually coconstructed. It is crucial at this stage of the supervisory relationship that the supervisor avoids interventions that may induce shame in the supervisee. Experiences of shame will discourage clinicians from disclosing and reflecting on the personal influences shaping their interventions. Shame-inducing comments parallel the implicit dissatisfaction of the client with the therapist and may rupture the supervisory alliance. An environment of safety and collaboration is required to facilitate examination of personal factors.

The process of resolving the alliance rupture begins with direct inquiry into the interactions and specific content that precipitated the negative interactions (Rhodes, Hill, Thompson, & Elliott, 1994; Safran & Muran, 1995; Safran, Muran, & Samstag, 1994). Through close analysis of these components, the supervisor assists the supervisee in developing an initial understanding of the origins of the mutual negative reactions, as well as to gain some training, through modeling by the supervisor, in ways to facilitate such an analysis with the client. Ruptures may be precipitated by a breach of the client's wants or needs, for example by doing something the client does not want, giving unwanted advice, not properly focusing on the client's concerns or failing to do something that the client wants or needs (Rhodes et al., 1994). Also, Omer (1994, 2000) identified three major roads to therapeutic impasse: (a) The therapist and the client develop a hopeless narrative about the client's difficulties; (b) the therapeutic strategy grinds to a halt; and (c) the therapeutic interaction becomes trapped in a negative pattern. When the therapist and client are faced with an impasse in which the therapeutic work is mired in nonproductive interactions, frustration often ensues, leading to threats to the alliance and a complete breakdown of the therapeutic relationship. Markers of ruptures in the therapeutic alliance include both confrontational behaviors, for example, overt expression of negative sentiments, disagreement about the goals or tasks of therapy, or through self-esteem enhancing operation; and nonconfrontational behaviors, for example, compliance (which is ineffectual), indirect communication of negative sentiments or hostility, or nonresponsiveness to therapist interventions. Sometimes, supervisors hear of the depth of frustration only after the fact, when supervisees report a sense of relief at an impasse being solved by a client leaving treatment. What goes unsolved, of course, is the rupture in the alliance.

The supervisory process is not intended to determine the nature of the rupture, in isolation of the client. Rather, supervision provides a means for the development of provisional observations and interpretations. The identification of the rupture marker and examination of the process are accomplished within the therapeutic process, as a collaborative effort that involves process metacommunication.

Although countertransference and its personal origins may be considered, we find it more useful to initially focus on the relational dimensions of the clinical interaction. We recommend this focus because therapists need to quickly gain an understanding of the interpersonal transactions taking place so that they may circumvent repetitions of negative interaction and commence rebuilding rapport. Through a sequential analysis of the transactions, including consideration of the therapist's cognitions, attributions, affects, and behaviors, the therapeutic relational pattern can be identified. The therapist is also encouraged to imagine the experience of the interaction from the point of view of the client. Perspective taking is necessary for the clinician to develop an empathic understanding of the motives behind the client's overt behaviors of aggression, withdrawal, or noncompliance. Supervisors may use role-playing, empty-chair, and focusing techniques in addition to inquiry and self-reflection to help the supervisee obtain a sense of what sessions may be like for the client. The focus on the interpersonal transactions does not mean that personal influences and reactions are summarily dismissed. However, exploration of countertransference is situated within the overarching goals of stabilizing the therapeutic relationship, eliminating "acting in" on the part of the therapist, and beginning the process of repairing the working alliance.

Supervising Metacommunication

A second task of supervision is to assist the supervisee to initiate the process of metacommunication (Kiesler, 1996), a task that is essential to the repair of the alliance. Metacommunication consists of the "attempt to step outside of the relational cycle that is currently being enacted by treating it as the focus of collaborative exploration: that is, communicating *about* the transaction or implicit communication that is taking place" (Safran & Muran, 2000b, p. 108, emphasis in original). This task is in keeping with Interpersonal Process Recall (Kagan, 1980; Kagan & Kagan, 1990; Kagan & Kagan, 1997), a widely used procedure in which the supervisee is encouraged to describe underlying thoughts and feelings that occurred during the therapeutic interaction. Such a procedure provides a means to process the dynamics that shaped the clinical process and builds skills in metacognition, which is essential in metacommunication.

Binder and Strupp (1997a) commented that what is required to metacommunicate "involves what Schön (1987) calls 'reflection in action,' the ability to observe process as one is participating in it and to improvise effective strategies while one is in the midst of acting" (pp. 134–135). Analysis of the relational and interpersonal transactions in addressing ruptures in the alliance should be emphasized rather than transference interpretations. The supervisee may require support and guidance, as such a process inevitably evokes personal vulnerability as well as the use of new clinical skills. Further, metacommunication requires the therapist to bring the relationship to a new level of collaboration in which the immediate interaction is the focus of inquiry. It involves a willingness to engage in the "here-and-now analysis of maladaptive cognitions, sentiments, and behaviors that are recurrently enacted in patterned form in the therapeutic relationship" (Binder & Strupp, 1997a, pp. 133–134).

The use of metacommunication, which includes challenging clients to disclose their experiences of the therapeutic interaction, has been found to be necessary to the reestablishment of a viable working alliance. Kivlighan and Schmitz (1992) found that improvement in poor working alliances was related to increases in counselor challenges and in the focus placed on the relationship. The process of metacommunication inevitably raises the anxiety of the supervisee and illuminates the influence of personal contributions to psychological treatment. The psychologist may find that his or her self-perceptions and behaviors are challenged by the client's observations and commentary. It is often difficult for therapists, no matter their level of training and experience, to hear that they are not as perceptive, empathic, attentive, or helpful than they believe themselves to be.

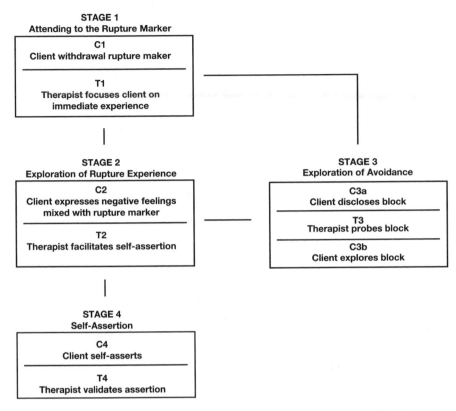

STAGE 1
Attending to the Rupture Marker

C1
Client withdrawal rupture maker
T1
Therapist focuses client on immediate experience

STAGE 2
Exploration of Rupture Experience

C2
Client expresses negative feelings mixed with rupture marker
T2
Therapist facilitates self-assertion

STAGE 3
Exploration of Avoidance

C3a
Client discloses block
T3
Therapist probes block
C3b
Client explores block

STAGE 4
Self-Assertion

C4
Client self-asserts
T4
Therapist validates assertion

Figure 5.1. Therapeutic alliance rupture resolution model (C = Client; T = Therapist). From "Resolving Therapeutic Alliance Ruptures: Diversity and Integration." *Journal of Clinical Psychology/In Session: Psychotherapy in Practice, 56*(2), 233–243 (2000), by J. D. Safran and J. C. Muran, © 2000 John Wiley & Sons, Inc. Reprinted with permission.

Stages of the Repair Process

Safran and Muran (2000b, 2000c) proposed a stage-process model in which the rupture marker is identified, the block to affective expression is explored, and the client is encouraged to explore and to assert his or her experience of the rupture. Ruptures in the alliance may take the form of withdrawal or confrontation. Withdrawal ruptures may manifest as disengagement from the therapist, the client's own emotions, or the therapeutic process. Confrontation ruptures involve overt expressions of anger, resentment, or dissatisfaction with the therapist or the treatment (Safran & Muran, 2000c). The stages of the repair process of the withdrawal rupture are presented in Figure 5.1 (see Safran & Muran, 2000b, for a presentation of the confrontation alliance and complete explication of the model).

Safran and Muran (2000c) provided a cogent description of the transition required of the therapist to commence the rebuilding of the alliance:

> Therapists often begin the resolution process as coparticipants in a maladaptive interpersonal cycle. Expressions of client hostility are often responded to defensively or with counterhostility. Compliant or avoidant responses to the rupture are often responded to with overbearing or controlling behavior. For example, clients who respond to an interpretation in a compliant fashion may elicit further attempts on the therapist's part to control, dominate them, or tell them what to do. In such situations, it is critical for therapists to become aware of the feelings evoked in them and to begin metacommunicating with the client about the interaction, rather than continuing to participate in the dysfunctional cognitive-interpersonal cycle. (p. 240)

Commencing with this initial stage, the therapist actively elicits exploration and disclosure of thoughts and feelings regarding the rupture, which implicitly include negative feedback to the therapist. The therapist must be in a posture of neutrality (or openness) and nondefensiveness to draw forth and empathize with the experience of the client.

Many supervisees need to be explicitly prepared to accept perceptions that differ from their own and to be reminded that the purpose is not to assign blame for the rupture, but rather to provide empathic understanding of the *client's* experience as well as to modify their own behavior. Further, therapists require support and encouragement to stay engaged and to facilitate a process of intense emotion, which will likely stimulate a host of personal reactions in the clinician.

Subsequent stages focus on the exploration of thoughts and feelings associated with the rupture; the factors or resistances restricting such exploration; the expression of negative sentiments, which initially includes a disowning of responsibility, followed by a deepening awareness on disavowed needs; and finally acceptance and communication to the therapist of wishes, needs, and feelings.

Differences in clinical theory determine the content and use of the material derived from the process of metacommunication (Safran & Muran, 1998). For example, psychodynamic clinicians may be interested in the parallels between the client's perceptions of the therapeutic interaction and the perceptions originating in developmentally salient relationships (Frawley-O'Dea & Sarnat, 2001); experiential therapists may focus explicitly on the conflicts in "experiencing" in the here and now; and cognitive psychologists may focus on the schemas that inform the interpersonal transactions in the clinical dyad (Greenwald & Young, 1998). Central to the process of repair, regardless of the technical differences inherent in clinical theories, is close attention to the here-and-now interpersonal dynamics. It is through the client and clinician collaboratively working to understand the natures of the transactions that the alliance can be rebuilt on a stronger foundation. It has been our clinical experience that the resolution of alliance ruptures not only is integral to maintaining the therapeutic relationship, but also facilitates change processes directly related to the relational difficulties that brought clients to psychotherapy in the first place. For clients, the process of repairing the alliance rupture involves in vivo learning and includes corrective emotional experiences, which may generalize to other relationships. For novice clinicians, the experience of learning how to metacommunicate, to face alliance ruptures and impasses directly, to understand firsthand the influence of personal factors and countertransference, and finally to successfully facilitate the repair of the alliance fosters the development of important clinical competencies.

Supervision plays an integral role by providing supervisees with a technical model to address threats to the alliance, a relationship that supports the processes of disembedding and metacommunication, and, importantly, empathic understanding. Beyond issues of training, the clinical task of repairing alliances is essential to the efficacy of the treatment and as such reflects the supervisor's commitment to provide the highest quality care of the client. For example, there are cases in which, despite the best efforts of the clinician, it appears that the alliance has been irreparably compromised. The supervisor, to safeguard the client's welfare and treatment, may initiate a number of interventions. For instance, the supervisor may conduct a consultation with the client; although the supervisor may not using metacommunication techniques, he or she will focus on the client's experience and attempt to reestablish an initial alliance between the client and the mental health institution. A useful entry point in such consultation is a discussion of the client's expectations of treatment; this topic addresses the goals and tasks components of the alliance, which have been found to affect outcome (Horvath & Symonds, 1991; Long, 2001; Tryon & Winograd, 2002). Following such clarification, collaboration can be aimed at reestablishing treatment with the same clinician, commending treatment with a different therapist, or initially conducting treatment with the supervisor serving as a cotherapist.

Misunderstanding and misalliances may develop at times within supervisory relationships. Using a metacommunication approach, supervisors can facilitate growth within the alliance in a manner similar to that in the clinical setting. Beyond repairing the alliance, such experiences provide essential modeling and implicit training in the skill of metacommunication. Conflicts that are not addressed in supervision may compromise the integrity of the supervisory process as well as communicate through the supervisor's behavior that avoidance and unresponsiveness are acceptable. The supervisor's willingness and ability to respond directly to misattunement within the supervisory relationship instill an ethic of responsiveness and counter any tendency on the supervisee's part toward unresponsiveness as a professional (Greben, 1985). In both clinical and supervisory settings, attention must be paid to the power differential in the relationship to ensure that process inquiry is used to forward mutual understanding rather than to stabilize or to reassert the authority status of the supervisor or clinician with respect to the supervisee or the client, respectively.

When difficulties emerge in a supervised case, novice clinicians understandably experience an increase in concern about their competence and how the treatment impasse will influence their clinical evaluation. In fact, fears regarding negative evaluations may actually play a role in weakening the working alliance (Burke, Goodyear, & Guzzard, 1998). To the extent that supervisees believe that their standing is in jeopardy, they may become defensive, less disclosing, less effective, and potentially retaliatory toward the client. However, if alliance ruptures are situated in the context of naturally occurring challenges within the treatment process and are not necessarily presented as indicators of therapist failure, students and interns may be better able to facilitate the repair of the alliance. Evaluations are best informed by how supervisees address ruptures and respond to recommendations, rather than by the fact that threats to the alliance occurred. However, it is of serious concern when supervisees are unable or unwilling to address their coconstruction of difficulties in therapeutic relationships and are noncompliant with supervisors' recommendations for addressing alliance ruptures. In situations where there are repeated threats to alliances across clients and these threats appear to be based primarily within the relational component, careful assessments of the supervisee's interpersonal and clinical competencies, as well as suitability for psychotherapy practice, are required.

Therapist attributes that can negatively affect the formation of an alliance with a client can equally influence the relationship between a supervisor and a supervisee. In fact, we believe that the adverse impacts can actually be as or more deleterious to the supervisor–supervisee relationship, in light of the unique power differential in supervision. For example, a client can easily, in some respects, leave a therapist without threat; a supervisee may be in a more precarious position should a destructive misalliance be established. We believe that the therapist personal attributes that positively influence the therapeutic alliance, for example, being flexible, honest, respectful, trustworthy, confident, warm, interested, and open (Ackerman & Hilsenroth, 2003, p. 1; see also Horvath, 2001), play a similar role in the supervisory alliance. Additionally, many of the techniques that were identified by Ackerman and Hilsenroth (2003) as positively related with therapeutic alliance, for example, exploration, reflection, noting past success, and accurate interpretation, also contribute to a positive supervisory alliance. Additional competencies, such as values sensitivity and perspective taking, conjoined with the relational qualities, establish a supervision alliance that encourages the examination of personal factors and countertransference.

Ruptures and Impasses in the Supervisory Alliance

The qualities and experiences that affect the development of therapeutic relationships similarly affect the supervisory relationship. Interpersonal and professional competencies, such as empathy, warmth, respect, clinical knowledge, and skill, as well as agreement concerning the goals and tasks of supervision, contribute to the formation of an effective supervisory working alliance in which personal influence and countertransference may be addressed. Inadequacies in those competencies or lapses in interpersonal or professional conduct may threaten the development of the working alliance. The Working Alliance Inventory (Bahrick, 1989, Appendix B, this volume) provides a useful self-report measure to assess alliance factors (i.e., task, bond, goal) in the supervisory relationship. Further investigation is required to establish its reliability and validity.

Ladany et al. (2000) reported that although the supervisees believed that supervisor countertransference initially weakened the relationship, they later stated that it strengthened the supervision. Part of the benefit was identified in the supervisor's facilitation of a discussion with the intern and in his or her efforts to deepen the intern's understanding of some of the interpersonal dynamics that occur in therapy (p. 109). Supervisors managed their reactions by consulting with colleagues, participating in a supervision group, or disclosing aspects of their experience with the intern (p. 110). Important to the resolution of the countertransference were identifying the reactions as countertransference, seeking consultation, and using disclosure. Such processing appears crucial to managing reactions that hold the potential to be expressed counterproductively.

Negative or counterproductive experiences may occur and, when not addressed, may result in ruptures and impasses. Such conditions threaten the viability of the working alliance, particularly with respect to the processing of personal factors, and in turn compromise the ability of the supervisor to adequately monitor the treatment and to safeguard the client. Ramos-Sanchez et al. (2002) reported that 21.4% of the participants in a survey of psychology interns and graduate students indicated having a negative experience in supervision (p. 199). Negative experiences were associated with weaker supervisory alliances, and the impact of the experiences appeared to be "global and long lasting, causing supervisees to question their choice of career and possibly change their career plans" (p. 200). Gray et al. (2001) conducted interviews with 13 psychotherapy trainees, each of whom reported experiencing a counterproductive event in supervision. The trainees described a wide range of emotional responses and believed that these incidents weakened the supervisory relationship, affected their work with clients, and changed their ways of approaching their supervisors; for example, most did not discuss the counterproductive event with their supervisors. These reports are consistent with previous research findings and point to the necessity of supervisors' addressing conflicts in supervisory relationships. The best cure is found in prevention.

Supervisors support this aim by being mindful of the effects of their personal and professional conduct and striving to be responsive to the needs of the supervisee by conveying a clear understanding of the objectives of the supervisor and the mutual responsibilities of the supervisor and supervisee. Events involving shame, parallel process, and boundary violations are of particular importance when addressing personal factors in supervision.

Shame

In supervision, novice clinicians are required to examine their use of personal influence and the intrusion of countertransference in treatment. Such exploration necessarily involves personal exposure, which may induce feelings of discomfort, anxiety, and shame. Inquiry into countertransference reactions, in addition to the ongoing evaluation of technical skills, focuses attention directly on the supervisee and may create a sense of vulnerability as well as amplify tendencies toward unreasonable self-criticism. Alonso and Rutan (1988) observed that, although psychotherapy supervision stimulates shame, shame is rarely addressed in supervision. Shame-inducing experiences may constitute counterproductive or negative events that not only foreclose the important examination of the clinician's personal influence on treatment, but may also lead to nondisclosure of the actual transactions occurring in psychotherapy. In such circumstances, the supervisory alliance may become so weakened that it is rendered incapable of fulfilling its responsibilities to the client, the supervisee, and the training institutions.

Shame is a consequence of interpersonal as well as intrapersonal dynamics. Supervisees may feel embarrassed when personal lapses or influences are discussed with valued supervisors, or they may feel shame when discovering a discrepancy between their performance and internally held standards. Shame inducement therefore is a product of both the relationship and the individual. That moments of shame or embarrassment appear in supervision should not be surprising, in light of the intrinsic demands of training in a very personally demanding profession, a profession that at times has been referred to as impossible. Talbot (1995), writing of her own experiences as a supervisee, offers the perspective that shame may arise when the therapist fears or experiences not being approved of or admired by an idealized supervisor. Although supervisors may be vigilant about not providing feedback in a shame-inducing manner, the supervisee may nonetheless feel shame. One should therefore be observant of—and in Talbot's (1995) view, "unearth" —the hidden manifestations of shame, such as increases in nondisclosure, avoidance of discussion of certain cases, intellectualization, and provision of experience-distant or insipid descriptions of clinical interactions. Hahn (2001), drawing on the work of Nathanson (1992), identified four reactions to shame that may affect supervision: withdrawal, avoidance, attack on the self, and attack on others.

Supervisors can initiate exploration or the supervisee's feeling of shame or embarrassment by focusing attention, in an empathic and supportive manner, on the supervisee's experience of the supervisor's commentaries and recommendations and by acknowledging the challenges involved in learning to conduct psychotherapy.

The supervisor must take a proactive stance, particularly if Gray et al.'s (2001) findings represent supervisees' beliefs that supervisors are not cognizant of counterproductive events and that supervisees are not disposed to bring such events into discussion. Supervisors need to examine any personal factors and their own transferences to their supervisees, as well as to consider institutional and social sources of shaming that may contribute to ruptures in the alliance. Talbot (1995) offers six recommendations for addressing shame in supervision: (1) Be alert to the supervisee's disguised shame, (2) encourage the supervisee to explore how the therapy and the supervision are experienced, (3) demonstrate the qualities of a psychotherapist by assisting the supervisee in uncovering personal material that affects the psychotherapy, (4) create an environment of safety where shame-related phenomena can be discussed with candor and curiosity, (5) ease insecurities by modeling the activities that supervisees seek to encourage from their clients, and (6) avoid attempts to dissuade the supervisee of an idealizing transference toward the activities.

Parallel Process

The concept of parallel process, originating within the psychoanalytic literature (Arlow, 1963; Bromberg, 1982; Doehrman, 1976; Ekstein & Wallerstein, 1958; Searles, 1955), suggests that dynamics of the therapeutic relationship stimulate and are reflected within the supervisory relationship. The therapist, through the process of identification with the client or, for some theorists, primarily by means of projective identification, enacts the client's dynamics with the supervisor. Rather than obtaining insight into the transference–countertransference matrix, therapists and supervisors replicate unconsciously derived roles and object relations (Grey & Fiscalini, 1987). Similarly, supervisors may bring into the interaction processes originating in contexts external to the supervisory relationship that result in parallelism as a triadic system (Gediman & Wolkenfeld, 1980). Frawley-O'Dea and Sarnat (2001) found that, "[w]hile a parallel process can originate in either the treatment relationship or the supervisory dyad, it is the supervisee who, by her overlapping membership in both dyads, necessarily is the interdyadic conduit of the relational material expressed through a parallel process" (p. 174). Symmetrical parallel processes, involving concordant or complementary countertransference, may lead to impasses in both the treatment and the supervisory relationship as enactments supersede the participants' abilities to gain awareness of the relational patterns being repeated. Despite the paucity of empirical support (Mothersole, 1999) and, for some clinicians, outright rejection of the concept (L. Miller & Twomey, 1999), the idea of parallel process appears within the literature to offer a theoretical vantage for considering possible dynamics influencing the supervisory relationship (Friedlander, Siegel, & Brenock, 1989; McNeill & Worthen, 1989; Morrissey & Tribe, 2001).

Caution should be exercised in applying this concept, as similarities at the surface may not reflect dynamic congruence (Baudry, 1993), independence may exist between similar relational patterns (Fosshage, 1997), and reactions originating in the supervisory relationship may be defensively relocated to the treatment. Appreciation of the intersubjective nature of interpersonal relationships (Fosshage, 1997; Ogden, 1994) allows for consideration of the numerous independent and interrelated influences that shape clinical and supervisory processes. The contents and processes that make up a given supervision draw on both independent and interrelated experiences of the therapist and the supervisee as well as the coconstruction of dynamics unique to the supervisory relationship. No matter their theoretical allegiance, supervisors need to be mindful of the range of influences and pressures existing within the treatment relationship that may come to be expressed within supervision. Failure to attend to such dynamics may lead to misunderstanding and ruptures in the working alliance. Parallel processes, to the extent that they exist, provide useful sources of information regarding the relational patterns associated with their interpersonal conflicts and psychological difficulties.

Boundary Violations

Maintenance of appropriate boundaries contributes to the formation and preservation of a safe and trusting professional relationship within which the novice clinician can explore his or her personal contributions to the therapeutic process. Violations of professional and personal boundaries undermine the supervision, particularly with respect to the addressing of personal material and countertransference. Breaches of professional ethics (e.g., sexual harassment and dual relationships) and unprofessional conduct (e.g., unavailability to supervisees and disinterest) may irrevocably compromise the supervisory relationship. Any misuse of the power differential in the relationship or any deviation from the legitimate uses of authority (which is ultimately vested in the power to evaluate) forecloses the possibility of an effective course of training and case management. The addressing of therapist countertransference constitutes a boundary that is at times difficult to clearly demarcate. Intrusions into the personal lives of clinicians through the quasiprovision of therapy, the use of personal information divulged in supervision for nonclinical or noneducational purposes, and breaches of confidentiality reflect significant violations. Beyond these overt behaviors, supervisors should be sensitive in addressing countertransference and inter-personal deficiencies and conflicts. A clear understanding, which could take the form of a contract, at the beginning of supervision regarding the responsibilities of the supervisor and the nature and processes of the evaluative, training, and case-management functions should be conveyed. Attention should be placed on the effects of countertransference and inter-personal shortcomings *specific to professional responsibilities* of the student or intern. The supervisor's responsibility is limited to safeguarding the client, ensuring the highest standards of care, and educating and training the supervisee. Although the empathy, support, understanding, and awareness obtained in supervision may in fact be therapeutic, a supervisor cannot and should not serve as a psychotherapist to the supervisee. Respect for this boundary ensures that the opportunity is extended to the supervisee to mature as a clinician and to gain awareness of the personal factors that influence the provision of psychological treatment.

Supervisors demonstrate and model competencies and ensure the integrity of the supervisory process by always being mindful of the nature of their influence, by being respectful of the supervisee, by minimizing shame-inducing processes, by directly addressing ruptures to the working alliance, by considering intrapersonal and interpersonal forces that affect the relationship, and by maintaining appropriate boundaries. Faithful attention to these factors not only builds a positive and mutually rewarding supervisory relation, but also ensures that appropriate supervision and counsel are obtained to provide competent client care.

Competencies

The competencies required to address the supervisory alliance include the following:

- Interpersonal skills involving the abilities to communicate, to understand the experience of the self and that of the supervisee (perspective taking); to experience and express empathy; to provide support; to trust; and to reflect on one's behavior and its impact on others, including the ability to identify alliance strain, rupture, and countertransference

- Values of integrity-in-relationship, ethical values-based practice, appreciation of diversity, and science-informed practice
- Knowledge of the literature regarding alliance and knowledge and skill in performing and teaching metacommunication through multiple learning strategies (e.g., instruction, demonstration, role-playing, and critiquing)

6

BUILDING DIVERSITY COMPETENCE IN SUPERVISION

Notwithstanding that it is a core component of psychology training, diversity is one of the most neglected areas in supervision training and research. The majority of attention to diversity has been devoted to culture— just one particular aspect—rather than to the broader construct. Diversity includes culture in all its aspects, as well as socioeconomic status, race, religion, disabilities or ableness, age, gender, and sexual orientation, all of which may converge and intersect (Bingham, Porche-Burke, James, Sue, & Vasquez, 2002). As Ridley, Mendoza, and Kanitz (1994) stated, "educators with the best of intentions find themselves caught between the press to provide MCT (multicultural training) and the dual disadvantage of their own inadequate training and the embryonic state of the field" (p. 228). This is the case not only for culture but also for all areas of diversity. Clinicians report lower self-perceived competence levels in work with clients with motor and sensory impairment and with Hispanic, Black Hispanic, Asian American, and Native American clients (Allison, Echemendia, Crawford, & Robinson, 1996). That consideration of diversity is essential to psychology training is unequivocal.

In this chapter, we describe the required role of diversity in psychology training, the current state of the art, barriers to integration of diversity into psychology training, and definitions of multicultural competence. Conceptualizations of culture are considered as well as approaches to acculturation as they apply to supervision. *Emic* (conceptions common to a particular ethnic or minority group and thus explicative) and *etic* (conceptions universal to people across culture) parameters are applied to training and to supervision. We then outline gender and sexual orientation as they have been approached in training models, providing a context to training efforts. We also review the relative deficits in training in disabilities and age as they affect supervision. The final sections focus on enhancing diversity competence and development of multicultural competence through understanding theories of racial and minority development and assessment techniques. These concepts serve as benchmarks and standards for diversity competency in programs such as internships and other training programs.

In "Domain D: Cultural and Individual Differences and Diversity," the Committee on Accreditation of the American Psychological Association (APA) lays out a framework for internship programs:

> The program recognizes the importance of cultural and individual differences and diversity in the training of psychologists.
>
> 1. The program has made systematic, coherent, and long-term efforts to attract and retain interns and staff from differing ethnic, racial, and personal backgrounds into the program. Consistent with such efforts, it acts to ensure a supportive and encouraging learning environment appropriate for the training of diverse individuals and the provision of training opportunities for a wide spectrum of individuals. Further the program avoids any action that would restrict program access on grounds that are irrelevant to success in internship training or a career in professional psychology.
> 2. The program has a thoughtful and coherent plan to provide interns with relevant knowledge and experiences about the role of cultural and individual diversity in psychological phenomena and professional practice. It engages in positive efforts designed to ensure that interns will have opportunities to learn about cultural and individual diversity as they relate to the practice of psychology. The avenues by which these goals are achieved are to be developed by the program." (APA, Committee on Accreditation, 2002e, p. 16).

The "Ethical Principles of Psychologists and Code of Conduct" (APA, 2002a) states the following:

> Where scientific or professional knowledge in the discipline of psychology establishes that an understanding of factors associated with age, gender, gender identity, race, ethnicity, culture, national origin, religion, sexual orientation, disability, language, or socioeconomic

status is essential for effective implementation of their services or research, psychologists have or obtain the training, experience, consultation, or supervision necessary to ensure the competence of their services, or they make appropriate referrals . . . . (2.01, Boundaries of Competence, ¶ b)

MULTICULTURAL DIVERSITY

Sheer demographics indicate that attention to cultural diversity is a necessity, not an option. The meanings of the terms *majority* and *minority* are no longer clear, as so-called minorities have become pluralities. With these changes, the Eurocentric bias of the field of psychology is evolving, but not fast enough. Guthrie (1998) titled his text *Even the Rat Was White: A Historical View of Psychology*, documenting the history of racism in the development of the field of psychology. It is time for supervisors and supervisees to integrate the strengths of culture and diversity into pedagogy and conceptual frameworks.

Through the appreciation of and education about diversity in supervision, underlying racism, prejudice, and negative cultural attitudes, albeit subtle, are addressed. Education and exposure lead to increased understanding, which in turn results in frames of respect for difference. Rather than conformity, stereotypes, or assimilation, the diversity-competent psychologist considers the strengths of the individual, culture, and community and how these factors can be integrated into a plan for treatment and development. It is a given that the culturally competent psychologist is cognizant of his or her own cultural background, its strengths, and the unique perspectives it casts on his or her worldview.

STATE OF THE ART

Reports of student training in diversity issues reflect mediocre efforts in training on counseling ethnic minorities and a lack of cultural infusion into training in general. "Such a lack of systematic instruction and evaluation in ethnic minority issues is particularly disturbing when one considers they had seen ethnic minority clients during both pre-internship and internship training" (Mintz, Bartels, & Rideout, 1995, p. 319). These authors concluded that the results of their survey of APA-approved graduate training sites (46% response rate) showed that these sites do not reflect the spirit of APA accreditation criteria nor are they in line with the APA Ethical Standard 2.01(b; stated previously). Much of the research and theorizing has focused on multiculturalism rather than on the broader realm of diversity. We would advocate a consideration of the entire spectrum of diversity; however, as multiculturalism has been a focus in the literature, we describe a significant amount of that research.

Mintz et al. (1995) reported that counseling-program interns were slightly better prepared than their clinical counterparts in coursework and examination of biases, a finding also reported by graduate students (Pope-Davis, Reynolds, Dings, & Nielson, 1995). However, Quintana and Bernal (1995) cautioned that any differences between the training given to the two groups are not meaningful, because both need to improve. Mintz et al. (1995) agreed. Bernal and Castro (1994) found that, among 104 APA-accredited doctoral programs, the "structural basics" (p. 803) are often lacking. Deficits exist in minority-related courses, faculty conducting minority mental health research, and use of off-campus clinical settings serving ethnic-minority students for practicum placement. In a study of psychology interns and their supervisors (57.4% response rate), 9 interns (30%) and 21 supervisors (70%) reported that they had never completed a course in multicultural or cross-cultural counseling (Constantine, 1997). A study of counseling, school, and clinical graduates who completed their training between 1985 and 1987 (48.7% response rate) revealed that small numbers of the respondents felt extremely or very competent to do clinical work with African Americans (37.5%), Asian Americans (15.8%), Black Hispanics (11.5%), Hispanics (25.9%), Native Americans (7.7 %), gay men (34.8%), lesbians (38.6%), bisexual individuals (33.2%), and individuals with sensory impairments (18.9%), even though they reported that they worked with a significant number of members of these populations (Allison, Crawford, Echemendia, Robinson, & Knepp, 1994). Allison et al. reported low rates of coursework or relevant training in practicum and internship on providing services to diverse populations. Graduate students in APA-approved settings felt even less prepared to work with bisexual clients than with lesbian or gay clients (Phillips & Fischer, 1998). It is interesting that in the Allison et al. (1996) study of self-rated competence, psychologists (49% return rate) rated themselves most competent in treating European Americans, females, and economically disadvantaged clients and least competent in treating Asian American, Black Hispanic, and Native American clients. The authors reported a correlation between higher diversity of caseload carried and perceived self-competence. A small group of psychologists in that study reported (8% response rate) that, although they did not view themselves as competent to provide services to that client group, they continued to do so. It is extremely worrisome that, according to self-reports, psychologists are practicing in an area outside their self-perceived competence—an ethical infraction.

BARRIERS TO THE INTEGRATION OF DIVERSITY INTO PSYCHOLOGY TRAINING

We are increasingly aware of the pain inflicted by supervisors and supervisees who function with inadequate knowledge of diversity. The pain is reflected in the supervisee's feeling hurt or misunderstood (Fukuyama, 1994a; McNeill et al., 1995; McRoy et al., 1986) client distress or withdrawal from treatment (Garnets, Hancock, Cochran, Goodchilds, & Peplau, 1991; Pope-Davis et al., 2002; Priest, 1994), and damage done by faulty assessments due to lack of a knowledge base (Goodman-Delahunty, 2000). In a small study of trainees in South Africa, Kleintjes and Swartz (1996) provide perspective on the difficulty of introducing race. Multiple reasons why Black students do not discuss color in supervision in a "White" university were presented. Trainees expressed difficulty with such discussion because they felt the setting was a "colourless zone (sic);" they felt that they could be perceived as making excuses for poor performance or be seen as using Blackness as a defense against other issues, or they feared being seen as pathologically preoccupied with color and discrimination. Also they may not have felt secure enough to raise the issue of color or may have wondered whether the issue should be dealt with personally. Without a structure for introduction of race as well as other aspects of diversity, these subjects may be ignored, at great cost.

One of the reasons that culture does not come up in supervision is that many supervisors are not meeting the minimum requirement of knowing at least as much as their trainees know about cultural competency (J. M. Bernard, 1994) or diversity. Graduate programs have a greater emphasis on cultural competence presently than was the case when most supervisors were themselves trained. Even in the current training climate, few curricula take an integrated cultural approach; most relegate culture to a single course or just a few courses (Yutrzenka, 1995). Although counseling-center training directors (49% return rate) reported that 88% of their centers offer a seminar on multicultural counseling, the mean duration of such seminars is nine sessions, and there is little emphasis on integrating multicultural issues into seminars and on religion (Lee et al., 1999). The low systematic emphasis on religion and spirituality was confirmed for counseling programs (Schulte, Skinner, & Claiborn, 2002) and for clinical training programs (Brawer, Handal, Fabricatore, Roberts, & Wajda-Johnston, 2002). Religion is reported highly salient by most persons (Gallup & Johnson, 2003; Gallup & Jones, 2000), as in many cultures spirituality and religion are inseparable from physical, mental, or health concerns (Fukuyama & Sevig, 1999). Transgender issues have been ignored or pathologized (Carroll & Gilroy, 2002), and gender has been dealt with mainly on a theoretical level (Granello, Beamish, & Davis, 1997). Nilsson, Berkel, Flores, Love, Wendler, & Mecklenburg

(2003) reported low attention to sexual orientation and religion in their review of 11 years of Professional Psychology Research and Practice. The role of religion in training is explored by Shafranske (in press) and Shafranske and Falender (2004). The number of courses offered in graduate programs has actually decreased in the area of disability; such courses are now rare (Olkin, 2002).

A barrier to implementing this critical curriculum is the lack of empirical support for the few existing models of ethnic and cross-cultural training and their relationship to treatment efficacy (Yutrzenka, 1995). Another is the lack of focus on self-knowledge and exploration, both cognitive and emotional, in psychology training (Carter, 2001). As a result, supervisors have an academic view of culture, distant from their own personal being. Supervisors who have less multicultural competence reinforce avoidance of racial issues in their White trainees (Steward, Wright, Jackson, & Jo, 1998), perhaps because race is not viewed as salient to their identities (T. L. Robinson, 1999). However, we are reminded that "cultural provincialism is not a disease that afflicts only Caucasians" (Myers, Echemendia, & Trimble, 1991, p. 9). That is, whatever the culture of the supervisor and supervisee, it is incumbent on the dyad to process and explore the implications of the cultural and diversity configuration among the client, supervisee–therapist, and supervisor and not to be complacent in one's preconceptions. Any cultural group can make incorrect judgments about another.

Some believe that White people do not have a culture. On the contrary, Whites are as diverse a population as any other group, and greater consciousness needs to be raised among Whites that they do have a culture, a history, and a story. Richardson and Molinaro (1996) suggested that the White emphasis on exploring the differences of others rather than looking at their own characteristics may promote unintentional ethnocentrism. Other barriers are guilt over being White and the existence of multitudes of other pressing and critical areas of training, making it hard to implement all of them (Lee et al., 1999). These findings are disappointing given the profound and intrinsic impact of culture on every aspect of training and psychotherapy. It is imperative that cultural-competence training be valued (Carter, 2001).

Another barrier may lie in the process of diversity education itself. The processes of self-discovery and acknowledging one's own cultural biases and prejudices may induce resistance, defensiveness, and inhibition (Abreu, 2001). Another problem has been the focus on particular groups as unitary, such as Black, White, Hispanic, gay, and lesbian. This unfortunate focus has resulted in increased stereotyping and less appreciation of the vast multitude of difference within groups when one considers the membership of each individual in other demographic groups. In fact, within-group differences have been shown to exceed between-group differences (Suzuki, McRae, & Short, 2001). The concept of "collective identities" derived from family, gender, race, and ethnicity (Fukuyama & Ferguson, 2000, p. 82) has not received adequate attention even though multiple factors determine one's identity, not a single one.

In attempting to explain why simply recruiting diverse faculty and students does not automatically result in a functioning multicultural program, Pope-Davis, Liu, Toporek, and Brittan-Powell (2001) described the necessity of a "complete contextual change" that encompasses not only a commitment to multicultural issues but also the creation and maintenance of a positive environment in which to nurture them (p. 124). For example, insertion of various ethnic–racial and gay, lesbian, and bisexual (GLB) content in application materials is associated with obtaining higher numbers of students with those identities (Bidell, Turner, & Casas, 2002).

MULTICULTURAL COMPETENCE DEFINED

Multicultural-counseling competency has been defined in a number of ways. Fuertes (2002) identified 16 different conceptual and theoretical approaches to multicultural competency and discussed how the perspectives supplement, but do not supplant, a theoretical approach. The most influential approach, presented by D. W. Sue, Arredondo, and McDavis (1992) in an APA Division 17 position paper, defined multicultural competency as a "therapist's awareness of assumptions about human behavior, values, biases, preconceived notions, personal limitations; understanding the worldview of the culturally different client without negative judgments; and developing and practicing appropriate, relevant, and sensitive intervention strategies and skills in working with culturally different clients" (p. 481). Thus, multicultural competency is organized into the three categories of attitudes and beliefs, knowledge, and skills. This organization has served as the basis for much of the subsequent research and conceptualization in the field. However, factor-analytic studies have shown little support for a tridimensional conceptualization and may suggest a unitary-factor construct (Ponterotto, Rieger, Barrett, & Sparks, 1994). Some have also suggested that the role of the relationship between client and therapist–supervisee (Sodowsky, Taffe, Gutkin, & Wise, 1994), racial identity (Ponterotto et al., 1994), and racial-identity development be added to the framework. The relationship between client and therapist–supervisee would include client disclosure, counselor behavior and approach, and equity and power in the relationship (Pope-Davis et al., 2002). Racial-identity development refers to the stage of development of each of the participants in his or her racial identity.

Adding social justice to the definition, D. W. Sue (2001) redefined cultural competence as follows:

The ability to engage in actions or create conditions that maximize the optimal development of client and client systems. Multicultural counseling competence is defined as the counselor's acquisition of awareness, knowledge, and skills needed to function effectively in a pluralistic democratic society (ability to communicate, interact, negotiate, and intervene on behalf of clients from diverse backgrounds), and on an organizational/societal level, advocating effectively to develop new theories, practices, policies, and organizational structures that are more responsive to all groups. (p. 802)

A definition more operationalized to a training setting was proposed by Ponterotto and Casas (1987):

Multicultural competence includes knowledge of clients' culture and status, actual experiences with these clients, and the ability to devise innovative strategies vis-à-vis the unique client's needs. A multiculturally competent program instills in its students these competencies, infuses minority issues into all program courses . . ., and has adequate representation of minority students and faculty members. (p. 433)

Although self-awareness is a component of cultural competence, incorporation of an integrated awareness, understanding, and competence with one's own cultural or multidiverse background has been slow to come in training environments. D. W. Sue et al. (1992) defined cultural self-awareness to include awareness of the influence of biases, awareness of personal limitations, awareness of how one's heritage affects definitions of normality and abnormality, awareness of one's individual racism, and ultimately an understanding of oneself as a racial and cultural being and movement to seek a nonracist identity. We believe that self-knowledge and awareness of one's own cultural self are critical preconditions to cultural awareness. Part of attaining awareness entails understanding the strengths inherent in one's own cultural heritage and how they translate into beliefs, values, and behavior. Until a supervisor has developed this level of competency, it is difficult, if not impossible, to be an excellent supervisor. Little, if any, attention is given to self-awareness in most psychology graduate training programs or in supervisor training. Thus, this vital precondition is usually not met.

The translation of the D. W. Sue et al. (1992) framework to interactions between the client and the therapist–supervisee has been problematic. S. Sue, Zane, and Young (1994) stated, "What is needed are approaches that propose specific hypotheses as to how the psychosocial experiences of ethnic minorities affect certain important processes in psychotherapy" (p. 809). Fischer, Jome, and Atkinson (1998) proposed common factors that contribute to client healing, including the therapeutic relationship, a shared worldview of client and therapist, meeting client's expectations, and use of rituals or interventions that both therapist and client view as appropriate.

These common factors are viewed as organizing factors of the trainee's conceptualizations, integration of multiculturalism into interventions, and instruction.

Building on the work of Fischer et al. (1998), Constantine and Ladany (2001) incorporated the component of self-awareness by proposing an extension in which multicultural competency consists of six dimensions:

- self-awareness: understanding one's own multiple cultural identities, personal biases, and how socialization affects values and attitudes;
- general knowledge of multicultural issues: general knowledge of psychological and social issues, prejudicial attitudes, discrimination, and knowledge of emics;
- multicultural-counseling self-efficacy: confidence in one's ability to perform successfully, based on a behavior set—not simply a self-perception of competence;
- understanding of unique client variables: understanding how personal attributes, situations, and other factors affect client behavior;
- formation of an effective counseling working alliance: includes addressing multicultural issues within the working alliance;
- multicultural-counseling skills: the ability to approach multicultural issues effectively in therapy.

The Fisher et al. (1998) and Constantine and Ladany (2001) frameworks integrate etic, universalistic approaches, with emic, culture-specific knowledge, as well as general-counseling competency.

Another very comprehensive approach is provided by the 12 "minimal multicultural competencies for practice" (N. D. Hansen, Pepitone-Arreola-Rockwell, & Greene, 2000). The following is a summary of the competencies that Hansen et al. distilled from the literature:

- "[a]wareness of how one's own cultural heritage, gender, class, ethnic-racial identity, sexual orientation, disability, and age cohort help shape personal values, assumptions, and biases related to identified groups;
- knowledge of the following factors:
  - historical and cultural embeddedness and change of psychological theory, inquiry methods, and professional practices,
  - history, manifestation, and psychological sequelae of oppression, prejudice, and discrimination,
  - sociopolitical influences (e.g., poverty, stereotyping, stigmatization, and marginalization) impinging on identified groups,

- culture-specific diagnosis; normative values about illness, worldview, family structures, and gender roles; impacts on personality formation; developmental outcomes; and manifestation of illness, and
- culture-specific assessment techniques;
- ability to do the following:
  - evaluate emic and etic hypotheses,
  - self-assess multicultural competence,
  - modify assessment tools and qualify conclusions, and
  - design and implement nonbiased effective treatment plans and interventions for multiple groups (condensed from Hansen, Pepitone-Arreola-Rockwell, & Greene, 2000, p. 654, with permission; please refer to the article for the full listing of competencies).

Hansen et al. (2000) proposed that use of these competencies could infuse multiculturalism into the entire training curriculum.

Another consequential framework of knowledge regarding cultural competence is the "Guidelines for Providers of Psychological Services to Ethnic, Linguistic, and Culturally Diverse Populations" (American Psychological Association, 1993a). Among the myriad important aspects is the directive that the counselor has the responsibility to gain knowledge of the client's culture rather than rely on the client to explain his or her understanding of his or her culture. Also, "[p]sychologists [should] respect clients' religious and/or spiritual beliefs and values, including attributions and taboos, since they affect world view, psychosocial functioning, and expressions of distress" (APA, 1993a, p. 46).

In its entirety, this document is very important, as it outlines the importance of consideration of bias or racism; cultural belief and value systems; family-member and community structures, hierarchies, and cultural beliefs; resources to be identified in the family; religious and spiritual beliefs; the role of the psychologist; indigenous beliefs and practices; and inclusion of religious and spiritual leaders, essentially providing a roadmap to culturally sensitive practice. It should be required reading for all supervisees and supervisors.

APA's "Guidelines on Multicultural Counseling Proficiency for Psychologists" (American Psychological Association, Division 45, Society for the Psychological Study of Ethnic Minority Issues, 2001) focus on racial and ethnic identity with an articulation of learning objectives and clinical-training guidelines in the areas of awareness, knowledge, and skills. These specific guidelines appear user friendly for training, but are not yet empirically supported.

Ancis and Ladany (2001) proposed domains of multicultural supervision competencies that are exceptionally useful in guiding supervisors, assessing supervision, and directing supervisees in the development of competencies. Ancis and Ladany (2001) proposed domains of supervisor-focused personal development, supervisee-focused development, skills and interventions, process, and outcome evaluation. They described particular competencies in self-awareness and knowledge of other cultures and worldviews, facilitation of supervisee diversity identity development, understanding of racism and oppression as well as indigenous resources and the creation of a climate that generally facilitates diversity discussion and consideration.

Our Definition of Diversity Competence

Our definition of diversity competency draws on many of the others. We believe that diversity competency includes incorporation of self-awareness by both supervisor and supervisee and is an interactive process of the client or family, supervisee–therapist, and supervisor, using all of their diversity factors. It entails awareness, knowledge, and appreciation of the interaction among the client's, supervisee–therapist's, and supervisor's assumptions, values, biases, expectations, and worldviews; integration and practice of appropriate, relevant, and sensitive assessment and intervention strategies and skills; and consideration of the larger milieu of history, society, and sociopolitical variables.

Conceptualizations of Culture

Several frameworks address multiple dimensions of cultural and personal identity, including those of Phinney (1996), Arredondo and Glauner (1992), Falicov (1988), and Hays (2001). Moving toward a way of integrating conceptualization, Phinney (1996) defined ethnicity as consisting of at least three aspects: (a) cultural values, attitudes, and behaviors distinguishing ethnic groups; (b) the subjective sense of membership or belonging in an ethnic group or identity; and (c) experiences associated with minority status, including powerlessness, discrimination, and prejudice, and ways in which individuals have responded to these experiences. She urged consideration of ethnicity not as a categorical variable, but as clusters of dimensions that affect individuals differently and according to which individuals vary. This approach is similar in part to that of Falicov (1995), who also advocated a multidimensional approach to consideration of culture, incorporating the multitude of other variables influential in identity (e.g., gender, age, and religion). It would appear that the more we understand and respect difference and the more training we are able to give to enhance understanding of the complexity, the more successful our efforts to build diversity competence will be.

Arredondo and Glauner (1992) addressed what they described as fixed and flexible dimensions contributing to identity and worldview. These dimensions are within a sociopolitical and historical context. Examples of fixed dimensions include age, gender, and race, whereas flexible dimensions include relationship status, hobbies, and educational background.

In contrast, Falicov (1988) described parameters of culture as jointly forming cultural membership. Her methodology elicits a kind of narrative regarding life experience in a variety of contexts. Falicov (1988) defined culture as the following:

> [t]hose sets of shared world views and adaptive behaviors derived from simultaneous membership in a variety of contexts, such as ecological setting (rural, urban, suburban), religious background, nationality and ethnicity, social, class, gender-related experiences, minority status, occupation, political leanings, migratory patterns and stage of acculturation, or values derived from belonging to the same generation, partaking of single historical moment, or particular ideologies. (p. 336)

Arredondo et al. (1996) provided a comprehensive articulation of dimensions of personal identity with a fuller conceptualization of contributing variables. It is important not to isolate variables such as race or religion, but instead to provide a framework for consideration of the individual and the family. It is critical to use a "cultural lens" to approach culture with respectful curiosity. Falicov (1988) concluded, "Each family is unique precisely because of its specific ecological niche, which is that combination of the multiple settings in which it is embedded" (p. 336). "Ecological niche" refers to the overlapping views, values, power, and access that an individual experiences and represents a narrative of contexts replacing labels such as "Black" or "Jewish." Emphasis is on interconnectedness as opposed to difference or separation of individuals by cultural group. One must consider the ecological niche of each member of the family, the therapist (trainee), and the supervisor.

Falicov (1995) described five parameters of culture, to which Wisnia and Falender (2004) added. Falicov's (1995) parameters are as follows:

- ecological context, or how the family lives and fits in its environment;
- migration and acculturation, or where the members of the family came from, why they came, what their respective journeys entailed, and what their aspirations are;
- family organization or family arrangements and values attached to that structure;

- family life cycle, which entails diversity in the developmental stage and transitions and their cultural patterning;
- The concept of health, healing, and wellness.

We encourage the addition of worldview which may be defined as including factors such as optimism and pessimism, traditional beliefs, attitude toward the present, social relations, time, one's relationship with nature, and living in harmony with nature (Ibrahim & Kahn, 1987). We also include aspects such as values (e.g., competition versus cooperation, emotional restraint versus expressiveness), guiding beliefs (e.g., independence versus interdependence; control and dominance versus harmony and deference), epistemology (e.g., cognitive versus affective or combined) logic (reasoning process), nature of reality (e.g., objective material versus subjective, spiritual versus material), and one's concept of self (Brown & Landrum-Brown, 1995). Also direct attention to spirituality and religion should be highlighted.

We advocate the use of therapist maps (Falicov, 1998) and supervisor maps to define each of these areas, not simply for the clients but also for the therapist or supervisee and the supervisor. It helps us to approach differing attitudes and values. For example, the issue of shared worldviews is complex. Some research indicates that while even culturally diverse therapists may share a somewhat common worldview, ignorance of differing client worldviews may result in negative attributions (D. W. Sue & Sue, 1990; Mahalik, Worthington, & Crump, 1999).

The issue of shared worldviews is increasingly complex. Some research indicates that although even culturally diverse therapists may share a somewhat common worldview, ignorance of differing client worldviews may result in negative attributions (Mahalik, Worthington, & Crump, 1999; D. W. Sue & Sue, 1990)

Hays (2001) proposed a framework that is in some ways similar to Falicov's (1995) method advocating approach of one's own culture and the culture of others. Using the acronym "ADDRESSING," the therapist lists one's own *a*ge and generational influences (familial, political, or social events), *d*evelopmental or acquired *d*isabilities, *r*eligion and spiritual orientation, *e*thnicity, *s*ocioeconomic status, *s*exual orientation, *i*ndigenous heritage, *n*ational origin, and *g*ender. Having completed this self-assessment, the therapist considers the role of privilege and culture on his or her clinical work and, finally, the role of values. Then the same process is followed to address the client's culture, so that similarities and differences between client and therapist are explored.

Although the two frameworks emphasize slightly different areas of functioning, they are parallel in their emphasis on comparing the cultural complexity between the therapist and the client—and, we urge, among therapist, client, and supervisor as well, as was advocated by Hird, Cavalieri, Dulko, Felice, and Ho (2001). M. T. Brown and Landrum-Brown (1995) also urged comparison of worldview congruence stances in which the client, supervisee–therapist, and supervisor complement or conflict with each other with respect to such dimensions as cooperation and competition.

Multicultural supervision is defined as "a supervisor–supervisee relationship in which there are cultural differences based on race and ethnicity" (Fukuyama, 1994a, p. 142). Furthermore, the institutional setting and administration are operative factors (Peterson, 1991). We suggest including the client and the complexity of the client's or family's, therapist–supervisee's, and supervisor's interactive diversity variables with respect to differences, preconceptions, and interactions in the equation of diversity supervision.

ACCULTURATION

Acculturation is a factor deemed important to consider in selecting therapist roles and strategies with clients of racial or ethnic minorities (Atkinson, Thompson, & Grant, 1993). Brislin (2000, derived from Berry, 1990) described acculturation as whether (a) the family retains selected aspects of its first culture and (b) the family pursues relations with members of the donor or host culture. If a family has achieved cultural "integration," it has done both (a) and (b). If a family has become "assimilated," it has done only (b). If a family is culturally "separated," it has done only (a). Finally, if a family is marginalized, it has done neither (a) nor (b). Another way of looking at acculturation is through the lens of ethnic identity, as a bidirectional process, with dimensions of degree of adoption of "Whiteness" and retention of one's other ethnic identity (Sodowsky, Kwan, & Pannu, 1995). The family's country of origin may be somewhat less important than where it is in this conceptual frame of assimilation, which encompasses ethnic identity. Acculturation across family members may be variable, with children's perceptions of their parents' acculturation (or relative lack thereof) affecting family acculturation conflict and acculturation stress. This point was highlighted by Roysircar-Sodowsky and Maestas (2000) as conflicts arising among traditional family kinship, traditional familial obligations, and deference to authority figures confronted with Westernized individualism, autonomy, egalitarianism, and assertiveness. Conflict can be intrapersonal as well, reflected in identity crisis, guilt, and anger. Greater complexity is added by the concept of "situational acculturation," which refers to the phenomenon of different acculturation responses, depending on the situational context (Trimble, 2003).

Formulation of acculturation status is very relevant for both trainees and supervisors. This factor should be another demographic dimension to put into the formulation of culture of supervisor, supervisee, and client (or family) in the context of strengths of each. Interestingly, Handelsman, Gottlieb, and Knapp (2002) applied Berry's (1990) cultural acculturation model to professional acculturation, or the socialization of trainees to integrate their personal morality with professional ethical standards so that they may acquire an ethical identity (see chap. 8, this volume).

EMIC PARAMETERS AND THEIR RELEVANCE TO TRAINING

Part of the difficulty of diversity competency lies in striking a balance between stereotyping and cultural knowledge. Understanding emic versus etic factors is essential to achieving this goal. An example of an emic factor is the concept of *personalismo,* or having a personal relationship with an individual, which is important in some Latino cultures. Another example is *familialism*—that is, emphasis on and value placed on family over the individual—a significant protective factor (Santisteban & Mitrani, 2003). Yet another example is nonverbal communication, including nuances of eye contact, how close individuals stand to each other during conversation, and other nonverbal cues that may have significant cultural loading. *Turn exchange,* or alternating dialogue typical of individuals conversing, may be uncomfortable for individuals from Latino or Asian cultural groups to engage in within therapy, as they may attribute a dominant role to the therapist and feel uncomfortable verbalizing in that cadence. They may also experience discomfort with the depth of disclosure required in initial intakes, especially if the expectation is a single-session intake. It may be that a longer time is required to establish rapport and proceed. The "I" emphasis in Eurocentric therapies may be problematic as well. A relationship or family focus rather than a focus on the individual may be more culturally syntonic for individuals from certain ethnic groups (Nwachuku & Ivey, 1991). Takushi and Uomoto (2001) urged consideration of environmental cues, including the general "cultural competence" of the setting, determined by factors such as the pictures on the wall of the counseling area and the ethnicities and languages highlighted by the magazines presented in the waiting area. Other areas of cultural incongruity may exist in the time orientation of the therapy: past, present, or future. However, to take any of the foregoing observations as set in stone would be stereotyping. Instead, knowledge can be used to provide a frame for reflection or to begin interpersonal understanding. Intensive coursework, reading, discussion, and multicultural life and therapy experience are necessities to increase one's cultural comprehension.

Client–Therapist Factors

There are numerous other examples of emic factors that are important to training, as they relate to the client–therapist interaction. Supervisees should thus receive training on verbal and nonverbal taboos, areas fraught with misunderstanding, and variables that could positively affect therapy and outcome. An individual's understanding of emic parameters has a profound influence on his or her assumptions and belief systems, which influence, for example, whether a family enters treatment or whether a trainee can synthesize his or her own beliefs with those of psychological pedagogy. As a result, seemingly simple concepts are very complex. For example, it is counterproductive to ask an American Indian, "How are you?", as this question has an ever-changing answer and is thus not culturally possible to evaluate (Trimble, 1991). With African American clients, it is essential to show genuine respect for complaints of racism, discrimination, and the underlying cultural mistrust, to avoid negative bias in diagnosis and ensuing treatment by professionals (Whaley, 2001). With Asian Americans, public verbal expression of feelings, a hallmark of traditional therapy, can be culturally discordant, as can focusing on painful, negative thoughts or feelings. Credibility of the therapist was found to be the best, and only, predictor of intent to use therapy for Chinese students, whereas empathic involvement *and* credibility were crucial for Caucasians. Credibility could be affected by problem conceptualization, means for problem resolution, and treatment goals formulated. Each of these factors needs to be compatible with the client's belief system and family structure (Zane & Sue, 1991). A symptom-focused approach, endemic to mental health, may be incongruent with how parents of some cultural groups look at children's problems. For example, behavior (e.g., truancy or school failure) may be the family's focus, not feelings of anger or depression (Cauce et al., 2002). Similarly, there are variations across cultures in "distress thresholds" for mental health problems (Weisz & Weiss, 1991). Other critical issues to consider include emic–etic distinctions in clinical conceptualization, nonverbal communication, disclosure depth, time, and general environmental cues (Takushi & Uomoto, 2001).

Supervision Factors

Emic factors relating to the supervisor–supervisee interaction have been discussed much less frequently (M. T. Brown & Landrum-Brown, 1995). Suggested dimensions include value placed on verbal communication, which is central to traditional supervisory roles; ways language systems are similar or different, and response to the power differential and social- and economic-status imbalances (M. T. Brown & Landrum-Brown, 1995). Examples of factors given by Ryan and Hendricks (1989) include cognitive orientation, or patterns of thinking and problem solving; motivational orientation, including the role of rewards and emphasis of locus of control; and value orientation, including family-versus-group and hierarchical-versus-egalitarian approaches. It is useful to consider all of the areas on the amended Falicov (1995) framework, which allows one to compare the respective life experiences of client or family, supervisee, and supervisor as a way of processing and formulating proposed interventions and the emotional response to these interventions. Putting the Falicov dimensions together with developmental frameworks of ethnic-identity development would provide even better means to understand the factors operating in the relationship. Consider, for example, a Latino trainee assigned to a Latino case by a White supervisor. The supervisor's expectation may be that the trainee and client or family will have much in common. However, the trainee may be a third-generation American who does not speak Spanish or identify with the Latino culture and has feelings of insecurity about this. The expectations of the supervisor and the family may thus impose a difficult burden on the supervisee–therapist who is struggling with issues of competence; these issues need to be addressed in supervision without stereotyping.

It has been suggested that for empirically supported treatments to be informed by multicultural thought, the treatments need to be decontextualized, to determine the cultural basis for the intervention, and then recontextualized according to relevant cultural features of the particular group (Quintana & Atkinson, 2002). To engage in this process, one would need to be well versed in emic understanding. Examples are available in Ancis (2004).

GENDER AND SEXUAL ORIENTATION IN TRAINING

Training in gender, sexual orientation, gender identity, and effective services for GLB (Bruss, Brack, Brack, Glickauf-Hughes, & O'Leary, 1997; Phillips & Fischer, 1998) and transgender clients (Carroll & Gilroy, 2002) has been neglected as well, although Murphy, Rawlings, and Howe (2002) raised the concern that perhaps training in GLB issues has not been adequately assessed and may be somewhat better than reported. Gender role identity may vary within and among cultural groups (Fassinger & Richie, 1997). The first step in addressing this area is to enhance supervisor self-awareness with respect to them so that supervisors take GLB issues into account when modeling for and training supervisees. Bruss et al. (1997) advocated a combination of didactic learning, encouragement of trainee independence in grappling with their value structure and possible homophobia, and ultimately learning to use "self-as-an-instrument" (p. 70). In the integration process, defenses are lowered and more self-disclosure can occur.

When working with a GLB trainee, one should not assume that the trainee will face no issues when working with the GLB population (Buhrke & Douce, 1991). Porter (1985) advocated exploration of internalized misogynist attitudes and described that facet as the most difficult part of feminist supervision. Understanding how one's own sexism or other prejudices affect one's work with clients is essential.

Biases revealed in an APA study of therapy with lesbians and gay men (Fassinger & Richie, 1997; Garnets et al., 1991) include pathologizing in assessment, focusing on sexual orientation when it is irrelevant, lacking understanding of identity development and the impact of its disclosure on others, minimizing the importance of same-sex intimate relationships, attributing poor parenting to sexual orientation, relying on the client for education, and teaching inaccurate information. One may not be conscious of one's own biases and stereotypes (Stevens-Smith, 1995), so great scrutiny is necessary.

Although more attention has been devoted to female gender issues, it is not correct to assume that male gender issues are less important. Introduction of feminist theories of supervision (Cummings, 2000; Porter, 1985), male socialization and its impact on the male as a therapist, gender pairing, and a general enhancement of awareness are all essential to diversity-sensitive training. Traditional patterns of male socialization, including a focus on independence and self-reliance, restriction of emotional expressivity, and toughness and aggression as coping styles, have specific consequences in psychology training programs (Wester & Vogel, 2002). Consequences of gender role conflict, a result of male socialization, might include the triggering of countertransference or interference by discussion of transference and countertransference phenomena. Wester and Vogel (2002) advocated fostering historical understanding, forging understanding of socialization, and encouraging male challenging of those aspects of their own socialization that are problematic to practice of psychology and supervisory relationships while balancing encouragement of aspects fostering successful practice.

Feminist supervision theory provides a model in which the power differential is minimized. According to this theory, those in power create meaning; reducing their power causes the context to change. As in solution-focused therapy, where the client is the expert and is empowered, the supervisee is empowered. Supervision exists within the context of relationship, enabling the supervisor to challenge the therapist with respect and to value emotional reactions (Prouty, 2001). Contracting is used to increase shared responsibility (Zimmerman & Haddock, 2001).

Higher levels of overall supervisory satisfaction were associated with discussion of gender and sexual-orientation similarities and differences in supervision (return rate, 36%; Gatmon et al., 2001). However, very low levels of such discussion occurred or were initiated by supervisors. It is the obligation of supervisors to keep abreast of changing demographics and dynamics. For example, in recent times, there is greater fluidity in gender and sexual identities in the gay male, lesbian, bisexual, and transgendered (GLBT) communities, and there is less identification of lesbian culture with feminism (DeAngelis, 2002). Current research directs trainees and supervisors to think of sexuality as a continuum with fluidity, not as sets of dichotomies or singular nouns (Reynolds & Hanjorgiris, 2000).

An interesting continuum between therapist attitudes and behavior toward GLB clients has been described. At one end are therapists with positive attitudes toward GLB clients; at the other extreme are therapists with negative attitudes, who have adopted judgmental or ignoring stances. However, even low levels of homophobia were associated with counselor avoidance of the topic of sexual orientation (Mohr, 2002). The outcome of avoidance of sexual orientation is a very serious consequence of therapist attitudes.

It is important to understand working models of sexual orientation. Heterosexuals may view individuals of all sexual orientations as essentially the same, where the only differences lie in the objects of sexual attraction and lifestyle. This approach is vulnerable to stereotyping and ignores differences in privilege, leading to assumptions by therapists that all clients are heterosexual. In compulsory heterosexuality, heterosexuality is the only acceptable sexual orientation, a view leading to the stigmatization of GLB individuals. It has been suggested that the most challenging aspect of working with GLB clients is dealing with the invisibility of the client's sexual orientation (Reynolds & Hanjorgiris, 2000). Thus, for a client with multiple identities—for example, GLB and another minority status (e.g., Latino, Black Hispanic, or African American)—the complexity and the likelihood of the therapist's focusing on only one of these factors, rather than multiple factors, increases.

Mohr (2002) proposed a series of supervisory questions to facilitate the competence of heterosexual supervisees in conducting therapy with GLB populations. These questions address the dominant working models that both supervisor and supervisee hold regarding sexual orientation and how these models might lead to errors or misconceptions.

TRAINING ISSUES IN DISABILITIES

The Americans With Disabilities Act of 1990 defines an individual's having a disability as

- having a physical or mental impairment that substantially limits one or more major life activities of such individual;

- having a record of such an impairment; or
- being regarded as having such impairment.

People with disabilities include individuals with limitations in walking, sight, hearing, speaking, learning, thinking, concentrating, or working; individuals who have a history of any of these limitations; individuals who experienced alcohol or substance addiction, but are in recovery; or individuals who suffer from any other type of impairment, such as facial scarring. There is a dearth of training for psychologists in working with clients who have disabilities, and APA has identified less than 2% of its membership as individuals with disabilities (Olkin, 2002). As a result, training programs provide little interaction with disabled individuals, even though approximately 15% of the U.S. population is disabled, making people with disabilities the largest minority group in the United States (Olkin, 2002). Olkin (2002) noted that the number of clinical-psychology graduate courses on disability decreased from 1989 to 1999: 24% of graduate programs offered disability courses in 1989, compared with 11% in 1999. In addition, the courses that were offered focused on cognitive impairment rather than physical, sensory, or psychiatric disabilities. As a result, "most able-bodied therapists are doing cross-cultural counseling with clients with disabilities without requisite training" (Olkin, 2002, p. 132). An additional unfortunate consequence is that inadequate evaluations are produced by mental health professionals who fail to understand disabilities or lack familiarity with the Americans With Disabilities Act of 1990 (Goodman-Delahunty, 2000). Specific prior training in disabilities results in more positive attitudes toward clients and prioritizing of extraneous variables in treatment, compared with treatment by therapists without such training (Kemp & Mallinckrodt, 1996).

AGE AS A DIVERSITY FACTOR

It has been predicted that, by the year 2020, more than 20% of the U.S. population will be over age 65. APA members surveyed (41% return rate) reported small numbers working with geriatric patients and little formal training (Qualls et al., 2002). As a result, aging and geriatric considerations will be significant for psychology training, as will combinations of all of the diversity factors with aging. Molinari et al. (2003) provided guidelines and recommendations regarding knowledge and skills required to work with these populations. These authors addressed seven competency areas, including normal aging, specialized assessment, diagnostic and treatment considerations, communication and interdisciplinary work, and special ethical concerns. Because of the significant constellations of cognitive physiological changes and negative life events unique to the population, specialized training is essential.

WHAT ENHANCES DIVERSITY COMPETENCE?

The study of a supervisee's abilities to conceptualize clients from a multicultural perspective has been neglected (Ladany, Inman, Constantine, & Hofheinz, 1997). Influences on interns' multicultural awareness has been studied following the finding that expression of the trainee's own perspectives and personal experiences increases the trainee's knowledge and skills, but is only slightly related to awareness on the Multicultural Counseling Awareness Scale (Pope-Davis, Reynolds, Dings, & Ottavi, 1994).

There is evidence that having had supervised training cases with individuals from a particular cultural group is associated with higher ratings of self-competence with that particular group (Allison et al., 1996). Ponterotto, Fuertes, and Chen (2000) concluded that personal experience combined with educational or training diversity experience results in higher competency scores. That is, life experience with diversity—one's own experiences and awareness and those of friends and family—combined with the formal training experience raises one's diversity competence. Pope-Davis et al. (1994) reported that supervision in a multicultural-counseling situation, completion of multicultural workshops, and a greater amount of multicultural coursework cumulatively contribute to greater knowledge and skills. However, Ladany, Inman, et al. (1997) found no relationship between multicultural case conceptualization skills and the trainee's completion of a graduate-level course on multicultural issues or experience with multiethnic clients. The area of outcome assessment in multicultural competence, and its impact on client outcome, requires substantial investigation, including whether particular coursework or experience enhances multicultural competency.

Another preliminary finding is that general-counseling competence may be an overlapping or predictive factor of multicultural-counseling competence: "The presence of multicultural competence is synonymous with general counseling competence" (Coleman, 1998, p. 153). Attempts by the therapist to present as culturally neutral resulted in clients' perceptions that the therapist had a lower level of general-counseling competence (Coleman, 1998). These findings are supported by Constantine (2002), who reported an approximate 60% shared variance between clients' perceptions of counselors' general-counseling competence and clients' perceptions of counselors' multicultural-counseling competence. These findings indicate that one cannot be an effective therapist unless one is multiculturally competent.

Constantine (2002) suggested that competence factors are even more critical to clients of color. Although Fuertes and Brobst (2002) found a 50% overlap between general-counseling competency (defined as conveyed empathy and trustworthiness) and multicultural-counseling competency, multicultural-counseling competency accounted for a significant portion of client satisfaction only for the ethnic-minority sample. In evaluation of the potential impact of multicultural-counseling training on White graduate-level trainees, the trainees demonstrated sustained increases in understanding of racism and Whiteness, identification of a nonracist definition of "White," and increased appreciation for multiculturalism after 45 hours of didactics and supplemental reading. The trainees reported that the most influential parts of the training were panels, guest speakers, and presentations, videotapes, and class discussion (Neville et al., 1996), with an emphasis on the opportunity to interact with racially and ethnically different individuals. Also, the more extensive the multicultural-counseling training that the White counseling trainees had received, the more differentiated were the ratings of culturally sensitive versus culturally insensitive videotapes of sessions and the more receptive were the trainees to the introduction of race as a critical issue (Steward et al., 1998). There is evidence that Black American and Latino American counseling trainees score higher than Whites on multicultural competency self-assessments, perhaps because of the salience of these issues in their lives (Constantine, 2001; Sodowsky, Kuo-Jackson, Richardson, & Corey, 1998). Increased intensive and personal understanding of individuals' cultural journeys and spiritual issues (Polanski, 2003), engenders more respect and competence in trainees. Also, the elements of knowledge of and self-respect for one's own cultural background constitute a core requirement of cultural competence. Paradigms for achieving this result will be discussed later in the chapter.

As previous multicultural training is predictive of self-assessment and other ratings of therapist multicultural competence, greater urgency is placed on the tasks of definition, conceptualization, and implementation of training to enhance multicultural competency (Constantine, 2001; Neville et al., 1996). Despite these findings, Gatmon et al. (2001) reported very low rates (12.5 to 37.9%) of actual discussion of ethnicity, gender, and sexual orientation in supervision, and a lack of initiation of such discussions by supervisors (response rate 36%). Initiation of discussion of race and other diversity issues is a supervisory competence. However, perceptions of whether these issues arise in supervision may differ between supervisee and supervisor. In a study of counseling-center cross-racial supervisory dyads (all containing one Caucasian member), over 93% of supervisors claimed that they had admitted to supervisees that they lacked cross-racial supervisory experience, but only 50% of the supervisees acknowledged being told. There were also differences in perceptions of supervisors' initiating discussions of cultural differences and of supervisors' efforts to understand the culture of the supervisee. Supervisees sensed that supervisors liked, valued, and respected them less than supervisors reported (Duan & Roehlke, 2001).

DEVELOPMENT OF MULTICULTURAL COMPETENCE

Supervisees

To understand the development of multicultural competence, one should consider multiple developmental theories: (a) the developmental model of multicultural-counseling competence (Carney & Kahn, 1984); (b) stages of effective multicultural supervision (Priest, 1994); (c) racial consciousness identity (Atkinson, Morten, & Sue, 1993; Helms, 1990; Sabnani et al., 1991); and (d) nonoppressive interpersonal development (Ancis & Ladany, 2001). In a developmental model paralleling those discussed in chapter 2 (this volume), Carney and Kahn (1984) proposed five stages of supervisee development of multicultural-counseling competence. In Stage 1, the supervisee has little knowledge of multicultural counseling and operates on assumptions based on ethnocentric attitudes. The supervisor focuses on structured and supportive approaches, trainee self-exploration, and exploration of how the client has been affected by membership in his cultural, ethnic, and racial group. Confrontation is avoided. In Stage 2, the supervisee's awareness of ethnocentric attitudes and behaviors is increased, but he or she still has a limited understanding of how the client's and counselor's level of development affects the therapy process. Carney and Kahn (1984) referred to this limited understanding as the "halo of naiveté" (p. 114), as the trainee has acquired elementary knowledge and may accordingly grow overconfident in his or her own perceived cultural competence. (This factor might account for the elevated self-ratings of cultural competence in trainee studies for which there is no correlation with multicultural conceptualization.) The supervisory task is to continue to provide a supportive and structured environment that builds the trainee's knowledge about barriers impeding intercultural communication, looks at ethnocentric belief structures, and examines client-held worldviews that differ from those of the trainee. Dissonance created in this stage may propel trainees toward Stage 3 or cause them to remain at Stage 2 through increasing resistance to change. In Stage 3, supervisees exhibit conflicting emotions about working with culturally different clients. They want to work in a respectful, culturally sensitive way, but are limited by their own biases, value conflicts, and previous training. This factor may result in a downplaying of the importance of race and culture. Supervisors are encouraged to support the trainees in their frustration, acknowledge their own awareness of the dissonance, and encourage incorporation of new cultural knowledge and skills. Supervisors may emphasize transformation of prejudice about cultural differences to respect through education and exposure.

At Stage 4, supervisees internalize a new professional identity as a competent multicultural therapist with validation of the worldview of others. They are in the process of incorporating their own ethnic–racial identity with an understanding of that of the client. At this stage, supervisors assist supervisees in understanding their own impact on clients and integrating all the operative, but disparate, components of culture. Supervisees should be taking a lead in supervision discussions of the rationale for particular culturally competent interventions. During Stage 5, supervisees advocate for the rights of individuals from diverse groups and take actions to promote and protect cultural pluralism and social equality. The supervisor moves to more of a consultant role. In this capacity, the supervisor assists in clarifying personal commitment and action strategies and understanding how to be an effective agent of change.

Although this model is developmentally based (à la Stoltenberg et al., 1998, for example), it omits the designation of the supervisor's level of cultural competency and the relationship of the myriad cultural variables of the client–supervisee–supervisor constellation. However, it is explicative of the finding that multicultural issues are integrated into conceptualizations later in training; it the rare novice who completes this process (J. M. Bernard, 1994; Falender, 2001).

Supervisors

Priest (1994) described stages for achieving effective multicultural supervision competency. The first stage is the supervisor's denial of cultural differences that affect supervision. The second stage is the supervisor's recognition that differences exist, but a lack of competence about what to do about it, possibly resulting in the supervisor's feeling overwhelmed. In stage three, the supervisor makes an attempt to identify similarities and differences among cultures that affect the supervisory relationship. In stage four, the supervisor determines where he or she fits in the cultural framework. In stage five, the supervisor develops a beginning appreciation of cultural distinctiveness, resulting in an enhanced supervisory process. In stage six, the supervisor can formulate methodologies that are respectful of the supervisee's culture and interaction while acquiring new skills. The client or family is not directly considered in this framework; however, this set of stages provides a useful outline for supervisors who are moving through the acquisition of cultural competence.

RACIAL AND IDENTITY DEVELOPMENT

Awareness of one's own racial identity and ethnocentric biases has been described as a developmental task (Sabnani et al., 1991) and as critical in understanding multicultural supervision (D'Andrea & Daniels, 1997). Most of the literature has focused on White and Black or African American identity development, overlooking the preponderance of other cultural groups. We now describe a model of White racial-identity development and a model of Minority Identity Development. The White racial-identity model put forth by Sabnani et al. (1991) provides an integration of previous models and a progression through stages. Cognizance of the supervisee and supervisor's stage of development is an oft forgotten ingredient of multicultural competence, accentuated by the fact that White individuals are at varying levels of readiness to assimilate multicultural training. Stage 1 is preexposure/precontact, which requires cultural emic knowledge acquisition and beginning etic counseling skills. Stage 2 is the conflict stage, in which the individual confronts the dilemma of conforming to White norms while upholding humanitarian values and beliefs. This stage requires a greater understanding of prejudice and racism and their emotional impact, definition of barriers to counseling, and development of counseling techniques more appropriate to individuals in particular cultural groups. Stage 3 is marked by a prominority and antiracism stance through which paternal attitudes of Whites are scrutinized; this stage requires cultural immersion and study. Role-playing and communication skills training are advocated in this stage as well. In Stage 4, "Retreat into White Culture," the focus is on fear or anger elicited during Stage 3. Emphasis on etic over emic approaches may facilitate dealing with the negative feelings aroused. Stage 5, or "Redefinition and Integration," entails the integration of "Whiteness" and its value as part of the supervisee or supervisor's identity. Enhanced respect for varying worldviews and deepening of culturally emic approaches are indicated. Sabnani et al. (1991) provided references for skill development exercises.

The model for Minority Identity Development (Atkinson et al., 1993) describes stages of integrating dominant White or Western values with the values of one's own racial group. Initially, at the "Conformity Stage," individuals prefer values and norms of the dominant group and express self-deprecating attitudes about their own ethnic–racial group as well as other non-White groups. They choose White colleagues to relate to, as they depreciate the value of the non-Whites. Moving to the "Resistance/Immersion Stage," there is an increase in ethnic pride and positivity combined with increased suspicion of White Americans. Next, in the "Synergistic Stage," a sense of self-fulfillment is associated with the individual's own ethnic, cultural, or racial identity, but the individual does not achieve a complete acceptance of all aspects. He or she may become an activist against oppression and discrimination, and the supervisor is well served to communicate respect for the synergy.

Dominance appears to be a significant difference between these two models. In the White racial-identity development model, one moves from

ethnocentrism and overvaluing one's own culture to greater cultural awareness and integration, whereas in the minority racial-identity development
model, movement is from overadoption of White values toward integration
of one's own cultural identity. In the White model, the individual is overly
dominant and wears blinders to others, whereas in the minority model, the
individual is overly nondominant and wears blinders to his or her own
culture, ethnicity, or race.

Helms (1990) proposed a way to conceptualize racial-identity development as a cognitive development continuum. There are two phases: Phase 1
involves relatively less complex strategies and lower levels of racial-identity
development. Ethnocentrism and conformity are elements of this phase.
Phase 2 involves more complex strategies and higher levels of racial-identity
development. This phase includes elements such as resistance, pseudoinde-
pendence, immersion, and autonomy. This continuum may be a particularly
useful way of conceptualizing the development of trainees, as it takes into
account the cognitive complexity and ability to integrate disparate information, concepts, and feelings.

Ancis and Ladany (2001) described a model of nonoppressive interpersonal development that integrates some of the previously discussed themes.
In this model, levels of identity are integrated with respect to multiple
demographic variables. There is also a strong emotional component to the
responses. Individuals are identified as belonging to a socially oppressed
group or a socially privileged group. Some individuals might belong to both
types of group, based on different demographic variables (e.g., sex and
socioeconic status). At the heart of the theory is a progression through
developing "means of interpersonal functioning," (p. 67) or thoughts, feelings, and behaviors based on feelings toward self and identification with
particular demographic factors. The first level of interpersonal functioning
is *adaptation*, or conformity, complacency, and apathy with a very superficial
understanding of cultural difference; stereotyping attitudes; and limited emotional awareness. This stage is marked by denial and resistance. In the
supervision context, supervisors in this stage minimize the trainee's expression of multicultural competence, use inaccurate stereotypes, and perceive
themselves as multiculturally competent. They have very limited ability to
integrate multicultural factors into the conceptualization, to address issues
of culture within the supervisor–supervisee or supervisee–client relationship,
and to assess strengths or weaknesses in this area. Supervisees at the adaptation level ignore the environment and miss cultural influences and issues
that substantially affect client behavior. The second stage is *incongruence*,
or a feeling that previously held beliefs of privilege and oppression are
inconsistent with their experience. Minimization and rationalization are
the operant defense mechanisms, and there are still remnants of the adaptation phase, such as stereotyping. Movement to this level could be precipitated

by a major event in which one could not longer overlook oppression. For supervisors in this phase, minimal, but some, attention is devoted to multicultural aspects. Supervisees may be aware of multicultural issues, but do not directly raise them in supervision. The third stage, *exploration*, is marked by anger regarding recognition of oppression, guilt and shame for not having seen it before, and increased insight. Ancis and Ladany (2001) emphasized that the following problem may occur in this stage of the supervisor–supervisee fit: As the supervisor increasingly raises multicultural issues, a supervisee in the adaptation or incongruence stage will resist. They cautioned that the zeal of this stage may result in an overemphasis on cultural factors. In the fourth and final stage, *integration*, proficiency and insight occur. Multicultural formulations are integrated into conceptualizations. Trainees use accurate empathy, analyze their own biases, and separate countertransference from transference phenomena.

Ancis and Ladany (2001) described supervisor–supervisee interactions in terms of whether each member is at the same or a different level or stage of development. The most effective combination in terms of client outcome, they posited, is when both are in the exploration or integration phase. The next best combination occurs when the trainee, at the integration level, is more advanced than the supervisor, at the adaptation level. They suggested that this combination may be the most frequent constellation at present. It is unclear exactly how the privilege or oppression on the part of the supervisor or supervisee plays out in the framework. Also, it seems that there is an abundance of other motivators to progress in sophistication beyond critical incidents. These motivators might include continuing education, clinical material, or personal life experience. In addition, it would be ideal if a model of development could also encompass the client or family, including their level of acculturation and their ethnic–racial–cultural identity.

All of the models that have been proposed fail to fully integrate trainee development of multicultural competence with that of the supervisor, as well as the multicultural competence reflected in the relationship (Ancis & Ladany, 2001). A major limitation is thinking that, to become culturally competent, one need only acquire knowledge and skills. "One cannot merely memorize cultural competence, but must learn and demonstrate it through a variety of active self-involving strategies and procedures" (Helms & Richardson, 1997, p. 69). Instead, one needs to assess the impact of cultural and racial attitudes of the therapist on the client–therapist interaction (Sodowsky et al., 1994).

The proposed models also lack empirical support and consideration of personality dynamics (Leong & Wagner, 1994) and are not typically concerned with the triad of client, supervisee (therapist), and supervisor, all of whom may be from different ethnic, racial, socioeconomic status, acculturation, religious, gender, gender-identity, and age categories.

Leong and Wagner (1994) concluded that we know very little about cross-cultural counseling supervision. However, they determined that empirical support has confirmed the following:

1. Race can profoundly influence supervision, including trainee expectations for supervisor "empathy, respect, and congruence" (p. 128).
2. Race can influence the supervisee's perception of whether the supervisor likes him or her.
3. Under some circumstances, race does not appear to influence supervision.

They resolved that we still need to know whether the evolution of cross-cultural supervision is in fact a developmental process and how specific the process is to race. That is, can we use a culture-general model, or do we need specific models for each racial–ethnic pair? Cook (1994) suggested that pairing of supervisors and supervisees with differing levels of racial-identity attitudes may lead to power differentials that result in lesser or greater expression and competency in "racial acknowledgement" (p. 136), especially if the acknowledgment remains unspoken and intellectualized. Cook (1994) encouraged more routine discussion of race of all (supervisee, supervisor, and client) participants in supervision.

STEPS TOWARD SUPERVISORY COMPETENCE

To achieve multicultural competency, one must complete a series of steps. First is the determination of the supervisor's self-competency, the competency of the program and site, and the supervisee's level of cultural competency. As described in the section on competency in ethics and legal considerations in chapter 7, it is incumbent on the supervisor to ascertain his or her own level of cultural and diversity competence. It is difficult, if not impossible, simply to remove oneself from supervision for clients in categories with which one feels less competent in a community setting. Therefore, the onus is on the supervisor to increase his or her cultural and diversity competence.

Program Assessment

Assessing the programmic "internal climate" (Suzuki et al., 2001, p. 848), including faculty, students, and administrators, is an essential step. An environment of openness with attitudes, values, and behaviors that exemplify administrative and clinical faculty support for respectful, culturally competent interchanges is desired (Priest, 1994). Challenges, input, and questions relating to culture are encouraged.

A tool for assessment of multicultural-counseling training settings, at least structurally, can be administered (D'Andrea & Daniels, 1991). The stages into which training settings are classified are "Culturally Entrenched," where multicultural training is rarely incorporated; "Cross-Cultural Awakening," where there is a developing awareness and some discussion of issues; "Cultural Integrity," where increased attention is given to culture and there are separate courses on various issues related to culture; and "Infusion," where multiculturalism is integrated into the whole curriculum. D'Andrea and Daniels (1991) found most counseling programs to be at the Cross-Cultural Awakening stage, although some programs were assessed to be at the Cultural Integrity or Infusion stage. This model provides a structure for determining a starting point and an aspirational end point for achieving cultural competency. It is reminiscent of Lefley's (1986) concern that training could be additive (new concepts are added to the standard clinical training), substitutive (new concepts replace traditional clinical content), or integrative (new concepts are integral to mental health training). Those who argue that they do not have space or time to add so many new components like cultural competency are missing the point of the integrative curriculum.

Alternatively, the Multicultural Competency Checklist (see Appendix E), developed for counseling-psychology programs, includes consideration of minority representation (a minimum benchmark of 30% racial- and ethnic-minority students, faculty, and staff), curricular issues (the addressing of multicultural issues in coursework and evaluation), counseling practice and supervision (competency promoted through training and supervision experiences), research (faculty research on multiculturalism being conducted and encouraged), student and faculty competency evaluation (staff and trainees being evaluated on multiculturally competent behavior), and physical environment (an environment reflective of multicultural appreciation) (Ponterotto, Alexander, & Grieger, 1995). Because of the importance of student and faculty diversity, and the broader spectrum this checklist analyzes, it would be useful to administer it in internship and other training settings. Both trainees and faculty should complete it, as there is some concern that student perceptions may differ from those of faculty members with respect to degree of cultural competence, with students perceiving less program competency in several areas (Constantine, Ladany, Inman, & Ponterotto, 1996).

Individual Multicultural Competency Assessment

Assisting supervisees to assess and work on the development of cultural self-awareness is an important step. Students feel more comfortable considering the culture, race, ethnicity, and differences of others than looking at themselves. They also are more eager to address cognitive-level aspects of what to do in situations with particular clients of particular ethnicities (Tomlinson-Clarke, 2000). Flexibility, openness, and adaptability to cultural difference and nuance seem to be predictors of success in multicultural competence (Tomlinson-Clarke, 2000).

To obtain at least a preliminary measure of individual multicultural-counseling competency, one of several measures should be applied for supervisors as well as supervisees. The Multicultural Awareness Knowledge and Skills Survey (D'Andrea, Daniels, & Heck, 1991), the Multicultural Counseling Inventory (Sodowsky et al., 1994), the Multicultural Counseling Knowledge and Awareness Scale (see Appendix D; Ponterotto, Gretchen, Utsey, Rieger, & Austin, 2002), and the Cross-Cultural Counseling Inventory–Revised (supervisor report form; see Appendix C; LaFromboise, Coleman, & Hernandez, 1991) are several that have been reviewed (Ponterotto & Alexander, 1995). The first three are self-report measures and have a social-desirability component (Constantine & Ladany, 2000; R. L. Worthington, Mobley, Franks, Tan, & Andreas, 2000), but perhaps less social desirability for those who rate themselves as high in multicultural competence (Ponterotto et al., 2002). That is, those who have high multicultural awareness may have a low need to appear socially desirable (Constantine & Ladany, 2000). Respondents rated themselves as more multiculturally competent than was reflected in their written multicultural conceptualization sophistication (Constantine & Ladany, 2000; Ladany, Inman, et al., 1997). Social desirability itself has cultural determinants; for example, Sodowsky et al. (1998) found that Asians generally had higher "multicultural social desirability" scores than their White, Black, and Hispanic peers. Sodowsky et al. explained this finding in terms of face saving in social situations or a desire to be less confrontational. In other words, to avoid confrontation, Asians in this sample responded as they thought the researcher wanted them to. Constantine and Ladany (2000) suggested use of the LaFromboise et al. (1991) supervisor-report measure of trainees as an alternative, assuming that supervisors are culturally competent enough to assess trainees (Constantine & Ladany, 2001).

Self-reported multicultural competence by trainees was not related to multicultural case conceptualization, which was contrary to expectation (Constantine, 2001; Constantine & Ladany, 2000) and may in fact be two theoretically divergent constructs (Constantine, 2001). Alternatively, self-reported multicultural-competence ratings might reflect anticipated rather than actual competency (Constantine, 2001). However, in an analog study, R. L. Worthington et al. (2000) reported a positive correlation between multicultural verbal content (verbal reference to culture, race, ethnicity, and other factors relating to culture, environment, and social conditions) and higher scores on the LaFromboise et al. (1991) scale, rated by graduate student judges based on transcripts of counselor verbal responses. For supervisors, it is important not to rely solely on supervisee self-report (Ladany, Inman, et al., 1997). The R. L. Worthington et al. (2000) study provides a potential methodology for describing multicultural competency in verbal content. As Torres-Rivera, Phan, Maddux, Wilbur, and Garrett (2001) summarized, multicultural competence involves self-knowledge of cultural (diversity) heritage; knowledge of how these personal factors affect attitudes, values, and beliefs related to the therapy process; recognition of limitations of one's own multicultural competency; and recognition of sources and instances of discomfort relating to clients of differing backgrounds. A more flexible worldview, a sense of personal adequacy, and belief in societal combating of racism are all associated with multicultural competency (Sodowsky et al., 1998). Constantine and Ladany (2001) proposed that empathy and interpersonal sensitivity may be correlates of multicultural counseling competence. Although there is need for additional reliability, validity, standardization, and treatment outcome data (Ponterotto & Alexander, 1995), it is still valuable to use one or more of the aforementioned measures to establish a baseline understanding of cultural competency and to begin to discuss and integrate culture into the training curriculum.

Another possible assessment device that has been proposed is portfolios, or collections of work (videos of sessions, reports, etc.) demonstrating the development of competence, even though they have been criticized as lacking in reliability in evaluation and as extremely time consuming (Coleman, 1997; Constantine & Ladany, 2001).

MULTICULTURAL-COMPETENCY IMPLEMENTATION

Once the cultural competency of a program, supervisor, and supervisee has been assessed, the next step is to implement a program to enhance competencies to reach the Infusion stage posited by D'Andrea and Daniels (1991). Use of a comprehensive model is imperative, such as the model defining competencies for multicultural counseling developed by D. W. Sue et al. (1992) and comprehensively operationalized by Arredondo et al. (1996). Their model articulates cultural attitudes and beliefs, knowledge, and skills. The first area of the model encompasses the therapist's awareness of his or her own cultural values and biases. For example, "Culturally skilled counselors believe that cultural self-awareness and sensitivity to one's own cultural heritage is essential" (Arredondo et al., 1996, p. 57). The second area involves the therapist's awareness of the client's worldview. "Culturally skilled counselors understand and have knowledge about sociopolitical influences that impinge on the life of racial and ethnic minorities" (Arredondo et al., 1996, pp. 64–65). The third area involves culturally appropriate intervention strategies. Although the component parts of each area of the model are operationalized, it is still necessary to translate them into a training curriculum. As Abreu (2001) concluded, "these conceptualizations do not clearly suggest the content of training needed to help . . . students achieve this competency" (p. 488). Fuertes, Mueller, Chauhan, Walker, and Ladany (2002) suggested an operationalizing step of measuring the introduction of the discussion of race into the therapeutic interaction at an early point.

Pope-Davis et al. (2002) presented some general direction for training. They suggested the importance of increasing one's cultural knowledge base; teaching counselors to disclose intentions and plans to clients, especially when cultural information is being collected or an intervention is being planned; training in the use of restraint in making assumptions based on cultural knowledge, to safeguard against stereotyping. For example, instead of making a blanket generalization about a cultural group, one could state the assumption and ask if it is one that applies to the particular client or family.

Experiential activities, including the labeling exercise (attaching stereotypic labels to individuals' backs), making implicit associations to words associated with race, and pairing up culturally different partners to share cultural information, have all been suggested (Abreu, 2001).

Wisnia and Falender (1999) described a specific training sequence for enhancing cultural competency, composed of a series of activities (all of which is described in program recruitment materials). Initially, several movies involving cultural passage or cultural assimilation are viewed and discussed in a Falicov (1995) or Hays (2001) framework. Another activity is the construction of supervisory and therapist (supervisee) maps such as the one illustrated in Figure 6.1. The task is to build a prioritized listing of considerations on the mind of the supervisor when he or she goes into the supervisory hour. The supervisor is to imagine a trainee with whom he or she is working and formulate a hierarchy of priorities approaching the next supervisory hour with that trainee: Exactly what areas of supervisory intervention are most critical, and in what order are they prioritized? The trainee constructs his or her own map as well. Then the supervisor and supervisee can compare these maps and discuss discrepancies and how they affect the supervisory relationship, the therapeutic relationship, and outcome. Contrasting priorities may exist for issues of safety, pragmatics, ethics and legalities, or many other possible considerations, many of which may be seen through the prism of diversity. Highlighting and discussing personal views on these issues adds perspective and enhances communication. This technique may also be useful in assisting a problematic trainee to address the substantial differences in approach to a particular client's situation. These maps are supplemental to maps constructed around dimensions

Safety of Client, Family and Therapist

Legal and Ethical Considerations

Cultural Overlay: Emic Considerations

Theoretical Orientation
Attention to Process Versus Content
View of Therapeutic Process
Role of Therapist
Attention to Past, Present, Integration of Two
Articulation of Treatment Goals

Transference-Countertransference Considerations

Responsiveness to Client
Cues
Affect
Nonverbal Communication
Process
Cultural Variables
Respect and Perspective Regarding These
Consistent Respect for Boundaries

Focus on Strengths

Interaction Between Supervisee and Supervisor
Open
Respectful
    Access to and Responsiveness to Therapeutic Data
    Responsiveness to Supervisory Input
    Cultural Respect

Looking Ahead
Integration of current data into plan for future intervention
    Ability to foresee possible consequences of particular interventions and plan ahead

    Look for Matches and Mismatches
    Contrast Map of Supervisor with Supervisee and Family/Client

Figure 6.1. An example of supervisor maps constructed by a supervisor.

described earlier in this chapter in conceptualizations of culture, the frameworks of Falicov (1995) and Hays (2001).

Next, the supervisors and supervisees describe an aspect of their own particular upbringing and personal cultural identification and development through one of four contexts: Falicov's journey of migration and culture change, an ecological context, family organization, or transitions in the structure of family life cycles. The supervisors and supervisees arrange these presentations around particular cultural variables or identity niches that are reflective of their cultural identity and comfortable for them to present. Presenters use food, music, poetry, photographic albums, video, or objects of significance to share their culture. The processing by the group includes reactions, expression of feelings elicited, and the forging of a sense of connectedness with aspects of each other's and one's own cultural experience. Next, the framework is applied to clinical material with discussion of how the maps of supervisor, supervisee, and client or family interface and influence the process. Myths, misconceptions, or stereotypes are discussed as awareness of some similarity of experience emerges. In the final portion of the seminar, personal and experiential understandings of prejudice and stereotyping are processed. In follow-ups, elaborate case analysis is conducted using Falicov's (1995) model and self-knowledge gleaned during the seminar about the cultural maps of supervisors and supervisees.

Zimmerman and Haddock (2001) presented a modified "In-the-box/Out-of-the-box" exercise (which they derived from Creighton and Kivel, 1992). In this activity, boxes are drawn on a board. One box is labeled male, and the other box is labeled female. Trainees brainstorm traits, attitudes, characteristics, and behaviors associated with each gender by society. These factors are "in-the-box" behaviors. Then the trainees describe consequences of "out-of-the-box" behaviors for men and women. For example, men could be considered "gay," "weak," or "passive" for exhibiting out-of-the-box behaviors, whereas women might be considered to "wear the pants in the family" as a result of their exhibiting out-of-box behaviors. Trainees also consider shared, or "common-box," behaviors that could occur, such as sharing of life tasks.

The appendices of Arredondo et al. (1996) provide excellent activities to enhance understanding of worldviews. These activities include readings, workshops and conferences, and strategies.

Simply training supervisees to raise the issue of race and diversity early in supervision is a preliminary step (Hird et al., 2001). The next step is to fully incorporate diversity into the supervisory process, which is the responsibility of the supervisor (Constantine, 1997). Particular processes, such as addressing the supervisor's or supervisee's feelings at the moment they occur, using video review to deal with assumptions and feelings elicited during the session, and determining what prompted particular interventions, are all useful in integrating affect, genuineness, and openness into discussions of diversity (Garrett et al., 2001). It is important to model and describe examples of what GLB and multiculturally competent therapists say or do in relevant situations—and what they tend not to say or do (Phillips, 2000). Awareness of the impact of language and assumptions is another critical part of supervision teaching. For example, use of words like "partner" rather than "boyfriend" helps the trainee avoid assumptions of sexual orientation.

Competencies

Cultural competencies required for supervisors include the following:

- Possesses a working knowledge of the factors that affect worldview (e.g., optimism and pessimism, the value of tradition, and relationship with nature)
- Possesses self-identity awareness and competence with respect to diversity in the context of self, supervisee, and client or family
- Exhibits competence in multimodal assessment of the multicultural competence of trainees, including self-ratings, observational ratings, and supervisor and client ratings
- Models diversity and multicultural conceptualizations throughout the supervision process
- Models respect, openness, and curiosity toward all aspects of diversity and its impact on behavior, interaction, and the therapy and supervision processes
- Initiates discussion of diversity factors in supervision

7

ETHICAL AND LEGAL PERSPECTIVES AND RISK MANAGEMENT

Even though supervisors are presumably the watchdogs, if not the bloodhounds, of the psychotherapy process (Slovenko, 1980), the ethics of supervision has only recently received significant attention. Prior to 1993, when the Association for Counselor Education and Supervision (ACES) first published the Ethical Guidelines for Counseling and Supervisors (Association for Counselor Education and Supervision, 1995), the set of ethics applied to supervision was extrapolated from the APA Ethical Principles and Code of Conduct (1992). This state of affairs led McCarthy et al. (1988) to conclude that the contention that "ethical standards exist for supervisors" is a supervision myth (p. 26). In the latest revision of the APA Ethical Principles and Code of Conduct, Section 7 is dedicated to education and training. Nonetheless, the ACES guidelines are the most comprehensive for supervisors, but have not been adopted by the American Psychological Association, only by the Association for Counselor Education and Supervision, a founding division of the American Counseling Association. Absent specific guidelines from the American Psychological Association, psychologists would be well advised to follow guidelines established by other, related professions (J. Younggren, personal communication, 2002).

The role of the supervisor entails being a role model for the trainee in the conscientious ethical practice of psychology, looking ahead for each area of practice and its special ethical considerations (e.g., psychodiagnostics;

see Rupert, Kozlowski, Hoffman, Daniels, & Piette, 1999), and considering the ethical issues of the entire administration–supervisor–supervisee–client chain, with all of its intricacies. Faculty and supervisor role modeling of ethical behavior is essential, but not sufficient to instilling ethical attitudes and behavior in students (Kitchener, 1992). As each party in the equation may (and typically does) wear multiple hats, the complexity grows. As Rest (1984) cautioned, "students. . .often have a mind set not to look for moral issues, do not expect that they are an inevitable part of professional life, and are usually ill-prepared to know how to approach a moral problem when one does smack them in the face" (p. 21). The message that needs to be communicated to the supervisees is that "holding ethical standards requires acting with benevolence and courage rather than donning protective armor and running for a safe place to hide" (Koocher & Keith-Spiegel, 1998, p. 4).

This chapter provides a review of ethical and legal dilemmas faced by psychologists, ethical violations that can be made by supervisors and supervisees, and supervision-related ethical issues. The latter may occur in areas including competence, due process, informed consent, confidentiality, multiple or dual relationships, ethical problem-solving approaches, ethics training, malpractice (including legal precedents in supervisory issues), duty-to-warn-and-protect issues, documentation, letters of recommendation, and risk management.

It is incumbent on the supervisor to introduce the supervisee to the state regulations for the practice of psychology (state licensing board regulations and welfare and institutional codes) as well as ethical and legal codes regulating practice.

CORE ETHICAL PRINCIPLES

It would be impossible for any ethics code to cover every possible contingency arising in clinical work or supervision. Thus, it is commendable that in the latest revision of the APA Ethical Principles of Psychologists and Code of Conduct (American Psychological Association, 2002a), general principles are defined. They are beneficence and nonmaleficence; fidelity and responsibility; integrity, justice, and respect for people's rights; and dignity. These ethical principles are derived from Beauchamp and Childress (1979) and others, as described by Kitchener (1984, 2000). Koocher and Keith-Spiegel (1998) added the following to the list of core ethical principles: according dignity or viewing others as worthy of respect, treating others with caring and compassion or being considerate within professional boundaries, pursuing excellence or maintaining competence and being considerate, and accepting accountability, which includes considering possible consequences, accepting responsibility for action or inaction, and acting with integrity.

Meara, Schmidt, and Day (1996) added veracity or truthfulness. These principles provide a frame for ethical behavior and a structure for supervisory ethical problem solving.

ETHICAL AND LEGAL DILEMMAS OF PSYCHOLOGISTS

It is useful to look at psychologists' ethical behavior across roles, to provide a context for their behavior in supervision. In Pope and Vetter's (1992) study of ethical dilemmas encountered by APA members, the most frequently cited instances out of 703 troubling ethical incidents were breaches of confidentiality (18%); blurred, dual, or conflictual relationships (17%); problems with payment sources, plans, settings, and methods (14%); and issues concerning academic settings, teaching dilemmas, and training (8%). Supervision accounted for 2% of the dilemmas. Pope and Vetter (1992) described difficulties regarding boundaries of confidentiality when multiple providers or clients were involved.

An analysis of licensing-related disciplinary actions from data collected by the Association of State and Provincial Psychology Boards revealed a different profile than APA members' reports of ethical dilemmas (Pope & Vasquez, 1998). The violations for which disciplinary actions were taken included sexual or dual relationships with clients (35%); unprofessional, unethical, or negligent practice (28.6%); fraudulent acts (9.5%); and conviction of crimes (8.6%), with disciplinary action for inadequate or improper supervision (4.9%) occurring slightly more frequently than for impairment (4.1%), breach of confidentiality (3.9%), and improper or inadequate record keeping (3.4%; Pope & Vasquez, 1998, pp. 32–33). Confidentiality issues, reported as the most frequent ethical dilemma by APA members, had a low frequency in the disciplinary-actions tally, whereas blurred, dual, or conflictual relationships, the second most prevalent dilemma in the study of APA members, corresponded to the high frequency of sexual or dual relationships in the disciplinary–actions tally. Supervision-related issues, although at a low frequency in the Pope and Vasquez (1998) study, were twice as prevalent as in the Pope and Vetter (1992) study. Interestingly, confidentiality issues were also reported to be the most frequently encountered dilemmas by college counselors (Hayman & Covert, 1986). It may be that, although confidentiality dilemmas are very prevalent among practitioners and supervisors, they are resolved informally and thus do not reach formal levels for resolution.

According to Pope and Vasquez (1998, from data from APA's Insurance Trust [APAIT]), the top five reasons psychologists were actually sued were sexual impropriety (20%), incorrect treatment (14%), loss from evaluation (11%), breach of confidentiality or privacy (7%), and failure to diagnose or establishment of an incorrect diagnosis (7%). Failure to supervise properly (2%) was the 12th most frequent reason in total claims. Although APAIT cautions in its risk management trainings that conducting supervision, through the sheer number of cases one oversees, increases one's risk quotient dramatically (Harris, 2002), this consideration has not been borne out in practice.

There appears to be a big difference between what the psychologist knows should be done and what the psychologist actually does (Bersoff, 1995), information that is directly relevant to supervision. An informal study by Pope and Bajt (1988) determined that over 50% of psychologists intentionally violated laws or ethical rules. J. L. Bernard & Jara (1995) presented graduate students in clinical psychology, the majority of whom had completed an ethics course, with two ethical-violation vignettes. There was a sizeable disparity between what the students reported they thought should be done and what they stated they actually would do. When J. L. Bernard, Murphy, and Little (1987) repeated a modified version of the study with psychologists who belonged to Division 12 of the American Psychological Association, they found that a greater proportion of psychologists reported that they would do what they stated they should do, but 25 to 37% still said that they would do less than what they should do. T. S. Smith, McGuire, Abbott, and Blau (1991) reported a similar finding.

For psychologists, child-abuse reporting was the area in which they were most likely to break the law and act on their beliefs (Pope & Vetter, 1992). However, more recently, Renninger, Veach, and Bagdade (2002) reported adequate knowledge of child-abuse reporting laws and fair satisfaction with them. The stress associated with child-abuse reporting is substantially higher for trainees, especially when making their first or second report. In addition, the dilemma of child-abuse reporting seems more complex in relationships where a supervisee is cotherapist and/or has multiple supervisors, because different value systems or thresholds for reporting may exist.

In situations of ethical conflict, clinicians act the way they feel they should when the situation involves a clear ethical code or law. There are myriad reasons for discrepancies between clinicians' actual actions and the actions they feel they should take in other situations. Personal values, belief structures, and practical considerations seem to temper resolution in less clear-cut ethical situations (T. S. Smith et al., 1991). The role of emotion over rationality has been suggested as another explanation of deviation from ethical principles (Betan & Stanton, 1999), indicating the need for the integration of emotionality, a factor that is often overlooked, into the problem-solving and training matrix of ethical decision making. Another factor that causes deviation from ethical principles is personal life history, especially history of abuse. Pope and Feldman-Summers (1992) reported that over two-thirds of female therapists and nearly one-third of male therapists had experienced abuse in their childhood or adult life. Thus, it is probable that a similar proportion of supervisees have had such a history. Greater emotional sensitivity or reactivity to abusive relationships might then skew reactions of therapists and lead them to deviate from the principles they would use under other circumstances. The therapist's own trauma history has been found to affect perceptions of safety, self-trust, and self-intimacy after dealing with client trauma. This finding was especially true for therapists with fewer years of experience (Pearlman & MacIan, 1995).

In the area of child clinical psychology, considerations of developmental status played a significant role in beliefs about ethical practice (Mannheim et al., 2002). Considerations of crossing boundaries (e.g., attending a client's major life event, hugging a client, buying fundraiser items from a client, giving gifts to a client) and confidentiality (even more imperative in protecting adolescents than young children) were subject to situational influences including the child's age and developmental status, accounting for possible deviation. In a study by J. R. Sullivan, Ramirez, Rae, Razo, and George (2002), the respondents, pediatric psychologists, were most likely to find it ethical to break confidentiality with adolescent clients to report the following behaviors to parents: suicidal behavior, drug use, sexual behavior, and alcohol use. Frequency, intensity, duration, and the actual type of behavior were considerations in the decision. These issues are particularly difficult for trainees, because of the greater identification with the child or adolescent that results from closer age proximity.

SUPERVISEE PERCEPTIONS OF SUPERVISORY ETHICS

Ladany, Lehrman-Waterman, Molinaro, and Wolgast (1999) studied supervisees' perceptions of their supervisor's ethical practices (49% return rate). Based on the premise that supervisees sometimes believed that their supervisors had engaged in unethical practices, Ladany et al. surveyed practicum students and interns and found that 51% of all supervisees reported at least one ethical violation by their supervisors. The average number of violations was 1.52, with a standard deviation of 2.35. The most frequent violations were failure to adhere to ethical guidelines regarding performance evaluation and general monitoring of student activities, violating areas of confidentiality with respect to supervision, and working with alternative theoretical perspectives. The most adhered-to guidelines by supervisors were those relating to sexual issues, the line between psychotherapy and supervision, and termination and follow-up issues. Thirty-five percent of supervisees reported that they discussed violations with their supervisors, 54% discussed them with someone else, 84% discussed them with a peer or friend in the field, 33% discussed them with a significant other, 21% discussed them with another supervisor, and 18% discussed them with a therapist. The supervisees reported that, 14% of the time, someone in a position of power knew of the violation, but did nothing about it. Supervisees reported that the violations had a mild to moderate negative impact on their quality of client care. Greater frequency of supervisors' unethical behavior was associated with less satisfaction with the supervisor. Conversely, supervisors who had lower frequencies of unethical behaviors were associated with more satisfied supervisees.

ETHICAL VIOLATIONS BY SUPERVISEES

In an exploratory survey by Fly, van Bark, Weinman, Kitchener, and Lang (1997) of graduate students in clinical and counseling programs, 89 ethical violations were self-reported by 47 respondents (19% return rate). As in the Pope and Vetter (1992) study of APA members, confidentiality was ranked the highest (25%) for types of violations reported. After that were the categories of professional boundaries, sexual and nonsexual (20%); plagiarism or falsification of data (15%); compromising of client welfare (10%); procedural breach with ethical implications (10%); competency (9%); integrity or dishonesty (8%); and misrepresentation of credentials (3%). Training directors learned of many of these violations through a third party (36%) or through either the training director or another faculty member having witnessed the transgression (25%). Fifty-four percent of the individuals who committed ethical transgressions had completed an ethics course. Unfortunately, the return rate in this study was extremely low, casting significant doubt on the reliability and validity of the findings.

R. L. Worthington, Tan, and Poulin (2002), bemoaning the lack of attention to ethical requirements and behavior for supervisees, explored categories of potentially problematic ethical areas for supervisees. Their questionnaire of ethically questionable practices revealed few discrepancies between supervisors' and supervisees' perceptions of what behaviors are unethical. Items that a high percentage of supervisees reported having done at least once included having negative feelings about the supervisor and not disclosing them (93%); not completing a timely documentation of client records (85%); gossiping about a supervisory conflict, but not discussing with the supervisor (83%); avoiding talking about problems or mistakes in client work (76%); not discussing negative feelings toward a client (72%); and not addressing a strong personal (countertransference) reaction (62%). These findings set the stage for other research that has been done on supervisee disclosure and negative incidents in supervision, to be discussed later in the chapter.

There is ample evidence that current approaches to training in ethics are not adequate because the transfer of ethical principles and their application and use in actual clinical and life situations are not reliable processes.

ETHICAL ISSUES RELATED TO SUPERVISION

General ethical issues identified as pertinent to supervision, extrapolated from Ladany, Lehrman-Waterman, et al.'s (1999) categories, which were culled from the ACES supervision ethics into a general framework (in bold print), include **competence** (Lamb, Cochran, & Jackson, 1991; Stoltenberg et al., 1998; Vasquez, 1992), **due process** (J. M. Bernard & Goodyear, 1998; Russell & Petrie, 1994), **informed consent** (J. M. Bernard & Goodyear, 1998; Russell & Petrie, 1994), **confidentiality** (J. M. Bernard & Goodyear, 1998; Ladany, Lehrman-Waterman, et al., 1999; Russell & Petrie, 1994), **multiple or dual relationships** (J. M. Bernard & Goodyear, 1998; Stoltenberg et al., 1998), and **ethical knowledge and behavior and personal functioning** (Lamb et al., 1991; Vasquez, 1992). Evaluation or performance valuation and monitoring of supervisee activities, also listed by Ladany, Lehrman-Waterman, et al. (1999) will be discussed in chapter 8, this volume. Ladany, Lehrman-Waterman, et al. (1999) identified multicultural sensitivity toward clients and supervisees (discussed in chap. 6, this volume) and client termination and follow-up as issues not addressed in the ACES ethical guidelines. Each of the foregoing bold categories will be discussed in this chapter, as well as preventative and problem-solving strategies for dealing with ethical dilemmas and supervisory approaches.

COMPETENCE

Competence entails functioning by the therapist within areas of established expertise, training, or experience, and ensuring the same functioning for the trainee, or providing structure, appropriate referral, or supervision and consultation. The APA Ethical Principles of Psychologists and Code of Conduct (American Psychological Association, 2002a, 2.01[a]) includes the following definition: Boundaries of competence are defined, "Psychologists provide services, teach, and conduct research with populations and in areas only within the boundaries of their competence based on their education, training, supervised experience, consultation, study, or professional experience."

Pope and Vasquez (1998) distinguished intellectual competence from emotional competence. Intellectual competence refers to education and knowledge of research, interventions, treatment efficacy, and theory, as well as critical thinking and conceptualization. A critical part of that area of competence is awareness of what one does not know. Emotional competence refers to knowledge of self, monitoring of self, and acceptance of self, areas relevant to supervisee training in self-care.

In the realm of supervisee competence, Sherry (1991) highlighted a significant issue in training: The supervisee is in training to learn and is not yet competent to perform many of the tasks that he or she is assigned. Simultaneously attending to the best interests of supervisee and client places the supervisor in a balancing act. The standard that applies to this issue is as follows, from the APA Ethical Principles of Psychologists and Code of Conduct (American Psychological Association, 2002a):

> 2.05: Psychologists who delegate work to . . . supervisees . . . take reasonable steps to . . . (2) authorize only those responsibilities that such persons can be expected to perform competently on the basis of their education, training, or experience, either independently or with the level of supervision being provided and (3) see that such persons perform these services competently.

Assessing One's Own Competence

An issue as central to supervision as it is to clinical practice is defining and supervising within one's own areas of competence. The assessment of one's own competence was addressed by Haas and Malouf (1989) with a series of guidelines that consider the existence of relevant standards, grounding of the approach in research or theory, contextual constraints, whether one is emotionally able to be of help, and whether one's decision could be justified to a group of one's peers. These guidelines are particularly useful in assessing one's competence to address or supervise problems new to or different from one's typical area of practice. Self-assessment is a valuable competency for supervisors to model for supervisees.

Competency in Supervision

Disney and Stephens (1994) asked whether, to be able to supervise, one must have had specific training in supervision. Considering that competence is a core ethical value, supervisory competence, derived through education, training, and experience, is essential to one's ability to supervise. However, apart from counseling programs, supervision training is new to professional training. It is incumbent on the supervisor to obtain the necessary training and to inform supervisees of the training he or she has received (Kurpius, Gibson, Lewis, & Corbet, 1991). Seventy-two percent of experienced licensed psychologists reported that they were not sure whether their supervisors had had training to provide supervision (McCarthy et al., 1994).

An important caution is that supervisors should monitor their own competence as well as that of their trainees (Russell & Petrie, 1994). A. S. Newman (1981) described the following components of supervisory competence: training in the theory and practice of supervision, experience in practicing the skills they help trainees learn, and training or experience in assessment or treatment of the types of client problems the trainee is seeing.

If the supervisor is not adequately qualified, supervision by a qualified clinician should be arranged or the client should be referred out. ACES Ethical Guidelines for Counseling Supervisors state the following (Association for Counselor Education and Supervision, 1995): "3.02: Supervisors should teach courses and supervise clinical work only in areas where they are fully competent and experienced." The issue of supervisor competence was addressed further in chapter 3, this volume.

Supervisor cultural competency also arises in this context. Besides coursework, the supervisor needs a framework to approach differences in culture, gender, race, socioeconomic status, religion, and other variables relevant to the case. The APA Ethical Principles of Psychologists and Code of Conduct states the following (American Psychological Association, 2002a):

> 2.01 (b): Where scientific or professional knowledge in the discipline of psychology establishes that an understanding of factors associated with age, gender, gender identity, race, ethnicity, culture, national origin, religion, sexual orientation, disability, language, or socioeconomic status is essential for effective implementation of services or research, psychologists have to obtain the training, experience, consultation, or supervision necessary to ensure the competence of their services or they make appropriate referrals, except as provided in Standard 2.02, Providing Services in Extraordinary Circumstances.

A controversy in the area of competence has been raised by Pedersen (2002), who suggested that neither APA's nor ACA's ethical guidelines are culturally sensitive. He argued that both are culturally encapsulated, the guidelines for applications are vague, and majority cultural values such as individualism serve as the norm. From a feminist perspective, Lerman and Porter (1990) found existing ethical codes reactive rather than proactive, dichotomizing behavior and ignoring issues of minorities and women.

DUE PROCESS

Ensuring due process, or that the supervisee's rights are not violated or ignored in supervision, is critical in all aspects of contracting and evaluation of training. It is incumbent on the supervisor to ensure that the supervisee has a clear understanding of the requirements of the internship or placement, specific knowledge of the evaluation tools, and means of assessing progress. "Supervisors are responsible for informing their supervisees about their roles, expectations, goals, and criteria for evaluation at the beginning of supervision" (Cormier & Bernard, 1982, p. 487). It is also essential to define what signifies successful completion of the training sequence and the consequences if these criteria are not satisfied. These tools and processes lead to definition of problematic students and establish a framework for dealing with grievances by the trainee or issues of competency discrepancy raised by the supervisor. Procedures need to be clearly operationalized and presented to the supervisee. Should there be a due-process case, the trainee must be given proper notice and opportunity for hearing, defense, and appeal.

INFORMED CONSENT

Informed consent refers to identification of parameters such as the qualifications and credentials of supervisor and supervisee, methods, logistics, requirements, responsibilities of the supervisor and supervisee, expectations for the interaction, evaluation format, and due process (J. M. Bernard & Goodyear, 1998). It also refers to limits of confidentiality for client, supervisee, and supervisor; supervision goals; risks and benefits of therapy (J. M. Bernard & Goodyear, 1998); and costs (Haas & Malouf, 1989). Business practices are not enforceable without informed consent. Ethical codes emphasize informed-consent requirements. For example, the state of Colorado requires psychologists to present certain written information to their clients, including therapist credentials, client rights, and the State Grievance Board address (Handelsman, 1990). Supervisors must be familiar with state regulations.

The APA Ethics Principles of Psychologists and Code of Conduct states the following (American Psychological Association, 2002a):

> 7.06 (a) In academic and supervisory relationships, psychologists establish a timely and specific process for providing feedback to students and supervisees. Information regarding the process is provided to the student at the beginning of supervision. (b) Psychologists evaluate students and supervisees on the basis of their actual performance on relevant and established program requirements.

Item 2.14 of the Ethical Guidelines for Counseling Supervisors by the Association for Counseling Education and Supervision (1995) specifies the following:

> Supervisors should incorporate the principles of informed consent and participation; clarity of requirements, expectations, roles and rules, and due process and appeal into the establishment of policies and procedures

of their institution, program, courses, and individual supervisory relationships. Mechanisms for due process appeal of individual supervisor actions should be established and made available to all supervisees.

There are multiple levels of informed consent in supervision and various pieces of descriptive information within each level. Falvey (2002) described five levels of informed consent. First, the client consents to treatment by the supervisee and that the supervisor will supervise the case. Second, the supervisor and supervisee consent to the supervisory responsibility and relationship. Third, the institution consents to comply with the clinical, ethical, and legal dimensions of supervision. Failure to obtain informed consent of the client has been ruled to be a form of malpractice (Falvey, 2002). Fourth, the client must be informed that his or her therapist is a trainee under the supervision of a named individual, the provision of whose license and contact information may be required. Fifth, the client must consent that confidential information and the therapy process will be shared with the supervisor. Failure to obtain this consent could "subject both the supervisor and the supervisee to a claim of negligent breach of confidentiality" (Disney & Stephens, 1994, p. 24).

McCarthy et al. (1995) outlined specific contents of each informed-consent category with respect to the supervisory relationship. In the professional disclosure statement spelled out by McCarthy et al. (1995), the supervisor should disclose multiple aspects regarding supervision. McCarthy et al. advocated disclosure of the supervisor's background information, including licensure, academic, clinical, and supervision training information; a list of the supervisor's professional associations; and the supervisor's theoretical orientation(s) for therapy and for supervision. Several of these factors should be listed in the contract (see chap. 8, this volume), namely, items concerning the logistics pertaining to supervision, including frequency and duration, location, and what occurs if either the supervisee or the supervisor cancels a session, and details of the learning contract for successful completion. Also contained in the contract are objectives of the supervision process, expectations of the contributions of each objective, advance preparation and presentation materials, and requirements for audio or videotaping. Finally, McCarthy et al. (1995) spelled out evaluation and due-process considerations to ensure knowledge of the type, expectations, criteria, specific format, and frequency of administration. Trainees have the right to know the performance competencies for satisfactory employment or completion of training (Disney & Stephens, 1994). Preferably, this information should be in written format and signed by supervisee and supervisor. The requirement of adherence to legal and ethical standards, often assumed, is clearly stated and agreed to as well. Finally, due-process procedures should be covered, either in this document or in a site handbook.

Inconsistency in informing supervisees of limits of confidentiality has been reported (McCarthy et al., 1994). The parameters of confidentiality should be articulated so that it is clear what information a supervisor may share, for example, among a training staff, with administrative supervisors, or with graduate faculty. McCarthy et al. (1994) found that one-fifth of the licensed clinicians receiving supervision were unsure whether their supervisors maintained confidentiality. Supervisees need to be informed about the limits of confidentiality: that information gleaned in supervisory encounters will be used for evaluation of their clinical skills, evaluation of the supervisee's competency to be an effective therapist (Patrick, 1989), and in supervisory team program planning.

In a study of informed consent, content areas covered for client service varied dramatically across psychologists (Handelsman, Kemper, Kesson-Craig, McLain, & Johnsrud, 1986), with differing content regarding confidentiality and risks of therapy (Talbert & Pipes, 1988) and inconsistency in informing clients of confidentiality parameters in child-abuse reporting (Nicolai & Scott, 1994). Nicolai and Scott (1994) found that 20% of the psychologists surveyed indicated that they sometimes, rarely, or never provided information to clients about confidentiality, and over 5% told clients that everything is confidential.

The situation is more complex with clients who are minors. In such cases, the supervisor–supervisee dyad must tailor the developmentally appropriate level of involvement in consent procedures (Gustafson & McNamara, 1999), communicate meaningfully with comprehensible language (L. Taylor & Adelman, 1995), and achieve great clarity in articulation of limits of confidentiality and what will be disclosed to parents. It is important to present the entire informed consent in understandable terms to the child or adolescent. Gray areas often pertain to substance use and sexuality. Gustafson and McNamara (1999) suggested a process for establishing the necessary and appropriate degree of confidentiality, including pretreatment family meetings with the parent and the adolescent and explanations of rationale for confidentiality decisions followed by a written professional-services agreement signed by all. Extra steps in this process would be added after thorough exploration and decision making between the supervisee and supervisor, prior to and during the process with the family. In some cases, the negotiation may be difficult, as the age of the supervisee may be close to that of the adolescent, resulting in the supervisee's identification with the adolescent, with the supervisor in the position of "parent."

Also at issue is the capacity of the client to competently assess treatment. Not only must clients be informed, but also they must be competent to make a decision about participation in treatment. Trainees must have developmental and cognitive assessment skills integral to such a decision.

CONFIDENTIALITY

Confidentiality is a general standard of professional conduct that may be based in statutes, case law, or ethics and has some legal recognition (Koocher & Keith-Spiegel, 1998). Privilege is the legal term that describes specific relationships that are protected from disclosure in legal proceedings. In *Jaffee v. Redmond*, the U.S. Supreme Court ruled in 1996 that communications which occur between a psychotherapist and patient are privileged in the federal courts (Mosher & Squire, 2002). All ethical and legal considerations must be applied to the rights of the client to confidentiality and to the maintenance of client information in the context of supervisor–supervisee or supervisor–supervisor communications. On-line supervision (Kanz, 2001) presents unique challenges in the area of confidentiality (and informed consent) because of the loss of objective control over transmitted data. With the adoption of the privacy rule of the Health Insurance Portability and Accountability Act (HIPAA), any health-care provider who transmits protected health information in electronic form or who acts on behalf of such an individual is required to be HIPAA compliant (www.apait.org/resources/hipaa). In HIPAA situations, great specificity is added to the form of consent and proximity in the timing of consent in relation to the release of information. The implications of HIPAA for training settings are just beginning to be explored.

Confidentially is governed by "the law of no surprises" and "the parsimony principle" (Behnke, Preis, & Bates, 1998). These terms refer to addressing the limits of confidentiality in a way that is relevant to the particular client and eliminates surprise disclosures. When it is necessary to disclose, only information that is necessary and sufficient to address the need is disclosed. It is essential to communicate this concept to supervisees.

Confidentiality in the context of supervision refers to the entire realm of client confidentiality, with added dimensions. Koocher and Keith-Spiegel (1998) stated, "In general, students (including psychology interns, unlicensed post-doctoral fellows or supervisees) are not specifically covered by privilege statutes. In some circumstances, trainees may be covered by privilege accorded to communication with a licensed supervisor, but state laws vary widely, and this cannot be assumed" (p. 118). The supervisor must be aware of the status of supervisees under his or her state law. A preferred modality of training is to observe videos of therapy sessions or to have teams observe live treatment. Protection of the client or family is paramount and may be difficult to achieve when supervision is involved. In the area of confidentiality within trainee behavior and records, informed consent is needed to articulate the entire range of review and information sharing that may occur as a matter of course within the operation of the training program.

This range may include client data as well as trainee data, and the parameters of disclosure need to be articulated to all parties involved.

The potential for "domestic violations of confidentiality" (Woody, 1999), or accidental disclosures made to significant others or in day-to-day life, needs to be discussed with supervisees. It is also important to introduce trainees to issues regarding accidental encounters with clients (Pulakos, 1994; Sharkin & Birky, 1992). A thoughtful approach to each area demonstrates in vivo for the trainee the application of ethical principles to day-to-day practice.

MULTIPLE AND DUAL RELATIONSHIPS

The term "multiple relationships" refers to instances when the therapist is in another, significantly different (perhaps social, financial, or professional) relationship with one of his or her clients (Pope, 1999). A multiple relationship exists when a therapist or supervisor has a concurrent or consecutive personal, social, business or professional relationship (Sonne, 1999) with a client or supervisee in addition to the therapist–client or supervisor–supervisee relationship, and these roles conflict or compete (Kitchener, 1988). Types of nonsexual and nonromantic relationships that might occur after therapy (or supervision) is terminated are personal-friendship, social, business, financial, collegial, professional, supervisory, evaluative, religious, social, and workplace relationships (Anderson & Kitchener, 1996). Our discussion focuses on the general ethical issues for the therapist and their translation to the supervisory relationship.

The Ethical Principles of Psychologists and Code of Conduct states the following (American Psychological Association, 2002a)

> 3.05 (a) A psychologist refrains from entering into a multiple relationship if the multiple relationship could reasonably be expected to impair the psychologist's objectivity, competence, or effectiveness in performing his or her functions as a psychologist, or otherwise risk exploitation or harm to the person with whom the professional relationship exists. . . . Multiple relationships that would not reasonably be expected to cause impairment or risk exploitation or harm are not unethical.

The ACES Ethical Guidelines for Counseling Supervisors (Association for Counselor Education and Supervision, 1995) state the following:

> 2.09 Supervisors who have multiple roles (e.g., teacher, clinical supervisor, administrative supervisor, etc.) with supervisees should minimize potential conflicts. Where possible, the roles should be divided among several supervisors. Where this is not possible, careful explanation should be conveyed to the supervisee as to the expectations and responsibilities associated with each supervisory role.

Section 2.05 of the APA Ethical Principles of Psychologists and Code of Conduct states, "Psychologists who delegate work to . . . supervisees . . . take reasonable steps to . . . avoid delegating such work to persons who have a multiple relationship with those being served that would likely lead to exploitation or loss of objectivity" (American Psychological Association, 2002a). Section 3.05c of the APA Ethical Principles of Psychologists and Code of Conduct states the following (American Psychological Association, 2002a):

> When psychologists are required by law, institutional policy, or extra-ordinary circumstances to serve in more than one role in judicial or administrative proceedings, at the outset they clarify role expectations and the extent of confidentiality and thereafter as changes occur.

Finally, Section 7.07 of the APA Ethical Principles of Psychologists and Code of Conduct states, "Psychologists do not engage in sexual relationships with students or supervisees who are in their department, agency, or training center or over whom psychologists have or are likely to have evaluative authority" (American Psychological Association, 2002a). Note that this section is a significant expansion on the guidelines for sexual relationships from the previous code. It includes the broader center or agency in internships and postdoctoral training sites rather than only individuals with evaluative function.

Sonne (1999) described dynamics of relationship-related and individual role-related expectations and responsibilities, emotional involvement with the therapist and the therapeutic process, and the power differential, all of which are affected by a multiple relationship. Such multiple or dual relationships may be tolerated and justified through selective inattention to evidence, lack of mention in therapy notes, citation of the relationship's benefits to the client, citation of prevalence data on dual relationships (e.g., "Everyone does it"), or belief that there was no alternative (Pope, 1999). Application of these codes to small communities or rural settings may be more complicated. Schank and Skovholt (1997) and Campbell and Gordon (2003) provided safeguards for minimizing risk in these contexts, including clarification of expectations and boundaries when out-of-therapy contact cannot be controlled.

This area is far from simple and thus deserves significant attention in supervision. The controversy associated with multiple relationships and their appropriate quality and even necessity for conducting therapy with individuals one knows in another context have been both espoused and argued against (Lazarus & Zur, 2002), and the latter approach is reflected in the 2002 revision of the APA Ethical Principles of Psychologists and Code of Conduct statement, in the last line of Section 3.05 (a): "Multiple relationships that would not reasonably be expected to cause impairment or risk exploitation or harm are not unethical" (American Psychological Association, 2002a). Lazarus and Zur (2002) explicitly supported Ebert's (2002) decision tree regarding "prohibited-class" relationships. They argued that, in a multitude of communities, including rural, religious, gay, feminist, and ethnic minorities, there are unavoidable multiple relationships. In addition, they cited numerous examples of planned clinical interventions (e.g., lunch with an eating-disordered client) that constitute boundary crossings in the eyes of some. Ethics committees and risk managers, they argued, are guided more by fear of attorneys and licensing boards than by clinically indicated considerations.

Another controversial example is the feminist-therapy position that self-disclosure is a way to build egalitarian relationships and is central to the therapy process. However, feminist therapists caution against careless use of self-disclosure or its use more for the benefit of the therapist than the client (Enns, 1993). In multicultural-counseling training, it is urged that the therapist also promote the use of self-help, outreach workers, ombudsmen, and facilitators of indigenous support systems (Atkinson, Morten, et al., 1993). These examples illustrate how alternative models challenge traditional ones.

Boundary Behaviors

The establishment and maintenance of boundary behaviors that mark limits of appropriate and ethical practice, including structural (e.g., roles, time, and place–space) and process (e.g., gifts, language, self-disclosure, physical contact, and interactional patterns) dimensions, is a central ethical dilemma of psychologists (Gutheil & Gabbard, 1993; Lamb & Catanzaro, 1998; D. Smith & Fitzpatrick, 1995). First we shall define some terms related to the concept of boundary behaviors. Then we will discuss modeling considerations and then their applications to supervision. A boundary is "defined as the 'edge' of appropriate or professional behavior, transgression of which involves the therapist stepping out of the clinical role" (Gutheil & Simon, 2002, p. 585). "Slippery slopes" refer to seemingly insignificant erosions in boundaries that transform into significant violations. Lamb and Catanzaro (1998) reviewed evidence that erosion of benign boundary crossings may be either a precipitant (Folman, 1991) or a predictor of a sexual relationship that ensues.

A boundary crossing is a "nonpejorative term that describes departures from commonly accepted clinical practice that may or may not benefit the client" (D. Smith & Fitzpatrick, 1995, p. 500). Boundary crossings may be harmless, nonexploitative, and supportive of the therapy (Gutheil & Simon, 2002). Thus, they are to be distinguished from boundary violations, which are defined as departures from accepted practice that place the client, supervisee, or the therapeutic process at serious risk (Gutheil & Gabbard, 1993) because they constitute exploitation of the client (Gutheil & Simon, 2002). It is important to consider boundary crossings as potentially high-risk behaviors and to remember that, ultimately, the supervisor is responsible for establishing and maintaining boundaries of professionalism (Gutheil & Simon, 2002). Gutheil and Gabbard (1993) divided boundary crossings and violations into categories of role, time, place and space, money, gifts, services and related matters, clothing, language, self-disclosure and related matters, and physical contact. A training activity is to list boundary crossings in the training setting and discuss them.

Dual Relationships During the Internship Year

Dual relationships may occur between supervisee and supervisor, between supervisee and client, or between supervisor and client. Dual relationships during the internship year include relationships related to business, social, therapy, and sexual factors (Slimp & Burian, 1994). Examples of business relationships are staff members hiring interns as employees to babysit, assist as research assistants, or conduct private practice. In such cases, issues arise of power differential, exploitation, transference, and placement of interns in a situation that is difficult, if not impossible, for them to refuse. The supervisor–employer may find objective evaluation clouded by the dual relationship or the possibility that the employment went awry, resulting in injury or other untoward outcomes. For sexual relationships, what was seen as love during the relationship is viewed as a mishandling of the transference after the end of the relationship (Caudill, 2002). Social relationships, a normative step on the road to the supervisor's and supervisee's becoming colleagues, can be problematic for the same reasons as business dual roles and should be viewed as a boundary crossing.

Prevalence of Sexual Misconduct

Sexual relationships between trainees and educators or supervisors have been extensively explored and are generally prohibited. Glaser and Thorpe (1986) reported that 17% of their respondents, female members of APA Division 12, Clinical Psychology, indicated that they had had sexual contact with psychology educators as graduate students. Thirty-one percent of the respondents reported having experienced sexual advances by teachers or supervisors during their training or psychotherapy. Nearly half of W. L. Robinson and Reid's (1985) sample experienced seductive behavior with educators while they were graduate students. However, Hammel, Olkin, and Taube (1996) reported substantially less student–educator sex, 10%. Lamb, Catanzaro, and Moorman (2003) reported a 10% incidence of sex during professionals' own training or psychotherapy and 3% during their professional careers. The probability of sexual seduction was greater for clinical-psychology students than for students in other areas of psychology (Glaser & Thorpe, 1986) and greater for female students than male students (Hammel et al., 1996). Sexual seduction was reportedly initiated prior to or during a working relationship (Hammel et al., 1996) or after the working relationship (Lamb et al., 2003).

The percentage of clinical supervisors who have had sexual relationships with their supervisees is estimated to range from 1.4% (W. L. Robinson & Reid, 1985) or 1.5% (Lamb & Catanzaro, 1998) to 4% (Pope, Levenson, & Schover, 1979), whereas the percentage of supervisees who have been sexually involved with their supervisors is reported to be 5–6% (Glaser & Thorpe, 1986; G. M. Miller & Larrabee, 1995) or as low as 1% (Lamb et al., 2003). Note that the frequency of therapist–client sex has declined to a 4 to 6% level (Lamb & Catanzaro, 1998; Rodolfa, Kitzrow, Vohra, & Wilson, 1990) or lower (Lamb et al., 2003; Pope & Vasquez, 1999) from the 12% figures reported for male therapists in the 1970s (Holroyd & Brodsky, 1977; Pope et al., 1979). However, some suspect that the rate is actually higher, but incidence of reporting is lower, because of compelling reasons for withholding such information (Samuel & Gorton, 1998; D. Smith & Fitzpatrick, 1995). Women were significantly more likely to have experienced a sexual-boundary violation as a client, supervisee, or student than were men (Lamb & Catanzaro, 1998). Rates of trainee–client sexual offense have been reported to be very low (Layman & McNamara, 1997). Fifty-three percent of female psychologists reported having experienced sexual harassment by a patient at some time during their career (deMayo, 1997), and 47% of clinical supervisors reported one or more incidents of a supervisee reporting sexual harassment by a client (deMayo, 2000).

Feelings of Sexual Attraction

Between 80 and 88% of psychologists report having been attracted to or having had sexual feelings for at least one client (Blanchard & Lichtenberg, 1998; Pope, Keith-Spiegel, & Tabachnick, 1986; Rodolfa et al., 1994). Slightly more than half of the student sample reported sexual attraction (Housman & Stake, 1999). Sixty-eight percent of clinical doctoral students surveyed did not know that it is acceptable and normative to have sexual feelings for clients. Thirty-four percent of clinical doctoral students did not understand that it is not acceptable to have sex with a client after termination or transfer; 7% did not know that sex with current clients is always prohibited (Housman & Stake, 1999). Of those supervisees who actually reported sexual feelings toward clients, 34 to 45% said that they did not discuss these feelings in supervision (Blackshaw & Patterson, 1992; Housman & Stake, 1999).

In a study of psychology interns (29% return rate), only about half of a small sample disclosed their feelings of sexual attraction toward clients to their supervisor, although they did typically discuss these issues with peers and therapists. They reported both beneficial and negative effects of the discussion of attraction on the supervision and on therapy with the clients (Ladany, O'Brien et al., 1997). Sixty-three percent of psychologists reported feeling guilty, anxious, or confused about their feelings of sexual attraction toward clients (Pope et al., 1986).

Housman & Stake (1999) were concerned that their results indicated that, although training in sexual ethics has increased, students have not gained greater understanding. In fact, attention to a wide range of sexual topics was "neutral," defined as neither excellent nor poor, in graduate training (M. P. Ford & Hendrick, 2003). Graduate student respondents felt that clinical-training programs do little to prepare them for sexual attraction to their clients and do not teach them ways of handling such attractions. Only 9% of psychologists believed that their training or supervision had been adequate to help them deal with this issue (Pope et al., 1986). Four percent overall (Rodolfa et al., 1994), or 9% of men and 2.5% of women (Pope et al., 1986), reported that they had acted on their feelings of sexual attraction.

Inadequate training in handling sexual feelings and in the ethics of sexual involvement with educators has been reported (Glaser & Thorpe, 1986; Pope & Tabachnick, 1993). Clinicians have reported that, when confronted with such feelings, they would introspect about the feelings (75.4%), consult with a colleague (50.7%), seek out supervision (36.4%), consult available literature (22.7%), do nothing (11.8%), refer the client to another professional (7.8%), begin or resume personal therapy (7%), tell the client about the sexual feelings (5.9%), or pursue a sexual relationship with the client (1.1%; Blanchard & Lichtenberg, 1998). Although consultation or supervision accounted for substantial numbers of the responses (and some respondents picked multiple choices), it is still worrisome that a substantial portion simply would introspect, do nothing, or pursue the sexual relationship by discussion or action with the client.

Supervisors need to be competent in their training in sexual-attraction and boundary issues, assertive in bringing these issues up in supervision, and aware of their own feelings that may deter such supervision or increase the probability of a parallel process (of sexual attraction) in supervision. In a study by Holmes, Rupert, Ross, and Shapera (1999), college undergraduates rated hypothetical relationships between a male faculty member and a student. The least appropriate potential dual relationships were the faculty member flirting with the student, telling the student he is attracted to him or her, getting drunk with the student, telling sexually explicit jokes during an office meeting with the student, and getting high with the student. It is encouraging that undergraduates identify such behaviors as inappropriate, but the power differential may mediate responsiveness of graduate students to such behavior. Training in identification of danger signals, use of role-play, and implementation of a nonjudgmental approach by supervisors to disclosures need to occur.

Sexual harassment of supervisees by clients must also be addressed, as must the place of sexual feelings in psychotherapy, so that supervisees may be prepared for such encounters (deMayo, 1997). The book by Pope, Sonne, and Holroyd (1993) *Sexual Feelings in Psychotherapy*, is an excellent training tool.

Supervisory discomfort with sexual issues and with sexual feelings between trainees and clients leads to dismissal of the topic or subtle communication that these issues are not to be discussed. Feelings of sexual attraction are more stressful for practicum and intern trainees than for professional staff (Rodolfa, Kraft, & Reilley, 1988) and thus are another factor that increases the risk of trainees' being overwhelmed.

Ninety-nine percent of training programs in psychiatry and psychology surveyed by Samuel and Gorton (1998) addressed the issue of therapist–client sexual misconduct. However, most offered only minimal training—perhaps a one-hour lecture (Samuel & Gorton, 1998). Training on this issue should come early in the graduate sequence (Housman & Stake, 1999), should spell out the differences between sexual misconduct and the natural phenomenon of sexual attraction, and should be thorough and integral to all training (Conroe & Schank, 1989).

Predictors of sexual-boundary risk were explored in a retrospective analysis of characteristics that sexually offending trainees had in common (Hamilton & Spruill, 1999). These characteristics included loneliness, prior quasi "counseling" experience, professional inexperience, training factors such as instruction on dealing with sexual feelings of attraction, failure to recognize ethical conflicts, and failure of supervisors to supervise in these areas. Brodsky (1989) described similar risk factors that increase therapist and client risk for sexual involvement: proneness to boundary crossings, situational vulnerability (perhaps because of a personal stressor), and isolation. A similar finding was reported for practicing psychologists: Boundary violations were associated with personal problems such as depression or divorce (Lamb et al., 2003).

Prevention of Client–Therapist Sexual Misconduct

One strategy to prevent sexual-boundary violations, presented by Hamilton and Spruill (1999), is education about the risks of such behavior. Under this approach, before trainees see clients, they are provided with education (and self-disclosure) by faculty and supervisors on sexual attraction, how to deal with it, and the necessity of seeking supervision. Specifically, trainees should learn warning signs and risk factors for therapist–client intimacy and the harmful effects that can occur as a result of it. Social-skills training and role-playing can be used to model and decrease anxiety related to dealing with sexual attraction and misconduct. Departmental policies on ethical infractions should be made clear, with differentiation between normally occurring feelings and actions that are unacceptable. Clear case conceptualization should be standard practice so that the supervisor can evaluate deviation in the therapeutic relationship. The Hamilton and Spruill (1999) approach is exceptionally useful (see Appendix F), as is working knowledge of the risk factors it describes.

Some traditional protective factors may have been decreased because of increased productivity requirements, the concomitant decrease in allotted supervision time, and movement away from psychodynamic theory, with its emphasis on countertransference reactions. However, Hamilton and Spruill (1999) concluded that boundary violations are more easily identified by cognitive behavioral therapists who use concretely operationalized assessment and treatment.

Intern–Supervisor Sexual Relationships

Because of the power differential and the supervisee vulnerability implicit in supervisee–supervisor sexual relationships, completely voluntary consent is impossible in trainee–supervisor sexual relationships (Koocher & Keith-Spiegel, 1998). Thus, to argue that such a relationship is consensual may be fallacious.

Consequences of a sexual relationship between supervisor and supervisee can be serious and pervasive. Such a relationship may arise out of "romantic or passionate love" (Pope, Schover, & Levenson, 1980, p. 159) or as a trade for academic advancement as a type of prostitution (Pope et al., 1980). Regardless of who initiates the sexual behavior, Conroe and Schank (1989) urged supervisory responsibility in dealing with this behavior systematically and conscientiously. Once the behavior occurs unchecked, interns may not feel able to confront or disagree with the supervisor or to discuss case material relating to sexuality or his or her personal responses to clinical material. The staff member's ability to evaluate the supervisee is also severely compromised (Conroe & Shank, 1989; Slimp & Burian, 1994). There is the subsequent danger that what started as a consensual sexual liaison evolves into what feels like coercion, a probability that increases with time (Glaser & Thorpe, 1986; Slimp & Burian, 1994) as recollections of events in the liaison grow harsher, seeming more coercive and harmful than they did when they occurred (Glaser & Thorpe, 1986; G. M. Miller & Larrabee, 1995). According to interviews that took place some time after the event, individuals involved in sexual liaisons while in training grew to perceive those relationships as ethically problematic and as hindering to their working relationships (Hammel et al., 1996). It is interesting that 40% of Lamb et al.'s (2003) sample of 13 individuals who had engaged in a sexual-boundary violation believed that no harm had been done, and a lesser number (28%) proceeded with the sexual relationship even though they understood that they were engaging in unethical or problematic behavior. The discrepancy between perceptions of the powerful member of the dyad and of the less powerful one is an important area for further research.

Legal jeopardy resulting from sexual-boundary violations increases because of inadequate supervision or the accusation of unfairness of evaluation after the sexual relationship ends (Slimp & Burian, 1994). The impact of an intern's sexual relationship with a staff member can be far reaching on the intern group, the staff, the agency, and the profession in general (Slimp & Burian, 1994). Isolation from the intern group, hostility over perceived preferential treatment or evaluation rivalry, fractionalization of staff members regarding the relationship, ostracism, or questioning of the professional judgment of the staff member are all possible results. In addition, engaging in sexual relations with a staff member is poor modeling and casts doubts on how the entire profession is viewed (Slimp & Burian, 1994). Because the professional community may be slow to acknowledge the potential damage of sexual contact between supervisor and supervisee, the supervisee may be stigmatized and the entire situation may ultimately go unacknowledged (Conroe & Schank, 1989). In a study conducted by W. L. Robinson and Reid (1985), 96% of the females who responded that they had experienced sexual contact or harassment as students felt that their relationship was harmful to one or both parties.

Although researchers had previously suggested that students or trainees sexually involved with their own therapists, supervisors, or educators would later have a greater probability of becoming offenders themselves (Bartell & Rubin, 1990; Pope et al., 1979), Lamb and Catanzaro's (1998) data did not fully support that prediction.

Risk Factors and Boundary Issues

Self-disclosure (Koocher & Keith-Spiegel, 1998) and touch are described as precursors of slippery slopes (Lamb, 2001). But whether self-disclosure is a facilitating factor in therapeutic and supervisory interactions or a risk factor is not clear. Lamb (2001) outlined levels of personal self-disclosure. First is the disclosure of public information that is easily accessible to clients. Second is the disclosure of private information not known to clients, such as the number of children one has. Third is the disclosure of private events experienced by the therapist, including divorce, loss, or trauma. Fourth is the disclosure of personal opinions, beliefs, or feelings related to the client or to the client's concerns, such as views on abortion and assisted suicide. This category includes the therapist's personal reactions to the client. Areas generally agreed on as not suitable for disclosure include details of current life stressors, dreams, fantasies, or social, sexual, or financial circumstances (Gutheil & Gabbard, 1993). A defining factor may be whether the disclosure is being made for the purposes of the therapist or in the context of treatment in consideration of the client's mental state (Caudill, 2002). It is critical that supervisees be given a framework for such disclosures over time so that they may explore the purpose of particular disclosures they make to clients.

In his or her multiple roles as supervisor, administrator, and evaluator, the supervisor may encounter further boundary issues. For example, the supervisee may be expected to self-disclose and be forthcoming. There may be seminars or groups in which discussion of one's personal cultural, ethnic, racial, sexual, or other background is expected. This situation may be difficult for supervisees who fear that disclosures may be included in evaluation and for supervisors when disclosures coupled with certain actions taken by the supervisee are indicative of problematic behavior.

Note 7.04 of the APA Ethical Principles of Psychologists and Code of Conduct has the following to say on this topic (American Psychological Association, 2002a):

> Psychologists do not require students or supervisees to disclose personal information in course- or program-related activities, either orally or in writing, regarding sexual history, history of abuse and neglect, psychological treatment, and relationships with parents, peers, and spouses or significant others except if (1) the program or training facility has clearly identified this requirement in its admissions and program materials or (2) the information is necessary to evaluate or obtain assistance for students whose personal problems could reasonable be judged to be preventing them from performing their training- or professionally related activities in a competent manner or posing a threat to the students or others.

Illfelder-Kaye (2002) suggested that it is essential that training programs which place particular value on personal exploration in supervision state this principle clearly in their program descriptions and brochures.

Patrick (1989) stated, "A unique ethical dilemma arises when, as a direct result of this dual relationship in the training laboratory, the supervisor becomes aware of personality traits in the client that the supervisor believes will interfere with that student's ability to function as a counselor. According to the ethical standards, the supervisor also has an ethical responsibility as a member of the counselor education faculty to screen and monitor graduate students in the counselor-training program" (p. 339). This situation is a dilemma for the empathic supervisor who encourages self-disclosure and who is also the evaluator and the liaison to the trainee's academic institution. An example of such circumstances is when the intense emotional tone or disclosure of a client triggers memories of traumatic events in the trainee's life experience. Alternatively, disclosures may cast doubt on the appropriateness of the trainee to function as a psychologist. The training contract should articulate procedures regarding confidentiality and disclosure.

Sherry (1991) emphasized the complexity of supervisors' simultaneous multiple roles. Kitchener (1986) further articulated the ways in which supervisees' and supervisors' roles may be problematical. For example, if a particular supervisee is also a supervisor to a younger trainee, there is a shift from the prior collegiality between the supervisee and his or her trainee to a relationship involving authority, which may cause role confusion or conflict. The danger of a boundary violation or assumption of multiple roles is very great. Kitchener (1986) pointed out that objectivity, confidentiality, the therapeutic process, and autonomy are at risk in such cases. It is useful to consider the Role Conflict and Role Ambiguity Inventory (see Appendix H) to assess role difficulties that may result in anxiety and dissatisfaction (Olk & Friedlander, 1992).

Another ethical issue in supervision is the establishment of appropriate boundaries between supervision and therapy. Section 7.05 (b) of the APA Ethical Principles of Psychologists and Code of Conduct states the following (American Psychological Association, 2002a): "Faculty who are or are likely to be responsible for evaluating students' academic performance do not themselves provide that therapy." The therapylike aspects of supervision that deal with countertransference may segue to actual therapy provided by supervisors apart from or within supervision. Boundaries need to be clearly defined, with a focus on the aspects that relate directly to the impact on the client or case. Supervisees' problems in the supervisory and therapeutic situations are addressed, but only to the extent that they affect the relationship with the supervisor or relationships with clients (Doehrman, 1976).

A specific strategy for approaching issues that may cross the line from supervision to therapy was proposed by Whiston and Emerson (1989) in building on a model by Egan (1986). A problematic situation, identified in supervision, is addressed, explored, and clarified. The supervisor determines whether personal problems are the reason the trainee is having difficulty with a particular case or whether the trainee's issue is being exacerbated in supervision. Depending on the result of the exploration, the emotional response of the trainee, countertransference phenomena, or other determinations, appropriate steps are taken, including a possible referral for therapy for the trainee and a decision about the future of the therapeutic relationship. It is important to delineate the trainee's rights of due process before recommending counseling services and to clearly differentiate supervision from a counseling relationship. Whiston and Emerson (1989) focused on the importance of remaining centered on the professional development of the trainee rather than proceeding to develop action-oriented understandings of the personal problems. In this way, the supervisor provides definition and avoids playing the dual role of counselor.

Prevention of Boundary Violations

There are three general categories of interventions and strategies for preventing boundary violations and other ethical breaches. First are psychoeducational approaches that enhance awareness and introduce environmental modifications to promote safety. Second are strategies to provide frameworks for decision making to prevent harmful multiple relationships. Third are more general decision-making models to approach ethical dilemmas.

Psychoeducational Approaches

Lamb (1999) described several strategies that include emotional tone or climate dimensions to prevent trainees from making boundary violations and the resulting burnout. First, orientation efforts could enhance bonding, provide support for stress, and allow for a safe place to discuss boundary dilemmas. There should be clearly articulated channels to discuss, report, and deal with inappropriate behavior by faculty, staff, or peers without fear of reprisal. Seminars on self-care, stress reduction, and identification of and dealing with boundary crossings and violation are desirable. Role-playing or in vivo techniques are strongly recommended as well (Lamb, 1999). The concept of preventative self-care training and especially the notion of education on monitoring factors that might contribute to ethical violations to prevent them are at the forefront of proactive feminist approaches to ethics (Porter, 1995).

Rodolfa et al. (1990) proposed a means of approaching the differentiation of normative sexual feelings and sexual acting out in their description of several training experiences, including a brief seminar and a one-day conference with opportunities for small-group discussion of critical issues in attraction and responding to innuendo. A critical concept in these training experiences was how to distinguish between sexual attraction (a normative response) and sexual acting out. It is very important for training directors to incorporate these areas into the training sequence from the onset.

Biaggo, Paget, and Chenoweth (1997) proposed a preventive model for faculty–student dual relationships. Because of enhanced risk from overlapping social, mentoring, and professional relationships that are normative, these authors described the training department as potentially a very small, closed community. They suggested particular guidelines for relationships to acknowledge the power and responsibility of faculty, develop an evaluative frame for faculty–student relationships to avoid exploitation, and foster a climate that supports ethical relationships with students, faculty role modeling of appropriate ethical behavior, and safety in discussion of perceived boundary issues.

Ethical Problem Solving and Decision Making in Dual Relationships: Strategies to Prevent Harm

Kitchener (1988) defined guidelines that should be identified or applied before entering a relationship, to decide which dual roles pose high risk. Her conceptualization of harm relates to the increasing divergence between the two individuals in the relationship. The potential for greater misunderstanding and harm increases with increasing incompatibility of expectations between roles. Also, divided loyalties and loss of objectivity occur as obligations associated with different roles diverge. In addition, as power and prestige between the psychologist's role and the other's role increase, the potential for exploitation and lack of objectivity widens. Areas of sexual intimacy and money are particularly high risk (Kitchener, 1988).

Gottlieb (1993) proposed an extension of this model. He concluded that there is a need for a decision-making model, as the aspirational goal of simply avoiding all dual relationships is unreasonable. The model uses three dimensions: power, duration, and termination. Power refers to amount or degree of power the psychologist has over the client, and thus the potential for exploitation. Duration, an aspect of power, is based on the assumption that power increases over time, so the length of time for which the relationship has existed is relevant. Termination relates to the probability that the client and the psychologist will have further professional contact. Gottlieb outlined a five-step process of assessing the current relationship according to the three dimensions, examining the contemplated relationship along those three dimensions, identifying role incompatibilities, obtaining consultation from a colleague, and discussing the decision with the client or consumer, including the ethical issues and the possible adverse consequences.

Anderson and Kitchener (1998) criticized Gottlieb's (1993) model as encouraging psychologists to overlook issues such as therapist motivation, confidentiality, the amount of time elapsed between the termination of therapy and the new relationship, and the effect of the new relationship on the client's progress made in therapy. Burian and Slimp (2000) pointed out that neither Kitchener's (1988) nor Gottlieb's (1993) model addressed the impact of others at training sites who are not directly in the multiple relationship. However, these models are useful to introduce in supervisee training to incorporate approaches to decision making in potentially high risk situations.

Burian and Slimp (2000) proposed a decision-making model for determining whether to proceed with a potential dual relationship with a trainee during the internship year. According to the model, there are three main issues to consider: each party's reasons and motivations to be in the relationship, the power differential between the staff member and intern, Likert scales, and the parameters of the social activities. Through the use of a decision tree (see Figure 7.1), the supervisor can obtain benefits of such social interactions while reducing the potential for harm.

It is important to consider the following hierarchy given in the ACES supervisory ethics guidelines (Association for Counselor Education and Supervision, 1995):

An arrangement of priorities in decision-making:
Client welfare
Supervisee welfare
Supervisor welfare
Program or agency service and administrative needs

Haas and Malouf (1989) proposed a useful general rule: "Make the fulfillment of personal needs subordinate to the needs of the client" (p. 64). This rule should apply to supervisors and their supervisees as well. Even though therapists or supervisors may find many situations emotionally gratifying, the supervisors' needs should be carefully monitored and should not be played out in the supervision.

Another useful guideline is to hold colleagues accountable. Approval is implied when colleagues observe or learn of unethical behavior and do nothing. Loyalty ties to colleagues, fear of personal costs or repercussions, and insufficient understanding of the ethical guidelines are all cited as reasons that misconduct may not be addressed between colleagues (Biaggio, Duffy, & Shaffelbach, 1998). Failure to address misconduct imposes secondary harm on trainees who witness such infractions and their supervisors doing nothing.

Gutheil and Gabbard (1993) advocated teaching limit-setting behavior for instances when clients begin to cross boundaries. They cited examples of clients who hug their therapists, who begin to take their clothes off, or who wear clothes open in provocative ways. Limit-setting, calm statements of the inappropriateness of the behavior in the therapy context, followed by a discussion and processing, are advocated.

GENERAL ETHICAL PROBLEM-SOLVING APPROACHES

A variety of other models have been proposed to assist in problem solving in situations that are not easily resolved by referring to law or ethics

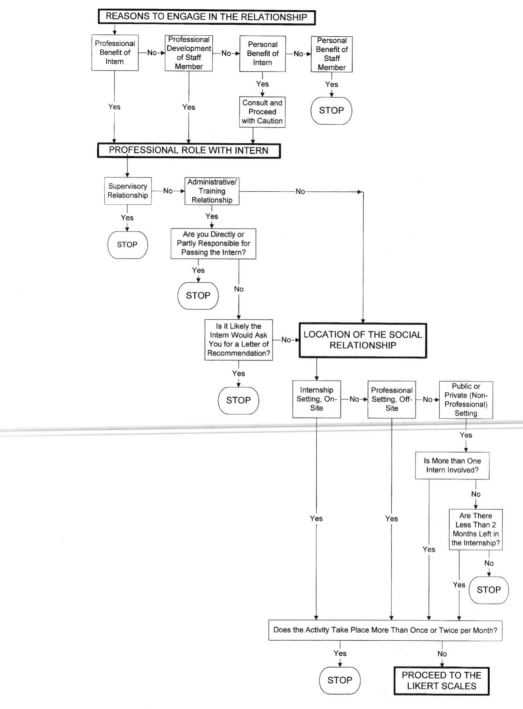

Figure 7.1. Supervisor decision-making model for determining whether to enter into a dual relationship with a trainee. From "Social Dual-Role Relationships During

LIKERT SCALES

Intern's ability to leave the social relationship/activity without repercussions:

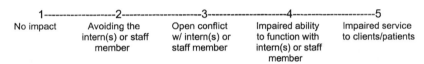

1	2	3	4	5
Freely exit with no repercussions	Mild repercussions e.g., intern's avoidance of staff member	Moderate repercuss., e.g., intern's open conflict with staff member	Severe repercuss., e.g., intern's impaired ability to function	Profound repercuss., e.g., intern leaving internship prematurely

Probable impact on uninvolved interns:

1	2	3	4	5
No impact	Avoiding the intern(s) or staff member	Open conflict w/ intern(s) or staff member	Impaired ability to function with intern(s) or staff member	Impaired service to clients/patients

Probable impact on uninvolved staff members:

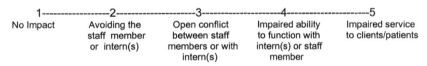

1	2	3	4	5
No Impact	Avoiding the staff member or intern(s)	Open conflict between staff members or with intern(s)	Impaired ability to function with intern(s) or staff member	Impaired service to clients/patients

If you have given a rating of 2 or higher on any of the above Likert Scales:

(STOP)

codes (Corey, Corey, & Callahan, 2003; Koocher & Keith-Spiegel, 1998; Tymchuk, 1986). These models are strongly advocated as structural tools for training. Generally, the series of steps in such models includes identification of the problem, interpretation, consultation, risk–benefit analysis, consultation and referral to ethics codes and legal guidelines, consideration of the five moral and ethical parameters described by Kitchener (1984), and choice of a course of action after considering consequences of outcomes. For example, Koocher and Keith-Spiegel's (1998) model, derived from Tymchuk (1981) and Haas and Malouf (1989), contains the following steps:

1. Determine that the matter is an ethical one.
2. Consult available ethical guidelines that might apply, to provide a possible mechanism for resolution.
3. Consider all sources that might influence the decision you will make.
4. Consult with a trusted colleague
5. Evaluate the rights, responsibilities, and vulnerability of all affected parties.
6. Generate alternative decisions.
7. Enumerate the consequences of making each decision.
8. Make the decision.
9. Implement the decision.

N. D. Hansen and Goldberg (1999) proposed the use of a seven-category matrix to approach ethical and legal dilemmas with considerations of moral principles and personal values (competence, integrity, responsibility, respect, concerns for others' welfare, and social responsibility); clinical and cultural factors; professional codes of ethics; agency or employer policies; federal, state, and local statues; rules and regulations; and case law. By arranging these considerations as a matrix rather than a hierarchy, this approach builds in greater flexibility, depending on the ethical dilemma.

Interestingly, all of these models omit the component of emotional response by the parties involved and by the person using the problem-solving framework. A systematic model of ethical decision making was originally developed for use in HIV-related ethical decisions, but has been applied much more generally (Barret, Kitchener, & Burris, 2001). The steps are as follows:

1. Pause and identify personal responses to the case.
2. Review the facts.
3. Conceptualize a preliminary plan.
4. Analyze the plan in terms of professional codes of ethics, foundational ethical principles (e.g., autonomy, beneficence,

do no harm, fidelity, and justice) (Kitchener, 1984) to determine whether the plan is congruent.

5. Examine the legal consequences of the preliminary plan.
6. Refine the plan to balance clinical, ethical, and legal considerations so that it
   - is congruent with one's personal values,
   - advances clinical interests as possible,
   - is operable within agency policies and professional ethics codes,
   - minimizes harm to client and relevant others,
   - maximizes the effect of all other ethical principles to the greatest extent possible, and
   - operates within the law.
7. Choose a course of action and share it with the client.
8. Implement the course of action, and monitor and document the outcomes.

Consultation and documentation are essential parts of this model as well.

The advantages of Barret et al.'s (2001) model are the integration of emotional response the provision of a complete review format to identify and resolve ethical dilemmas within multiple relevant contexts (e.g., legal, ethical, moral, personal). In the case of supervisor–supervisee dilemmas, Steps 1 and 6 necessitate multilevel considerations of supervisor, supervisee, and client.

Kitchener's (2000) protocol is different in that possible options and alternative plans are generated in Step 3. Her Step 7 entails the reassessment of options and identification of a plan, and at the conclusion (Step 9) she advocates reflection on the outcome of the decision, so that its lessons may be applied in the future.

INTEGRATING CULTURE INTO EVERY STEP OF DECISION MAKING

Culture was not explicitly included as a factor in any of the aforementioned decision-making models. In articulating how cultural considerations must be integrated into the decision-making model, Ridley, Liddle, Hill, and Li (2001) encouraged flexibility in representing ethical concerns and determining whether a cultural conflict is implicit or explicit in the ethical issue. Implicit cultural assumptions must be made explicit and factored into the decision-making process both from the personal perspective and from the systemic perspective.

ETHICS TRAINING

There is significant concern that our current teaching of ethics does not generalize adequately to actual therapy situations. In an article titled, "Problems with Ethics Training by Osmosis," Handelsman (1986) described how the informal teaching of ethics by supervisor to supervisee is fraught with peril. If, as Tymchuk et al. (1995) reported, almost 60% of doctoral-level psychologists felt inadequately informed about ethical issues, then leaving the substantive training of ethics to these same individuals in the course of their supervision is erroneous. Welfel (1995) reported that 67% of clinical-psychology programs had a formal structure for the teaching of ethics, and Houseman and Stake (1999) found that 94% of students in clinical programs had had an average of six hours training in sexual ethics. However, even though trainees or supervisors may have had course content in ethics, it does not follow that they are using it clinically, connecting it to real-life experience, or making a conscious decision to do what they ethically should.

A framework derived from Rest (1984) provides insight into the breach. Failure to act ethically is defined as a deficiency in one of four component parts. The first component is interpreting the situation as a moral one. This component entails recognizing ethical dimensions of situations in the context of other aspects (e.g., clinical or pragmatic), including how one's actions affect the welfare of others. The second component is deciding which course of action is just, right, or fair. It involves moral reasoning to differentiate ethical choices from unethical choices. The third component is deciding what one intends to do, which entails choosing whether to carry out the ethical action in the face of competing forces. Finally, the fourth component is implementing the moral action, or carrying it out despite costs to self or external pressures to act otherwise. Rest (1984) noted that it requires ego strength to take such actions.

It may be that the very concept of ethics training is flawed in that the trainee is attuned to ethics only as examples of dilemmas are presented in the context of a particular seminar. It is a much more difficult task to identify ethical issues within the broader spectrum of day-to-day clinical activities—that is, to determine which events or issues are ethical ones and then proceeding to act accordingly. In our own supervision, we have noted that, immediately after the conclusion of an ethics training sequence with highly trained supervisees, very similar dilemmas to those just studied arose and were not identified in the clinical caseloads of our trainees, but came to light only incidentally in supervision. In support of this finding, Welfel (1992) described several unpublished studies in which trainees had only moderate rates of identifying ethical dilemmas from general clinical material.

Beyond identification, supervisors must model implementation of the proper action, which may not be popular.

A formulation (Handelsman et al., 2002) derived from Berry's (1990) acculturation framework is useful in explaining some of the pitfalls in our current ethics training. Essentially, our questions are, Do trainees retain their original moral and ethical values and traditions as they move into and through graduate training, and how do they identify and adopt the ethics and values of professional psychology? Berry (1990) provided four categories of development: professional assimilation, or adopting the professional psychology ethics and discarding one's own values; separation, or maintaining one's own values and having low levels of identification with the professional code or values; marginalization, or having both an undeveloped personal moral sense and a low internalized professional ethical sense; and integration, or both maintaining one's moral and ethical values and adopting the professional codes. Handelsman et al. (2002) lead us to believe that, unless trainees integrate their own ethical identity with professional psychology's ethical identity, through acculturation, trainees may be at higher risk for ethical difficulty. The important lesson of this conclusion for training is that trainees' personal ethical and moral codes should be encouraged, highlighted, and valued rather than discounted in favor of total reliance on the professional codes of ethics. This area warrants empirical investigation.

Areas for which training directors have reported intern ethical competency as lowest are HIV-positive clients, fee-setting arrangements, involuntary commitment, and therapy with gays and lesbians, whereas confidentiality has been rated as an area of high competence (a finding incongruous with the self-reports of supervisees [Fly et al., 1997]). According to Welfel's (1992) study, 63% of training directors had seen improvement in interns' ethics abilities in the previous few years. They recommended increasing the focus on clinical application of ethical principles, using case studies more often to discuss ethics, and paying more attention to dual-relationship issues (Welfel, 1992). Plante (1995) proposed a model for training predoctoral interns and postdoctoral fellows in practical, applied ethics and professional issues.

In addition to more adequate training, an environment of safety needs to be maintained within the therapy setting and in supervision (Rodolfa et al., 1994). Such an environment includes the absence of sexual harassment and innuendo, so that disclosure can occur comfortably.

Ironically, the emotions of psychologists have also been overlooked in training. Pope and Tabachnick (1993) reported that respondents to their survey rated graduate training regarding fear, anger, and sexual arousal as inadequate. Fear can be elicited by the possibility of client suicide, client deterioration, or risk of the client attacking a third party, for example.

Anger may be directed toward the client for being uncooperative. Over half of the respondents reported feeling sexually aroused in the presence of a client. We have noted the omission of emotion from decision-making protocols and from many training contexts as a possible reason that clinicians do not act as they know they should in ethical dilemmas. This area warrants immediate attention and intervention.

MALPRACTICE

Increased attention has recently been paid to supervisor liability and malpractice. Pivotal to the concern is the principle of *respondeat superior*, or vicarious liability. This term refers to the legal doctrine which holds that "one who occupies a position of authority or direct control over another (such as a master and servant, employer and employee, or supervisor and supervisee) can be held legally liable for the damages of another suffered as a result of the negligence of the subordinate" (Disney & Stephens, 1994, p. 15). Thus, liability can be based on a supervisor's erroneous actions or omissions, even if the intern was the therapist seeing the client and implementing the intervention. Malpractice is a form of negligence and is therefore a tort (Behnke et al., 1998). A tort refers to negligent or intentional wrongs to a party, resulting in civil lawsuits for which another party may be financially liable (Stromberg et al., 1988). A malpractice lawsuit is described as consisting of "four D's": "Dereliction of a Duty Directly causing Damages." Demonstration that all four "D's" are present by a preponderance of evidence is essential for a successful malpractice suit (Behnke et al., 1998). Direct liability could arise from the supervisor's inattention to the trainee's comments or from the supervisor's failing to carry out supervision. To help avert this problem, the supervisor should know the level of skill of the supervisee (Harrar, VandeCreek, & Knapp, 1990).

In 1980, Slovenko predicted that litigation involving supervisors might be the "suit of the future" (p. 468). If malpractice insurance rates for psychologists are any indication, this prediction has been proven to have some validity. In 1990, APAIT data revealed that the probability of a psychologist being sued was less than half of 1% (Bennett, Bryant, VandenBos, & Greenwood, 1990). In contrast, Pope and Tabachnick (1993) found that 11.6% of their respondents reported that at least one malpractice lawsuit or complaint against them had been filed. M. Miller (2002) stated that the possibility of an adverse disciplinary event is 10 to 15% during a 15-year career. Montgomery, Cupit, and Wimberley (1999) reconciled the differences in these reports by explaining that insurance data may not include malpractice lawsuits dismissed, dropped, or settled, as well as data on uninsured practitioners. Furthermore, different statistical methods are applied to malpractice suits, disciplinary actions, and complaints. Welch (2000) cautioned that "malpractice lawsuits and licensing board complaints represent a serious threat to the welfare of psychologists" (p. xiv).

It is important to bear in mind the differing burden of proof across contexts. For example, it must be established that harm was done to the plaintiff for damages to be awarded in a malpractice suit. However, a licensing board can discipline professionals for improper conduct without harm having been inflicted. Licensing boards have a much broader range of admissible evidence (hearsay and prior acts, for example) than does the court (N. D. Hansen & Goldberg, 1999).

Although the ACES Ethical Guidelines for Supervisors (Association for Counselor Education and Supervision, 1995) have not been adopted by the American Psychological Association, a psychologist who is facing legal proceedings regarding supervision may encounter these documents and the related standards in cross-examination in the courtroom. The psychologist should have a rationale for why documents and standards don't apply if he or she is not in compliance with them (Younggren, personal communication, 2002). Standard of care for supervision are determined by available guidelines, the law, and practices in the community.

A small, but growing, number of malpractice suits arise from failure to supervise adequately (Sherry, 1991). C. L. Guest and Dooley (1999) predicted that malpractice litigation brought against supervisors by supervisees may be significant in the future of risk management. To date, psychotherapist–patient sexual violations are the major source of financial loss in malpractice suits (Pope & Vasquez, 1998) and are increasingly excluded from malpractice insurance coverage.

Bennett et al. (1990) described four criteria of malpractice:

1. A professional *relationship* was formed between the psychologist and the client. Only thus does a practitioner incur a legal duty of care.
2. There is a *demonstrable* standard of care, and the practitioner breached that standard. He or she is said to have practiced "below the standard of care."
3. The client suffered *harm or injury*, which must be demonstrated and established.
4. The practitioner's breach of duty to practice within the standard of care was the *proximate cause* of the client's injury; that is, the injury was a reasonably foreseeable consequence of the breach. (p. 35, emphasis in original)

C. L. Guest and Dooley (1999) further refined these concepts in the context of supervision. For the first criterion, relationship, they suggested that the legal duty was established through an implied contract on the supervisee's acceptance by the supervisor. They cited Kurpius et al. (1991), who concluded that transference, countertransference, power, dependency, dual relationships, and stereotyping are all ethical issues involved in the supervisory relationship and have counterparts in client–therapist relationships. For the second criterion, standard of care, C. L. Guest and Dooley (1999) referred to ethical codes and standards for supervision, including ACES. A breach of standard of care might then be any deviation from the established set of standards. Overextension beyond the supervisee's level of competence, dual relationships, and boundary violations were cited as examples of the third criterion, or harm. Finally, for the fourth criterion, to establish the supervisor as the proximate cause of harm, it is necessary to prove the aspect of reasonable forseeability (Bennett et al., 1990; C. L. Guest & Dooley, 1999).

For the special case of supervisory malpractice, Disney and Stephens (1994) further clarified factors that aid in the determination of whether the supervisee's alleged negligence implicates the supervisor. These factors are as follows:

- the supervisor's power to control the supervisee (e.g., ability to control the supervisee on the basis of administrative authority or ability to gain knowledge of what is being done);
- the supervisee's duty to perform the act (e.g., failure to perform an act or perform in a manner that a reasonable supervisor in the same situation would assume);
- the time, place, and purpose of the act (e.g., during formal supervision or within the course and scope of the relationship);
- the motivation of the supervisee for committing the act (e.g., beneficence or malfeasance);
- whether the supervisor could have reasonably expected that the supervisee would commit the act. (pp. 15–16).

The fifth factor is related to forseeability, in the sense of whether the act would be reasonably expected to result in harm. Also to be considered is standard of care in supervision, or what a reasonable professional would do in the same circumstances (Falvey, 2002).

Another consideration in malpractice is the supervisor's responsibility to carry out supervision. This responsibility includes diligence or supervising on a regular basis, awareness of what transpires in the therapy sessions, and provision of adequate supervision (see also the section Competency in Supervision, this chapter). In particular, supervisors engaged in dual, sexual relationships with their supervisees are vulnerable to vicarious liability or direct liability, because the supervision was inadequate or because the supervisee felt abused or unfairly evaluated after receiving less than positive feedback after the termination of the dual relationship (Slimp & Burian, 1994).

Some risk management specialists urge, especially in the case of third-party payment, that the supervisor have a face-to-face contact with the client on at least one occasion. Cormier and Bernard (1982) suggested that giving the client the opportunity to meet the supervisor and learn about the supervision gives the supervisor additional, firsthand information about the client and the level of supervision required. It also provides a channel of communication in the case of client dissatisfaction or other trouble. If the supervisor learns that a supervisee is having difficulty with a particular client, the supervisor must take steps to increase the amount of supervision or other actions in response to the difficulty. It is critical to remember that the goal of treatment is to protect the welfare of the client and do no harm.

The "borrowed-servant" rule, a legal term, relates to situations in which a university places a student in another setting, perhaps a community mental health center. Supervisory liability may be shared between the university and the other setting. Saccuzzo (2002) described that the university would be considered the general employer, whereas the placement site would be the special employer. If a negligent act occurs, the task is to determine which employer had control of the supervisee, by examining affiliation agreements that define the conditions of placement. Saccuzzo (2002) suggested that, if no such agreements exist, the university may be liable as the general employer. It is thus extremely important to have clearly defined relationships between training institutions and placements.

Montgomery et al. (1999) reported a very important finding regarding supervision practices and liability: Respondents to their survey did not recognize negligent clinical supervision or incorrect diagnosis as potential sources of malpractice liability. In fact, the largest category of complaints (over 20%) reportedly filed with state licensing boards dealt with supervisory issues, such as the supervisee's performance with clients and the relationship between the supervisee and the supervisor. Respondents instead recognized the high-risk categories of sexual misconduct with a client; failure to warn, with resulting injury; child custody case decisions; and client suicide as potential sources of malpractice liability. Although over 70% of the respondents knew a colleague who had had a complaint filed against him or her with the state licensing board, only 14% had actually been threatened with a complaint themselves. Most (over 70%) thought it was highly unlikely that they would have a malpractice lawsuit filed against them at any point in their career.

A case involving forseeability in child psychiatry and psychoanalytic training is *Almonte v. New York Medical College* (1994). The U.S. District Court for the District of Connecticut found that the supervisor has a duty to the clients of the supervisee if there is reasonable forseeability of harm. In this case, the resident disclosed to his psychoanalyst that he was a pedophile (that he had such fantasies which the court construed to constitute pedophilia) and that he planned to practice child psychiatry. The psychoanalyst, who was a school faculty member, was found to have had the responsibility to inform the school that the resident had not successfully completed his analysis, a requirement for graduation, or to take reasonable steps to prevent the resident from taking up a child practice. These steps could have been taken without compromising the confidentiality of the resident's disclosures (Falvey, 2002; *Garamella v. New York Medical College*, 1998; "Jury finds," October 9, 1998).

Disney and Stephens (1994) discussed the growing number of malpractice claims alleging sexual relations or other unethical boundary crossings between supervisees and clients. They urged supervisors to have a formal policy in place, in writing, in which each supervisee is informed of the legal and ethical standards and consequences of such actions. This statement must be signed as understood by the supervisee. In addition, there should be practices in place for case review, treatment planning, and a review of goals set for and the ongoing progress of each client. As supervisees, like supervisors, are held to a standard of ethics of their profession, it is a standard of practice for these ethics to be incorporated into and articulated as a minimum ethical standard. *Andrews v. United States* (1982), cited by Harrar et al. (1990), is an example of a physician supervisor who did not adequately investigate a report that a physician's assistant was having a sexual relationship with a patient. By not speaking with the patient, conducting a thorough investigation, or filing a written report, the supervisor was found liable. Had the supervision been proper, the relationship would have been terminated and the emotional harm prevented (Bray, cited by Falvey, 2002).

C. L. Guest and Dooley (1999) expressed concern that potential or current supervisors will be frightened away from supervision by the threat of liability. They urged that the same risk management procedures used in one's practice be used in supervision. They especially urged that attention be paid to the slippery slopes of dual relationships, competence, accountability, and contracting, with the goal of supervising as one would like to live, with honesty, integrity, and responsibility.

DUTY TO WARN AND DUTY TO PROTECT

Ultimate responsibility in duty-to-warn cases lies with the supervisor, to ensure that full responsibility for diagnosis and treatment has been assumed. It is essential that the supervisor document steps taken. It is critical for supervisors to understand completely the privilege statutes, duty-to-warn-

and-protect concept, and confidentiality status of the state(s) in which one practices. Supervisors should bear in mind that what is required as far as breaching confidentiality as part of the duty to warn in one state may be prohibited in other states (Herlihy & Sheeley, 1988).

Tarasoff v. Regents of University of California (1976), the case that established duty to warn, stands at the forefront. A less attended-to part of the Tarasoff case is that the supervisor was found liable, along with the psychologist, for failing to take steps to warn and protect the client. The plaintiff's attorney later acknowledged that if the supervisor of the clinic had examined the patient (Poddar) himself and made a determination that he was not dangerous to himself or others, there would have been no cause of action under forseeability (Slovenko, 1980). However, he did not and instead disregarded his staff's medical records. What protects a therapist from liability is the capacity to identify what specific values are relevant to a particular circumstance and to apply those values thoughtfully to a problem that lacks a clear answer (Behnke et al., 1998). It is important for the trainee to understand that the duty to protect arises only when the victim is identifiable, could be identifiable after "a moment's reflection," (p. 345) or is part of an identifiable class of reasonably foreseeable victims (Vandecreek & Knapp, 2001). In the case of Tarasoff, the supervisee, entitled to the psychotherapist–patient privilege, a special relationship, must hear the communication of a specific threat of serious physical violence (with intent and ability to carry out the threat) against a reasonably identifiable victim (Behnke et al., 1998). *Hedlund v. The Superior Court of Orange County* (1983) extended the definition of victim to anyone who is foreseeably at risk—in that case, the child of the individual (the mother) who should have been warned. The court ruled that the child was identifiable as someone who might be injured if the mother was attacked, as one of the people in close proximity.

In instances in which the supervisee should have been aware of potential danger, there is a significant risk factor if a novice trainee is responsible for implementation of the requisite steps. It is imperative the supervisor monitor very closely or even work along with the supervisee under such difficult circumstances. It is important to remember that the entire process is predicated by a very specific set of behaviors identified by the supervisee. One less understood part of *Tarasoff* is that there is a "duty to warn, protect, and predict" (Behnke et al., 1998, p. 21). Making reasonable efforts to communicate the expressed threat to the victim(s) and to the police as well as developing action steps for the client fulfill the duty.

In *Jablonski v. United States* (1983), at issue was the failure to obtain past medical records or to interview relevant individuals regarding the client's potential for violence. The case also highlighted the critical nature of communication among professionals regarding high-risk clinical situations.

In *Peck v. the Counseling Service of Addison County* (1985), the counselor did not take seriously a client's threat to burn down his parents' barn, did not consult her supervisor, and did not issue any warnings. The counseling center was found negligent, as there were no written policies or procedures for when a client constitutes a significant danger. The counselor was also found negligent, as she did not take an adequate history, consult her supervisor, or obtain past medical records quickly (Harrar et al., 1990).

A series of steps compiled from multiple sources (Herlihy & Sheeley, 1988; VandeCreek & Knapp, 2001) can be adapted as steps to introduce to trainees in duty-to-warn-and-protect situations. These steps include warning the intended victim, increasing frequency of treatment, referring for changing or adding appropriate medication, making plans to eliminate access of the client to a lethal weapon, dealing with aggression in the treatment, subjecting the client to involuntary commitment, notifying the police, consulting with colleagues, and documenting every step of every action the supervisor and supervisee take. Chenneville (2000) provided guidelines dealing with duty to protect in the case of HIV.

Supervisees should be introduced to state-of-the-art techniques for assessment of risk (Rosenberg, 1999) and for management of violent clients (J. C. Beck, 1987; Borum, 1996; Tishler, Gordon, & Landry-Meyer, 2000), as almost half of all psychotherapists are threatened, physically attacked, or harassed by clients at some time in their career (Guy, Brown, & Poelstra, 1992), with supervisees and those licensed less than five years at greater risk. Supervisees also need to learn suicide risk assessment (Kleespies, Penk, & Forsyth, 1993) and guidelines for working with potentially violent clients (VandeCreek & Knapp, 1993), two other neglected areas in graduate training (Bongar & Harmatz, 1991).

As graduate training in dealing with feelings of anger, fear, and sexual arousal has been determined to be inadequate, and as any of these feelings could increase stress and potential burnout, these topics are areas of concern. Specifically, fear of a client committing suicide, fear that a client could get worse, anger at a client for being uncooperative, or fear that a client will attack a third party was so severe that it affected the eating, sleeping, or concentration of over half of the therapists who responded to Pope and Tabachnick's (1993) study.

Kleespies et al. (1993) reported that 40% of psychology trainees experienced a client's suicide or suicide attempt during their training. Coping with the aftermath is highly stressful and traumatic, more so the earlier in the training sequence it occurs (Kleespies et al., 1993). Preparation for this eventuality as well as for all the other categories of danger is essential. Preparation could take the form of presentation of vignettes, presentation of actual cases, and group problem-solving and processing exercises. Kleespies and Dettmer (2000) cautioned against defensive supervision in the instance of trainee debriefings or postmortem case reviews should a suicide occur. Such a strategy might be geared toward fear that such information would be revealed in legal proceedings. Kleespies and Dettmer (2000) urged support and learning to ensue in the aftermath of such an event.

In *Cohen v. State of New York* (1975), a first-year psychiatric resident released a client who had documented suicidal risk. The client killed himself the same day. The court found that the unsupervised resident did not possess enough skill or judgment for reasonable treatment and was acting beyond his competence. Therefore, the decisions of student therapists need to be reviewed and altered as determined by the supervisor (Moline, Williams, & Austin, 1998).

DOCUMENTATION

Harrar et al. (1990) stated, "Just as practitioners maintain case records on their clients to document their services, it would be prudent for supervisors to also document their supervisory work" (p. 38). And Falvey (2002) cautioned that "[d]ocumentation is no longer an option in supervision" (p. 117). Besides being a measure of professional accountability, establishment of whether, for example, a liability claim meets criteria for malpractice documentation is definitely a risk management strategy. Documentation on supervisees includes the supervisory contract, the supervisee's application materials (or, at minimum, a curriculum vitae), all performance evaluations that have been conducted, and a monitoring log. The log could consist of a list of cases the supervisee is carrying; dates of supervision of each; when supervision actually occurred; presentation of problems and critical issues; directives or directions the supervisee is following in treatment; changes in the diagnosis or treatment plan; discussions of case progress; details of safety, ethical, legal, or risk management concerns raised and their resolution; follow-up reports on previous interventions or concerns; details of supervisory or supervisee problems and their resolution; and supervisee attendance records for supervision appointments and any associated make-up information. If past or present medical records, audiotapes, videotapes, or assessment reports are reviewed, this factor should be noted in the recommendations the supervisor makes (Bernstein & Hartsell, 1998; Bridge & Bascue, 1990). There should also be a termination summary documenting circumstances of termination, as well as recommendations or referrals and follow-up by the supervisee (Falvey, 2002).

Like progress notes, supervision notes should be objective, nonjudgmental, nonderogatory, clear, and concrete (Stromberg et al., 1988). Falvey (2002) recommended that, as there is no statute of limitations regarding complaints of professional ethics, supervisory records should be kept as long as clinical records are required to be kept in one's particular state—anywhere from 5 to 30 years. In their guidelines for record keeping, APA suggests that records be retained for a minimum of 3 years after the last contact with the client. Records or a summary of the records is then maintained an additional 12 years before disposal.

Letters of Recommendation

Ethical and legal issues arise in writing letters of recommendation. Such letters are extremely influential and among the most important criteria for selection for internships and multiple other settings (Grote, Robiner, & Haut, 2001). Writing such a letter is an informed-consent issue, as students may be asked to protect the confidentiality of the writer by waiving rights to review the letter before they have an indication of what the contents will be (Ford, 2001). Some agencies and institutions refuse to write letters of recommendation beyond a simple statement verifying dates of employment, because of concerns about legal jeopardy. It has even been suggested that a balanced, accurate letter can appear negative because of the preponderance of inflated letters that are exaggerated and unrealistic in their claims (R. K. Miller & Van Rybroek, 1988). If a letter of recommendation includes *any* negative evaluation, even if the letter is predominantly positive, it is very likely to result in the applicant's rejection (Koocher & Keith-Spiegel, 1998). This tendency exists because the predominance of letters of recommendation are extremely glowing and positive, resulting in "letter inflation" (Range, Menyhert, Walsh, Hardin, Craddick, & Ellis, 1991, p. 390). In fact, a majority of supervisors (53%) in one study believed that they had written letters of recommendation which were biased. Only 5% of the respondents believed supervisors' letters were not biased (Robiner, Saltzman, Hoberman, Semrud-Clikeman, & Schirvar, 1997).

An ethical progression is to model integrity by discussing with the individual what will be contained in the letter, especially should there be areas of weakness or concern. An ethical dilemma for the supervisor regards the obligation to communicate accurate information to colleagues or institutions in the interests of the profession of psychology. The writer of the recommendation may also be at risk for failing to disclose negative or dangerous facts. In fact, Grote et al. (2001) reported that nearly half (46.5%) of their respondents (return rates of 64% and 78%) said that they would refuse to write a letter for a student they knew had alcohol or drug abuse problems, whereas a "nontrivial minority" of respondents (12.4%) indicated that they would exclude all mention of alcohol and drug abuse problems from their letter of recommendation (p. 658). They also reported significant rates of respondents who would exclude mention of the applicant's anxiety or depression (43.2%), motivation (14.1%), and interpersonal problems (13.2%).

R. K. Miller and Van Rybroek (1988) proposed guidelines for what a helpful letter might contain. These elements include a caveat about how many letters overstate desirable qualities, and the writer's intent to avoid that trap by highlighting strengths and weaknesses in specific skills, experience, commitments, and traits; examples or reasons that the individual should be selected over others; and suggestions of the types of internship experiences that the candidate might most benefit from. Grote et al. (2001) urged use of Likert scales rather than binary yes–no decisions. They suggested an acknowledgment in all letters of recommendation that "no applicant is perfect and that the writer will describe some areas of personal or professional growth that the applicant should work toward in his or her internship year" (p. 659–660). We urge movement toward standardization with inclusion of details on the scope of experience with the supervisee, mention of Grote's recommendations and one's relationship with the supervisee (e.g., primary supervisor or director of training), description of the context of the relationship (e.g., internship or professional organization), discussion of the special skills or attributes the supervisee would bring to the setting, and clear description of what was supervised. If one is not able to write a positive letter for a supervisee, this factor should have been dealt with in ongoing supervision, but needs to be clearly discussed with the supervisee.

As the APA Ethical Principles of Psychologists and Code of Conduct states in Principle C, Integrity, "Psychologists seek to promote accuracy, honesty, and truthfulness in the science, teaching and practice of psychology. In these activities psychologists do not steal, cheat, or engage in fraud, subterfuge, or intentional misrepresentation of fact" (American Psychological Association, 2002a, p. 4). Section 7.06 (b) of the same document states, "Psychologists evaluate students and supervisee on the basis of their actual performance on relevant and established program requirements" (American Psychological Association, 2002a).

RISK MANAGEMENT

The major components of supervisory risk management have been outlined in this chapter. Adherence to informed consent, competency, confidentiality, due process, duty to warn, and the approach of taking reasonable steps to think through and document the process in identified situations are sound preventative steps. Both legally and with respect to common sense, the supervisor needs to do what a reasonable supervisor would do under the particular set of circumstances. The ethical problem-solving models described in this chapter provide a framework for determining appropriate actions; the step entailing consultation with a colleague or colleagues is particularly important. Harris (2002) advocated "worst case thinking," or considering the worst possible outcomes of the scenario in question. This technique is very useful in preparing trainees for sessions during times of high uncertainty or crisis.

Competencies

The competencies for addressing ethical and legal considerations are as follows:

- Supervisors function within their areas of competency in all clinical practice and supervision
- Supervisors have knowledge and training in ethics of mental health professions and conduct themselves in a manner that models such behavior. This competency encompasses all areas of ethical functioning, including boundary definition
- Supervisors have knowledge of laws and regulations of the mental health disciplines and conduct themselves accordingly. They seek consultation as needed
- Supervisors develop goals and contracts with supervisees and translate these objectives into training, giving ongoing constructive feedback and evaluation and documenting all parts of the process

8

EVALUATION OF THE SUPERVISORY PROCESS

Feedback and evaluation are core components of psychology training programs. However, they are two of the most difficult areas in psychology training. Evaluation has been described as "typically a weak suit for most supervisors" (Cormier & Bernard, 1982, p. 490). Ironically, as psychologists, we pride ourselves on our training in research, methodology, psychodiagnostics, and evaluation, yet find that in the area of evaluation of our students—and ourselves—our techniques are sorely lacking, as is our will to do the task.

In this chapter, we introduce a protocol for evaluation. First, we discuss the role of evaluation in psychology training, in terms of both the current state of the art and aspirations for its future. We then define the psychologist's role as evaluator and describe specific types of evaluation. In particular, we devote attention to qualitative versus quantifiable forms of evaluation and to the focus of evaluation: assessment of the client interactions between the client and the supervisee–therapist and among the client, supervisee–therapist, and supervisor, obtained through observation, assessment-of-process, and client-outcomes measures. Next, we discuss the variant of manualized treatment evaluation. Nuances that differentiate formative and summative evaluation, including examples of frames, are laid out as steps in the development of competency-based criteria that use an interwoven contract as a centerpiece. We then present 360-degree evaluation as an alternative to supervisor evaluation and discuss contextual factors that influence evaluation and satisfaction of supervisees. Relevant ethical issues introduced in evaluation or in lack of an evaluation process are significant factors. We also briefly discuss admissions criteria for psychology training and licensure programs. Finally, we examine aspects of dealing with a supervisee with problematic behavior as defined through the evaluation process, including identification, remediation, addressing of legal issues, dismissal, and preventative strategies. In this analysis, we do not neglect the problematic supervisor or program evaluation, factors that only recently have received attention in the context of supervision.

REASONS FOR DIFFICULTY IN EVALUATION

The reasons for the evaluation deficit seem multifaceted. First, there is the perceived incongruity between developing a supportive supervisory relationship or alliance and then giving negative feedback. Central to this problem is the belief that feedback may disturb the unmitigated positive regard in the relationship (Hahn & Molnar, 1991) or otherwise disrupt the relationship. Ladany, Ellis, et al. (1999) suggested that evaluation may even moderate the relationship between working alliance and supervision outcome, such that, for example, a trainee may not self-disclose relevant personal information, out of the fear that doing so may adversely affect his or her evaluation. However, effective evaluation practices appear to be positively associated with and predictive of a stronger working alliance (Lehrman-Waterman & Ladany, 2001). Because most evaluations are positive (Robiner, Saltzman, Hoberman, Semrud-Clikeman, et al., 1997), it is even more difficult to provide negative evaluations.

Second, there is a profound misunderstanding of the task of evaluation in training: Evaluation is viewed as punitive and worrisome, whereas it should be viewed simply as part of the effective learning process and as a method of dealing with problematic behavior and remediation in a small minority of cases. Multiple studies cited in chapter 2, this volume, reported that trainees viewed high levels of feedback and evaluation as a highly desirable characteristic of supervision (Gandolfo & Brown, 1987; Henderson et al., 1999; Leddick & Dye, 1987; C. D. Miller & Oetting, 1966; Nerdrum & Ronnestad, 2002). However, the differences in the supervisory role between giving formative (ongoing) and summative evaluations are complex.

Third, evaluation has typically been a unidirectional process, given from supervisor to supervisee, rather than bidirectional. However, it is important to consider the impact of supervisees' evaluations of supervisors on the relationship and on the supervisees' satisfaction. Potentially, such evaluations would provide supervisors with feedback on their own performance and effectiveness, creating a spiral of supervisory improvement.

Fourth, Robiner et al. (1993) have done an admirable job outlining the myriad reasons that we convince ourselves to avoid, be lenient in, or inflate evaluation. They described the definitional and measurement issues, including lack of clear criteria and definition of competency; legal and administrative issues, such as fear of liability, fear of institutional censure, concern for program status, and concern for institutional reputation; interpersonal issues, including fear of diminished rapport or damaging a trainee's career; and supervisor issues, such as a wish to avoid scrutiny of one's own work, inexperience with or minimization of impairment, low assertiveness, a wish to avoid the time and energy expenditure required in the effort, and inappropriate optimism. Norcross, Stevenson, and Nash (1986) found time constraints, inadequate measures and methods, lack of personnel, and insufficient funding to be primary obstacles, rather than staff resistance and theoretical disparity. Much traditional evaluation to date has been single-measure, supervisor-reported, and often global evaluation (Hahn & Molnar, 1991) or measurement of a single, global factor (Newman & Scott, 1988). In terms of methodology, without the use of observation of therapy, videotape review, or a 360-degree procedure, the validity of the evaluation may be compromised; discomfort on the part of both parties when feedback is based on small segments of data is warranted. In addition, few supervisors have been formally trained in supervision, and the majority feels less than adequately prepared to work with "unsuitable" interns (Robiner, Saltzman, Hoberman, & Schirvar, 1997).

Last, there is the underlying reality that negative evaluation of a supervisee may lead to remediation plans and possibly culminate in the supervisee's dismissal from the program (Olkin & Gaughen, 1991), thus adding the role of judge to that of supervisor.

That evaluation is a critical part of supervision is unequivocal. One need only look at the APA Guidelines and Principles for Accreditation of Programs in Professional Psychology to confirm this condition (American Psychological Association, Committee on Accreditation, 2002e):

> At the time of admission, the program provides interns with written policies and procedures regarding program requirements and expectations for interns' performance and continuance in the program and procedures for the termination of students. Interns receive, at least semiannually, written feedback on the extent to which they are meeting these requirements and performance expectations. The feedback should address the intern's performance and progress in terms of professional conduct and psychological knowledge, skills and competencies in the areas of psychological assessment, intervention, and consultation. Such feedback should include:

Timely written notification of all problems that have been noted and the opportunity to discuss them, guidance regarding steps to remediate all problems (if remediable); and substantive written feedback on the extent to which corrective actions are or are not successful in addressing the areas of concern.

Further confirmation of this point is given by section 7.06, "Assessing Student and Supervisee Performance," of the APA Ethical Principles of Psychologists and Code of Conduct 7.06 (American Psychological Association, 2002a)

(a) In academic and supervisory relationships, psychologists establish a timely and specific process for providing feedback to students and supervisees. Information regarding the process is provided to the student at the beginning of supervision.
(b) Psychologists evaluate students and supervisees on the basis of their actual performance on relevant and established program requirements.

Together, these guidelines leave no doubt that evaluation, feedback, and clear performance expectations need to be the hallmark of psychology training. However, evidence reveals a significant schism between what should be a competence of psychologists and what actually occurs in practice.

STATE OF THE ART

Even though it would be reasonable to expect a comparable level of methodological rigor for assessment of supervisees and peers as that required for client assessments, that has not been the case. In a review of psychometric properties of existing competency assessment tools, Scofield and Yoxtheimer (1983) concluded that existing measures were lacking in reliability and validity of data. The area most frequently assessed was interpersonal competencies, including empathy, expertness, interpersonal nonverbal responses, and overall therapeutic effectiveness. Ponterotto and Furlong (1985) extended the inquiry into rating scales used to assess competency of therapists, concluding that use of the rating scales was "based more on convention than on sound psychometric evidence" (p. 614). Rater bias has been shown to be significant. Rater bias in evaluation includes leniency (giving ratings that are more positive than warranted), the central tendency (the tendency to skew ratings more toward average than warranted), and strictness (giving ratings that are more negative than warranted; Robiner, Saltzman, Hoberman, Semrud-Clikeman, et al., 1997). Robiner, Saltzman, Hoberman, Semrud-Clikeman, et al.'s (1997) survey of 62 supervisors revealed that 58% of the supervisors believed their evaluations were biased in some way, mainly because of leniency or the central tendency.

Ladany, Lehrman-Waterman, et al. (1999) found that supervisees cited performance evaluation and monitoring of supervisees' activities as the most frequent ethical violation. In a survey of counseling training sites, there was high variability among programs in the type of evaluation and exit criteria. Out of 60 counseling centers, only 1 had complete formal exit criteria (Hahn & Molnar, 1991). In a survey of 179 APA-accredited internships, the most frequently used procedures were informal qualitative procedures; quantitative comparison procedures were used the least (Norcross et al., 1986). Forrest, Elman, Gizara, and Vacha-Haase (1999) concluded,

> Our review of the literature describing evaluation criteria used by academic and internship programs suggest minimal consensus across programs about evaluation criteria and procedures. There does not appear to be a systematic and comprehensive evaluation schema that is widely accepted within professional psychology training programs. (p. 641)

Ellis and Ladany (1997) also concluded that, although supervisees *can* be evaluated effectively, currently "there is little evidence indicating how or what is being evaluated" (p. 484). There is a significant gap between what is ethically and programmatically indicated for evaluation and what is actually practiced.

PSYCHOLOGIST AS EVALUATOR

Cormier and Bernard (1982) described three pivotal skills in the training of the psychologist to be an evaluator:

> (a) the ability to evaluate efficiently using some objective criteria as a yardstick or measure; (b) the ability to communicate feedback clearly and to have some method of checking the counselor's understanding of the feedback; (c) the ability to be comfortable and effective with the power inherent in the role of supervisor. (p. 490)

These skills are basic competencies that all supervisors should possess. In addition, Ellis and Ladany (1997) delineated the parameters for evaluating supervisee competence. They suggested consideration of scope of competency, the particular domain and modality of therapy behavior, skills and behaviors desired, a designated period of time, and the method of assessment.

TYPES OF EVALUATION

The following are some of the types of evaluation used in supervision:

- qualitative or quantitative evaluation of material presented by the supervisee regarding the client and interactions between the client and the supervisee–therapist, based on recollection (described by Cone [2001] as indirect, because of the temporal gap and lack of direct observation);

- qualitative or quantitative evaluation of observational (live or videotaped) data of interactions between the client or family and the supervisee–therapist (described by Cone [2001] as direct with no temporal gap), which may include responses to the following variables or others that can be operationalized and coded from the observed session or Likert scales developed to assess the following:
  - affective component,
  - cultural and diversity competency,
  - relationship and interpersonal skills,
  - conceptualization,
  - diagnosis,
  - technical skills,
  - adherence to the model, and
  - empathy;
- evaluation of the progress of the supervisee toward predesignated therapy goals;
- analysis of client-report outcome data on the client's progress;
- use of rating scales for role induction or to structure formative feedback;
- Use of unobtrusive measures, such as comparing tallies of client attendance and cancellations, analyzing rates of client retention, and determining the number of clients seen per week or psychodiagnostics sessions completed, assessing supervisee timely and credible completion of paperwork;
- analysis of client satisfaction data, based on client reports and attendance records;
- assessment of case presentations at grand rounds or diagnostic team meetings;
- analysis of portfolios or examinations (adapted from Sumerall et al., 2000);
- ratings of a work sample, including diagnostic assessment, case formulation, and course of treatment (Dienst & Armstrong, 1988);
- analysis of critical incidents (Norman, 1985) or incidents that were major turning points in supervision, resulting in change to the supervisee's approach or effectiveness;
- study of diagnostic thinking, clinical judgment, or problem solving in which physicians are observed and questioned as they solve a clinical problem (Norman, 1985).

Frame and Stevens-Smith (1995) identified and operationalized particularly salient variables that can be converted to an evaluation format. They identified nine characteristics to be imperative to counselor development, compiled through analysis of counselor literature by the counseling psychology department at the University of Colorado–Denver: openness, flexibility, positivity, cooperativeness, willingness to use and accept feedback, awareness of one's impact on others, ability to deal with conflict, ability to accept personal responsibility, and ability to express feelings effectively and appropriately. On a 5-point Likert scale, a minimum rating of 3 points per item is required.

Evaluation of the Process of Supervision

Evaluation of the process of supervision is another approach. The measure by Worthen and Isakson (2000) shown in Appendix J provides for supervisee introspection regarding multiple aspects of suitability, conceptualization, relationship, technique, results, and satisfaction with supervision. Although this approach has not been empirically validated, the authors reported good reliability of data. It appears to be useful in providing structured, somewhat less judgmental feedback from supervisee to supervisor.

A Supervisory Utilization Rating Form (SURF) was developed by Vespia et al. (2002). Although it has not been psychometrically supported, they suggested its use as a tool in role induction, to help supervisees define their task and what is entailed in being a supervisee. It might also be useful in identifying differences between importance assigned to various supervisory activities by supervisors and supervisees. For example, two items rated as more important by supervisees than supervisors were "critiques own work" and "invites feedback from supervisor" (Vespia et al., 2002, p. 60).

The observational instrument (Process Evaluation of Teaching and Supervision) described by Milne and James (2002) provides another format for assessment. By coding supervisee behaviors of reflecting, experimenting, conceptualizing, experiencing, and planning in the context of supervisor behaviors of managing, listening, supporting, informing and educating, and guiding experiential learning, the authors provide a framework which could be adapted to other assessment and guiding functions.

The Evaluation Process Within Supervision Inventory (see Appendix I; Lehrman-Waterman & Ladany, 2001) is a self-report measure designed to assess supervisees' perceptions of the degree of effectiveness of supervision goal setting and feedback. Supervisees use a 7-point Likert scale, where 1 = strongly disagree and 7 = strongly agree. The scale consists of two groupings of items: goal setting and feedback. An example of a goal-setting item is, "My supervisor and I created goals that were realistic." An example of a feedback item is, "The feedback I received was directly related to the goals we established" (Lehrman-Waterman & Ladany, 2001, p. 171). The authors reported that the two scales were highly correlated, but conceptually distinct. They accounted for the relatively lower internal consistency of the feedback scale by explaining that feedback is very heterogeneous and includes input solicited by a supervisor and whether summative evaluation was given. This inventory appears useful in providing the supervisor with feedback on the supervisee's perspective and satisfaction and as a springboard for discussion of the supervision process.

Evaluating Client Outcome

Another type of supervision evaluation examines client-outcome data on changes in the client's symptoms. There is not a complete correlation between client outcome and competence of supervisees, as client's symptom status is a significant factor, and assessment of this variable occurs informally anyway (Ward, Friedlander, Schoen, & Klein, 1985) and plays a role in evaluation. Although client outcome is considered the acid test of supervision efficacy (Ellis & Ladany, 1997; Stein & Lambert, 1995), to date we do not have clear, methodologically sound data on client outcome and its relationship to supervision.

Several methodologies have been described to track client change (Clement, 1999; Frazier, Dik, Glaser, Steward, & Tashiro, 2002; Lambert et al., 2002) or to relate monitoring of client outcome to supervision (Lambert & Hawkins, 2001, Worthen & Isakson, 2002). The Outcome Questionnaire, or OQ-45, a self-report measure, consists of three subscales: symptom distress, interpersonal relations, and social role performance. A youth version, the Youth Outcome Questionnaire (Y-OQ), is geared to clients ages 4 to 17 and contains six subscales: intrapersonal distress, somatics, interpersonal relations, critical items, social problems, and behavioral dysfunction (Wells, Burlingame, Lambert, Hoag, & Hope, 1996). A noteworthy methodology combines the OQ-45 and, based on the results, a therapeutic-alliance assessment (Horvath & Greenberg, 1994) or analysis of the client's motivation for change (McConnaughy, Prochaska, & Velicer, 1983) to determine which factors are influencing inadequate client progress (Lambert & Hawkins, 2001). Under this approach, the therapist is given a weekly graph with white, green, yellow, and red dots signifying different degrees of the client's self-reported functioning and the probability of achieving a positive outcome. White corresponds to normal functioning indicative of a need for termination of treatment, whereas green signifies adequate progress without a need for treatment-plan changes. Yellow reflects less than adequate progress, a need for treatment-plan change, and consideration that treatment is not helping. Finally, red signifies that the client is not progressing at an expected level and may withdraw from treatment prematurely or end up with a negative treatment effect. However, significant changes need to be made to this methodology; for example, readiness for change could be assessed (Lambert & Hawkins, 2001).

Lambert and Hawkins (2001) believed that the kinds of feedback evinced by their approach are not systematically elicited in the supervisory process and have been associated with client improvement in therapist–client feedback studies (Lambert et al., 2001). In one case described by Lambert and Hawkins (2001), after a series of very negative feedback reports about the client's symptom severity, evidence of the need to rethink the treatment plan, the client began to improve on self-reports, a change that went unnoticed by the novice therapist. When questioned, the client described that the extreme discomfort of the symptoms was unmanageable, thereby increasing the client's motivation to improve.

Worthen and Isakson (2002) used Lambert's OQ-45 (Lambert & Burlingame, 1996) to provide weekly client-outcome data. They posited client feedback to be value neutral and easier for trainees to tolerate and incorporate. Lambert et al. (2002) found this feedback to enhance therapy outcome. Although the results from the Worthen and Isakson (2002) study were equivocal because of pretreatment between-group differences, this technique may provide a way to incorporate client outcome into the supervisory process. Frazier et al.'s (2002) application of Clement (1999) used scales with fixed behavioral points for client self-monitoring, which could be used in supervision as well.

A somewhat different approach to evaluation is provided in the feminist supervision model. Under this approach, the supervisor and the supervisee each gives the other evaluative feedback both on an ongoing basis and in written form on completion of the supervision. Responsibility is shared for evaluating success and limitations in goal attainment (Zimmerman & Haddock, 2001). However, it is clearly established that the supervisor must provide direct and valid evaluations and feedback and if necessary, recommend the supervisee's termination from the training program. All feedback is provided in a humane manner (Porter & Vasquez, 1997).

Evaluation of Manualized Treatment

Supervisors in manualized-treatment programs rate each supervisory hour on how closely it adhered to the manual and to the parameters of treatment. Attention is given to how well the supervisee completed the stated goals of the session, individualized the session for the benefit of the client, and stayed within the treatment protocol (Kendall & Southam-Gerow, 1995). This type of tracking could be modified so that trainees and supervisors rate these variables session by session. Henggeler and Schoenwald (1998) developed a manual for supervision of multisystemic therapy, or MST; their manual is one of the only efforts to create a supervisory model to accompany a transportable evidence-based mental health treatment for the community. Particularly interesting is the Supervisor Adherence Measure (Henggeler et al., 2002), a questionnaire that articulates and assesses multiple aspects of the supervisor's role in implementing the model. This questionnaire is a noteworthy effort to organize the elements of supervision in a measurable format, to demystify the process, and to provide a roadmap to evaluation of the supervision process within a particular model.

Lambert and Ogles (1997) came to the following conclusions regarding existing measures of training outcome: (a) Focusing on observable behavior of trainees, with frequency counts, is most useful; (b) evaluation of training through criteria from several sources is most desirable (i.e., from clients, supervisor, and trainees themselves); (c) it is ideal to evaluate the effects of supervision by looking at client-outcome and relationship (e.g., trainee–client) variables, but this goal is aspirational; (d) most outcome measures are "homemade" and lack reliability and validity, so we need to move toward criterion measures instead.

FORMATIVE AND SUMMATIVE EVALUATION

Formative and summative evaluations are two types of evaluation in the psychology traineeship, each of which may have a different emotional valence (Robiner et al., 1993). Formative evaluation, which is seen as a way to assist in skill refinement and identification of personal issues that may be impeding clinical practice, is viewed more positively than summative evaluation. Because psychologists believe in positive change and in the power of feedback, formative evaluation may be syntonic. However, summative evaluation, or the objective assessment of competence and performance, is not viewed so positively. Because of the outcomes it yields (completion and passing, probationary status, or termination), there is greater ambivalence or negativity associated with this form of evaluation. There may be specific reasons that either form of evaluation, but especially summative, is difficult. To some supervisors, being an evaluator may feel like a dual role: On one hand, the supervisor is supportive, personal, and growth focused, whereas on the other hand he or she is the one to give hard facts on how the trainee is not measuring up to the requirements of the traineeship. Other reasons for supervisor discomfort with these forms of evaluation include unfamiliarity with the process of evaluation, because of a lack of supervision evaluation training (Borders & Leddick, 1988). In addition, there are all the aforementioned reasons that supervisors avoid or are lenient in evaluation.

Formative and Summative Feedback

Because of the structure of the supervisory relationship, the definition of its parameters and expectations, its use as a vehicle and process for formal feedback, etc., an early expectation should be established for a structure of goals and for ongoing qualitative feedback. These elements should be dictated by the goals of the trainee, the developmental level at which the trainee is functioning, and attention to the evaluation form that will be used for the summative evaluation. Supervisors must have competency in providing formative and summative feedback to trainees.

There are multiple levels of evaluation within the larger categories of formative and summative evaluation, including evaluative feedback, corrective feedback, and general feedback. In particular, giving corrective feedback to trainees is an essential part of supervision. When goals are clearly defined, as in a training contract, and updated as appropriate, a skillful supervisor uses the contract as the overarching framework for supervision. Thus, tangible behavioral feedback can be linked to the training goals. In the case, for example, of a trainee who continues to be content oriented as opposed to process oriented, corrective feedback might include identification of the shifts to content, analysis of the trainee's feeling state and thinking process at these junctures when the transition to content occurs, and analysis of alternative explanations of why the shifts occurred.

Ronnestad and Skovholt (1993) discriminated between confirmatory feedback given to beginning trainees and corrective feedback given to more advanced trainees. Summative evaluation takes the form of grades, ratings, passing or failing the training sequence, and feedback to the school or graduate institution. Formative feedback can take on many forms:

- Reflective:
  - "I wonder how that felt to you.";
  - "I wonder what you were thinking or feeling when. . .";
  - reflection on the impact of a particular client on the supervisee;
  - observation of a behavior or event that was unnoticed in the session;
  - a general observation about the role of the therapist vis à vis the clients.
- Integrative:
  - "Let's think about that and how it fits in the direction in which you see the family moving";

- "Where would pursuing that option have led?";
- "What was your thought process when you let that opportunity pass?"
- Neutral: "It would be interesting to know. . .."
- Empowering:
  - "Your skill set has markedly enlarged, and with it your integration of clinical material";
  - "Your use of the metaphor far surpasses your self-assessment of play-therapy competence";
  - "Think about how well you approached the same problem last month when the mother was so angry";
  - "Remember how your research experience with anxiety provides you with a perspective on how to approach this situation";
  - "I am struck by the contrast between how self-effacing you are in supervision and how effective you are with this family";
  - "Your skillful use of the metaphor paved the way for the child's disclosure about her level of pain."
- Analytic:
  - "Let's analyze the pattern of what has been happening in the past three sessions";
  - "I'm wondering what your thought process would have been if there were any other ways to have linked that situation to the history of abuse."
- Responsive:
  - "It seemed like you were wondering which way to proceed";
  - "What emotions were elicited in you when your client accused you of being unfeeling?"
- Corrective:
  - "It would be interesting to see what prefaces besides disclaimers you could use";
  - "I am wondering what other ideas you and I can come up with to get around the problem of the mother's continuing to ignore the child's appropriate behavior."
- Level-I Concern—specification of concern and context: "I'm concerned that the mother started to broach punishment and you changed the subject. Why do you think that happened?" (Assume, in this example, that there was a previous report of child abuse, and thus it is critical to monitor the types of punishment that are being used.)
- Level-II Concern: "The fact that you did not follow up with the input about exploring possible child abuse in this case is a legal breach as well as a breach of professionalism."

- Evaluative feedback:
  - Positive:
    - "You are responding much more clearly and empathically to this family, a direction we indicated in your goals. Good job";
    - "Your intervention had the desired effect on the adolescent."
  - Negative:
    - "You are continuing to ignore affective expression of this child. Attending to the child's affective expression is a goal in your contract, and I am increasingly concerned that the efforts we are making to improve this area are not succeeding";
    - "I am continuing to be concerned about how you do not seem to be integrating the concept of process in your clinical work. For your level of training and experience, I am very surprised that you are not progressing more easily."

Supervisors need to develop their own individual styles of imparting feedback. Some very seasoned supervisors prefer to give very positive feedback throughout most of the supervisory hour and, at most, one negative or corrective piece of feedback toward the end, interwoven with statements of the trainee's strengths. In a strength-based approach, it is essential to be honest, as emphasis on strengths to the extent that areas needing improvement are not mentioned is not an ethical, creditable, or educational approach.

PROCEDURE FOR COMPETENCY-BASED EVALUATION

The first step in the competency-based approach is to compile the learning assessment, determining areas of strength and weakness within each trainee's prior experience and academic training. Reviews of self-reports, the elaborate internship or trainee application forms, and, in some cases, descriptions from graduate training directors may be included in the assessment. Hahn and Molnar (1991) suggested that evaluation of interns actually begins during the internship application process, when training committees review applicants, view their areas of strength and weakness, and build a class or intern group out of the successful applicants. The next step in the establishment of the evaluation process could be to obtain postadmission direct input from training directors or professors of practicum, internship, or fellowship programs on the supervisee's areas of strength and weakness, perhaps through the use of a checklist or Likert-scaled items geared to the specific focus and competencies of the training program that the supervisee is entering. Early observations by the new supervisors and supervisee self-reports of competencies are done to establish the format for goals within a training contract. It may be useful to break down particular tasks into component parts (for an example, see chap. 3, this volume) and have the trainee complete a self-assessment on the incremental steps. Alternatively, larger increments can be self-assessed, with confirmation provided from one or more supervisors on observing or supervising performance in each area.

Supervision Contract

The written training contract, or working agreement (Proctor, 1997), is a key to the establishment of the training relationship between trainee and setting or supervisor. It is also an important part of ethical structuring, relationship building, and evaluation. The contract can be described as an "Individualized Learner Contract" (Cobia & Boes, 2000) and should be in writing (Osborne & Davis, 1996). It should be initiated by the supervisor (Sherry, 1991) prior to or at the very beginning of the training sequence and signed by both supervisor and supervisee, with copies for both (Bridge & Bascue, 1990). It should be brought to supervision regularly for reference, as a review of the goals and expectations. The training contract has a structural function analogous to the supervisory relationship per se (Ronnestad & Skovholt, 1993). Besides satisfying due-process and informed-consent rights of supervisees, the document contributes to the clear articulation of goals and expectations, which should be frequently addressed and reviewed. Such practices result in effective supervision (Leddick & Dye, 1987). The process of involving the trainee in formulating a working agreement in the form of a contract may enhance the supervisee's sense of responsibility for learning (Osborne & Davis, 1996) and perhaps the supervisee's dominance.

Although we have proposed one sample supervision contract in Appendix A, it is intended mainly to be an example. Multiple systems can be generated as a function of theoretical orientation, incorporating procedures such as manualized treatments, systems, and modalities (Shaw & Dodson, 1988). It is important to note the significance of psychometrically sound assessments of competencies with excellent interrater reliability as a goal. We suggest that developmental gradients for metaphor, process, sense of self, and relationship may be built into the evaluation process and serve as competency anchors in the process of supervision and in evaluation. There are multiple examples of competency-assessment programs available at the APPIC Web site (http://www.appic.org), most of which are based on an analysis of the components of the tasks that compose each respective training program. Use of behaviorally anchored, specific categories with ratings given by supervisors appears to be the norm. Some ratings are based on observation, whereas others are based on responses to a vignette.

Goals and objectives should be mutually agreed up by the supervisor and supervisee and should include a definition of how progress toward the goals will be evaluated, a statement of expected periods of time for the accomplishment of the goals, and a list of responsibilities of supervisor and supervisee if the goals are not met (Cobia & Boes, 2000). Cornerstones of the contract are the developmental needs and strengths of the supervisee; the competencies of the supervisor; the duties and responsibilities of both the supervisor and supervisee; procedural considerations; opportunities provided within the setting, including those afforded by unique characteristics of the clients; and supervisory goals, methods, and foci (Ronnestad & Skovholt, 1993). Lehrman-Waterman & Ladany (2001) summarized their research findings on desirable qualities of goals as including specificity, realistic quality, measurability, prioritization, and early definition. Within this context, we may also include the amount and length of supervision, where and how supervision is to be conducted, and the types of monitoring activities as elements that should be articulated in the contract (Osborne & Davis, 1996).

Specifying available resources ensures clear communication regarding realistic possibilities within a particular setting. For example, trainees would do well to formulate goals that are compatible with the organization and mission of the agency. Methods that need to be spelled out include procedures such as for reviewing required videotapes, audiotapes, or live observations or for supervisory interventions such as role-playing, midsession supervision with feedback, didactics, or observation of a clinician or supervisor. Live supervision serves as an ethical safeguard (Cormier & Bernard, 1982). The functions of observation are to enhance compliance with a training model, to refine supervisory communication, and to address process, transference, and countertransference. Articulation of theoretical orientation in this context is critical. For example, a critical issue may be determining whether the supervisory relationship is conceptualized as a significant agent for change (Ronnestad & Skovholt, 1993).

Clearly articulating the evaluation process is a critical component of the supervisory contract (Osborne & Davis, 1996). Components of the evaluation process include amount, type (e.g., formal vs. informal, or written vs. verbal), timing, and frequency. In addition, the supervisory contract should specify that a "primary role of the supervisor is that of evaluation" (Osborne & Davis, 1996, p. 129). Also, methods by which information is to be recorded (e.g., a formal evaluation format provided by the school or by the setting, verbal feedback provided to the school, or a narrative in letter form) should be specified, and the parties who will be receiving parts of the evaluation and which parts they will be receiving should be identified so that clear limits of confidentiality are established (Osborn & Davis, 1996).

A prototypical or standard contract with potential for individualization provides a structure through which the needs of the trainee and of the setting can be met. A program can be designed carefully by drawing on areas of strength and areas that need improvement within the structure of the clinical services and requirements of the setting. We advocate greater rather than lesser specificity in requirements, all of which may be individualized for the particular program.

Within the training contract are some quantitative-evaluation components that constitute program requirements (e.g., productivity, number of videos made, number of psychodiagnostic batteries completed, client diversity, diagnoses, and family compositions served). A more qualitative evaluation is based on aspects of performance (as enumerated by the evaluation form).

Supervision Contract Prototypes

Osborn and Davis (1996) provided an outline for a supervision contract, and Sutter, McPherson, and Geeseman (2002) provided a prototype of a contract for supervision that includes multiple sections. In Sutter et al.'s (2002) prototype, supervisee and supervisor agree to the length and purpose of training, payment arrangements, malpractice insurance, and record-keeping expectations. Supervisors agree to follow all ethical, legal, and office codes and policies; to be available; to identify coverage for absences; to document supervision; and to provide evaluation. Supervisees agree to document supervised activities; follow all ethical, legal, and office codes and policies; and inform clients of the supervisees' status as an unlicensed supervisee under supervision. In contrast, Osborn and Davis (1996) described the contract as consisting of purpose, goals, objectives, a context of services, evaluation methods, the duties and responsibilities of both supervisor and supervisee, procedural considerations (e.g., with respect to notes, taping, and conflict resolution), and a definition of the supervisor's scope of competency.

The Sutter et al. (2002) contract addresses many structural, ethical, and procedural aspects, but not the qualitative, individualized, or programmatic factors relating to the growth and development of the trainee. Osborne and Davis (1996) included more of the latter factors, but did not lay out competencies or specific, individualized training goals. Ideally, a contract would address all of these aspects. An example of a contract is given in Appendix A. This contract is not intended to be exemplary, but simply to serve as an example on which one can build.

The level of specificity of the training contract is a critical area. Ronnestad and Skovholt (1993) described the importance of balancing goals generally enough to be meaningful, but specifically enough to allow their assessment. They also highlighted the dangers of changing goals too frequently and of maintaining goals too rigidly. In a model of "goal-directed supervision plans" (Talen & Schindler, 1993), goals relating to conceptual models, therapy skills, diagnosis and treatment planning, and personal and professional issues were developed. It was noted that secondary benefit of treatment-plan development included enhancement of the supervisory relationship and facilitation of evaluation. Under this model, trainees defined specific needs or problem areas; then, based on sample models of training plans, objectives or goals for supervision were developed and supervisory procedures and strategies were identified to assist in accomplishing the goals. Some of the suggested supervision strategies included supervisory integration of data (assessment and therapy process), expansion of trainees' alternative responses, and use of case examples to amplify a particular intervention plan.

360-DEGREE FEEDBACK

A conclusion shared by many who have studied evaluation is that it is highly desirable to use multiple sources of data (Fuqua, Newman, Scott, & Gade, 1986; Lambert & Ogles, 1997). The greater the amount of inference required, the lower is interrater reliability (Shaw & Dodson, 1988). At issue are the finite quality of the behavior to be measured and determination of the specific behaviors that comprise a particular outcome. If information is not collected in a systematic way, these uncertainties and unreliabilities are incorporated into the evaluation process of the student. Ideally, multiple sources of input are used to assess the same dimension, such as the trainee's development as a therapist. When looking at client outcomes, Cone (2001) advocated measurement of multiple aspects of the client constructs, to gauge their relative effectiveness.

Multirater feedback is commonplace in business, where ratings are often obtained from a complete circle (360 degrees) of viewpoints, including those of peers, managers, clients, and direct reports (Sala & Dwight, 2002). There is evidence that such feedback is important in increasing self-awareness of performance (J. R. Williams & Johnson, 2000). Self-monitoring and self-rating are of questionable validity, because they have very low correlations with others' perceptions. In contrast, peer, direct-report, and managerial ratings correlate moderately (Sala & Dwight, 2002). J. R. Williams and Johnson (2000) found self-ratings to be higher (i.e., more lenient) than ratings by supervisors. However, the high self-ratings in one study were only in the domains of relationships with clients (e.g., understanding, communication, and trust) and in problem-solving-oriented behaviors (Church, 1997). Clients also rated more highly in these areas. And the greater the agreement in these areas for a given observer group, the higher were the overall performance ratings of that group, especially with respect to creativity (Church, 1997). Researchers concluded that different types of competencies might be best analyzed by different types of assessment; thus, multirater surveys are most desirable (Church, 1997; Sala & Dwight, 2002).

However, there is also evidence that the more individuals seek feedback, through inquiry about their comparative performance, by monitoring or covertly comparing their own performance with that of others, and by assessing how others respond to them, the more congruent self-ratings are to supervisory ratings. Individuals who seek less feedback have less congruence between self-ratings and supervisory ratings (J. R. Williams & Johnson, 2000). In fact, J. R. Williams and Johnson (2000) found monitoring to be associated with higher congruence between self-ratings and supervisor ratings. No such results were found for inquiry, and monitoring occurred more frequently than inquiry. An association has been shown between managerial self-awareness, vis-à-vis ratings agreement, and enhancement in managerial performance (Church, 1997) and between self-monitoring and job-related interpersonal effectiveness (Warech, Smither, Reilly, Millsap, & Reilly, 1998). A high convergence between 360-degree ratings and self-ratings is conceptualized as self-awareness (Church, 1997). However, these results are from supervisory relationships in business. While they should be considered with caution, they provide an interesting entrée into training-performance analysis. Falender and Shafranske (2004) consider applications of 360-degree feedback to psychology training.

RUBRICS

As an alternative, and in conjunction with the accreditation standards of many programs, Hanna and Smith (1998) proposed development of a rubric for performance assessment. A rubric is defined as a quantitative method for assessment of students' performance targets in light of agreed-on standards. Because of the need to evaluate performance, as well as theoretical and technical skills, the rubric allows for assessment with specific standards, anchors, and defined levels of performance for various training levels. Hanna and Smith (1998) described the need to clearly describe each dimension to be evaluated; in addition, a scale and very specific examples of achievement at each level must be provided. In a sample scoring rubric, they defined the competency of "establishing counseling relationship" and assigned the highest rating, 5, to performance described as follows: "At least

97% of the time, makes a conscious effort to use the core conditions of counseling: empathy, unconditional positive regard, genuineness, and concreteness/intentionality" (Hanna & Smith, 1998, p. 276). They assigned the lowest rating, 1, to, performance described as, "has significant difficulty exhibiting a knowledge of, or a use of (the same previously mentioned) core conditions" (Hanna & Smith, 1998, p. 276). Advantages of rubrics are that they can be individually tailored to reflect the particular competencies of an individual program, can be scaled, and allow evaluation of inter-rater reliability.

EVALUATION, SUPERVISORY RATINGS, AND SUPERVISION SATISFACTION

There is some evidence that supervisees who rate their supervisory experiences more highly are evaluated more highly by their supervisor (Kennard et al., 1987). Factors such as strength of the emotional bond between supervisor and supervisee may be indicative of whether supervisees like their supervisors, as in Ladany, Ellis, et al.'s (1999) study, in which a relationship was found between emotional bond, positive perceptions of supervisors' personal qualities, and positive judgment of one's own behavior in supervision, all of which were associated with greater comfort in supervision. "Liking" one's supervisor may be related to the whole evaluative process and may be even stronger if rating scales completed by supervisors are the exclusive means of evaluating.

However, it may be that the most effective supervision is not the most satisfying supervision (Ladany, Ellis, et al., 1999). In other words, supervisors who give serious feedback may not be among a trainee's favorites, at least at the time that the feedback is given. More research is needed on effective feedback and how it relates to other variables of client outcome, supervisee satisfaction, supervisee developmental level, and supervisee progress.

POTENTIAL FORMAL MODELS FOR COMPETENCY-BASED SUMMATIVE EVALUATION

Individual, goal-centered evaluations may be developed for use by supervisors and trainees in live or videotaped sessions. In a Microcounseling paradigm, Daniels, Rigazio-Diglio, and Ivey (1997) outlined a process of training that we believe has a built-in evaluation component that results from the definition of baseline levels of functioning with predetermined criteria levels. Training behaviors are shaped through development of a common language and the use of modeling, self-observation, and copious feedback from the supervisor. A hierarchy of skills is a developmental sequence that the counselor needs to accrue, passing from the basic skill of attending to the highest skill of individualizing a personal style and theory. However, it has been pointed out that use of direct confrontation and self-disclosure may be culturally dystonic (M. T. Brown & Landrum-Brown, 1995), causing discomfort that could be avoided by use of a less confrontational, less demanding style until rapport is established.

EVALUATION OR LACK OF SUCH AS AN ETHICAL ISSUE

Ethical considerations, addressed more fully in chapter 7, this volume, are critical for consideration in evaluation. It may be difficult for trainees, who are dependent on their supervisors for evaluation, letters of recommendation to their schools, and future employment, to be honest in feedback regarding supervisor weaknesses or deficiencies. Although supervisees perceive supervisory ethical lapses (Ladany, Lehrman-Waterman, et al., 1999), counterproductive events in supervision (Gray et al., 2001), and conflict (Moskowitz & Rupert, 1983), they may be reluctant to give feedback on these issues. When collecting feedback on supervisory performance from supervisees, the reports should therefore be viewed tentatively.

Evaluating supervisees ex post facto in areas not clearly defined from the onset violates their due-process and informed-consent rights (Forrest et al., 1999). For example, intrapersonal functioning is a frequently cited area of supervisee difficulty; however, almost half of the programs in one survey did not routinely evaluate in that area (Olkin & Gaughen, 1991), nor is it likely that most programs indicate their intention to do so. An exception is the Professional Counseling Performance Evaluation, which includes such areas as maturity, competence, and integrity and has items on self-control, honesty, fairness, and respect (Kerl, Garcia, McCullough, & Maxwell, 2002). Effectiveness of an individual in the role of supervisee is an area often only implicitly evaluated (Vespia et al., 2002). Supervisees are frequently unclear as to whether their supervisors discuss the supervisory relationship or simply solicit supervisee feedback (Kurpius et al., 1991). McCarthy et al. (1994) found that 48% of their sample said that the supervisor–supervisee relationship was rarely discussed; 27% said it was never discussed.

ADMISSION CRITERIA

Whether there should be requisite fitness or character-trait requirements for admission to psychology training and licensure programs is controversial. In contrasting psychology's stance with admission to the bar, which has requirements of good moral character and fitness, Johnson and Campbell (2002) stated that there is no mention of such character or fitness requirement in psychology accreditation guidelines (American Psychological Association, 2002e), nor do programs interview specifically for those domains. They urged that fitness requirements be developed and proposed inclusion of psychological stability, integrity, personality adjustment, responsible use of substances, prudence, and caring as additional requirements.

REMEDIATION

As mentioned at the beginning of this chapter, evaluation may precipitate a process of remediation; in a very small number of extreme problem cases, evaluation precipitates due-process steps leading up to dismissal. Much of the literature refers to such students as "impaired." However, it is better to use a different identifier, so as to distinguish such supervisees from designation in the Americans With Disabilities Act (ADA) categorizations of "impairment." ADA impairment refers to "any mental or psychological disorder such as mental retardation, organic brain syndrome, emotional or mental illness, and specific learning disabilities." Disability is defined as "a physical or mental impairment that substantially limits one or more of the major life activities of an individual" (Americans With Disabilities Act of 1990, 42 U.S.C. §12102(2)(A)), has a record of such, or is regarded as having such an impairment (U.S. EEOC, 1992, p. I-3; Bruyere, 2002).

In this book, we use the designation "trainee with problematic behavior" to describe trainees who are not meeting set performance criteria. If a trainee meets criteria for disability under the ADA, reasonable accommodations are required. However, "[e]ven when an applicant/intern/postdoc claims he/she is a qualified disabled person, entitled to protection under the Rehabilitation Act or ADA, the internship/program site has no obligation to do so, unless the applicant/intern/postdoc also shows he/she can perform the essential functions of his/her position, with or without reasonable accommodation" (Mitnick, 2002).

TRAINEE WITH PROBLEMATIC BEHAVIOR

Identification of problematic qualities is a major training issue. First, there is the problem of lack of congruence between a program's established evaluation criteria and processes for identifying problematic aspects of students' behavior (Forrest et al., 1999). In addition, definition of "problematic" varies from program to program and even within the same setting, depending on the criteria used (Forrest et al., 1999). Hahn and Molnar (1991) found that "evaluation procedure at 8 of 33 institutions (surveyed) had failed at the most gross level—that of distinguishing the unacceptable candidates for graduation from the acceptable ones" (p. 415).

Overholser and Fine (1990) distinguish types of professional incompetence due to lack of knowledge, inadequate clinical skills, deficient technical skills, poor judgment, and disturbing interpersonal attributes.

Lamb et al. (1991) defined impairment (what we refer to as "problematic behavior") in a training context as

> [a]n interference in professional functioning that is reflected in one or more of the following ways: (a) an inability or unwillingness to acquire and integrate professional standards into one's repertoire of professional behavior; (b) an inability to acquire professional skills to reach an acceptable level of competency; (c) an inability to control personal stress, psychological dysfunction and/or excessive emotional reactions that may affect professional functioning. (pp. 291–292)

They defined unethical behavior on the part of supervisees and impairment (or a problematic quality) as overlapping concepts: "All unethical behaviors are a reflection of impairment, whereas impairment may involve other aspects of professional behavior that may or may not eventuate in unethical behavior" (p. 292). However, these authors pointed out the importance of ensuring that the program itself abides by ethical practices, such as providing training on the topics covered on the evaluation, ensuring due process, and using timely evaluation procedures (Lamb et al., 1991).

In the controversy over definitions of incompetent, problematic, and unethical, Forrest et al. (1999) concluded that an all-encompassing, broad definition of the student with problematic performance is difficult "because some unethical and incompetent professional behavior may not be the result of diminished professional functioning but rather an inability to reach a minimal acceptable standard of professional functioning" (p. 632). Thus, they concluded that a subset of individuals considered as problematic may *never* have met acceptable clinical or ethical standards of practice, but this condition was not identified during their training.

Competent and problematic trainees were further differentiated by Lamb et al. (1986):

> (a) The [problematic] intern does not acknowledge, understand, or address the problem when it is identified, (b) the problem is not merely a reflection of a skill deficit that can be rectified by academic or didactic training, (c) the quality of services delivered by the intern is consistently negatively affected, (d) the problem is not restricted to one area of professional functioning, (e) a disproportionate amount of attention by training personnel is required, and/or (f) the intern's behavior does not

change as a function of feedback, remediation efforts, and/or time. (p. 599)

Even with intensive remediation efforts, change is not observed.

The number of trainees with problematic behavior annually ranges from 3.3% (Olkin & Gaughen, 1991; 54% return rate) to 4.2% or 4.8%, and 66% of programs reported at least one such intern in the past 5 years (Boxley, Drew, & Rangel, 1986 [29% return rate]; Forrest et al., 1999). Areas that may lead to remediation include ethical violation, psychopathology, poor academic performance, inadequate therapy (clinical) skills, inadequate assessment skills, poor clinical judgment, poor interpersonal skills, problematic response to supervision, poor theoretical skills, and immaturity (Biaggio, Gasparikova-Krasnec, & Bauer, 1983; Forrest et al., 1999; Olkin & Gaughen, 1991). Procidano et al. (1995) found that 89% of departments in graduate programs reported at least one instance of nonacademic, professional deficiency in the past 5 years with, the majority of failings being limited clinical skills and personality or emotional problems.

In Mearns and Allen's (1991) investigation of difficulties that graduate students experience having to deal with peers' problematic behavior (response rate 30% for students and 18% for faculty), 95% of psychology graduate student respondents reported having been aware of some serious problematic qualities in a peer that interfered with professional functioning. Faculty underestimated how many graduate students confronted their peers and the intensity of student emotional response (e.g., worry, sorrow, or guilt) and overestimated how many students did nothing about the problems. In fact, many problematic trainees come to faculty attention through peer report or community field placement or internship-site supervisors, especially when the problems are in the area of intra- or interpersonal functioning (Olkin & Gaughen, 1991).

The immediate concerns with trainee problematic behavior are the potential for harm to clients (Frame & Stevens-Smith, 1995) and to the public and the potential for violation of the ethical standard of nonmaleficence. There is concern that in states which have abolished their oral exam, one level of screening has been removed, placing greater onus on supervisors in practicum, internship, and post-doctoral programs to identify trainees who exhibit problematic behavior.

The percentage of practicing psychologists with significant problematic issues is estimated to be 15 to 27%, with 7–14% not seeking help (Wood, Klein, Cross, Lammers, & Elliott, 1985). Problematic behavior includes mental illness, sexual misconduct, burnout, substance abuse, and offenses resulting in license revocation (Laliotis & Grayson, 1985). Personal-relationship problems and work with particularly difficult clients may also result in stress and problematic qualities (Sherman & Thelen,

1998). Problematic psychologists should be distinguished from incompetent (Kutz, 1986) and unethical (Stadler, Willing, Eberhage, & Ward, 1988) professionals. Koocher and Keith-Spiegel (1998) estimated that almost half of the psychologists who have had complaints filed against them appear to have a personal problem that contributed to the alleged ethical violation.

A very small percentage of Wood et al.'s (1985) sample had reported someone they perceived as a problematic colleague to a regulatory agency. It is unknown how many individuals approach their colleagues regarding perceived areas of distress or problems. It is noteworthy that the new APA ethics code (American Psychological Association, 2002a) does not contain section 1.13(b) of the 1992 code: "obligation to be alert to signs of, and obtain assistance for, their personal problems at an early stage" (Lamb, personal communication, 2002). The number of problematic psychologists who are supervisors is unknown.

Dismissal

The process leading to dismissal is variable. Biaggio et al. (1983) found that a large number of programs did not have procedures for dismissing clinical students. Boxley et al. (1986) reported that 44% of internship programs that responded to their survey (29% response rate) had no formal due-process procedures for trainees to be dismissed and no proactive approach. Another 10% of the respondents felt no need to establish such procedures. Sixty-six percent of the responding internships had no means of ensuring due process to the interns who were to be dismissed. However, Procidano et al. (1995; 32% return rate) reported that 74% of all graduate programs had a policy for responding to students' professional deficiencies. There was a relationship between having such a policy and reporting instances of such deficiencies, indicating either that the policies arose as a result of the deficiencies or that the policy facilitated their identification.

It is important to caution supervisors to focus solely on specifically describing inadequate performance or behavior rather than looking for explanatory factors. It is also important for supervisors to be aware of legal precedent in the dismissal process. Dismissed students may file suits for violation of due-process protection under the 14th Amendment of the U.S. Constitution or under provisions of other employment laws. Procedures used by supervisors may not be arbitrary, capricious, prejudicial, or discriminatory (Knoff & Prout, 1985).

Dismissal rates vary. The percentages of programs reporting at least one student being terminated have ranged from 52% (Vacha-Haase, 1995, as reported by Forrest et al., 1999) to 86% (Biaggio et al., 1983). Within the preceding 3 to 5 years, a mean of one student was reported to have been terminated from a selected number of APA-approved counseling-psychology programs (Gallessich & Olmstead, 1987, response rate 67%). According to a survey by Tedesco (1982), 51 out of 3,325 interns in APA-approved programs (63% response rate) failed to complete the training, and 89 others were considered for premature termination but did not proceed. Twenty-four interns left by their own choice, and 27 were asked to leave. Criteria for termination were unsatisfactory academic performance, lack of timely progress, failure of a course or practicum, unethical behavior, lack of interpersonal maturity, or unsatisfactory clinical performance or judgment (Biaggio et al., 1983; Gallessich & Olmstead, 1987). Tedesco's (1982) most frequent reasons were emotional instability and manifestation of a personality disorder.

Several judicial precedents provide guidance regarding dismissal criteria. Professionally related interpersonal skills are viewed to be within the academic domain (*Greenhill v. Bailey*, 1975, cited in Knoff & Prout, 1985), and remedial measures are within the domain of a program's faculty if they are relevant to identified areas of deficit (*Shuffer v. Trustees of California State University and Colleges*, 1977, cited in Knoff & Prout, 1985). In the Supreme Court decision *Board of Curators of the University of Missouri v. Horowitz* (1978), dismissal of a medical student for deficient clinical performance, peer and patient relationships, and personal hygiene was upheld. The court ruled that all rights under the 14th Amendment were sufficiently protected (Knoff & Prout, 1985). In another case, *Alanis v. University of Texas Health Sciences Center* (1992), unsuitability to practice medicine was deemed an academic reason to be dismissed from medical school (Kerl et al., 2002). The court appears to defer to schools in academic evaluation, with appropriate due process following standard academic norms (Kerl et al., 2002).

Responding to Trainee Problematic Behavior

Lamb et al. (1991) discussed a four-step model for responding to trainee problematic behavior. In Step 1, which occurs early in the evaluation process, supervisors who have identified problematic areas in trainee functioning consult to clarify their concerns. Consultations, modifications in the trainee's program, and the concerns themselves must be documented in keeping with the due-process procedure, giving the trainee ample chance to remediate the deficiencies and provide a formal reply.

If the measures in Step 1 do not result in performance improvement, additional documentation and discussion of problematic behaviors ensue, constituting Step 2. The training staff implements a full range of interventions and observes the impact. Modifications are made to the supervision procedure itself, and further elements of supervision and other interventions are added as deemed necessary. We add the institution of a remediation plan in Step 1 or, at the latest, Step 2, with specific timelines and clearly articulated performance expectations. We also advocate notification of the trainee's school at this point.

If further intervention is required, Step 3, or expulsion from the program, is considered. If probation is necessary, the intern is notified in writing. This information is shared with the academic institution as well; in general, feedback is shared with the institution and the trainee throughout the entire process. Due-process steps are followed, including the appeal-process steps if the trainee chooses to appeal. Should expulsion occur, the school and the trainee are simultaneously notified, and a process and time for departure are planned.

In Step 4, the impact of the probation or expulsion is addressed sensitively with all the remaining trainees, staff members, the academic program, and the trainee him- or herself.

PROBLEMATIC SUPERVISORS

Supervisors may also be unable to perform their functions, perhaps because of personal or external factors. Like discussion of trainees with problematic behavior, discussion of problematic supervisors contains the guiding assumption that the individual was previously functioning at a higher level of competence, as discussed by Forrest et al. (1999). Muratori (2001) proposed a continuum of ineffective supervisors from those who may be improved through guided supervision to those who are frankly problematic in one of the areas previously articulated for trainees. Muratori (2001) suggested that the danger factor is grave for trainees with problematic supervisors, because of the power differential and the fact that the supervisees may be trapped in the supervisory relationship, with no options. We suggest that, because this topic is such a new area of discussion, the supervisee working with a problematic supervisor carries a greater burden than the supervisor working with a problematic supervisee, as there typically are no established procedures or guidelines to follow in the former case and because of the power differential.

PREVENTION OF PROBLEMATIC BEHAVIOR

Coster and Schwebel (1997) proposed ways for psychologists who believe they are experiencing symptoms of difficulty to proceed. These methods should also be useful in the longer range prevention of problematic symptoms in supervisees and supervisors. The suggested interventions include interpersonal support from people such as peers, spouse, companions, family, and friends and intrapersonal activities such as self-awareness monitoring. The latter might include reduction of workload, increase of leisure activities, increase of sleep, and heightening of awareness of the professional life cycle. Other interventions are professional and civic activity and activism and self-care, including forms of professional involvement. Coster and Schwebel (1997) posed a series of questions for psychologists who have identified themselves as being at risk of or on the road to severely problematic behavior. These questions elicit responses about the progression from rigorous self-awareness or metacognitive skills to assistance by peers and consultation with a therapist (Coster & Schwebel, 1997). It is essential that supervisees receive training to ensure proactive awareness, prevention, and self-monitoring of dysfunction. Guy and Norcross (1998) provide an excellent self-care checklist.

Lamb (1999) suggested that more effective identification and negotiation of professional boundary dilemmas in the training setting would serve as a preventative strategy in some instances of problematic behavior. These approaches would include a comprehensive orientation, with social networking, bonding opportunities, and general provision of a supportive environment; distribution of specific written guidelines about performance expectations and their relationship to problematic behavior; provision of open avenues for challenging evaluations or dealing with boundary issues; seminars on self-help and stressors, including means of dealing with the stressors; guidelines for addressing boundary dilemmas; and opportunities to identify and address boundary issues through role-playing or other means.

Slimp and Burian (1994) outlined steps that could be taken to prevent ethical violations. They suggested that organizations establish an internal ethics committee comprising both interns and staff. They also urged either having an ethics consultant who is unaffiliated with the program, using the local or APA ethics committee, or establishing policies and procedures that address how to consult the ethics committee and for what reasons it may be consulted, procedures for remediation and sanctions, guidelines that address whether recommendations of the committee are binding, and methods by which formal actions would follow.

REMEDIATION

The Association for Counselor Education and Supervision (1995) provided a guideline regarding remediation:

> 2.12. Supervisors, through ongoing supervisee assessment and evaluation, should be aware of any personal or professional limitations of supervisees which are likely to impede future professional performance.

Supervisors have the responsibility of recommending remedial assistance to the supervisee and of screening from the training program, applied counseling setting, or state licensure those supervisees who are unable to provide competent professional services. These recommendations should be clearly and professionally explained in writing to the supervisees who are so evaluated.

Olkin and Gaughen (1991) strongly recommended that reactivity be replaced with proactivity in dealing with problem students. Ideally, this task includes establishing, at the onset of training, clear contracts with supervisees about policies and expectation, articulation and operationalization of expected behaviors, and routine evaluation and feedback on the articulated requirements.

It has been suggested that the training years are prime for identification and amelioration of problems. Psychologists believe strongly in remediation. Behaviors become problematic only when not addressed and when they persist in severity (Vasquez, 1988). Through monitoring and evaluation, case-load modifications, intensive interventions such as live observation, cotherapy with the supervisor, required supplemental courses, and leaves of absence (Lamb et al., 1987), some remediation can occur. Goal setting and provision of more frequent feedback are steps that could be instituted to enhance the working alliance (Lehrman-Waterman & Ladany, 2001). Personal therapy and additional clinical field experiences are other options (Knoff & Prout, 1985). However, although repeating coursework and personal therapy are the frequent forms of remediation, Olkin and Gaughen (1991) cautioned that therapy goals and timelines may be unclear or undesignated, and the program does not set them. Instead, the student and his or her therapist do. Furthermore, because of confidentiality, the program will not be privy to the trainee's progress or lack of such.

It is not clear that therapy is the remediation of choice for academic or clinical functioning problems (Olkin & Gaughen, 1991). In the case of remediating trainee sexual misconduct, Layman and McNamara (1997) expressed concern that the low rates of sexually offending trainees preclude the real possibility of a significant impact of early identification and intervention during the training years. Conditions such as alcoholism might be more evident during internship, as a retrospective analysis revealed that psychologists in recovery reported they had exhibited harmful effects from drinking as early as age twenty-four (Skorina, Bissell, & DeSoto, 1990), which would in many cases be during graduate training.

Training programs must establish specific steps to remediate trainee problematic functioning. Risk factors are implicit in the internship year (Kaslow & Rice, 1985; Lamb et al., 1987; Lipovsky, 1988). Directors and supervisors in internship programs know that the cycle of the training year is fraught with peril regarding intern stress, potential for burnout or fatigue, and general vulnerability (Lamb et al., 1982). Besides the due-process steps and action plans with timelines, supportive relationships with training staff, and monitoring of progress, a strength-based orientation with an emphasis on small increments of improvement is indicated. It is also note-worthy that there may be differences in perception between trainees and supervisors as far as the degree of supportiveness of the training environment, with faculty perceiving the training environment to be highly supportive and supervisees feeling unsupported. This possibility warrants further exploration.

Wise, Lowery, and Silverglade (1989) described remediation methods that focus on skill development, workshops, supervision groups, consultation, and continuing-education experiences. However, if there is still a need to deal with specific issues or if skill development is blocked by personal issues, they urged suggesting personal counseling. They identified the periods of time before seeing clients and when the individual's identity as a therapist has been partially established and he or she is gaining greater insight as optimal times for referral.

EVALUATION OF THE SUPERVISOR

Providing feedback to the supervisor regarding his or her performance should be an integral part of the evaluation process. In fact, Sherry (1991) proposed that, as part of supervisory competence assessment, all supervisees should evaluate their supervision and provide feedback to supervisors, prog-ress toward supervisory contract goals should be reviewed regularly, and supervision of supervisors should be provided. In addition, supervisors should self-assess, taking into account success, failures, and areas in which they feel they could improve or grow. However, any type of evaluation of the supervisor has been relatively neglected in the literature (Dendinger & Kohn, 1989). Logically, it appears that multisource evaluations are indicated, including self-evaluations and evaluations by the supervisor of the supervisor, fellow supervisors, supervisees, and individuals outside the agency who can give an expert assessment of the supervisor's skill base (Dendinger & Kohn, 1989). (It has been suggested that supervisors be evaluated by supervisees on relationship, agreement levels, knowledge, and communication and that administrators might evaluate productivity, error rate, and complaints [as reported by Dendinger & Kohn, 1989]). There are a number of evaluation instruments for this purpose, including "Supervision Satisfaction Question-naire" (Ladany, Hill, Corbett, & Nutt, 1996), "Supervisee Perceptions of

Supervision" (Olk & Friedlander, 1992), and "Supervisee/Trainee Self Assessment of Supervision-Related Knowledge and Skills" (Borders & Leddick, 1987). The Ladany, Hill, Corbett, and Nutt (1996) form addresses overall satisfaction without eliciting specific feedback about areas where less satisfaction is indicated. The Olk and Friedlander (1992) form found in Appendix H combines supervisees' perceptions of supervision with assessments of the level of uncertainty elicited. The best form for gathering feedback specific to particular tasks is that provided by Borders and Leddick (1987; see Appendix G), which breaks down items into teaching, counseling, consultation, and research-skills components. Another form, developed by Hall-Marley (personal communication; and modified by Falender in Appendix L), is linked to overall expectations for supervisee competencies. Another measure developed by Hall-Marley (personal communication; see Appendix K) gathers supervisor feedback that can be organized to coordinate with program goals and the training contract.

Herrmann (1996) developed a three-part format for evaluation of supervisors in medical education. In the first part, a critical-incident approach is used to determine the number of hours the supervisee had spent per week with the supervisor, the number of live or taped interviews with the supervisor in the past six months, and the number of times detailed feedback about progress was received. In the second section, residents rate supervisors on enthusiasm, organization, clarity, knowledge, clinical supervision skills, availability, and modeling ability, with descriptive factors listed to guide the rating (e.g., factors on role modeling; regular feedback and constructive criticism; and sensitivity to gender, ethical, cultural, and SES [socio-economic status] issues). Residents assign an overall rating to the supervisor, using a 5-point Likert scale with a range from poor to excellent. Finally, in the third part, residents have a chance to provide narrative comments on the supervisor's strengths, major weaknesses, and possible areas of improvement of supervision quality. Herrmann (1996) found that having residents return the forms to the program office, with a cover sheet identifying the resident (which was removed and destroyed once the form was checked in), as a requirement for completion of the rotation dramatically increased the number of evaluations returned. The large size of the training program allowed anonymity. Generally, very positive outcomes resulted from feedback given to supervisors. In another format adopted by Ramsbottom-Lucier, Gillmore, Irby, and Ramsey (1994), residents evaluated their clinical supervisors on knowledge and analytic ability, accessibility, establishment of rapport, organization and clarity, enthusiasm, involvement of learner, feedback and direction, and demonstration of clinical skills, using a 6-point Likert scale. Residents also rated their perceived degree of involvement with their supervisors on a 4-point scale. Reliability scores were high, especially in outpatient settings.

PROGRAM EVALUATION

Although it would seem to be a high-priority area, little attention is devoted to program evaluation outside of the self-study that evaluates self-imposed criteria. Norcross and Stevenson (1984) found that the major factors used by training directors of doctoral programs to evaluate the programs were the quality of internships the students attained and feedback from internship supervisors. Another important measure was quantitative evaluation of supervisors by supervisees. Some efforts have been made to compare groups of trainees under different conditions of training (Aronson, Akamatsu, & Page, 1982) and to monitor acquisition of particular skills deemed requisite to psychology training (e.g., empathy). Methodological issues such as the need for more sophisticated instruments possibly beyond paper and pencil, context–specific issues, and assessment of impact on client outcome have been raised as future directions for program evaluation.

SUMMARY

In conclusion, the area of evaluation is central to the training of psychologists. As Robiner, Saltzman, Hoberman, Semrud-Clikeman, et al. (1997) summarized,

> Evaluation requires judgments about supervisees' capability for exercising appropriate clinical judgment and their level of clinical proficiency. Administrative determinations of supervisees' ability to proceed to more advanced stages of training and ultimately to achieve autonomy in clinical activities are based on supervisory evaluations. (p. 50)

The competencies necessary to do a creditable job entail the ability to create self-assessments, performance assessments, and competency-based evaluations and to provide formative and summative evaluation. A number of tools have been cited that pave the way for more comprehensive formative evaluation and feedback. A competent supervisor must weave evaluation considerations, feedback, and formal evaluation into the supervisory relationship.

Competencies

The competencies in the area of evaluation of the supervisory process are as follows:

- Ability to administer a format for assessment of incoming supervisees, to identify their strengths and areas that need improvement, as well as a plan for their development during the training period

- Ability to construct a supervision contract
- Ability to construct tools to assess the supervisee's performance and behavior during the training sequence
- Skill at self-assessment for oneself and for administering self-assessment measures for the supervisee
- Skill at providing formative and summative feedback on an ongoing basis
- Skill at eliciting feedback about oneself from supervisees and using this feedback

9

THE EVOLVING PRACTICE OF
CLINICAL SUPERVISION

Our study of supervision leads to the conclusion that the landscape of supervision is changing. We have been impressed by the range of competencies that are required to provide quality supervision. These competencies include not only the knowledge and skills of a clinician, educator, supervisor, and consultant, but also a host of personal and interpersonal qualities. The requisite competencies to perform supervision will continue to evolve in step with developments in professional psychology, the needs of an increasingly diverse populace, continuing changes in the nature of service delivery, and the requirements of accountability in assessing the competence of supervisees and outcomes of their clients. Supervision is at the center of these developments.

Our intent is to distinguish supervision from clinical practice and to elevate its status as a unique specialty, which requires education and training, and receives adequate administrative support. Supervision is a distinct specialty area and deserves recognition as such. It is our hope that our work will contribute to the legitimatization of the field of supervision and increase interest in competency articulation and development through the introduction of an appropriate methodology.

This volume has intended to provide a conceptual, research-based, and scholarly foundation on which to consider advances in the practice of clinical supervision. We have made recommendations and provided conceptual and assessment tools to assist in putting these ideas to work. We have placed an emphasis on the integration of theory and practice, with attention to evaluation at all steps in the process. Integrity-in-relationship, ethical values-based practice, appreciation for diversity, and science-informed practice were identified as superordinate values, informing the practice of both psychotherapy and supervision. We have also advocated the use of a competency-based approach to supervision, because such an educational model complements the goals of supervision and readily supports empirical study. With increased understanding of the supervisory process, the ideas and approaches presented may be applied in the local clinical supervisory setting. Programs of development require tailoring to the specific needs and unique characteristics of a particular training clinic, hospital, agency, program, or university. Initiatives to improve supervisory practice require commitment at each level in the system—i.e., institution, clinical faculty, and individual supervisor—to support program development. Such initiatives taken at the individual or institutional level reflect professional values and commitment to competent supervision practice.

IMMEDIATE OPPORTUNITIES AND CHALLENGES

Opportunities and challenges exist no matter how high the present quality of clinical training and supervision provided. In keeping with the understanding that competence, by definition, can always be enhanced, individual supervisors and their institutions have an opportunity, as well as a responsibility, for continuous improvement in quality (Nelson, Batalden, & Ryer, 1998). In addition to the ongoing development of competence as individuals (described in chap. 3, this volume), in diversity (described in chap. 6, this volume), and in ethics and legal applications (described in chap. 7, this volume), training institutions can initiate programs, tailored to their unique local situation, to systematically enhance supervisor competence. Practice improvement models (PIMs) that have been developed to improve the quality of clinical practice and influence clinician behavior may be appropriated to enhance supervision competencies.

Cape and Barkham (2002) identified the following methods for improving clinical practice: training workshops, clinical supervision, clinical guidelines, evidence-based clinical methods, practice-based methods, clinical audit, outcomes monitoring and management, outcomes benchmarking, and continuous quality improvement (pp. 285–286). Of these approaches, training workshops, supervision of clinical supervision, supervision guidelines, practice-based methods, and outcomes monitoring offer particularly useful strategies in the enhancement of the practices of clinical supervision at the local level. Workshops and in-service training seminars, particularly those that use experiential rather than just didactic methods, offer straightforward approaches to training and professional development. Ongoing peer supervision and review, as per APA's Ethical Guidelines for Clinical Supervisors (Association for Counselor Education and Supervision, 1995), provide a means for formative feedback and offer learning opportunities for each of the participants. Provision of ongoing supervision and support for all levels of supervisors is an intervention that will strengthen practice. Supervision guidelines such as those presented in this text provide tools to orient the process to particularly salient content areas in supervision, such as cultural or diversity competency (American Psychological Association, 1993a, 2000, 2002b). Clinical guidelines offer the advantage of simplicity and, when well developed, "focus attention on areas of agreement about appropriate practice, whether based on research evidence or consensus" (Cape & Barkham, 2002, p. 291).

Practice-based methods are focused directly on the practices of the clinician or, in this case, the supervisor. The implementation of supervisor self-report measures in conjunction with supervision guidelines and objective analysis of supervisor behavior, as illustrated in Milne and James's (2002) competency-based model of supervision (see chap. 1, this volume), as well as elaborate self-assessment (see chap. 3, this volume; Belar et al., 2001) provide tools to improve supervisor behaviors. Monitoring and management directly relate to the assessment of supervisory outcomes. Presently, most assessment procedures rely on supervisee self-reports of competence and satisfaction with supervision, which do not actually measure outcomes in either client progress or the development of clinical competencies. Assessments of outcome can be conducted by observing skills demonstrated in therapy sessions and through client response measures (Lambert & Hawkins, 2001).

Benchmarks can also be used to assess competence. Levels of competence can be operationalized and specific benchmarks of behavior defined. Supervisor effectiveness can then be evaluated, in part, by the benchmarks achieved by the supervisee during the course of training. Such a method complements the competency-based approach to supervision, in which specific components of competency are identified, training goals are defined, and procedures for assessing performance objectives are established. It is anticipated that that the use of multiple PIMs is more likely to affect supervisor behavior and supervisee and patient outcomes than the use of a singular intervention strategy. We advocate that individuals and programs self-assess their competence at supervision in general and in each of the prescribed areas (e.g., personal factors, diversity, ethics and legal, and evaluation) and begin to build on existing structures to enhance program functioning.

We draw on Cape and Barkham's (2002) recommendations for clinical-practice improvement in our consideration of steps to ensure continuous improvement in supervision:

Improvement Cycle. Individual supervisors and clinical faculty teams would benefit from taking an integrated approach to practice improvement, starting from a clear idea about what areas of clinical and supervisory practice need to be improved. Areas of practice where the individual or team believes they are weak or where there have been new developments are a good place to start. Plans for practice improvement in the chosen area that include focus on all three stages—process guidance, process monitoring, and outcomes management—are likely to have the greatest impact.

Process Guidance. There is a need for development of clinical and supervisory practice guidelines focused on skillful practice of interventions and supervision approach over time. Workshops and peer supervision and review can be used to support the implementation of guidelines.

Process Monitoring. Structured process-monitoring methods need to be developed for key aspects of interventions that, when fed back, can prompt adjustments to supervision and clinical practice. This factor provides formative evaluation and allows for reflection-in-action to affect the improvement cycle.

Outcomes Management. The range of methods composing outcomes management needs to be standardized and owned by supervisors so that it is consistent with a bottom-up approach in which empirical data are viewed on par with clinical wisdom.[1]

Clinical supervision programs can ensure systematic, continuous improvement through the use of collaborative initiatives in which skills developed as clinical scientists are applied to program development.

In addition to formal methods of improving supervisory practice, we suggest that the development of reflective and reflexive skills, as discussed in Chapter 1, this volume contributes to both the supervisor's and supervisee's ability to make metacognitive observations and to perform self-assessment. These skills are particularly important in monitoring the supervisory working alliance and in applying the superordinate values of integrity-in-relationship, ethical values-based practice, appreciation for diversity, and science-informed practice.

These values, in our view, are critical to clinical and supervisory practices in professional psychology. As important as these values are, how-

[1]From "Practice Improvement Methods: Conceptual Base, Evidence-Based Research, and Practice-Based Recommendations," by J. Cape and M. Barkham, 2002, *British Journal of Clinical Psychology,* 41, pp. 285–307. Copyright 2002 by the British Psychological Society. Reprinted with permission.

ever, their full expression in the supervisory relationship requires thoughtful and deliberate attention. Supervisors may assume that there is integrity in the relationship, because there are no breaches or boundary violations. However, subtle affirmations or detractions influence the full development of integrity in the relationship, which will support and enhance the supervisory working alliance. For example, consistently being on time or fully attending to a supervisee's exploration of an issue rather than simply offering a suggestion affects the relationship's integrity. Similarly, appreciation of diversity requires consistent attention and skill, particularly if one aims for a comprehensive understanding of the ever present influence of culture rather than a superficial and stereotypic assessment of the role of ethnicity in treatment. Attention to these values, as well as to faithfully fulfilling each of the responsibilities of a supervisor (i.e., case management, teaching, consultation, supervision, and evaluation), contributes to values-based ethical practice. Maintenance of boundaries with respect to overt behavior, the subtlety of attraction, respectfulness in the use of authority, avoidance of inappropriate dual relationships of any kind, including conducting psychotherapy in the guise of supervision, supports ethical practice. Further, as a values-based relationship, supervision can provide the experience of a host of human values—genuineness, empathy, commitment to another's welfare, and fidelity to professionalism and to the highest standards of client care, to name a few. Also, values are expressed in facilitating the development of competencies by identifying talents that will become strengths, rather than focusing on weaknesses and creating an environment composed solely of criticism. Respect infused throughout the program goes a long way toward creating an environment in which evaluation can be accepted and integrated. The task of integrating science and practice requires that a trusting collaborative relationship be formed that will allow for application of evidence-based practices and a scientific perspective to the analysis of the psychotherapy and supervisory processes.

LOOKING TO THE FUTURE

Supervision practices are at the front line of efforts to train practitioners to address the needs of an increasingly diverse population within health care systems that are continuing to reshape the nature of service delivery. Psychologists, more than ever before, must be able to apply their clinical skills in novel ways within the changing clinical landscape. Clinical competencies viewed as knowledge, skills, and values, which are uniquely assembled to address the needs of the local clinical situation, provide a useful orientation. Supervisors can enhance this perspective by focusing on the portability of competencies rather than orienting training in a parochial manner, which focuses learning exclusively on how to conduct a particular form of treatment. Norcross and Halgin (1997), in presenting an approach to integrative approaches to supervision, opined, "The emphasis should be placed squarely on 'how to think' rather than on 'what to think.' This modified focus engenders informed pluralism and self-evolving clinical styles, in contrast to young disciples or mindless imitators" (p. 218). Plato differentiated two classes of doctors, the slave doctors, who "acquire their knowledge of medicine by obeying and observing their masters" and "never talk to their patients individually, [merely prescribing] what mere experience suggests," and the true doctors, "who have learned scientifically[,] . . . attend[ing] and practic[ing] on freemen[,] . . . [carrying their] enquires far back and [going] into the nature of the disorder" (as cited in Jackson, 1999, p. 41). Supervision endeavors to instill reflective professional practice (Schön, 1983, 1987) and the perspective of a clinical scientist, which requires the ability to know how to think clinically. Supervision must also be responsive to developments in psychology (Norcross, Hedges, & Prochaska, 2002), such as advances in empirically supported treatments (Addis, 2002), changes in the roles of psychologists to include facets of primary health-care provision (R. T. Brown et al., 2002), the inclusion of psychopharmacology, and innovation in science-based practice (Beutler, 2000).

The practice of clinical supervision requires further investigation to ensure the development of effective methods, particularly with respect to the integration of science and practice, the integration of legal and ethical considerations into all levels, the development of cultural and diversity competency, and formative and summative evaluation, leading to benchmarks of competency. An empirical, evidence-based, theoretical foundation is required. As with other competencies, training in supervision will best occur through coordinated articulation between graduate education and clinical training experiences, through which knowledge, skills, and attitudes are assembled, leading to competent practice. We need not be bewildered by the changing clinical landscape; new perspectives can lead supervisors to look forward to ever expanding opportunities to contribute to the professional development of the next generation of psychologists who will serve the community.

APPENDIX A
Sample Supervision Contract Outlin

The Sample Supervision Contract Outline is designed to illustrate dimensions that could be included in such a document. It is organized with sections to represent definition of supervisor roles, definition of supervisee roles, and definition of the relationship. Development of such a contract serves an important role in the development of the relationship and supervisory alliance. Furthermore, it serves a significant role in invocation of the role of the supervisee by clearly defining the expectations and parameters the supervisor requires. This document is intended to be an example. Individual programs will develop contracts to correspond to their specific settings and requirements. The contract was developed by Falender in 2003.

This is an agreement between _____ (Supervisee)

and _____ (Supervisor and Agency/Setting).

Effective Dates: _____

The purpose of supervision is (e.g., to meet requirements for internship,

to prepare the supervisee for licensure) _____

_____

- **Clear definition of what the supervisor will provide to the setting (which will be included in a supervision contract during the first two weeks of the supervision period).**
  - Frequency, length, duration, and type of supervision to be provided (specify individual or group) and attendance requirement.
  - Specific areas of supervisory competence (please define), including educational and supervisory experience and multicultural competence.
    - Supervisor will be respectful of and address cultural and diversity differences in the supervisor–supervisee–client(s) triad.
  - Supervision model(s) and theories, including the developmental model.

233

- Theoretical orientation(s) directing interventions.
- How client assignments are made.
- Expectation that the supervisor will focus on professional development, learning and teaching, mentoring, and the personal development of the trainee.
  - Expectation that the relationship will include open communication and two-way feedback.
  - Expectation that the supervision will not include therapy.
  - Expectation that the supervision will include exploration of values, beliefs, interpersonal biases, and conflicts considered to be sources of countertransference in the context of case material.
- Supervision format, including role of the supervisor and expectations for the supervisee.
- Review of record keeping, including statement of deadlines for submission.
- Availability.
- Procedure for cancellation and rescheduling.
- Emergency contact procedures to follow in defined emergency situations.
- Requirement of adherence to agency, ethical, licensing, and legal codes and principles.
- Evaluation, both formative and summative, the details of which are drawn from the supervision contract and which are clearly defined, measurable, and occur at designated intervals.
  - Evaluation measures to be provided at the onset of supervision.
  - Self- and peer-assessment forms.
- Professionalism.
  - Statement that the supervisor will model professionalism.
  - Informed consent for supervisee regarding evaluation, confidentiality, due process, and grievances about the supervisee.
- Statement that the supervisor bears liability in supervision, and thus it is essential that supervisee share complete information regarding clients and files and abide by the supervisor's final decisions, as the welfare of the client is tantamount.
  - The supervisor expects the supervisee to express disagreements and differences in opinion with supervisor.
  - The supervisor expects the supervisee to discuss conflicts in the supervisory relationship.
- Attention will be addressed to personal factors such as values, belief systems, biases, conflicts, and predispositions.

- Attention will be addressed to assessment of individual learning needs at the onset of and throughout the training sequence.
- Space and resources for trainee.
- Clarification of financial arrangements.
- Malpractice insurance arrangement.

- **Clear definition of what the supervisee is expected to provide in the supervisory setting and in setting in general.**
  - Time commitments, including dates of traineeship, hours required, and attendance at supervision hours designated in advance.
  - Adherence to agency, ethical, licensing, regulatory, and legal codes and principles.
  - Adherence to specifics of codes in terms of respect for boundaries (or avoidance of multiple relationships, which could result in loss of objectivity or exploitation) with clients, staff, and others in the setting.
  - Many contracts include the stipulation of no sex with clients. We believe that such a clause is redundant; however, it is an option.
  - Disclosure of previous experience, including areas of competency.
  - Record-keeping practices, including notes to be completed before supervisory sessions and given to the supervisor to review prior to supervision. The notes are to be in compliance with APA record-keeping guidelines or other established standards.
  - Audio- and videotape requirements.
  - Productivity expectations, with specific itemization of each area—e.g., groups, families, adult, child, diversity factors, developmental levels, empirically supported models, and consultation.
  - Requirements and procedures for attendance, cancellations, and rescheduling.
  - Expected preparation for supervision sessions.
  - Attendance requirements for seminars, case conferences, and other meetings.
  - On-call responsibilities.
  - Expectation that the supervisee is to include the following in conceptualization: theoretical framework, multicultural conceptualization, empirical and research support and background, developmental considerations, and attention to differential diagnoses.

- Openness to learning as a continuous, developmental, life-long process.
- Openness and receptivity to feedback.
- Requirement that clients be informed of trainee's status as supervisee and be given the name and contact information of the supervisor.

- **Relationship.**
  - Statement that the supervisory relationship is a two-way process through which growth is enhanced and mentoring is accomplished.
  - Goals to be jointly developed for the supervisor and the trainee.
  - Expectation that the supervisor will possess skills to facilitate a positive learning relationship that encompasses respect, encourages autonomy, and enhances the training experience.
  - Expectation that the supervisee will be open to the facilitation of a positive learning relationship that encompasses respect, encourages autonomy, and enhances the training experience.
  - Expectation that attention and respect will be accorded to diversity competence within the supervisory dyad and across the client–trainee–supervisor relationship.

Signature Supervisee   Date

Signature Supervisor   Date

APPENDIX B
Working Alliance Inventory

"The Working Alliance Inventory: Supervisee and Supervisor Forms" provides useful tools to evaluate alliance factors in the supervisory relationship. Alliance and relationship factors are TASK, BOND, and GOAL, which define agreement from the supervisor and the supervisee's perspective on the tasks of supervision, the supervisory bond, and the goals of supervision. The forms are conceptually sound and are useful in enhancing communication and strengthening the supervisory alliance. However, until additional reliability and validity data are accumulated, they should not be used as definitive measures.

WORKING ALLIANCE INVENTORY: SUPERVISEE FORM

Developed by Audrey Bahrick, University of Iowa Counseling Center

Instructions: On the following pages there are sentences that describe some of the different ways a person might think or feel about his or her supervisor. As you read the sentences, mentally insert the name of your supervisor in place of _____ in the text. Beside each statement there is a seven point scale:

1	2	3	4	5	6	7
Never	Rarely	Occasionally	Sometimes	Often	Very Often	Always

If the statement describes the way you always feel (or think), circle the number "7;" if it never applies to you, circle the number "1." Use the numbers in between to describe the variations between these extremes.

Please work fast. Your first impressions are what is wanted.

1. I feel uncomfortable with _____.
2. _____ and I agree about the things I will need to do in supervision.
3. I am worried about the outcome of our supervision sessions.
4. What I am doing in supervision gives me a new way of looking at myself as a counselor.
5. _____ and I understand each other.
6. _____ perceives accurately what my goals are.

1	2	3	4	5	6	7
Never	Rarely	Occasionally	Sometimes	Often	Very Often	Always

7. I find what I am doing in supervision confusing.
8. I believe _____ likes me.
9. I wish _____ and I could clarify the purpose of our sessions.
10. I disagree with _____ about what I ought to get out of supervision.
11. I believe the time _____ and I are spending together is not spent efficiently.
12. _____ does not understand what I want to accomplish in supervision.
13. I am clear on what my responsibilities are in supervision.
14. The goals of these sessions are important to me.
15. I find what _____ and I are doing in supervision is unrelated to my concerns.
16. I feel that what _____ and I are doing in supervision will help me to accomplish the changes that I want in order to be a more effective counselor.
17. I believe _____ is genuinely concerned for my welfare.
18. I am clear as to what _____ wants me to do in our supervision sessions.
19. _____ and I respect each other.
20. I feel that _____ is not totally honest about his or her feelings toward me.
21. I am confident in _____'s ability to supervise me.
22. _____ and I are working towards mutually agreed-on goals.
23. I feel that _____ appreciates me.
24. We agree on what is important for me to work on.
25. As a result of our supervision sessions, I am clearer as to how I might improve my counseling skills.
26. _____ and I trust one another.
27. _____ and I have different ideas on what I need to work on.
28. My relationship with _____ is very important to me.
29. I have the feeling that it is important that I say or do the "right" things in supervision with _____.
30. _____ and I collaborate on setting goals for my supervision.
31. I am frustrated by the things we are doing in supervision.

1	2	3	4	5	6	7
Never	Rarely	Occasionally	Sometimes	Often	Very Often	Always

32. We have established a good understanding of the kinds of things I need to work on.
33. The things that _____ is asking me to do don't make sense.
34. I don't know what to expect as a result of my supervision.
35. I believe the way we are working with my issues is correct.
36. I believe _____ cares about me even when I do things that he or she doesn't approve of.

WORKING ALLIANCE INVENTORY: SUPERVISOR FORM

1. I feel uncomfortable with _____.
2. _____ and I agree about the things he or she needs to do in supervision.
3. I have some concerns about the outcome of our supervision sessions.
4. _____ and I both feel confident about the usefulness of our current activity in supervision.
5. _____ and I have a common perception of her or his goals in supervision.
6. I feel I really understand _____.
7. _____ finds what we are doing in supervision confusing.
8. I believe _____ likes me.
9. I sense a need to clarify the purpose of our supervision sessions for _____.
10. I have some disagreements with _____ about the goals of these sessions.
11. I believe the time _____ and I are spending together is not spent efficiently.
12. I have some doubts about what we are trying to accomplish in supervision.
13. I am clear and explicit about what _____'s responsibilities are in supervision.
14. The current goals of these sessions are important for _____.
15. I find what _____ and I are doing in supervision is unrelated to his or her concerns.

1	2	3	4	5	6	7
Never	Rarely	Occasionally	Sometimes	Often	Very Often	Always

16. I feel that what _____ and I are doing in supervision will help him or her to accomplish the changes needed for him or her to become a more effective counselor.
17. I am genuinely concerned for _____'s welfare.
18. I am clear as to what I expect _____ to do in our supervision sessions.
19. _____ and I respect each other.
20. I feel that I am not totally honest about my feelings toward _____.
21. I am confident in my ability to supervise _____.
22. _____ and I are working towards mutually agreed-on goals.
23. I appreciate _____ as a person.
24. We agree on what is important for _____ to work on.
25. As a result of our supervision sessions, _____ is clearer as to how to improve his or her counseling skills.
26. _____ and I have built a mutual trust.
27. _____ and I have different ideas on what he or she needs to work on.
28. Our relationship is important to _____.
29. _____ has some fears that I will disapprove if she or he says or does the "wrong" thing.
30. _____ and I have collaborated on setting goals for our supervision sessions.
31. _____ is frustrated by what I am asking her or him to do in supervision.
32. We have established a good understanding of the kinds of things _____ needs to work on.
33. The things that we are doing in supervision don't make much sense to _____.
34. _____ doesn't know what to expect as a result of supervision.
35. _____ believes that the way we are working with his or her issues is correct.
36. I respect _____ even when he or she does things that I don't approve of.

SCORING KEY FOR THE WORKING ALLIANCE INVENTORY
(BOTH FORMS)

TASK Scale:	2,	4,	7,	11,	13,	15,	16,	18,	24,	31,	33,	35
Polarity	+	+	−	−	+	−	+	+	+	−	−	+

BOND Scale	1,	5,	8,	17,	19,	20,	21,	23,	26,	28,	29,	36
Polarity	−	+	+	+	+	−	+	+	+	+	−	+

GOAL Scale	3,	6,	9,	10,	12,	14,	22,	25,	27,	30,	32,	34
Polarity	−	+	−	−	−	+	+	+	−	+	+	−

Note. From *Working Alliance Inventory–Training (WAI-T),* by A. Bahrick, 1989. Unpublished dissertation, Ohio State Counseling Department. Reprinted with permission of the author.

APPENDIX C
Cross-Cultural Counseling Inventory— Revised

The Cross-Cultural Counseling Inventory was designed as a supervisor report form to assess the trainee's cultural awareness by Hernandez and LaFromboise (1983). It is a 20-item, 6 point Likert scale measure developed on the basis of the cross-cultural counseling competencies as defined by the Society of Counseling Psychology (Division 17) of the American Psychological Association (D. W. Sue et al., 1982). The scale consists of items including cross-cultural counseling skill, sociopolitical awareness, and cultural sensitivity. The scale has good construct, criterion-related, and content-validity. However, the supervisor must possess good cultural competency to be an adequate rater of the trainee. LaFromboise et al. (1991) emphasized that, until it is further refined, this instrument should be used primarily as a tool in training to decrease anxiety related to cross-cultural work and for self-evaluative reflection. It is useful as a training exercise to enhance staff members' or trainees' cultural awareness and identify areas for their further education and training.

CROSS-CULTURAL COUNSELING INVENTORY—REVISED

Rating Scale: 1 = strongly disagree   4 = slightly agree
2 = disagree   5 = agree
3 = slightly disagree   6 = strongly agree

1. Counselor is aware of his or her own cultural heritage.	1	2	3	4	5	6
2. Counselor values and respects cultural differences.	1	2	3	4	5	6
3. Counselor is aware of how own values might affect this client.	1	2	3	4	5	6
4. Counselor is comfortable with differences between counselor and client.	1	2	3	4	5	6
5. Counselor is willing to suggest referral when cultural differences are extensive.	1	2	3	4	5	6

Rating Scale: 1 = strongly disagree   4 = slightly agree
                2 = disagree   5 = agree
                3 = slightly disagree   6 = strongly agree

6. Counselor understands the current socio-political system and its impact on the client.	1	2	3	4	5	6
7. Counselor demonstrates knowledge about client's culture.	1	2	3	4	5	6
8. Counselor has a clear understanding of counseling and therapy process.	1	2	3	4	5	6
9. Counselor is aware of institutional barriers which might affect client's circumstances.	1	2	3	4	5	6
10. Counselor elicits a variety of verbal and nonverbal responses from the client.	1	2	3	4	5	6
11. Counselor accurately sends and receives a variety of verbal and nonverbal messages	1	2	3	4	5	6
12. Counselor is able to suggest institutional intervention skills that favor the client.	1	2	3	4	5	6
13. Counselor sends messages that are appropriate to the communication of the client.	1	2	3	4	5	6
14. Counselor attempts to perceive the presenting problem within the context of the client's cultural experience, values, and/or lifestyle.	1	2	3	4	5	6
15. Counselor presents his or her own values to the client.	1	2	3	4	5	6
16. Counselor is at ease talking with this client.	1	2	3	4	5	6
17. Counselor recognizes those limits determined by the cultural differences between client and counselor.	1	2	3	4	5	6
18. Counselor appreciates the client's social status as an ethnic minority.	1	2	3	4	5	6
19. Counselor is aware of the professional and ethical responsibilities of a counselor.	1	2	3	4	5	6
20. Counselor acknowledges and is comfortable with cultural differences.	1	2	3	4	5	6

Note. From "Development and Factor Structure of the Cross-Cultural Counseling Inventory—Revised," by T. D. LaFromboise, H. L. K. Coleman, and A. Hernandez, 1991, *Professional Psychology: Research and Practice, 22,* 380–388. Copyright 1983 by A. Hernandez & T. D. LaFromboise. Reprinted with permission.

APPENDIX D
Multicultural Counseling Knowledge and Awareness Scale

Ponterotto's (2002) Multicultural Counseling Knowledge and Awareness Scale is a 32-item 7 point Likert scale measure of both general knowledge related to multicultural counseling and Eurocentric worldview bias. The two factors are knowledge (20 items, all positively worded) and awareness (12 items of which 10 are negatively worded). This widely used self-report instrument has been shown in preliminary studies to possess construct validity and is useful as a training tool to enhance focus on self-appraisal of multicultural counseling knowledge and awareness. However, caution is warranted in using it for individual evaluative purposes (Ponterotto, Gretchen, et al., 2002).

MULTICULTURAL COUNSELING KNOWLEDGE AND AWARENESS SCALE (MCKAS)

Using the following scale, rate the truth of each item as it applies to you:

1	2	3	4	5	6	7
Not at All True			Somewhat True			Totally True

1. I believe all clients should maintain direct eye contact during counseling.
2. I check up on my minority/cultural counseling skills by monitoring my functioning—via consultation, supervision, and continuing education.
3. I am aware some research indicates that minority clients receive "less preferred" forms of counseling treatment than majority clients.
4. I think that clients who do not discuss intimate aspects of their lives are being resistant and defensive.
5. I am aware of certain counseling techniques or approaches that are more likely to transcend culture and be effective with any clients.

1	2	3	4	5	6	7
Not at All True			Somewhat True			Totally True

6. I am familiar with the "culturally deficient" and "culturally deprived" depictions of minority mental health and understand how these labels serve to foster and perpetuate discrimination.

7. I feel all the recent attention directed toward multicultural issues in counseling is overdone and not really warranted.

8. I am aware of individual differences that exist among members within a particular ethnic group based on values, beliefs, and level of acculturation.

9. I am aware some research indicates that minority clients are more likely to be diagnosed with mental illnesses than are majority clients.

10. I think that clients should perceive the nuclear family as the ideal social unit.

11. I think that being highly competitive and achievement oriented are traits that all clients should work for.

12. I am aware of the differential interpretations of nonverbal communication (e.g., personal space, eye contact, handshakes) within various racial/ethnic groups.

13. I understand the impact and operations of oppression and the racist concepts that have permeated the mental health professions.

14. I realize that counselor–client incongruities in problem conceptualization and counseling goals may reduce counselor credibility.

15. I am aware that some racial/ethnic minorities see the profession of psychology functioning to maintain and promote the status and power of the White Establishment.

16. I am knowledgeable of acculturation models for various ethnic minority groups.

17. I have an understanding of the role of culture and racism play in the development of identity and worldview among minority groups.

18. I believe that it is important to emphasize objective and rational thinking in minority clients.

19. I am aware of culture-specific, that is culturally indigenous, models of counseling for various racial/ethnic groups.

1	2	3	4	5	6	7
Not at All True			Somewhat True			Totally True

20. I believe that my clients should view a patriarchal structure as the ideal.
21. I am aware of both initial barriers and benefits related to the cross-cultural counseling relationship.
22. I am comfortable with differences that exist between me and my clients in terms of race and beliefs.
23. I am aware of institutional barriers which may inhibit minorities from using mental health services.
24. I think my clients should exhibit some degree of psychological mindedness and sophistication.
25. I believe that minority clients will benefit most from counseling with a majority who endorses the White middle-class values and norms.
26. I am aware that being born a White person in this society carries with it certain advantages.
27. I am aware of the value assumptions inherent in major schools of counseling and understand how these assumptions may conflict with the values of culturally diverse clients.
28. I am aware that some minorities see the counseling process as contrary to their own life experiences and inappropriate or insufficient to their needs.
29. I am aware that being born a minority in this society brings with it certain challenges that White people do not have to face.
30. I believe that all clients must view themselves as their number-one responsibility.
31. I am sensitive to circumstances (personal biases, language dominance, stage of ethnic identity development) which may dictate referral of minority client to a member of his/her own racial/ethnic group.
32. I am aware that some minorities believe counselors lead minority students into non-academic programs regardless of student potential, preferences, or ambitions.

Thank you for completing this instrument. Please feel free to express in writing below any thoughts concerns, or comments you have regarding this instrument.

SCORING DIRECTION FOR THE 32-ITEM MCKAS

A number of items ($n=10$) in the Awareness Scale are reverse-worded (i.e., low scores indicates high awareness) and need to be reverse-scored prior to any data analysis. To reverse-score these items use the following conversion table

1 = 7
2 = 6
3 = 5
4 = 4
5 = 3
6 = 2
7 = 1

The MCKAS yields two scores that are mildly correlated ($r = 0.36$), supporting the independent interpretation of separate subscales. (See the review in Ponterotto & Potere, in press).

Knowledge Scale (20 items): 2, 3, 5, 6, 8, 9, 12, 13, 14, 15, 16, 17, 19, 21, 22, 23, 27, 28, 31, and 32.

These items are all worded in a positive direction where high score indicate higher perceived knowledge of multicultural counseling issues. The score range for the Knowledge scale ranges from 20 to 140 using aggregate score, or 1–7 using a mean score (the mean subscale score is derived by dividing the total aggregate score by the number of subscale items, $n=20$).

Awareness Scale (12 items): (1), (4), (7), (10), (11), (18), (20), (24), (25), 26, 29, and (30).

Ten items in the parentheses need to be reversed scored. After reverse-scoring, the total score range for the Awareness Scale range from 12 to 84 (or 1 to 7 for mean score; that is the total score divided by number of subscale items, $n=12$) with higher scores indicating higher awareness of multicultural counseling issues.

Note. No cutoff scores establishing "satisfactory" knowledge or awareness of multicultural-counseling issues exist. From "A Construct Validity Study of the Multicultural Counseling Awareness Scale (MCAS)," by J. G. Ponterotto, D. Gretchen, S. O. Utsey, B. P. Rieger, and R. Austin, 2002, *Journal of Multicultural Counseling and Development, 30*, p. 153–180. Copyright 2002 by Joseph Ponterotto. Reprinted with permission. The MCKAS is copyrighted by Joseph G. Ponterotto, PhD. This instrument should not be photocopied or distributed without his consent. He can be contacted at the Division of Psychological and Educational Services, Room 1008, Fordham University at Lincoln Center, 113 West 60th Street, New York, New York 10023-7478 (Jponterott@aol.com).

APPENDIX E

Multicultural Competency Checklist
for Counseling Psychology

The Multicultural Competency Checklist (Ponterotto, Alexander, & Grieger, 1995) is designed to assist faculty and staff in assessing their status with reference to providing multicultural training for their students. The measure may be completed by the program head or by a group of program faculty. It is divided into categories of minority representation, curriculum issues, clinical practice and supervision, research considerations, student and faculty competency evaluation, and physical environment. This scale is an excellent tool to assess the multicultural competency of a training program. Although it was developed for assessing counseling-psychology programs, it has applications in other training settings for identifying and enhancing awareness of dimensions of competency.

MULTICULTURAL COMPETENCY PROGRAM CHECKLIST FOR COUNSELING PSYCHOLOGY PROGRAMS

	Competency	
Minority Representation	Met	Not Met
1. 30%+ faculty represent racial/ethnic minority populations.	_____	_____
2. 30%+ faculty are bilingual.	_____	_____
3. 30%+ students represent racial/ethnic minority populations.	_____	_____
4. 30%+ support staff (secretaries, graduate assistants) represent minority populations.	_____	_____
Curriculum Issues		
5. Program has a required multicultural course.	_____	_____
6. Program has one or more additional multicultural courses that are required or recommended.	_____	_____
7. Multicultural issues are integrated into all coursework. Faculty can specify how this is done and syllabi clearly reflect this inclusion.	_____	_____

| | Competency | |
Curriculum Issues	Met	Not Met

Curriculum Issues

8. Diversity of teaching strategies and procedures employed in class, e.g., individual achievement and cooperative learning models are utilized. _____ _____

9. Varied assessment methods used to evaluate student performance and learning, e.g., written and oral assignments. _____ _____

Clinical Practice and Supervision

10. Students are exposed to 30%+ multicultural clientele. _____ _____

11. Multicultural issues are integral to on-site and on-campus clinical supervision. _____ _____

12. Students have supervised access to a cultural immersion experience such as study abroad for at least one semester, or an ethnographic immersion in a community culturally different from that of the campus or the student's own upbringing. _____ _____

13. Program has an active "Multicultural Affairs Committee" composed of faculty and students. Committee provides leadership and support with regard to multicultural initiatives. _____ _____

Research Considerations

14. The program has a faculty member whose primary research interest is in multicultural issues. _____ _____

15. There is clear faculty research productivity in multicultural issues. This is evidenced by faculty publications and presentations on multicultural issues. _____ _____

16. Students are actively mentored in multicultural research. This is evidenced by student–faculty co-authored work on multicultural issues and completed dissertations on these issues. _____ _____

	Competency	
Research Considerations	Met	Not Met

17. Diverse research methodologies are apparent in faculty and student research. Both quantitative and qualitative research methods are utilized.   _____   _____

Student and Faculty Competency Evaluation

18. One component of students' yearly (and end of program) evaluations is sensitivity to and knowledge of multicultural issues. The program has a mechanism for assessing this competency.   _____   _____

19. One component of faculty teaching evaluations is the ability to integrate multicultural issues into the course. Faculty are also assessed on their ability to make all students, regardless of cultural background, feel equally comfortable in class. The program has a mechanism to assess this competency.   _____   _____

20. Multicultural issues are reflected in comprehensive examinations completed by all students.   _____   _____

21. The program incorporates a reliable and valid paper-and-pencil self-report assessment of student multicultural competency at some point in the program.   _____   _____

22. The program incorporates a content-validated portfolio assessment of student multicultural competency at some point in the program.   _____   _____

Physical Environment

23. The physical surroundings of the Program Area reflect an appreciation of cultural diversity (e.g., artwork, posters, paintings, languages heard).   _____   _____

	Competency	
Physical Environment	Met	Not Met

24. There is a "Multicultural Resource Center" of some form in the Program Area (or within the Department or Academic Unit) where students can convene. Cultural diversity is reflected in the décor of the room and in the resources available (e.g., books, journals, films, etc.).   _____   _____

APPENDIX F
Trainee–Client Sexual Misconduct

Hamilton and Spruill (1999) developed "Risk Management: A Checklist for Trainees and Supervisors" from information culled retrospectively from students who became sexually involved with clients while on internship. The checklist includes therapist responses to clients, therapist needs, session characteristics, accountability, other, and checklist for supervisors. The checklist should be valuable as a psychoeducational and preventative measure as well as a means to identify risk. The red flags elicited by positive answers to this checklist should serve to alert supervisors as to possible indices of risk for sexual misconduct.

TRAINEE–CLIENT SEXUAL MISCONDUCT

RISK MANAGEMENT: A CHECKLIST FOR TRAINEES AND SUPERVISORS

Checklist for Trainees

Therapist Responses to Clients

- Do you find it difficult to set limits on the demands your client makes of you?
- Do you accept phone calls from your client at home or in your office when the client needs you to (a) help with a "crisis," (b) deal with minor problems, or (c) alleviate his or her loneliness or meet his or her need to talk to someone who "understands"?
- Do you make such statements such as, "This is not my usual practice; I ordinarily don't do this, but in your case. . ." or "Under the circumstances, it seems OK to. . ."?
- Do you find yourself wanting to rescue your client from some situation or behavior that is detrimental to him or her?
- Do you find yourself talking about your client to others?
- Does your client occupy your thoughts outside office hours?
- Do you hope you will "run into" your client at the grocery store, social settings, and so forth?
- Is it becoming progressively easier and more satisfying to share intimate details of your own life with your client?

- Do you find opportunities to talk about nontherapy issues with your client?
- Do you take care to dress or look more attractive than usual for a particular client?
- Do you find yourself wondering what the client thinks about you?
- Do you make excuses to talk to your client by phone?
- Do you accept friends of your client as therapy clients, and then find yourself spending a lot of the session talking about the original client to the current client rather than focusing on the current client's problems?
- Do you find yourself looking forward to seeing a particular client (or type of client) and feeling disappointed if he or she cancels the session?

Therapist's Needs

- Does your primary satisfaction come from your work with therapy clients?
- Do you have more clients than required or more than your fellow practicum students?
- Are you lonely and feeling as if your needs are not being met by anyone?
- Do you have a circle of friends with whom you engage in pleasurable social activities?
- Do you have a circle of friends to whom you can turn for support?
- Do you have one or more close friends in whom you could confide in about fears, anxieties, and self-doubts?
- What are the important stressors in your life, and what steps are you taking to resolve or cope with them?

Session Characteristics

- Do you regularly extend the session for one client but not the others?
- Do you regularly start the session early, end it late, or both for one client?
- Do you schedule a particular client at times that afford the opportunity to linger, or to walk out of the clinic altogether, and so forth?
- Do you schedule the client after regular office hours because your schedule or the client's schedule does not permit regular office hours?

Accountability

- Do you find yourself forgetting to document phone calls from your client?
- Do you find yourself getting defensive about particular clients or certain issues (e.g., you bristle when a superior suggests that there is no progress being made and a referral is in order)?
- Are you reluctant to talk about transference or boundary issues, particularly feelings regarding sexual attraction by or to the client?
- Do you find it difficult to tell your treatment team or supervisor some details related to your client?
- Is there anything that you "try not to talk about" concerning a particular client?
- Do you find yourself putting off seeking supervision or consultation about a particular client or issue?
- Does the tape always run out or mess up at a "sensitive" point in the session? Does the therapy session regularly extend beyond the length of the tape?
- If you make phone calls, extend sessions, and so forth, how much of this information is recorded in the client's file? Do you find yourself unwilling, or "forgetting" to document information with regard to a particular client?

Other

- Have the secretaries or other people commented on your behavior toward a client?
- Have you offered to do such things as give the client a ride home, give tutoring in a difficult class, or arrange a meeting outside the therapy hour or place?
- Are you concerned about the client's feelings toward you, or the feelings toward the client?

Checklist for Supervisors

- Have I discussed how to establish professional therapist–client relationships with my practicum students?
- Have I reviewed the issue of sexual attraction to clients and shared my own feelings, what have I done about this?
- Have I created an atmosphere of openness and willingness to discuss the fears, uncertainties, and so forth, of my practicum students?

- Do my practicum students know about boundary violations and the reasons for establishing boundaries?
- Have I discussed the checklist for students with them?

Note. From "Identifying and Reducing Risk Factors Related to Trainee–Client Sexual Misconduct," by J. C. Hamilton and J. Spruill, 1999, *Professional Psychology: Research and Practice, 30,* p. 327. Copyright 1999 by the American Psychological Association. Reprinted with permission.

APPENDIX G
Competencies of Supervisors

Borders and Leddick (1987) provided this comprehensive list of supervisor competencies provides a framework that can be adapted to a particular setting to evaluate and identify parameters of the supervisor's performance. This list of supervision competencies was adopted by the ACES Supervision Interest Network (C. VanZandt, Chair), at the AACD Convention, New York, April 2, 1985. Please note that the rating scale is from Needs Development (1) to Expertise (6).

COMPETENCIES OF SUPERVISORS

I. CONCEPTUAL SKILLS AND KNOWLEDGE

A. *Generic Skills*
THE SUPERVISOR IS ABLE TO DEMONSTRATE KNOWLEDGE AND CONCEPTUAL UNDERSTANDING OF THE FOLLOWING:

1. the methodology of supervision, including   1 2 3 4 5 6
  a. facilitative processes (consultation, counseling, education, or training and evaluation).   1 2 3 4 5 6
  b. basic approaches (e.g., psychotherapeutic, behavioral, integrative, systems, developmental).   1 2 3 4 5 6
2. a definition or explanation of supervision.   1 2 3 4 5 6
3. the variety of settings in which counselor supervisors work.   1 2 3 4 5 6
4. the counselor's roles and functions in particular work settings.   1 2 3 4 5 6
5. the developmental nature of supervision.   1 2 3 4 5 6
6. appropriate supervisor interventions, including   1 2 3 4 5 6
  a. role-playing.   1 2 3 4 5 6

b. role reversal.	1	2	3	4	5	6
c. live observation and live supervision.	1	2	3	4	5	6
d. reviewing audio- and video-tapes.	1	2	3	4	5	6
e. giving direct suggestions and advice.	1	2	3	4	5	6
f. leading groups of 2 or more supervisees.	1	2	3	4	5	6
g. providing didactic experiences.	1	2	3	4	5	6
h. Microtraining.	1	2	3	4	5	6
i. IPR.	1	2	3	4	5	6
j. Other _____.	1	2	3	4	5	6
7. credentialing standards for counselors.	1	2	3	4	5	6
8. counselor ethical practices.	1	2	3	4	5	6
9. various counseling theories.	1	2	3	4	5	6
10. his or her own personal theory of counseling.	1	2	3	4	5	6
11. his or her assumptions about human behavior.	1	2	3	4	5	6
12. models of supervision.	1	2	3	4	5	6
13. the meaning of accountability and the supervisor's responsibility in promoting this condition.	1	2	3	4	5	6
14. human growth and development.	1	2	3	4	5	6
15. motivation and needs theory.	1	2	3	4	5	6
16. learning theory.	1	2	3	4	5	6
17. resources and information to assist in addressing program goals and client needs.	1	2	3	4	5	6

B. *Supervision of Practicing Counselors*
THE SUPERVISOR IS ABLE TO DEMONSTRATE
KNOWLEDGE AND CONCEPTUAL UNDERSTANDING
OF THE FOLLOWING:

18. legal considerations affecting counselor practice.	1	2	3	4	5	6
19. various intervention activities and strategies that would complement the counseling program's goals.	1	2	3	4	5	6

C. *Supervision of Counselors-in-Training*
(covered in Generic Skills above)

D. *Program Management/Supervision*
   THE SUPERVISOR IS ABLE TO DEMONSTRATE
   KNOWLEDGE AND CONCEPTUAL UNDERSTANDING
   OF THE FOLLOWING:

   20. his or her basic management
       theory.   1   2   3   4   5   6
   21. various program development
       models.   1   2   3   4   5   6
   22. decision-making theory.   1   2   3   4   5   6
   23. organization development theory.   1   2   3   4   5   6
   24. conflict-resolution techniques.   1   2   3   4   5   6
   25. leadership styles.   1   2   3   4   5   6
   26. computerized information systems.   1   2   3   4   5   6
   27. time-management techniques.   1   2   3   4   5   6

II. DIRECT INTERVENTION SKILLS

A. *Generic Skills*
   THE SUPERVISOR IS ABLE TO DEMONSTRATE INTER-
   VENTION TECHNIQUES IN THE FOLLOWING WAYS:

   1. provide structure for supervision
      sessions, including   1   2   3   4   5   6
      a. stating the purposes of
         supervision.   1   2   3   4   5   6
      b. clarifying the goals and
         direction of supervision   1   2   3   4   5   6
      c. clarifying his/her own role
         in supervision.   1   2   3   4   5   6
      d. explaining the procedures
         to be followed in
         supervision.   1   2   3   4   5   6
   2. identify the learning needs
      of the supervisee.   1   2   3   4   5   6
   3. determine the extent in which
      the supervisee has developed and
      applied his/her own personal
      theory of counseling.   1   2   3   4   5   6
   4. provide specific feedback about
      supervisee's   1   2   3   4   5   6
      a. conceptualization of client
         concerns.   1   2   3   4   5   6
      b. process of counseling.   1   2   3   4   5   6

c. personalization of counseling.	1	2	3	4	5	6

d. performance of other related
duties.

	1	2	3	4	5	6

5. implement a variety of supervisory
interventions (see Conceptual
Skills & Knowledge).

	1	2	3	4	5	6

6. negotiate mutual decisions regarding the needed direction of learning experiences for the supervisee.

	1	2	3	4	5	6

7. use media aids for assisting with
supervision.

	1	2	3	4	5	6

8. develop evaluation procedures and
instruments to determine program
and supervisee goal attainment.

	1	2	3	4	5	6

9. monitor the use of tests and test
interpretations.

	1	2	3	4	5	6

10. assist with the referral process,
when appropriate.

	1	2	3	4	5	6

11. facilitate and monitor research to
determine the effectiveness of programs, services, and techniques.

	1	2	3	4	5	6

B. *Program Management/Supervision*
THE SUPERVISOR IS ABLE TO DEMONSTRATE INTER-
VENTION TECHNIQUES IN THE FOLLOWING WAYS:

12. develop role descriptions for all
staff positions.

	1	2	3	4	5	6

13. conduct a needs assessment.	1	2	3	4	5	6
14. write goals and objectives.	1	2	3	4	5	6

15. monitor the progress of program
activities.

	1	2	3	4	5	6

16. monitor the progress of staff's
responsibilities.

	1	2	3	4	5	6

17. utilize decision-making
techniques.

	1	2	3	4	5	6

18. apply problem-solving techniques.	1	2	3	4	5	6

19. conduct and coordinate staff development training.

	1	2	3	4	5	6

20. implement management information systems.

	1	2	3	4	5	6

21. employ group management
strategies.

	1	2	3	4	5	6

22. schedule tasks and develop time
lines according to the needs of
supervisees and the program.   1   2   3   4   5   6
23. maintain appropriate forms and
records to assist with supervisory
duties.   1   2   3   4   5   6
24. monitor supervisee report-writing
and record-keeping skills.   1   2   3   4   5   6
25. diagnose organizational problems.   1   2   3   4   5   6
26. employ systematic observation
techniques.   1   2   3   4   5   6
27. plan and administer a budget.   1   2   3   4   5   6
28. conduct follow-up studies and
applied research.   1   2   3   4   5   6
29. establish consistent and quality
hiring and affirmative action
practices.   1   2   3   4   5   6
30. delegate responsibility.   1   2   3   4   5   6

III. HUMAN SKILLS

A. *Generic Skills*
THE SUPERVISOR IS ABLE TO APPLY THE FOLLOWING
INTERACTION SKILLS IN A SUPERVISORY CAPACITY:

1. deal with the supervisee from the
perspective of   1   2   3   4   5   6
    a. teacher.   1   2   3   4   5   6
    b. counselor.   1   2   3   4   5   6
    c. consultant.   1   2   3   4   5   6
    d. evaluator.   1   2   3   4   5   6
2. describe his/her own pattern
of dealing with interpersonal
relations.   1   2   3   4   5   6
3. integrate knowledge of supervision
with own style of interpersonal
relations.   1   2   3   4   5   6
4. create facilitative conditions
(empathy, concreteness, respect,
congruence, genuineness, and
immediacy).   1   2   3   4   5   6
5. establish a mutually trusting relationship with the supervisee.   1   2   3   4   5   6

6. establish a therapeutic relationship
   when appropriate.   1 2 3 4 5 6
7. identify supervisee's professional
   and personal strengths as well as
   weaknesses.   1 2 3 4 5 6
8. clarify supervisee's personal needs
   (behavior mannerisms, personal
   crises, appearance, etc.), as well as
   professional needs that affect
   counseling.   1 2 3 4 5 6
9. elicit supervisee feelings during
   counseling or consultation
   sessions.   1 2 3 4 5 6
10. elicit supervisee perceptions of
    counseling dynamics.   1 2 3 4 5 6
11. use confrontation skills when iden-
    tifying supervisee's inconsistencies.   1 2 3 4 5 6
12. elicit new alternatives from super-
    visee for identifying solutions,
    techniques, responses, etc.   1 2 3 4 5 6
13. demonstrate skill in the applica-
    tion of counseling techniques
    (both individual and group) that
    are appropriate for the work
    setting.   1 2 3 4 5 6
14. assist the supervisee in structuring
    his/her own self-supervision.   1 2 3 4 5 6
15. conduct self-evaluations as a
    means of modeling appropriate
    professional growth.   1 2 3 4 5 6
16. identify own strengths and weak-
    nesses as a supervisor.   1 2 3 4 5 6
17. model appropriate behaviors
    expected of supervisees.   1 2 3 4 5 6
18. demonstrate and enforce ethical/
    professional standards.   1 2 3 4 5 6

B. *Traits and Qualities*
   THE SUPERVISOR POSSESSES THE FOLLOWING TRAITS
   OR QUALITIES:

   1. demonstrates a commitment to the
      role of supervisor.   1 2 3 4 5 6

2. is comfortable with the authority
   inherent in the role of supervisor.   1 2 3 4 5 6
3. has a sense of humor.   1 2 3 4 5 6
4. is encouraging, optimistic, and
   motivational.   1 2 3 4 5 6
5. expects supervisees to own the
   consequences of their actions.   1 2 3 4 5 6
6. is sensitive to individual
   differences.   1 2 3 4 5 6
7. is sensitive to supervisee's needs.   1 2 3 4 5 6
8. is committed to updating his/her
   own counseling and supervisory
   skills.   1 2 3 4 5 6
9. recognizes that the ultimate goal
   of supervision is helping the client
   of the supervisee.   1 2 3 4 5 6
10. maintains open communication
    between supervisees and the
    supervisor.   1 2 3 4 5 6
11. monitors the "energy level" of
    supervisees to identify possible
    signs of counselor burnout in
    advance of possible crises.   1 2 3 4 5 6
12. recognizes own limits through
    eliciting self-evaluation and
    feedback from others.   1 2 3 4 5 6
13. enjoys and appreciates the role
    of supervisor.   1 2 3 4 5 6

Note. From *Handbook of Counseling Supervision* (pp. 65–70), by L. D. Borders and G. R. Leddick, 1987, Alexandria, VA: American Association for Counseling and Development. Copyright 1987 by Association for Counselor Education and Supervision. Reprinted with permission.

APPENDIX H
Role Conflict and Role Ambiguity Inventory

The Role Conflict and Role Ambiguity Inventory developed by Olk and Friedlander (1992) consists of a 16-item Role Ambiguity and a 13-item Role Conflict scale. Items were empirically derived and focus on role ambiguity including uncertainty about supervision expectation and how to perform within these, and uncertainty about evaluation by supervisors. The role conflict items relate to situations in which expectations of the role of the student are in conflict with those associated with the role of counselor and colleague. These particularly are particularly concerned with making autonomous decisions versus following supervisory directives. The authors conclude that this measure is a reliable and valid measure of trainee experience in supervision with respect to role conflict and role ambiguity. This scale is useful as both a preventative and a remedial tool.

Instructions:

The following statements describe some problems that therapists-in-training may experience during the course of clinical supervision. Please read each statement and then rate the extent to which you have experienced difficulty in supervision in your most recent clinical training. Please rank them on a 1 to 5 scale from Not at All (1) to Very Much So (5).

I have experienced difficulty in my current or most recent supervision because:

ROLE AMBIGUITY SCALE

1. I was not certain about what material to present to my supervisor.
2. I wasn't sure how best to use supervision as I become more experienced, although I was aware that I was expected to behave more independently.
3. My supervisor expected me to come prepared for supervision. But I had no idea what or how to prepare.
4. I wasn't sure how autonomous I should be in my work with clients.
5. My supervisor's criteria for evaluating my work were not specific.

6. I was not sure that I had done what the supervisor expected me to do in a session with a client.
7. The criteria for evaluating my performance in supervision were not clear.
8. The feedback I got from my supervisor did not help me to know what was expected of me in my day-to-day work with clients.
9. Everything was new, and I wasn't sure what would be expected of me.
10. I was not sure if I should discuss my professional weaknesses in supervision because I was not sure how I would be evaluated.
11. My supervisor gave me no feedback, and I felt lost.
12. My supervisor told me what to do with a client but didn't give me very specific ideas about how to do it.
13. There were no clear guidelines for my behavior in supervision.
14. The supervisor gave no constructive or negative feedback, and as a result, I did not know how to address my weaknesses.
15. I didn't know how I was doing as a therapist, and as a result, I didn't know how my supervisor would evaluate me.
16. I was unsure of what to expect from my supervisor.

ROLE CONFLICT SCALE

1. I have felt that my supervisor was incompetent or less competent than I. I often felt as though I were supervising him or her.
2. I have wanted to challenge the appropriateness of my supervisor's recommendations for using a technique with one of my clients, but I thought it better to keep my opinions to myself.
3. My orientation to therapy was different from that of my supervisor. She or he wanted me to work with clients using his or her framework, and I felt that I should be allowed to use my own approach.
4. I have wanted to intervene with one of my clients in a particular way, and my supervisor wanted me to approach the client in a very different way. I am expected both to judge what is appropriate for myself and also to do what I am told.
5. My supervisor told me to do something I perceived to be illegal or unethical, and I was expected to comply.

6. I disagreed with my supervisor about how to introduce a specific issue to a client, but I also wanted to do what the supervisor recommended.
7. Part of me wanted to rely on my own instincts with clients, but I always knew that my supervisor would have the last word.
8. I was not comfortable using a technique recommended by my supervisor; however, I felt that I should do what my supervisor recommended.
9. I disagreed with my supervisor about implementing a specific technique, but I also wanted to do what the supervisor thought best.
10. My supervisor wanted me to use an assessment technique that I considered inappropriate for a particular client.
11. I have believed that my supervisor's behavior in one or more situations was unethical or illegal, and I was undecided about whether to confront her or him.
12. I got mixed signals from my supervisor and I was unsure of which signals to attend to.
13. When using a new technique, I was unclear about the specific steps involved. As a result, I wasn't sure how my supervisor would evaluate my performance.

Note. From "Trainees' Experiences of Role Conflict and Role Ambiguity in Supervisory Relationships," by M. Olk and M. L. Friedlander, 1992, *Journal of Counseling Psychology, 39,* p. 394. Copyright 1992 by the American Psychological Association. Reprinted with permission.

APPENDIX I
Evaluation Process Within Supervision Inventory

Lehrman-Waterman and Ladany (2001) developed this 21-item self-report measure to assess the degree trainees thought their supervision was characterized by effective goal setting and feedback. A 7-point Likert scale is used with two subscales. Thirteen items address goal setting and 8 items address feedback. One third of the items are reverse scored to control for error. Negatively scored items are Goal Setting: 5, 6, 8, 10, 11, 12; Feedback: 4. The authors concluded that their results indicated that the measure is reliable and valid.

This measure, designed to assess the extent to which trainees perceived their supervision as characterized by effective goal setting and feedback, can be an important part of relationship building and refining and provides a framework for structuring and assessing the process of supervision. Effective goal setting and feedback as defined in this measure are associated with a stronger working alliance and trainee satisfaction.

EVALUATION PROCESS WITHIN SUPERVISION INVENTORY

Goal Setting

1. The goals my supervisor and I generated for my training seemed important.
2. My supervisor and I created goals which were easy for me to understand.
3. The objectives my supervisor and I created were specific.
4. My supervisor and I created goals that were realistic.
5. I think my supervisor would have been against my reshaping/ changing my learning objectives over the course of our work together.
6. My supervisor and I created goals which seemed too easy for me.
7. My supervisor and I created objectives which were measurable.
8. I felt uncertain as to what my most important goals were for this training experience.

9. My training objectives were established early in our relationship.
10. My supervisor and I never had a discussion about my objectives for my training experience.
11. My supervisor told me what he or she wanted me to learn from the experience without inquiring about what I hoped to learn.
12. Some of the goals my supervisor and I established were not practical in light of the resources available at my site.
13. My supervisor and I set objectives which seemed practical given the opportunities available at my site (e.g., requiring videotaping and providing equipment).

Feedback

1. My supervisor welcomed comments about his or her style as a supervisor.
2. The appraisal I received from my supervisor seemed impartial.
3. My supervisor's comments about my work were understandable.
4. I didn't receive information about how I was doing as a counselor until late in the semester.
5. I had a summative, formal evaluation of my work at the end of the semester.
6. My supervisor balanced his or her feedback between positive and negative statements.
7. The feedback I received from my supervisor was based on his or her direct observation of my work.
8. The feedback I received was directly related to the goals we established.

Note. From "Development and Validation of the Evaluation Process Within Supervision Inventory," by D. Lehrman-Waterman and N. Ladany, 2001, Journal of Counseling Psychology, 48, p. 171. Copyright 2001 by the American Psychological Association. Reprinted with permission.

APPENDIX J
Supervision Outcomes Survey

Worthen and Isakson (2000) developed the Supervision Outcomes Survey to assess the supervisee's view of supervision. It is a 20-item measure with ratings on a 7-point Likert scale. The total score is useful in tracking the supervisee's changing impressions of supervision. Worthen and Isakson suggest using it at intervals during supervision or as an ongoing measure. Its formative use seems most effective, as it enables the results to be fed back into the supervisory process.

SUPERVISION OUTCOMES SURVEY

Supervisor's Name: _____ Date: _____

Please respond to the following questions in terms of your current supervisor. The terms "therapy" and "therapist" have been used as generic terms to apply to both counseling and psychotherapy. Use the following rating scale for all items:

1 ------- 2 ------- 3 ------- 4 ------- 5 ------- 6 ------- 7
Not at all   Moderately   Greatest Degree Possible

1. My supervisor helps me develop by providing both challenge and support.	1 2 3 4 5 6 7
2. The supervision I am receiving has helped me grow as a professional.	1 2 3 4 5 6 7
3. My supervisor helps me feel strengthened and affirmed in my efforts to become a professional.	1 2 3 4 5 6 7
4. My supervisor helps me identify areas where I need to continue to develop by identifying my strengths and weaknesses.	1 2 3 4 5 6 7
5. Supervision helps me better see the complexity in my cases.	1 2 3 4 5 6 7

271

1 ------ 2 ------ 3 ------ 4 ------ 5 ------ 6 ------ 7

Not at all   Moderately   Greatest Degree Possible

6. Supervision helps me improve my ability to conceptualize my cases.	1	2	3	4	5	6	7
7. Supervision helps me examine, modify, and refine my approaches to therapy.	1	2	3	4	5	6	7
8. Supervision helps me take risks that have led to professional growth and more effective therapy.	1	2	3	4	5	6	7
9. The relationship I have with my supervisor is characterized by acceptance, trust, and respect.	1	2	3	4	5	6	7
10. My supervisor's feedback encourages me to keep trying to improve.	1	2	3	4	5	6	7
11. Supervision helps me see my mistakes as learning experiences.	1	2	3	4	5	6	7
12. The modeling of my supervisor helps me learn more about therapy.	1	2	3	4	5	6	7
13. Self-disclosure by my supervisor helps to normalize my experience as a therapist.	1	2	3	4	5	6	7
14. My supervisor helps me to be open and receptive to supervision.	1	2	3	4	5	6	7
15. I feel comfortable sharing my perceived weaknesses and failures with my supervisor.	1	2	3	4	5	6	7
16. Supervision helps me develop specific skills that have made me a more effective therapist.	1	2	3	4	5	6	7
17. Supervision is helping me better understand and facilitate effective therapy outcomes with my clients.	1	2	3	4	5	6	7
18. As a result of supervision, I feel more confident and comfortable in working with my therapy cases.	1	2	3	4	5	6	7
19. Overall, I feel satisfied with my supervision.	1	2	3	4	5	6	7
20. I feel that supervision is contributing to my overall effectiveness in my therapy cases.	1	2	3	4	5	6	7

Note. From *Supervision Outcomes Survey* by V. E. Worthen and R. L. Isakson, 2000. Copyright 2000 by V. E. Worthen. Reprinted with permission.

APPENDIX K
Supervisor Feedback

Hall-Marley (2001) developed this supervisor feedback form as an instrument to provide feedback to supervisors on the trainee's experience of supervision. The form consists of sections including atmosphere for learning, supervision style, supervision conduct, and supervision impact. It is recommended a supervisor feedback form be used a minimum of four times during the training year and ideally more frequently. It is a tool in establishing a dialogue and a feedback loop which should enhance the supervisory alliance. This form is a sample tool by which trainees may provide their supervisors with feedback. Although this process is difficult, because of the power differential, use of the tool sets a tone of interest and openness to such feedback and may strengthen communication.

SUPERVISOR FEEDBACK

This form was designed by clinic training staff to increase the effectiveness of supervisory relationships early in the academic year and thus improve the clinic's quality of service to client families, as well as enable you to formally reevaluate your training needs. The items listed in the form are intended to represent the goals of supervision. The form is not designed to be used to evaluate staff. Your supervisors need your most honest feedback. You may wish to use checkmarks to indicate areas where you are receiving adequate help; "n" to indicate areas where you could use more help; and "?" to indicate areas where you are not sure. You may provide any written narrative as you wish. Please give these forms to your supervisor or discuss them with him or her in the coming week.

Atmosphere for Learning

_____ Promotes a sense of acceptance and support.
_____ Establishes clear boundaries (not parental, peer, or therapeutic).
_____ Recognizes therapist strengths.
_____ Establishes clear and reasonable expectations of therapist performance.
_____ Conveys active interest in helping therapist with clients.
_____ Conveys active interest in helping therapist grow professionally.
_____ Sensitive and adaptive to stresses attendant to internship.

_____ Treats mistakes as a learning experience.
_____ Deals explicitly with the formal evaluation process.

Supervision Style

_____ Openly discusses and is respectful of differences in style, orientation, and case conceptualizations.
_____ Balances instruction with exploration, conforming directiveness in style to therapist's needs.
_____ Encourages therapist to question, challenge, or doubt supervisor's opinions.
_____ Allows therapist to structure sessions.
_____ Encourages reflection on implications of alternative interventions.
_____ Makes supervision a collaborative enterprise.
_____ Offers critical case-centered or general feedback with respect.
_____ Openly processes any conflicts that arise in supervisory relationship.
_____ Admits errors or limitations without undue defensiveness.
_____ Enables the relationship to evolve over the year from advisory to consultative to collegial.
_____ Openly discusses and is respectful of differences in culture, ethnicity, or other individual diversity

Supervision Conduct

_____ Reliably available for scheduled meetings.
_____ Available in emergencies.
_____ Makes decisions and takes responsibility when appropriate.
_____ Makes concrete and specific suggestions when needed.
_____ Maintains appropriate and useful level of focus in sessions.
_____ Assists therapist in making dynamic or other theoretical case formulation.
_____ Defines and clarifies problems in treatment.
_____ Raises ethical and legal considerations.
_____ Offers practical and useful case-centered suggestions.
_____ Offers suggestions appropriate to therapist's level of training.
_____ Can present theoretical rationale for suggestions.
_____ Assists therapist to integrate different techniques.
_____ Addresses countertransference issues between therapist and client.
_____ Provides general knowledge about psychotherapy or psychology as a science.
_____ Raises cultural and individual diversity issues.

Supervision Impact

_____ Provides teaching that generalizes or transcends individual cases to strengthen therapist's general skill level.

_____ Shows concern for therapist's personal development as well as internship performance.

_____ Furthers therapist's self-understanding as professional.

_____ Facilitates therapist's self-confidence to accept new challenges.

_____ Assists therapist in forming a more crystallized theoretical orientation or professional identify.

Comments:

Note. From _Supervisor Feedback_ by S. Hall-Marley, 2001. Copyright 2001 by S. Hall-Marley. Reprinted with permission.

APPENDIX L
Therapist Evaluation Checklist

Hall-Marley (2000) developed the Therapist Evaluation Checklist, an evaluation form used to give feedback to trainees. Sections include contributes to clinical team, capacity for professional development, general psychotherapy skills (case management, assessment, intervention), and evaluator comments. This sample trainee evaluation form provides a basic structure for performance and competency assessment. It is essential to yoke the evaluation to the contract and stated programmatic expectations for completion.

THERAPIST EVALUATION CHECKLIST

The present level of each skill should be rated as follows:

s   Strength
/   Ability commensurate with level of training
?   Insufficient data
n   Needs improvement (must specify)
na Not applicable

Any rating of "needs improvement" must be accompanied by specific recommendations in the comments section. Raters are encouraged to provide narrative commentary as opposed to simple ratings when possible.

I. CONTRIBUTES TO CLINICAL TEAM

_____ is conscientious, fulfills responsibilities without reminders, and is productive
_____ is accepting and cooperative toward staff at all levels; forms positive relationships
_____ establishes effective supervisory alliance
_____ exercises good judgment in seeking help
_____ exercises good judgment when acting independently
_____ contributes to task completion and cohesion in meetings
_____ has exhibited increased autonomy over the course of the year
_____ makes outside communications that reflect positively on the agency

II. CAPACITY FOR PROFESSIONAL DEVELOPMENT

_____ approaches supervision in an open and collaborative manner
_____ acknowledges the impact of own feelings and cultural values on practice
_____ is appropriately self-critical and accurate in assessing self
_____ incorporates new ideas and critical feedback
_____ is motivated to learn (e.g., seeks information and help)
_____ actively participates in diagnostic teams and seminars
_____ appropriately questions and challenges colleagues and supervisors
_____ has demonstrated improvement in skills over the course of the year
_____ exhibits conduct that consistently reflects knowledge of and conformance to APA ethical principles and state laws

III. GENERAL PSYCHOTHERAPY SKILLS

A. CASE MANAGEMENT SKILLS

_____ documents services fully, but concisely
_____ assesses nonpsychological needs
_____ initiates referrals as needed
_____ completes work in a timely manner
_____ is able to network and coordinate services with external agencies and other service providers

B. ASSESSMENT SKILLS

1. Therapeutic Alliance

_____ conveys warmth, genuineness, and empathy
_____ conveys credibility
_____ facilitates depth of self-disclosure
_____ establishes alliance with all family members
_____ respects client as a whole person with strengths and needs
_____ maintains objectivity
_____ is able to include cultural variables in alliance building

2. Data Gathering Skills

_____ is aware of impact of own behavior and culture on client behavior
_____ understands cultural background in client's presentation
_____ assesses dangerousness to self and others
_____ handles child maltreatment issues appropriately
_____ recognizes and understands nonverbal communication
_____ recognizes and understands metaphorical communication
_____ understands clinical-process issues

3. Diagnostic–Analytic Skills

_____ conceptualizes and organizes data from a definite theoretical view
_____ recognizes impact of multicultural variables on psychological differences and response to treatment
_____ incorporates empirical findings in literature into diagnostic formulation
_____ generates accurate differential diagnosis
_____ develops assessment plan to rule out differential diagnosis
_____ generates accurate case formulation, integrating development, self-report, interview-process, projective, and other data
_____ communicates findings orally in case presentations
_____ generates accurate and timely written reports

C. INTERVENTION SKILLS

1. Maintenance of Working Alliance

_____ tracks or reflects (particularly affect) client statements in session
_____ maintains client's motivation to work (without overwhelming the client or causing the client to become dependent)
_____ balances tracking functions with guiding functions consistent with theoretical perspective
_____ demonstrates multicultural competence
_____ maintains appropriate case load

2. Focusing of Therapy

_____ formulates realistic short- and long-term behavioral goals
_____ formulates methods (process goals) for achieving outcome
_____ establishes shared sense of outcome and process goals with client
_____ fosters positive expectations of hope
_____ recognizes therapeutic impasses
_____ realistic in assessing and reassessing progress and revising formulation and diagnosis as indicated
_____ undertakes interventions that are consistent with theoretical formulation
_____ undertakes interventions that are culturally and ethically appropriate
_____ undertakes interventions that potentiate change
_____ is able to focus on process issues in session
_____ undertakes interventions that are prescriptive rather than generic
_____ undertakes interventions that reflect basic knowledge of cognitive–behavioral, dynamic, time-limited, crisis-intervention, and systemic interventions

3. Understanding of Interpersonal Process Issues

_____ uses personal response to client to aid assessment
_____ selectively responds to accurate self-reports, distortions, and client demands
_____ responds appropriately to metaphoric and nonverbal content
_____ recognizes and highlights underlying affect, cognition, or themes from content
_____ accurately intuits culturally meaningful behavior

4. Psychological Assessment

_____ is able to accurately administer cognitive tests
_____ is able to accurately score cognitive tests
_____ is able to accurately interpret cognitive tests
_____ is able to accurately administer personality tests
_____ is able to accurately score personality tests
_____ is able to accurately interpret personality tests
_____ is able to accurately integrate findings in a comprehensive report
_____ is able to formulate a dynamic conceptualization of personality functioning
_____ is sensitive to cultural issues in terms of the appropriateness of the instruments selected to the interpretation of data
_____ is able to generate appropriate treatment recommendations based on the results of the assessment

IV. EVALUATOR COMMENTS:

Note. From *Therapist Evaluation* Checklist by S. Hall-Marley, 2000. Copyright 2000 by S. Hall-Marley. Adapted with permission.

REFERENCES

Abreu, J. M. (2001). Theory and research on stereotypes and perceptual bias: A didactic resource for multicultural counseling trainers. *The Counseling Psychologist, 29*, 487–512.

Academy of Psychological Clinical Science. (2002). *Mission and Specific Goals.* Retrieved May 1, 2003, from http://psych.arizona.edu/apcs/purpose.html

Accreditation Council for Graduate Medical Education. (2000). *ACGME outcome project.* Retrieved May 1, 2003, from http://www.acgme.org/outcome/project/OutIntro.html

Ackerman, S. J., & Hilsenroth, M. J. (2001). A review of therapist characteristics and techniques negatively impacting the therapeutic alliance. *Psychotherapy: Theory/Research/Practice/Training, 38*, 171–185.

Ackerman, S. J., & Hilsenroth, M. J. (2003). A review of therapist characteristics and techniques positively impacting the therapeutic alliance. *Clinical Psychology Review, 23*,1–33.

Addis, M. E. (2002). Methods for disseminating research products and increasing evidence-based practice: Promises, obstacles, and future directions. *Clinical Psychology: Science & Practice, 9*, 367–378.

Allen, G. J., Szollos, S. J., & Williams, B. E. (1986). Doctoral students' comparative evaluations of best and worst psychotherapy supervision. *Professional Psychology: Research and Practice, 17*, 91–99.

Allison, K. W., Crawford, I., Echemendia, R. J., Robinson, L., & Knepp, D. (1994). Human diversity and professional competence: Training in clinical and counseling psychology revisited. *American Psychologist, 49*, 792–796.

Allison, K. W., Echemendia, R. J., Crawford, I., & Robinson, W. L. (1996). Predicting cultural competence: Implications for practice and training. *Professional Psychology: Research and Practice, 27*, 386–393.

Almonte v. New York Medical College, 851 F.Supp.34 (D.Conn.1994).

Alonso, A., & Rutan, S. (1988). Shame and guilt in psychotherapy supervision. *Psychotherapy, 25*, 576–581.

American Psychological Association. (1965a). Preconference materials prepared for the conference on the professional preparation of clinical psychologists. Washington, DC: Author.

American Psychological Association. (1965b, August–September). Professional preparation of clinical psychologists. *Proceedings of the Conference on the Preparation of Clinical Psychologists meeting at the Center for Continuing Education, Chicago.* Washington, DC: Author.

American Psychological Association. (1992). Ethical principles of psychologists and code of conduct. *American Psychologist, 47*, 1597–1611.

American Psychological Association. (1993a). Guidelines for providers of psychological services to ethnic, linguistic, and culturally diverse populations. *American Psychologist, 48*, 45–48.

American Psychological Association. (1993b). Recordkeeping guidelines. *American Psychologist, 48*, 984–986.

American Psychological Association. (2000). Guidelines on multicultural education, training, research, practice, and organizational change for psychologists. Washington, DC: Author.

American Psychological Association. (2002a). *Ethical principles of psychologists and code of conduct 2002.* Retrieved May 1, 2003, from http://www.apa.org/ethics/code2002.html

American Psychological Association. (2002b). Guidelines for multicultural education, training, research, practice, and organizational change for psychologists. Washington, DC: Author.

American Psychological Association. (2002c). *PsycINFO.* Washington, DC: Author.

American Psychological Association. (2002d). *Yearly membership, American Psychological Association.* Archives of the American Psychological Association. Retrieved May 1, 2003, from http://www.apa.org/archives/yearlymembership.html#30

American Psychological Association, Committee on Accreditation. (2002). *Guidelines and principles for accreditation of programs in professional psychology.* Washington, DC: Author.

American Psychological Association, Committee on Training in Clinical Psychology. (1947). Recommended graduate training program in psychology. *American Psychologist, 2*, 539–558.

American Psychological Association, Division 29, Task Force on Empirically Supported Therapy Relationships. (2002). *Empirically supported therapy relationships: Conclusions and recommendations of the Division 29 Task Force.* Washington, DC: Author.

American Psychological Association, Division 45, Society for the Psychological Study of Ethnic Minority Issues. (2001). *Guidelines for multicultural counseling proficiency for psychologists: Implications for education and training, research and clinical practice*. Washington, DC: Author.

American Society for Healthcare Education and Training. (1994). *Competency assessment allied health*. Chicago: American Hospital Association.

Americans With Disabilities Act of 1990, 42 U. S.C.A. §12101 *et seq.* (West, 1993).

Ancis, J., (Ed.). (2004). *Culturally responsive interventions: Innovative approaches to working with diverse populations*. New York: Brunner-Routledge.

Ancis, J. R., & Ladany, N. (2001). A multicultural framework for counselor supervision. In L. J. Bradley & N. Ladany (Eds.), *Counselor supervision: Principles, process, and practice* (3rd ed., pp. 63–90). Philadelphia: Brunner-Routledge.

Anderson, S. K., & Kitchener, K. S. (1996). Nonromantic, nonsexual posttherapy relationships between psychologists and former clients: An exploratory study of critical incidents. *Professional Psychology: Research and Practice, 27*, 59–66.

Anderson, S. K., & Kitchener, K. S. (1998). Nonsexual posttherapy relationships: A conceptual framework to assess ethical risks. *Professional Psychology: Research and Practice, 29*, 91–99.

Andrews v. United States, 732 F.2d 366 (4th Cir. 1984).

Andrusyna, T. P., Tang, T. Z., DeRubeis, R. J., & Luborsky, L. (2001). The factor structure of the working alliance inventory in cognitive–behavioral therapy. *Journal of Psychotherapy Practice and Research, 10*, 173–178.

Arlow, J. A. (1963). The supervisory situation. *Journal of the American Psychoanalytic Association, 11*, 576–594.

Arnoult, L. H., & Anderson, C. A. (1988). Identifying and reducing causal reasoning biases in clinical practice. In D. C. Turk & P. Salovey (Eds.), *Reasoning, inference, and judgment in clinical psychology* (pp. 209–232). New York: Free Press.

Aron, L. (1991). The patient's experience of the analyst's subjectivity. *Psychoanalytic Dialogues, 1*, 29–51.

Aronson, D. E., Akamatsu, T. J., & Page, H. A. (1982). An initial evaluation of a clinical psychology practicum training program. *Professional Psychology, 13*, 610–619.

Arredondo, P., & Glauner, T. (1992). *Personal dimensions of identity model*. Boston, MA: Empowerment Workshops.

Arredondo, P., Toporek, R., Brown, S. P., Jones, J., Locke, D. C., Sanchez, J., et al. (1996). Operationalization of the multicultural counseling competencies. *Journal of Multicultural Counseling and Development, 24*, 42–78.

Asa, T. P., & Lambert, M. J. (2002). Therapist relational variables. In D. J. Cain (Ed.), *Humanistic psychotherapies: Handbook of research and practice* (pp. 531–557). Washington, DC: American Psychological Association.

Association for Counselor Education and Supervision. (1990). Standards for counseling supervisors. *Journal of Counseling and Development, 69*, 30–32.

Association for Counselor Education and Supervision. (1995). Ethical guidelines for counseling supervisors. *Counseling Education and Supervision, 34,* 270–276.

Association of Psychology Postdoctoral and Internship Centers. (2002). *2002 Competencies Conference. Future Directions in Education and Credentialing in Professional Psychology.* Scottsdale, AZ: Author.

Association of State and Provincial Psychology Boards, Task Force on Supervision Guidelines. (1998). *Final report of the ASPPB Task Force on Supervision Guidelines.* Montgomery, AL: Author.

Atkinson, D. R., Morten, G., & Sue, D. W. (Eds.). (1993). *Counseling American minorities: A cross-cultural perspective* (4th ed.). Dubuque, IA: Brown & Benchmark.

Atkinson, D. R., Thompson, C. E., & Grant, S. K. (1993). A three-dimensional model for counseling racial/ethnic minorities. *The Counseling Psychologist, 21,* 257–277.

Atwood, G. E., & Stolorow, R. D. (1984). *Structures of subjectivity: Explorations in psychoanalytic phenomenology.* Hillsdale, NJ: The Analytic Press.

Bachelor, A., & Horvath, A. (1999). The therapeutic relationship. In M. A. Hubble, B. L. Duncan, & S. D. Miller (Eds.), *The heart and soul of change. What works in therapy* (pp. 133–178). Washington, DC: American Psychological Association.

Bachelor, A., & Salame, R. (2000). Participants' perceptions of dimensions of the therapeutic alliance over the course of therapy. *Journal of Psychotherapy Practice and Research, 9*(1), 39–53.

Bahrick, A. (1989). *Working alliance inventory–training* (WAI-T). Unpublished dissertation, Ohio State University, Columbus.

Baker, R. (2000). Finding the neutral position: Patient and analyst perspectives. *Journal of the American Psychoanalytic Association, 48*(1), 129–153.

Barlow, D. H. (1981). On the relation of clinical research to clinical practice: Current issues, new directions. *Journal of Consulting and Clinical Psychology, 49,* 147–155.

Barret, B., Kitchener, K. S., & Burris, S. (2001). A decision model for ethical dilemmas in HIV-related psychotherapy and its application in the case of Jerry. In J. R. Anderson & B. Barret (Eds.), *Ethics in HIV-related psychotherapy: Clinical decision making in complex cases* (pp. 133–154). Washington, DC: American Psychological Association.

Bartell, P. A., & Rubin, L. J. (1990). Dangerous liaisons: Sexual intimacies in supervision. *Professional Psychology: Research and Practice, 21,* 442–450.

Baudry, F. D. (1993). The personal dimension and management of the supervisory situation with a special note on the parallel process. *Psychoanalytic Quarterly, 62,* 588–614.

Beauchamp, T. L, & Childress, J. F. (1979). *Principles of biomedical ethics.* Oxford, NY: Oxford University Press.

Beck, A. T. (1976). *Cognitive therapy and the emotional disorders.* New York: International Universities Press.

Beck, J. C. (1987). The potentially violent patient: Legal duties, clinical practice, and risk management. *Psychiatric Annals, 17*, 695–699.

Behnke, S. H., Preis, J., & Bates, R. T. (1998). *The essentials of California mental health law.* New York: Norton.

Beidel, D. C., Phillips, S. D., & Zotlow, S. (2003). The future of accreditation. In E. M. Altmaier (Ed.) *Setting standards in graduate education* (pp. 113–134). Washington, DC: American Psychological Association.

Belar, C. D., Brown, R. A., Hersch, L. E., Hornyak, L. M., Rozensky, R. H., Sheridan, E. P., et al. (2001). Self-assessment in clinical health psychology: A model for ethical expansion of practice. *Professional Psychology: Research and Practice, 32*, 135–141.

Belar, C. D., & Perry, N. W. (1992). The national conference on scientist–practitioner education and training for the professional practice of psychology. *American Psychologist, 47*, 71–75.

Benjamin, L. T. (2001). American psychology's struggles with its curriculum: Should a thousand flowers bloom? *American Psychologist, 56*, 735–742.

Bennett, B. E., Bryant, B. K., VandenBos, G. R., & Greenwood, A. (1990). *Professional liability and risk management.* Washington, DC: American Psychological Association.

Bent, R. J., Schindler, N., & Dobbins, J. E. (1991). Management and supervision competency. In R. Peterson (Ed.), *Core curriculum in professional psychology* (pp. 121–126). Washington, DC: American Psychological Association Press.

Bergin, A. E., & Garfield, S. L. (Eds.) (1994). *Handbook of psychotherapy and behavior change* (4th ed.). New York: Wiley.

Bernal, M. E., & Castro, F. G. (1994). Are clinical psychologists prepared for service and research with ethnic minorities? Report of a decade of progress. *American Psychologist, 49*, 797–805.

Bernard, J. L., & Jara, C. S. (1995). The failure of clinical psychology graduate students to apply understood ethical principles. In D. N. Bersoff (Ed.), *Ethical conflicts in psychology* (pp. 67–70). Washington, DC: American Psychological Association.

Bernard, J. L., Murphy, M., & Little, M. (1987). The failure of clinical psychologists to apply understood ethical principles. *Professional Psychology: Research and Practice, 18*, 489–491.

Bernard, J. M. (1994). Multicultural supervision: A reaction to Leong and Wagner, Cook, Priest, and Fukuyama. *Counselor Education and Supervision, 34*, 159–171.

Bernard, J. M. (1997). The discrimination model. In C. E. Watkins (Ed.), *Handbook of psychotherapy supervision* (pp. 310–327). New York: Wiley.

Bernard, J. M., & Goodyear, R. K. (1998). *Fundamentals of clinical supervision* (2nd ed.). Boston: Allyn & Bacon.

Bernstein, B. E., & Hartsell, T. L. (1998). *The portable lawyer for mental health professionals.* New York: Wiley.

Berry, J. (1990). Psychology of acculturation: Understanding individuals moving between cultures. In R. Brislin (Ed.), *Applied cross-cultural psychology* (pp. 232–253). Newbury Park, CA: Sage.

Bers, T. H. (2001). Measuring and reporting competencies. *New Directions for Institutional Research, 110*, 29–40.

Bersoff, D. N. (1995). *Ethical conflicts in psychology*. Washington, DC: American Psychological Association.

Betan, E. J., & Stanton, A. L. (1999). Fostering ethical willingness: Integrating emotional and contextual awareness with rational analysis. *Professional Psychology: Research and Practice, 30*, 295–301.

Beutler, L. E. (1979). Values, beliefs, religion and the persuasive influence of psychotherapy. *Psychotherapy: Theory, Research & Practice, 16*, 432–440.

Beutler, L. E. (1981). Convergence in counseling and psychotherapy: A current look. *Clinical Psychology Review, 1*, 79–101.

Beutler, L. E. (2000). David and Goliath: When empirical and clinical standards of practice meet. *American Psychologist, 55*, 997–1007.

Beutler, L. E., & Harwood, H. T. (2002). What is and can be attributed to the therapeutic relationship. *Journal of Contemporary Psychotherapy, 32*(1), 25–33.

Beutler, L. E., Machado, P. P. P., & Neufeldt, S. A. (1994). Therapist variables. In A. E. Bergin & S. L. Garfield (Eds.), *Handbook of psychotherapy and behavior change* (4th ed., pp. 229–269). New York: Wiley.

Bevan, W. (1991). Contemporary psychology: A tour inside the onion. *American Psychologist, 46*(5), 475–483.

Biaggio, M. K., Duffy, R., & Shaffelbach, D. F. (1998). Obstacles to addressing professional misconduct. *Clinical Psychology Review, 18*(3), 273–285.

Biaggio, M. K., Gasparikova-Krasnec, M., & Bauer, L. (1983). Evaluation of clinical psychology graduate students: The problem of the unsuitable student. *Professional Practice of Psychology, 4*(1), 9–20.

Biaggio, M. K., Paget, T. L., & Chenoweth, M. S. (1997). A model for ethical management of faculty-student dual relationships. *Professional Psychology: Research and Practice, 28*, 184–189.

Bidell, M. P., Turner, J. A., & Casas, J. M. (2002). First impressions count: Ethnic/racial and lesbian/gay/bisexual content of professional psychology application materials. *Professional Psychology: Research and Practice, 33*, 97–103.

Binder, J. L., & Strupp, H. H. (1997a). "Negative process": A recurrently discovered and underestimated facet of therapeutic process and outcome in the individual psychotherapy of adults. *Clinical Psychology: Science and Practice, 4*, 121–139.

Binder, J. L., & Strupp, H. H. (1997b). Supervision of psychodynamic therapies. In C. E. Watkins, Jr. (Ed.), *Handbook of psychotherapy supervision* (pp. 44–62). New York: Wiley.

Bingham, R. P., Porche-Burke, L., James, S., Sue, D. W., & Vasquez, M. J. T. (2002). Introduction: A report on the National Multicultural Conference and Summit II. *Cultural Diversity and Ethnic Minority Psychology, 8*(2), 75–87.

Blackshaw, S. L., & Patterson, P. G. R. (1992). The prevention of sexual exploitation of patients: Educational issues. *Canadian Journal of Psychology, 37,* 350–353.

Blanchard, C. A., & Lichtenberg, J. W. (1998). Counseling psychologists' training to deal with their sexual feelings in therapy. *The Counseling Psychologist, 26,* 624–639.

Board of Curators of the University of Missouri v. Horowitz, 430 U.S. 964 (1978).

Bob, S. (1999). Narrative approaches to supervision and case formulation. *Psychotherapy, 36*(2), 146–153.

Bongar, B., & Harmatz, M. (1991). Clinical psychology graduate education in the study of suicide: Availability, resources, and importance. *Suicide and Life Threatening Behavior, 21,* 231–244.

Borders, L. D. (1992). Learning to think like a supervisor. *Clinical Supervisor, 10,* 135–148.

Borders, L. D., Bernard, J. J., Dye, H. A., Fong, M. L., Henderson, P., & Nance, D. W. (1991). Curriculum guide for training counseling supervisors: Rationale, development, and implementation. *Counselor Education and Supervision, 31,* 58–82.

Borders, L. D., & Leddick, G. R. (1987). *Handbook of counseling supervision.* Alexandria, VA: American Association for Counseling and Development.

Borders, L. D., & Leddick, G. R. (1988). A nationwide survey of supervision training. *Counselor Education and Supervision, 27,* 271–283.

Bordin, E. (1979). The generalizability of the psychoanalytic concept of the working alliance. *Psychotherapy, 16,* 252–260.

Bordin, E. S. (1983). Supervision in counseling: II. Contemporary models of supervision: A working alliance based model of supervision. *The Counseling Psychologist, 11,* 35–42.

Bordin, E. S. (1994). Theory and research in the therapeutic working alliance: New directions. In A. O. Horvath & L. S. Greenberg (Eds.), *The working alliance: Theory, research and practice* (pp. 13–37). New York: Wiley.

Borkovec, T. D., Echemendia, R. J., Ragusea, S. A., & Ruiz, M. (2001). The Pennsylvania Practice Research Network and future possibilities for clinically meaningful and scientifically rigorous psychotherapy effectiveness research. *Clinical Psychology: Science & Practice, 8*(2), 155–167.

Borum, R. (1996). Improving the clinical practice of violence risk assessment: Technology, guidelines, and training. *American Psychologist, 51,* 945–956.

Bouchard, M.-A., Normandin, L., & Seguin, M.-H. (1995). Countertransference as instrument and obstacle: A comprehensive and descriptive framework. *The Psychoanalytic Quarterly, 64,* 717–745.

Boxley, R., Drew, C. R., & Rangel, D. M. (1986). Clinical trainee impairment in APA approved internship programs. *Clinical Psychologist, 39,* 49–52.

Brady, M., Leuner, J. D., Bellack, J. P., Loquist, R. S., Cipriano, P. F., & O'Neil, E. H. (2001). A proposed framework for differentiating the 21 Pew competencies by level of nursing education. *Nursing Health Care Perspectives, 21*(1), 30–35.

Brawer, P. A., Handal, P. J., Fabricatore, A. N., Roberts, R., & Wajda-Johnston, V. A. (2002). Training and education in religion/spirituality within APA-accredited clinical psychology programs. *Professional Psychology: Research and Practice, 33*, 203–206.

Breunlin, D. C., Karrer, B. M., McGuire, D. E., & Cimmarusti, R. A. (1988). Cybernetics of videotape supervision. In H. A. Liddle, D. C. Breunlin, & R. C. Schwartz (Eds.), *Handbook of family therapy training and supervision* (pp. 194–206). New York: Guilford Press.

Breunlin, D. C., Rampage, C., & Eovaldi, M. L. (1995). Family therapy supervision: Toward an integrative perspective. In R. H. Mikesell, D.-D. Lusterman, & S. H. McDaniel (Eds.), *Integrating family therapy: Handbook of family psychology and systems theory* (pp. 547–560). Washington, DC: American Psychological Association.

Bridge, P., & Bascue, L. O. (1990). Documentation of psychotherapy supervision. *Psychotherapy in Private Practice, 8*(1), 79–86.

Bridges, N. A. (2001). Therapist's self-disclosure: Expanding the comfort zone. *Psychotherapy: Theory, Research, Practice, Training, 38*(1), 21–30.

Brislin, R. (2000). *Understanding culture's influence on behavior*. Fort Worth, TX: Harcourt College Publishers.

Brodsky, A. M. (1989). Sex between patient and therapist: Psychology's data and response. In G. O. Gabbard (Ed.), *Sexual exploitation in professional relationships* (pp. 15–25). Washington, DC: American Psychiatric Publishing.

Bromberg, P. M. (1982). The supervisory process and parallel process in psychoanalysis. *Contemporary Psychoanalysis, 18*, 92–111.

Brown, M. T., & Landrum-Brown, J. (1995). Counselor supervision: Cross-cultural perspectives. In J. M. Casas & J. G. Ponterotto (Eds.), *Handbook of multicultural counseling* (pp. 263–286). Thousand Oaks, CA: Sage.

Brown, R. T., Freeman, W. S., Brown, R. A., Belar, C., Hersch, L., Hornyak, L. et al. (2002). The role of psychology in health care delivery. *Professional Psychology: Research and Practice, 33*, 536–545.

Browning, D. (1987). *Religious thought and the modern psychologies*. Philadelphia: Fortress.

Bruss, K. V., Brack, C. J., Brack, G., Glickauf-Hughes, C., & O'Leary, M. (1997). A developmental model for supervising therapists treating gay, lesbian, and bisexual clients. *The Clinical Supervisor, 15*(1), 61–73.

Bruyere, S. M. (2002). Disability nondiscrimination in the employment process: The role for testing professionals. In D. K. Smith (Ed.), *Assessing individuals with disabilities in educational, employment, and counseling settings* (pp. 205–220). Washington, DC: American Psychological Publishing.

Bugental, J. F. T. (1965). *Search for authenticity*. New York: Holt, Rinehart & Winston.

Buhrke, R. A., & Douce, L. A. (1991). Training issues for counseling psychologists in working with lesbian women and gay men. *Counseling Psychologist, 19*, 216–234.

Burian, B. K., & Slimp, A. O. (2000). Social dual-role relationships during internship: A decision-making model. *Professional Psychology: Research and Practice, 31*, 332–338.

Burke, W. R., Goodyear, R. K., & Guzzard, C. R. (1998). Weakenings and repairs in supervisory alliances. *American Journal of Psychotherapy, 52*, 450–463.

Campbell, C. D., & Gordon, M. C. (2003). Acknowledging the inevitable: Understanding multiple relationships in rural practice. *Professional Psychology: Research and Practice, 34*, 430–434.

Cape, J., & Barkham, M. (2002). Practice improvement methods: Conceptual base, evidence-based research, and practice-based recommendations. *British Journal of Clinical Psychology, 41*, 285–307.

Carifio, M. S., & Hess, A. K. (1987). Who is the ideal supervisor? *Professional Psychology: Research and Practice, 18*, 244–250.

Carney, C. G., & Kahn, K. B. (1984). Building competencies for effective cross-cultural counseling: A developmental view. *The Counseling Psychologist, 12*, 111–119.

Carroll, L., & Gilroy, P. J. (2002). Transgender issues in counselor preparation. *Counselor Education and Supervision, 41*, 233–242.

Carroll, M. (1999). Training in the tasks of supervision. In E. Holloway & M. Carroll (Eds.), *Training Counselling Supervisors* (pp. 44–66). London: Sage.

Carter, R. T. (2001). Back to the future in cultural competence training. *The Counseling Psychologist, 29*, 787–789.

Cauce, A. M., Domenech-Rodriguez, M., Paradise, M., Cochran, B. N., Shea, J. M., Srebnik, D., & Baydar, N. (2002). Cultural and contextual influences in mental health help seeking: A focus on ethnic minority youth. *Journal of Consulting and Clinical Psychology, 70*, 44–55.

Caudill, B. (2002). Risk management for psychotherapists: Avoiding the pitfalls. In L. VandeCreek & T. L. Jackson, (Eds.), *Innovations in clinical practice: A source book* (Vol. 20; p. 307) . Sarasota, FL: Professional Resource Press.

Celenza, A. (1995). Love and hate in the countertransference supervisory concerns. *Psychotherapy: Theory, Research, Practice, Training, 32*, 301–307.

Chambless, D. L., & Hollon, S. D. (1998). Defining empirically supported therapies. *Journal of Consulting and Clinical Psychology, 66*(1), 7–18.

Chenneville, V. (2000). HIV, confidentiality, and duty to protect: A decision-making model. *Professional Psychology: Research and Practice, 31*, 661–670.

Cherniss, C., & Equatios, E. (1977). Styles of clinical supervision in community mental health programs. *Journal of Consulting and Clinical Psychology, 45*, 1195–1196.

Chung, Y. B., Baskin, M. L., & Case, A. B. (1998). Positive and negative supervisory experiences reported by counseling trainees. *Psychological Reports, 82*, 752.

Church, A. H. (1997). Do you see what I see? An exploration of congruence in ratings from multiple perspectives. *Journal of Applied Social Psychology, 27*, 983–1020.

Chused, J. (1991). The evocative power of enactments. *Journal of the American Psychoanalytic Association, 39*, 615–639.

Clark, R. A., Harden, S. L., & Johnson, W. B. (2000). Mentor relationships in clinical psychology doctoral training: Results of a national survey. *Teaching of Psychology, 27*, 262–268.

Clement, P. W. (1999). *Outcomes and incomes: How to evaluate, improve, and market your psychotherapy practice by measuring outcomes.* New York: Guilford Press.

Clinical Treatment and Services Research Workgroup. (1998). *Bridging science and service.* Washington, DC: National Institute of Mental Health. Retrieved December 1, 2002 from http://www.nimh.nih.gov/research/bridge.htm

Cobia, D. C., & Boes, S. R. (2000). Professional disclosure statements and formal plans for supervision: Two strategies for minimizing the risk of ethical conflicts in post-master's supervision. *Journal of Counseling and Development, 78*, 293–296.

Cohen v. State of New York, 382 N.Y.S. 2d 128 (1975).

Coleman, H. L. K. (1997). Portfolio assessment of multicultural counseling competence. In D. B. Pope-Davis & H. L. K. Coleman (Eds.), *Multicultural counseling competencies* (pp. 43–59). Thousand Oaks, CA: Sage.

Coleman, H. L. K. (1998). General and multicultural counseling competency: Apples and oranges? *Journal of Multicultural Counseling and Development, 26*, 147–156.

Cone, J. J. (2001). *Evaluating outcomes: Empirical tools for effective practice.* Washington, DC: American Psychological Association.

Conroe, R. M., & Schank, J. A. (1989). Sexual intimacy in clinical supervision: Unmasking the silence. In G. R. Schoener, J. H. Milgrom, J. C. Gonsiorek, E. T. Leupker, & R. M. Conroe (Eds.), *Psychotherapists' sexual involvement with clients: Intervention and prevention* (pp. 245–262). Minneapolis, MN: Walk-in Counseling Center.

Constantine, M. G. (1997). Facilitating multicultural competency in counseling supervision. In D. B. Pope-Davis & H. L. K. Coleman (Eds.), *Multicultural counseling competencies* (pp. 310–324). Thousand Oaks, CA: Sage.

Constantine, M. G. (2001). Predictors of observer ratings of multicultural counseling competence in Black, Latino, and White American trainees. *Journal of Counseling Psychology, 48*, 456–462.

Constantine, M. G. (2002). Predictors of satisfaction with counseling: Racial and ethnic minority clients' attitudes toward counseling and ratings of their counselors' general and multicultural counseling competence. *Journal of Counseling Psychology, 49*, 255–263.

Constantine, M. G., & Kwan, K. K. (2003). Cross-cultural considerations of therapist self-disclosure. *JCLP/In Session, 59*, 581–588.

Constantine, M. G., & Ladany, N. (2000). Self-report multicultural counseling competence scales: Their relation to social desirability attitudes and multicultural case conceptualization ability. *Journal of Counseling Psychology, 47*, 155–164.

Constantine, M. G., & Ladany, N. (2001). New visions for defining and assessing multicultural counseling competence. In J. G. Ponterotto, J. M. Casas, L. A. Suzuki, & C. M. Alexander (Eds.), *Handbook of multicultural counseling* (2nd ed., pp. 482–498). Thousand Oaks, CA: Sage.

Constantine, M. G., Ladany, N., Inman, A. G., & Ponterotto, J. G. (1996). Students' perceptions of multicultural training in counseling psychology program. *Journal of Multicultural Counseling and Development, 24*, 241–253.

Cook, D. A. (1994). Racial identity in supervision. *Counselor Education and Supervision, 34*, 132–138.

Cooper, S. H. (1998). Countertransference disclosure and the conceptualization of analytic technique. *The Psychoanalytic Quarterly, 67*, 128–154.

Corey, G., Corey, M., & Callahan, P. (2003). *Issues and ethics in the helping professions.* Pacific Grove, CA: Brooks/Cole.

Cormier, L. S., & Bernard, J. M. (1982). Ethical and legal responsibilities of clinical supervisors. *The Personnel and Guidance Journal, 60*, 486–491.

Coster, J. S., & Schwebel, M. (1997). Well-functioning in professional psychologists. *Professional Psychology: Research and Practice, 28*, 5–13.

Creighton, A., & Kivel, P. (1992). *Helping teens stop violence: A practical guide for educators, counselors, and parents.* Alameda, CA: Hunter House.

Cummings, A. L. (2000). Teaching feminist counselor responses to novice female counselors. *Counselor Education and Supervision, 40*, 47–57.

D'Andrea, M., & Daniels, J. (1991). Exploring the different levels of multicultural counseling training in counselor education. *Journal of Counseling and Development, 70*, 78–85.

D'Andrea, M., & Daniels, J. (1997). Multicultural counseling supervision: Central issues, theoretical considerations, and practical strategies. In D. B. Pope-Davis & H. L. K. Coleman (Eds.), *Multicultural counseling competencies: Assessment, education and training, and supervision* (pp. 290–309). Thousand Oaks, CA: Sage.

D'Andrea, M., Daniels, J., & Heck, R. (1991). Evaluating the impact of multicultural counseling training. *Journal of Counseling and Development, 70*, 143–150.

Daniels, T. G., Rigazio-Diglio, S. A., & Ivey, A. E. (1997). Microcounseling: A training and supervision paradigm for the helping profession. In C. E. Watkins, Jr. (Ed.), *Handbook of psychotherapy supervision* (pp. 277–295). New York: Wiley.

DeAngelis, T. (2002). A new generation of issues for LGBT clients. *American Psychological Association Monitor on Psychology, 33*(2), 42–44.

deMayo, R. A. (1997). Patient sexual behavior and sexual harassment: a national survey of female psychologists. *Professional Psychology: Research and Practice, 28*, 58–62.

deMayo, R. A. (2000). Patients' sexual behavior and sexual harassment: A survey of clinical supervisors. *Professional Psychology: Research and Practice, 31,* 706–709.

Dendinger, D. C., & Kohn, E. (1989). Assessing supervisory skills. *The Clinical Supervisor, 7*(1), 41–55.

Dewald, P. (1987). Learning process in psychoanalytic supervision: Complexities and challenges. Madison, CT: International Universities Press.

Dewald, P. A. (1997). The process of supervision in psychoanalysis. In C. E. Watkins, (Ed.), *Handbook of psychotherapy supervision* (pp. 31–43). New York: Wiley.

Dickinson, S. C., & Johnson, W. B. (2000). Mentoring in clinical psychology doctoral programs: A national survey of directors of training. *The Clinical Supervisor, 19*(1), 137–152.

Dienst, E. R., & Armstrong, P. M. (1988). Evaluations of students' clinical competence. *Professional Psychology: Research and Practice, 19,* 339–341.

Disney, M. J., & Stephens, A. M. (1994). *The ACA Legal Series (Vol. 10): Legal issues in clinical supervision.* Alexandria, VA: American Counseling Association.

Doehrman, M. J. (1976). Parallel processes in supervision and psychotherapy. *Bulletin of the Menninger Clinic, 40,* 9–104.

Duan, C., & Roehlke, H. (2001). A descriptive "snapshot" of cross-racial supervision in university counseling center internships. *Journal of Multicultural Counseling and Development, 29,* 131–146.

Dubin, S. S. (1972). Obsolescence or lifelong education: A choice for the profession. *American Psychologist, 27,* 486–498.

Dunn, J. (1995). Intersubjectivity in psychoanalysis: A critical review. *The International Journal of Psychoanalysis, 76,* 723–738.

Dye, H. A., & Borders, L. D. (1990). Counseling supervisors: Standards for preparation and practice. *Journal of Counseling and Development, 69,* 27–32.

Ebert, B. W. (2002). Dual-relationship prohibitions: A concept whose time never should have come. In A. A. Lazarus & O. Zur (Eds.), *Dual relationships and psychotherapy* (pp. 169–211). New York: Springer Publishing Company.

Eby, L. T., McManus, S. E., Simon, S. A., & Russell, J. E. A. (2000). The protégé's perspective regarding negative mentoring experiences: The development of a taxonomy. *Journal of Vocational Behavior, 57,* 1–21.

Efstation, J. F., Patton, M. J., & Kardash, C. M. (1990). Measuring the working alliance in counselor supervision. *Journal of Counseling Psychology, 37,* 322–329.

Egan, G. (1986). *The skilled helper: Models, skills and methods for effective helping* (3rd ed.). Monterey, CA: Brooks/Cole.

Ekstein, R., & Wallerstein, R. S. (1958). *The teaching and learning of psychotherapy.* New York: Basic Books.

Ekstein, R., & Wallerstein, R. S. (1972). *The teaching and learning of psychotherapy* (2nd ed.). New York: International Universities Press.

Ellis, M. V. (1991a). Critical incidents in clinical supervision and in supervisor supervision: Assessing supervisory issues. *Journal of Counseling Psychology, 38,* 342–349.

Ellis, M. V. (1991b). Research in clinical supervision: Revitalizing a scientific agenda. *Counselor Education and Supervision, 30,* 238–251.

Ellis, M. V. (2001). Harmful supervision, a cause for alarm: Comment on Gray et al. (2001) and Nelson and Friedlander (2001). *Journal of Counseling Psychology, 48,* 401–406.

Ellis, M. V., & Dell, D. M. (1986). Dimensionality of supervisor roles: Supervisors' perceptions of supervision. *Journal of Counseling Psychology, 33,* 282–291.

Ellis, M. V., & Douce, L. A. (1994). Group supervision of novice clinical supervisors: Eight recurring issues. *Journal of Counseling and Development, 72,* 520–525.

Ellis, M. V., Krengel, M., & Beck, M. (2002). Testing self-focused attention theory in clinical supervision: Effects on supervisee anxiety and performance. *Journal of Counseling Psychology, 49,* 101–116.

Ellis, M. V., & Ladany, N. (1997). Inferences concerning supervisees and clients in clinical supervision: An integrative review. In C. E. Watkins, Jr. (Ed.), *Handbook of psychotherapy supervision* (pp. 447–507). New York: Wiley.

Ellis, M. V., Ladany, N., Krengel, M., & Schult, D. (1996). Clinical supervision research from 1981 to 1993: A methodological critique. *Journal of Counseling Psychology, 43,* 35–50.

Enns, C. Z. (1993). Twenty years of feminist counseling and therapy. *The Counseling Psychologist, 21,* 3–87.

Enyedy, K. C., Arcinue, F., Puri, N. N., Carter, J. W., Goodyear, R. K., & Getzelman, M. A. (2003). Hindering phenomena in group supervision: Implications for practice. *Professional Psychology: Research and Practice, 34,* 312–317.

Epstein, R. M., & Hundert, E. M. (2002). Defining and assessing professional competence. *Journal of the American Medical Association, 287,* 226–235.

Falender, C. (1999). *Supervisor's maps.* Unpublished manuscript.

Falender, C. (2000, October). Education and training in the 21st century. *California Psychologist,* 18–20.

Falender, C. (2001). Development of supervisees during the training year. Unpublished manuscript.

Falender, C. (2003). *Supervision contract outline.* Unpublished measure.

Falender, C. A., Cornish, J. A. E., Goodyear, R., Hatcher, R., Kaslow, N. J., Leventhal, G., et al. (in press). Defining competencies in psychology supervision: A consensus statement. *Journal of Clinical Psychology.*

Falender, C. A., & Shafranske, E. P. (2004). 360-degree evaluation applied to psychology training. Manuscript in preparation.

Falicov, C. J. (1988). Learning to think culturally. In H. A. Liddle, D. C. Breunlin, & R. C. Schwartz (Eds.), *Handbook of family therapy training and supervision* (pp. 335–357). New York: Guilford Press.

Falicov, C. J. (1995). Training to think culturally: A multidimensional comparative framework. *Family Process, 34,* 373–388.

Falicov, C. J. (1998). *Latino families in therapy: A guide to multicultural practice.* New York: Guilford.

Falvey, J. E. (2002). Managing clinical supervision: Ethical practice and legal risk management. Pacific Grove, CA: Brooks/Cole.

Fantuzzo, J. W. (1984). Mastery: A competency-based training model for clinical psychologists. *The Clinical Psychologist, 37*(1), 29–30.

Fantuzzo, J. W., & Moon, G. W. (1984). Competency mandate: A model for teaching skills in the administration of the WAIS-R. *Journal of Clinical Psychology, 40,* 1053–1059.

Fantuzzo, J. W., Sisemore, T. A., & Spradlin, W. H. (1983). A competency-based model for teaching skills in the administration of intelligence tests. *Professional Psychology: Research and Practice, 14,* 224–231.

Fassinger, R. E., & Richie, B. S. (1997). Sex matters: Gender and sexual orientation in training for multicultural counseling competency. In D. B. Pope-Davis & H. L. K. Coleman (Eds.), *Multicultural counseling competencies: Assessment, education and training, and supervision* (pp. 83–110). Thousand Oaks, CA: Sage.

Finkelstein, H., & Tuckman, A. (1997). Supervision of psychological assessment: A developmental model. *Professional Psychology: Research and Practice, 28,* 92–95.

Fischer, A. R., Jome, L. M., & Atkinson, D. R. (1998). Reconceptualizing multicultural counseling: Universal healing conditions in a culturally specific context. *Counseling Psychologist, 26,* 525–588.

Fischer, C. T. (1998). Phenomenological, existential and humanistic foundations for psychology as a human-science. In M. Hersen & A. Bellack (Series Eds.), *Comprehensive clinical psychology*; C. E. Walker (Vol. Ed.). *Vol. 1: Foundations* (pp. 449–472). London: Elsevier Science.

Fly, B. J., van Bark, W. P., Weinman, L., Kitchener, K. S., & Lang, P. R. (1997). Ethical transgression of psychology graduate students: Critical incidents with implications for training. *Professional Psychology: Research and Practice, 28,* 492–495.

Folman, R. Z. (1991). Therapist-patient sex: Attraction and boundary problems. *Psychotherapy, 28,* 168–173.

Ford, G. G. (2001). *Ethical reasoning in the mental health professions.* Boca Raton, FL: CRC Press.

Ford, M. P., & Hendrick, S. S. (2003). Therapists' sexual values for self and clients: Implications for practice and training. *Professional Psychology: Research and Practice, 34,* 80–87.

Forrest, L., Elman, N., Gizara, S., & Vacha-Haase, T. (1999). Trainee impairment: A review of identification, remediation, dismissal, and legal issues. *The Counseling Psychologist, 27,* 627–686.

Fosshage, J. L. (1997). Towards a model of psychoanalytic supervision from a self-psychology/intersubjective perspective. In M. H. Rock (Ed.), *Psychodynamic supervision* (pp. 189–212). Northvale, NJ: Jason Aronson.

Frame, M. W., & Stevens-Smith, P. (1995). Out of harm's way: Enhancing monitoring and dismissal processes in counselor education programs. *Counselor Education and Supervision, 35*, 118–129.

Frank, J. D., & Frank, J. B. (1991). *Persuasion and healing* (3rd ed.). Baltimore: John Hopkins University Press. (Original work published 1961)

Franklin, G. (1990). The multiple meanings of neutrality. *Journal of the American Psychoanalytic Association, 38*(1), 195–220.

Frawley-O'Dea, M. G., & Sarnat, J. E. (2001). *The supervisory relationship: A contemporary psychodynamic approach.* New York: Guilford Press.

Frazier, P., Dik, B. J., Glaser, T., Steward, J., & Tashiro, T. (2002). *Integrating science and practice in advanced practica.* Roundtable discussion at the Annual Meeting of the American Psychological Association, Chicago, IL.

Freud, S. (1910). The future prospects of psycho-analytic therapy. In J. Strachey (Ed. & Trans.), *Standard edition of the collected works of Sigmund Freud* (Vol. 10, pp. 139–151). London: Hogarth Press. (Original work published 1923)

Freud, S. (1912). Recommendations to physicians practicing psycho-analysis. In J. Strachey (Ed. & Trans.), *Standard edition of the collected works of Sigmund Freud* (Vol. 12, pp. 111–125). London: Hogarth Press. (Original work published 1923)

Friedberg, R. D., & Taylor, L. A. (1994). Perspectives on supervision in cognitive therapy. *Journal of Rational-Emotive & Cognitive Behavior Therapy, 12*(3), 147–161.

Friedlander, M. L., Siegel, S., & Brenock, K. (1989). Parallel process in counseling and supervision: A case study. *Journal of Counseling Psychology, 36*, 149–157.

Friedlander, M. L., & Ward, L. G. (1984). Development and validation of the supervisory styles inventory. *Journal of Counseling Psychology, 31*, 541–557.

Friedman, D., & Kaslow, N. J. (1986). The development of professional identity in psychotherapists. In F. W. Kaslow (Ed.), *Supervision and training: Models, dilemmas, and challenges* (pp. 29–49). New York: Haworth Press.

Friedman, S. C., & Gelso, C. J. (2000). The development of the inventory of countertransference behavior. *Journal of Clinical Psychology, 56*, 1221–1235.

Fruzzetti, A. E., Waltz, J. A., & Linehan, M. M. (1997). Supervision in dialectical behavior therapy. In C. E. Watkins, Jr. (Ed.), *Handbook of psychotherapy supervision* (pp. 84–100). New York: Wiley.

Fuertes, J. N. (2002). *Facilitating trainees' multicultural counseling competence.* Paper presented at the 110th Annual Convention of the American Psychological Association, Chicago, IL.

Fuertes, J. N., & Brobst, K. (2002). Clients' ratings of counselor multicultural competency. *Cultural Diversity & Ethnic Minority Psychology, 8*(3), 214–223.

Fuertes, J. N., Mueller, L. N., Chauhan, R. V., Walker, J. A., & Ladany, N. (2002). An investigation of European American therapists' approach to counseling African American clients. *The Counseling Psychologist, 30,* 763–788.

Fukuyama, M. A. (1994a). Critical incidents in multi-cultural counseling supervision: A phenomenological approach to supervision. *Counselor Education and Supervision: 34,* 142–151.

Fukuyama, M. A. (1994b). Multicultural training: If not now when? If not you who? *The Counseling Psychologist, 22,* 296–299.

Fukuyama, M. A., & Ferguson, A. D. (2000). Lesbian, gay, and bisexual people of color: Understanding cultural complexity and managing multiple oppressions. In R. M. Perez, K. A. Debord, & K. Bieschke (Eds.), *Handbook of counseling and psychotherapy with lesbian, gay, and bisexual clients* (pp. 81–105). Washington, DC: American Psychological Association.

Fukuyama, M. A., & Sevig, T. D. (1999). *Integrating spirituality into multicultural counseling.* Thousand Oaks, CA: Sage.

Fuqua, D. R., Newman, J. L., Scott, T. B., & Gade, E. M. (1986). Variability across sources of performance ratings: Further evidence. *Journal of Counseling Psychology, 33,* 353–356.

Gabbard, G. O. (2001). A contemporary psychoanalytic model of countertransference. *Journal of Clinical Psychology, 57,* 983–991.

Gabbard, G., Horwitz, L., Frieswyk, S., Allen, J., Colson, D., Newsom, G., et al. (1988). The effect of therapist interventions on the therapeutic alliance with borderline patients. *Journal of the American Psychoanalytic Association, 36,* 697–727.

Gabbard, G. O., & Wilkinson, S. M. (1994). *Management of countertransference with borderline patients.* Washington, DC: American Psychiatric Publishing.

Gadamer, H.-G. (1962/1976). On the problem of self understanding. In D. E. Linge (Ed. & Trans.), *Philosophical hermeneutics* (pp. 44–58). Berkeley, CA: University of California Press.

Gallessich, J., & Olmstead, K. M. (1987). Training in counseling psychology: Issues and trends in 1986. *The Counseling Psychologist, 15,* 596–600.

Gallup, G., Jr., & Johnson, B. R. (2003, January 28). New index tracks "Spiritual State of the Union." The Gallup Organization. Retrieved February 2, 2003 from http://www.gallup.com/poll/tb/religValue/20030128.asp#rm

Gallup, G., Jr., & Jones, T. (2000). *The next American spirituality: Finding God in the twenty-first century.* Colorado Springs, CO: Cook Communications.

Gandolfo, R. L., & Brown, R. (1987). Psychology intern ratings of actual and ideal supervision of psychotherapy. *The Journal of Training and Practice in Professional Psychology, 1*(1), 15–28.

Garamella, Conservator for the estate of Denny Almonte v. New York Medical College et al., CIV.NO.3:93CV116(HBF). United States District Court for the District of Connecticut, 23 F. Supp. 2d 167; 1998 U.S. Dist. Lexis 16696.

Garb, H. N. (1989). Clinical judgment, clinical training, and professional experience. *Psychological Bulletin, 105,* 387–396.

Garnets, L., Hancock, K. A., Cochran, S. D., Goodchilds, J., & Peplau, L. A. (1991). Issues in psychotherapy with lesbians and gay men: A survey of psychologists. *American Psychologist, 46,* 964–972.

Garrett, M. T., Borders, L. D., Crutchfield, L. B., Torres-Rivera, E., Brotherton, D., & Curtis, R. (2001). Multicultural superVISION: A paradigm of cultural responsiveness for supervisors. *Journal of Multicultural Counseling and Development, 29,* 147–159.

Gaston, L., Thomson, L., Gallagher, D., Cournoyer, L.-G., & Gagnon, R. (1998). Alliance, technique, and their interactions in predicting outcome of behavioral, cognitive, and brief dynamic therapy. *Psychotherapy Research, 8,* 190–209.

Gatmon, D., Jackson, D., Koshkarian, L., Martos-Perry, N., Molina, A, Patel, N., et al. (2001). Exploring ethnic gender and social orientation variables in supervision: Do they really matter? *Journal of Multicultural Counseling and Development, 29,* 102–113.

Gediman, H. K., & Wolkenfeld, F. (1980). The parallelism phenomenon in psychoanalysis and supervision: Its reconsideration as a triadic system. *Psychoanalytic Quarterly, 49,* 234–255.

Gelso, C. J., & Hayes, J. A. (2001). Countertransference management. *Psychotherapy, 38,* 418–422.

Gelso, C. J., Latts, M. G., Gomez, M. J., & Fassinger, R. E. (2002). Countertransference management and therapy outcome: An initial evaluation. *Journal of Clinical Psychology, 58,* 861–867.

Gergen, K. J. (1994). Exploring the postmodern: Perils or potentials? *American Psychologist, 49,* 412–416.

Gerson, B. (Ed.). (1996). *The therapist as a person: Life crises, life choices, life expectancies, and their effects on treatment.* Hillsdale, NJ: Analytic Press.

Gerson, S. (1996). Neutrality, resistance, and self-disclosure in an intersubjective psychoanalysis. *Psychoanalytic Dialogues, 6,* 623–645.

Getz, H. G. (1999). Assessment of clinical supervisor competencies. *Journal of Counseling and Development, 77,* 491–497.

Gill , M. (1994). *Psychoanalysis in transition: A personal view.* Hillsdale, NJ: Analytic Press.

Giorgi, A. (1970). *Psychology as a human science.* New York: Harper & Row.

Glaser, R. D., & Thorpe, J. S. (1986). Unethical intimacy: A survey of sexual contact and advances between psychology educators and female graduate students. *American Psychologist, 41,* 43–51.

Gold, J. H., & Nemiah, J. C. (Eds.). (1993). When the therapist's real life intrudes. In M. R. Goldfried & G. C. Davison (Eds.), *Clinical behavior therapy.* New York: Holt, Rinehart & Winston.

Gonsalvez, C. J., Oades, L. G., & Freestone, J. (2002). The objectives approach to clinical supervision: Towards integration and empirical evaluation. *Australian Psychologist, 37*(1), 68–77.

Goodman-Delahunty, J. (2000). Psychological impairment under the Americans With Disabilities Act: Legal guidelines. *Professional Psychology: Research and Practice, 31*, 197–205.

Goodyear, R. K., & Bernard, J. M. (1998). Clinical supervision: Lessons from the literature. *Counselor Education and Supervision, 38*, 6–22.

Goodyear, R. K., & Guzzardo, C. R. (2000). Psychotherapy supervision and training. In S. D. Brown & R. W. Lent (Eds.), *Handbook of counseling psychology* (3rd ed., pp. 83–108). New York: Wiley.

Goodyear, R. K., & Nelson, M. L. (1997). The major formats of psychotherapy supervision. In C. E. Watkins, Jr. (Ed.), *Handbook of psychotherapy supervision* (pp. 328–344). New York: Wiley.

Goodyear, R. K., & Robyak, J. E. (1982). Supervisors' theory and experience in supervisory focus. *Psychological Reports, 51*, 978.

Gottlieb, M. C. (1993). Avoiding exploitative dual relationships: A decision-making model. *Psychotherapy, 30*, 41–48.

Gould, L. J., & Bradley, L. J. (2001). Evaluation in supervision. In L. J. Bradley & N. Ladany (Eds.), *Counselor education: Principles, process, and practice* (pp. 271–303). Philadelphia: Brunner-Routledge.

Granello, D. H., Beamish, P. M., & Davis, T. E. (1997). Supervisee empowerment: Does gender make a difference? *Counselor Education and Supervision, 36*, 305–317.

Grater, H. A. (1985). Stages in psychotherapy supervision: From therapy skills to skilled therapist. *Professional Psychology: Research and Practice, 5*, 605–610.

Gray, L. A., Ladany, N., Walker, J. A., & Ancis, J. R. (2001). Psychotherapy trainees' experience of counterproductive events in supervision. *Journal of Counseling Psychology, 48*, 371–383.

Greben, S. E. (1985). Dear Brutus: Dealing with unresponsiveness through supervision. *Canadian Journal of Psychiatry, 30*, 48–53.

Greenberg, J. (1986). The problem of analytic neutrality. *Contemporary Psychoanalysis, 22*, 76–86.

Greenson, R. (1967). *The technique and practice of psychoanalysis.* New York: International Universities Press.

Greenwald, M., & Young, J. (1998). Schema-focused therapy: An integrative approach to psychotherapy supervision. *Journal of Cognitive Psychotherapy: An International Quarterly, 12*(2), 109–125.

Grey, A. G., & Fiscalini, J. (1987). Parallel process as countertransference-countertransference interaction. *Psychoanalytic Psychology, 4*, 131–144.

Grote, C. L., Robiner, W. N., & Haut, A. (2001). Disclosure of negative information in letters of recommendation: Writers' intentions and readers' experiences. *Professional Psychology: Research and Practice, 32*, 655–661.

Guest, C. L., Jr., & Dooley, K. (1999). Supervisor malpractice: Liability to the supervisee in clinical supervision. *Counselor Education and Supervision, 38,* 269–279.

Guest, P. D., & Beutler, L. E. (1988). Impact of psychotherapy supervision on therapist orientation and values. *Journal of Consulting and Clinical Psychology, 56,* 653–658.

Gustafson, K. E., & McNamara, J. R. (1999). Confidentiality with minor clients: Issues and guidelines for therapists. In D. N. Bersoff (Ed.), *Ethical conflicts in psychology* (2nd ed., pp. 200–204). Washington, DC: American Psychological Association.

Gutheil, T. G., & Gabbard, G. O. (1993). The concept of boundaries in clinical practice: Theoretical and risk-management dimensions. *American Journal of Psychiatry, 150,* 188–196.

Gutheil, T. G., & Simon, R. I. (2002). Non-sexual boundary crossings and boundary violations: The ethical dimension. *Psychiatric Clinics of North America, 25,* 585–592.

Guthrie, R. V. (1998). *Even the rat was white: A historical view of psychology* (2nd ed.). Boston: Allyn & Bacon.

Guy, J. D., Brown, C. K., & Poelstra, P. L. (1992). Safety concerns and protective measures used by psychotherapists. *Professional Psychology: Research and Practice, 23,* 421–423.

Haas, L. J., & Malouf, J. L. (1989). *Keeping up the good work: A practitioner's guide to mental health ethics.* Sarasota, FL: Professional Resource Exchange.

Hahn, W. K. (2001). The experience of shame in supervision. *Psychotherapy, 38,* 272–282.

Hahn, W. K., & Molnar, S. (1991). Intern evaluation in university counseling centers. *The Counseling Psychologist, 19,* 414–430.

Hall-Marley, S. (2000). Therapist evaluation checklist. Unpublished measure.

Hall-Marley, S. (2001). Supervision feedback. Unpublished measure.

Hamacek, D. E. (1985). *Psychology in teaching, learning, and growth.* Boston: Allyn & Bacon.

Hamilton, J. C., & Spruill, J. (1999). Identifying and reducing risk factors related to trainee–client sexual misconduct. *Professional Psychology: Research and Practice, 30,* 318–327.

Hammel, G. A., Olkin, E., & Taube, D. O. (1996). Student-educator sex in clinical and counseling psychology doctoral training. *Professional Psychology: Research and Practice, 27,* 93–97.

Handelsman, M. M. (1986). Problems with ethics training by osmosis. *Professional Psychology: Research and Practice, 17,* 371–372.

Handelsman, M. M. (1990). Do written consent forms influence clients' first impressions of therapists? *Professional Psychology: Research and Practice, 21,* 451–454.

Handelsman, M. M., Gottlieb, M. C., & Knapp, S. (2002, August). *Training ethical psychologists: An acculturation model.* Paper presented at the American Psychological Association annual meeting, Chicago.

Handelsman, M. M., Kemper, M. B., Kesson-Craig, P., McLain, J., & Johnsrud, C. (1986). Use, content, and readability of written informed consent forms for treatment. *Professional Psychology: Research and Practice, 17,* 514–518.

Hanna, M. A., & Smith, J. (1998). Innovative Methods: Using rubrics for documentation of clinical work supervision. *Counselor Education and Supervision, 37,* 269–278.

Hansen, J. C. (1965). Trainees' expectations of supervision in the counseling program. *Counselor Education and Supervision, 2,* 75–80.

Hansen, N. D., & Goldberg, S. G. (1999). Navigating the nuances: A matrix of considerations for ethical-legal dilemmas. *Professional Psychology: Research and Practice, 30,* 495–503.

Hansen, N. D., Pepitone-Arreola-Rockwell, F., & Greene, A. F. (2000). Multicultural competence: Criteria and case examples. *Professional Psychology: Research and Practice, 31,* 652–660.

Harrar, W. R., VandeCreek, L., & Knapp, S. (1990). Ethical and legal aspects of clinical supervision. *Professional Psychology: Research and Practice, 21,* 37–41.

Harris, E. (2002). *Legal and ethical risk management in professional psychological practice—Sequence I.* Presentation sponsored by the APA Insurance Trust and the California Psychological Association, Los Angeles, CA.

Hayes, J. A., Riker, J. R., & Ingram, K. M. (1997). Countertransference behavior and management in brief counseling: A field study. *Psychotherapy Research, 7,* 145–153.

Hayman, P. M., & Covert, J. A. (1986). Ethical dilemmas in college counseling centers. *Journal of Counseling and Development, 64,* 318–320.

Hays, K. A., Rardin, D. K., Jarvis, P. A., Taylor, N. M., Moorman, A. S., & Armstead, C. D. (2002). An exploratory survey on empirically supported treatments: Implications for internship training. *Professional Psychology: Research and Practice, 33,* 207–211.

Hays, P. A. (2001). Addressing cultural complexities in practice: A framework for clinicians and counselors. Washington, DC: American Psychological Association Press.

Hedlund v. The Superior Court of Orange County. 34 Cal. 3d 695; 194 Cal. Rptr. 805, 669 P. 2d 41 (Sept. 1983).

Heimann, P. (1950). On counter-transference. *International Journal of Psychoanalysis, 31,* 81–84.

Helms, J. E. (1990). *Black and white racial identity: Theory, research, and practice.* Westport, CT: Greenwood Press.

Helms, J. E., & Richardson, T. Q. (1997). How "multiculturalism" obscures race and culture as differential aspects of counseling competency. In D. B. Pope-Davis, & H. L. K. Coleman (Eds.), *Multicultural counseling competencies: Assess-*

ment, education and training, and supervision (pp. 60–82). Thousand Oaks, CA: Sage.

Henderson, C. E., Cawyer, C. S., & Watkins, C. E., Jr. (1999). A comparison of student and supervisor perceptions of effective practicum supervision. *The Clinical Supervisor, 18,* 47–74.

Henggeler, S. W., & Schoenwald, S. K. (1998). *The MST supervisory manual: Promoting quality assurance at the clinical level.* Charleston, SC: MST Institute.

Henggeler, S. W., Schoenwald, S. K., Liao, J. G., Letourneau, E. J., & Edwards, D. L. (2002). Transporting efficacious treatments to field settings: The link between supervisory practices and therapist fidelity in MST programs. *Journal of Clinical Child Psychology, 31*(2), 155–167.

Heppner, P. P., & Roehlke, H. J. (1984). Differences among supervisees at different levels of supervision. *Journal of Consulting Psychology, 31,* 76–90.

Herlihy, B., & Sheeley, V. L. (1988). Counselor liability and the duty to warn: Selected cases, statutory trends, and implications for practice. *Counselor Education and Supervision, 27,* 203–215.

Herman, K. C. (1993). Reassessing predictors of therapist competence. *Journal of Counseling and Development, 72,* 29–32.

Herrmann, N. (1996). Supervisor evaluation: From theory to implementation. *Academic* Psychiatry, *20*(4), 205–211.

Hernandez, A., & Lafromboise, T. D. (1983). *Cross-cultural counseling inventory.* Unpublished measure.

Hess, A. K. (Ed.), (1980a). *Psychotherapy supervision: Theory, research and practice.* New York: Wiley.

Hess, A. K. (1980b). Training models and the nature of psychotherapy supervision. In A. K. Hess (Ed.), *Psychotherapy supervision: Theory, research and practice* (pp. 15–28). New York: Wiley.

Hess, A. K. (1986). Growth in supervision: Stages of supervisee and supervisor development. *The Clinical Supervisor, 4,* 51–67.

Hess, A. K. (1987a). Advances in psychotherapy supervision: Introduction. *Professional Psychology: Research and Practice, 18,* 187–188.

Hess, A. K. (1987b). Psychotherapy supervision: Stages, Buber, and a theory of relationship. *Professional Psychology: Research and Practice, 18,* 251–259.

Hill, C. E., Helms, J. E., Tichenor, V., Spiegel, S. B., O'Grady, K. E., & Perry, E. S. (1988). The effects of therapist response modes in brief psychotherapy. *Journal of Counseling Psychology, 35,* 222–233.

Hill, C. E., & Knox, S. (2001). Self-disclosure. *Psychotherapy, 38,* 413–417.

Hill, C. E., Mahalik, J. R., & Thompson, B. J. (1989). Therapist self-disclosure. *Psychotherapy, 26,* 290–295.

Hill, C. E., Nutt-Williams, E., Heaton, K. J., Thompson, B. J., & Rhodes, R. H. (1996). Therapist retrospective recall of impasses in long-term psychotherapy: A qualitative study. *Journal of Counseling Psychology, 43,* 207–217.

Hird, J. S., Cavalieri, C. E., Dulko, J. P., Felice, A. A. D., & Ho, T. A. (2001). Visions and realities: Supervisee perspectives of multicultural supervision. *Journal of Multicultural Counseling and Development, 29,* 114–130.

Hirsch, I. (1998). The concept of enactment and theoretical convergence. *Psychoanalytic Quarterly, 67,* 78–101.

Hoch, E. L., Ross, A. O., & Winder, C. L. (Eds.). (1966). *Professional preparation of clinical psychologists.* Washington, DC: American Psychological Association.

Hoffman, I. (1983). The patient as interpreter of the analyst's experience. *Contemporary Psychoanalysis, 19,* 389–422.

Hoffman, I. (1991). Discussion: Toward a social-constructivist view of the psychoanalytic situation. *Psychoanalytic Dialogues, 1,* 74–105.

Hogan, R. A. (1964). Issues and approaches in supervision. *Psychotherapy: Theory, Research, and Practice, 1,* 139–141.

Holloway, E. L. (1995). *Clinical supervision: A systems approach.* Thousand Oaks, CA: Sage.

Holloway, E. L. (1997). Structures for the analysis and teaching of supervision. In C. E. Watkins, Jr. (Ed.), *Handbook of psychotherapy supervision* (pp. 249–276). New York: Wiley.

Holloway, E. L. (1999). A framework for supervision training. In E. Holloway & M. Carroll (Eds.), *Training counselling supervisors* (pp. 8–43). London: Sage.

Holloway, E. L., & Carroll, M. (1996). Reaction to the special section on supervision research: Comment on Ellis et al. (1996), Ladany et al. (1996), Neufeldt et al. (1996), and Worthen & McNeill (1996). *Journal of Counseling Psychology, 43,* 51–55.

Holloway, E. L., & Neufeldt, A. A. (1995). Supervision: Its contributions to treatment efficacy. *Journal of Consulting and Clinical Psychology, 63*(2), 207–213.

Holloway, E. L., & Wolleat, P. L. (1994). Supervision: The pragmatics of empowerment. *Journal of Educational and Psychological Consultation, 5*(1), 23–43.

Holmes, D. L., Rupert, P. A., Ross, S. A., & Shapera, W. E. (1999). Student perceptions of dual relationships between faculty and students. *Ethics and Behavior, 9*(2), 79–107.

Holroyd, J. C., & Brodsky, A. (1977). Psychologists' attitudes and practices regarding erotic and nonerotic physical contact with clients. *American Psychologist, 32,* 843–849.

Horvath, A. O. (1994). Research on the alliance. In A. O. Horvath & L. S. Greenberg (Eds.), *The working alliance: Theory, research, and practice* (pp. 259–286). New York: Wiley.

Horvath, A. O. (2000). The therapeutic relationship: From transference to alliance. *Journal of Clinical Psychology/In Session: Psychotherapy in Practice, 56*(2), 163–173.

Horvath, A. O. (2001). The alliance. *Psychotherapy, 38,* 365–372.

Horvath, A. O., & Greenberg, L. S. (Eds.) (1994). *The working alliance: Theory, research, and practice.* New York: Wiley.

Horvath, A. O., & Symonds, D. B. (1991). Relationship between working alliance and outcome in psychotherapy: A meta-analysis. *Journal of Counseling Psychology, 38,* 139–149.

Hoshmand, L. T. (1994). *Orientation to inquiry in a reflective professional psychology.* Albany: State University of New York Press.

Hoshmand, L. T., & Polkinghorne, D. E. (1992). Redefining the science-practice relationship and professional training. *American Psychologist, 47,* 55–66.

Housman, L. M., & Stake, J. E. (1999). The current state of sexual ethics training in clinical psychology: Issues of quantity, quality, and effectiveness. *Professional Psychology: Research and Practice, 30,* 302–311.

Hutt, C. H., Scott, J., & King, M. (1983). A phenomenological study of supervisees' positive and negative experiences in supervision. *Psychotherapy: Theory, Research, and Practice, 20*(1), 118–123.

Ibrahim, F. A., & Kahn, H. (1987). Assessment of worldviews. *Psychological Reports, 60,* 163–176.

Illfelder-Kaye, J. (2002). Tips for trainers: Implications of the new Ethical Principles of Psychologists and Code of Conduct on Internship and Post-Doctoral Training Program. *APPIC Newsletter, 27*(2), 25.

Jablonski v. United States, 712 F.2d 391 (9th Cir. 1983).

Jackson, S. W. (1999). *Care of the psyche: A history of psychological healing.* New Haven, CT: Yale University Press.

Jacobs, T. (1986). On countertransference enactments. *Journal of the American Psychoanalytic Association, 34,* 289–307.

Jaffee v. Redmond, 51 F.3d 1346, 1357 (7th Cir. 1995).

Johan, M. (1992). Enactments in psychoanalysis. *Journal of the American Psychoanalytic Association, 40,* 827–841.

Johnson, W. B. (2002). The intentional mentor: Strategies and guidelines for the practice of mentoring. *Professional Psychology: Research and Practice, 33,* 88–96.

Johnson, W. B., & Campbell, C. D. (2002). Character and fitness requirements for professional psychologists: Are there any? *Professional Psychology: Research and Practice, 33,* 46–53.

Johnson, W. B., & Huwe, J. M. (2002). Toward a typology of mentorship dysfunction in graduate school. *Psychotherapy: Theory, Research, Practice, Training, 39*(1), 44–55.

Johnson, W. B., Koch, C., Fallow, G. O., & Huwe, J. M. (2000). Prevalence of mentoring in clinical versus experimental doctoral programs: Survey findings, implications, and recommendations. *Psychotherapy, 37,* 325–334.

Johnson, W. B., & Nelson, N. (1999). Mentor-protégé relationships in graduate training: Some ethical concerns. *Ethics and Behavior, 9,* 189–210.

Jones, S. L. (1994). A constructive relationship for religion with the science and profession of psychology: Perhaps the boldest model yet. *American Psychologist, 49,* 184–199.

Jury finds psychiatrist was negligent in pedophile case. (1998, October 9). *The New York Times*, p. B4.

Kadushin, A. (1968). Games people play in supervision. *Social Work, 13,* 23–32.

Kagan, H., & Kagan, N. (1997). Interpersonal process recall: Influencing human interaction. In C. E. Watkins, Jr. (Ed.), *Handbook of psychotherapy supervision* (pp. 296–309). New York: Wiley.

Kagan, N. (1980). Influencing human interaction—eighteen years with IPR. In A. K. Hess (Ed.), *Psychotherapy supervision: Theory, research, and practice* (pp. 262–286). New York: Wiley.

Kagan, N. I., & Kagan, H. (1990). IPR—A validated model for the 1990s and beyond. *The Counseling Psychologist, 18,* 436–440.

Kanfer, F. H. (1990). The scientist-practitioner connection: A bridge in need of constant attention. *Professional Psychology: Research and Practice, 21,* 264–270.

Kanz, J. E. (2001). Clinical-supervision.com: Issues in the provision of online supervision. *Professional Psychology: Research and Practice, 32,* 415–420.

Kaslow, N. J. (2002). Future directions in education and credentialing in Professional Psychology. Paper presented at the 2002 Competencies Conference, Scottsdale, AZ.

Kaslow, N. J., & Deering, C. G. (1994). A developmental approach to psychotherapy supervision of interns and postdoctoral fellows. *The Psychotherapy Bulletin, 28*(4), 20–23.

Kaslow, N. J., & Rice, D. G. (1985). Developmental stresses of predoctoral internship training: What training staff can do to help. *Professional Psychology: Research and Practice, 23,* 369–375.

Kauderer, S., & Herron, W. G. (1990). The supervisory relationship in psychotherapy over time. *Psychological Reports, 67,* 471–480.

Kelly, E. W. (1990). Counselor responsiveness to client religiousness. *Counseling & Values, 35*(1), 69–72.

Kemp, N. T., & Mallinckrodt, B. (1996). Impact of professional training on case conceptualization of clients with a disability. *Professional Psychology: Research and Practice, 27,* 378–385.

Kendall, P. C., & Southam-Gerow, M. A. (1995). Issues in the transportability of treatment: The case of anxiety disorders for youth. *Journal of Consulting and Clinical Psychology, 63,* 702–708.

Kennard, B. D., Stewart, S. M., & Gluck, M. R. (1987). The supervision relationship: Variables contributing to positive versus negative experiences. *Professional Psychology: Research and Practice, 18,* 172–175.

Kerl, S. B., Garcia, J. L., McCullough, C. S., & Maxwell, M. E. (2002). Systematic evaluation of professional performance: Legally supported procedure and process. *Counselor Education and Supervision, 41,* 321–334.

Kernberg, O. (1965). Notes on countertransference. *Journal of the American Psychoanalytic Association, 13,* 38–56.

Kiesler, D. J. (1996). *Contemporary interpersonal theory and research. Personality, psychopathology, and psychotherapy.* New York: Wiley.

Kitchener, K. S. (1984). Intuition, critical evaluation and ethical principles: The foundation for ethical decisions in counseling psychology. *The Counseling Psychologist, 12,* 43–56.

Kitchener, K. S. (1986). Teaching applied ethics in counselor education: An integration of psychological processes and philosophical analysis. *Journal of Counseling and Development, 64,* 306–310.

Kitchener, K. S. (1988). Dual role relationships: What makes them so problematic? *Journal of Counseling and Development, 67,* 217–221.

Kitchener, K. S. (1992). Psychologist as teacher and mentor: Affirming ethical values throughout the curriculum. *Professional Psychologist: Research and Practice, 23,* 190–195.

Kitchener, K. S. (2000). *Foundations of ethical practice, research, and teaching in psychology.* Mahwah, NJ: Erlbaum.

Kivlighan, D. M., Jr., & Quigley, S. T. (1991). Dimensions used by experienced and novice group therapists to conceptualize group process. *Journal of Counseling Psychology, 38,* 415–423.

Kivlighan, D. M., & Schmitz, P. J. (1992). Counselor technical activity in cases with improving working alliances and continuing-poor working alliances. *Journal of Counseling Psychology, 39,* 32–38.

Kleespies, P. (1993). The stress of patient suicidal behavior: Implications for interns and training programs in psychology. *Professional Psychology: Research and Practice, 24,* 477–482.

Kleespies, P., & Dettmer, E. L. (2000). The stress of patient emergencies for the clinician: Incident, impact, and means of coping. *Journal of Clinical Psychology, 56,* 1353–1369.

Kleespies, P., Penk, W., & Forsyth, J. (1993). The stress of patient suicidal behavior during clinical training: Incidence, impact, and recovery. *Professional Psychology: Research and Practice, 24,* 293–303.

Kleintjes, S., & Swartz, L. (1996). Black clinical psychology trainees at a "White" South African University: Issues for clinical supervision. *Clinical Supervisor, 14*(1), 87–109.

Knoff, H. M., & Prout, H. T. (1985). Terminating students from professional psychology programs: Criteria, procedures, and legal issues. *Professional Psychology, 16,* 789–797.

Kolb, D. A. (1984). *Experiential learning: Experience as the source of learning and development.* Englewood Cliffs, NJ: Prentice Hall.

Koocher, G. P. (2002). Mentor revealed: Masculinization of an early feminist construct. *Professional Psychology: Research and Practice, 33,* 509–510.

Koocher, G. P., & Keith-Spiegel, P. (1998). *Ethics in psychology: Professional standards and cases* (2nd ed.). New York: Oxford University Press.

Kratochwill, T. R., & Bergan, J. R. (1978). Training school psychologists: Some perspectives on a competency-based behavioral consultation model. *Professional Psychology: Research and Practice, 13*, 71–82.

Kratochwill, T. R., Lepage, K. M., & McGivern, J. (1997). Child and adolescent psychotherapy supervision. In C. E. Watkins, Jr. (Ed.), *Handbook of psychotherapy supervision* (pp. 347–365). New York: Wiley.

Kratochwill, T. R., Van Someren, K. R., & Sheridan, S. M. (1989). Training behavioral consultants: A competency-based model to teach interview skills. *Professional School Psychology, 4*, 41–58.

Kurpius, D., Gibson, G., Lewis, J., & Corbet, M. (1991). Ethical issues in supervising counseling practitioners. *Counselor Education and Supervision, 31*(1). 48–57.

Kutz, S. L. (1986). Comment: Defining "impaired psychologist." *American Psychologist, 41*, 220.

Ladany, N. (2002). Psychotherapy supervision: How dressed is the emperor? *Psychotherapy Bulletin, 37*, 14–18.

Ladany, N., Constantine, M. G., Miller, K., Erickson, C. D., & Muse-Burke, J. L. (2000). Supervisor countertransference: A qualitative investigation into its identification and description. *Journal of Counseling Psychology, 47*, 102–115.

Ladany, N., Ellis, M. V., & Friedlander, M. L. (1999). The supervisory working alliance, trainee self-efficacy, and satisfaction. *Journal of Counseling and Development, 77*, 447–455.

Ladany, N., & Friedlander, M. L. (1995). The relationship between the supervisory working alliance and trainees' experience of role conflict and role ambiguity. *Counselor Education and Supervision, 34*, 220–231.

Ladany, N., Hill, C. E., Corbett, M. M., & Nutt, E. A. (1996). Nature, extent and importance of what psychotherapy trainees do not disclose to their supervisors. *Journal of Counseling Psychology, 43*, 10–24.

Ladany, N., Inman, A. G., Constantine, M. G., & Hofheinz, E. W. (1997). Supervisee multicultural case conceptualization ability and self-reported multicultural competence as functions of supervisee racial identity and supervisor focus. *Journal of Counseling Psychology, 44*, 284–293.

Ladany, N., & Lehrman-Waterman, D. (1999). The content and frequency of supervisor self-disclosures and their relationship to supervisor style and the supervisory working alliance. *Counselor Education and Supervision, 38*, 143–160.

Ladany, N., Lehrman-Waterman, D., Molinaro, M., & Wolgast, B. (1999). Psychotherapy supervisor ethical practices: Adherence to guidelines, the supervisory working alliance, and supervisee satisfaction. *The Counseling Psychologist, 27*, 443–475.

Ladany, N., & Melincoff, D. S. (1999). The nature of counselor supervisor nondisclosure. *Counselor Education and Supervision, 38*, 161–176.

Ladany, N., O'Brien, K. M., Hill, C. E., Melincoff, D. S., Knox, S., & Petersen, D. A. (1997). Sexual attraction towards clients, use of supervision, and prior training: A qualitative study of psychology predoctoral interns. *Journal of Counseling Psychology, 44,* 413–424.

Ladany, N., & Walker, J. A. (2003). Supervisor self-disclosure: Balancing the uncontrollable narcissist with the indomitable altruist. *JCLP/In Session, 59,* 611–621.

LaFromboise, T. D., Coleman, H. L. K., & Hernandez, A. (1991). Development and factor structure of the Cross-Cultural Counseling Inventory—Revised. *Professional Psychology: Research and Practice, 22,* 380–388.

Laliotis, D., & Grayson, J. (1985). Psychologist heal thyself: What is available to the impaired psychologist? *American Psychologist, 40,* 84–96.

Lamb, D. H. (1999). Addressing impairment and its relationship to professional boundary issues. *The Counseling Psychologist, 27,* 702–711.

Lamb, D. H. (2001). *Sexual and non-sexual dual relationship dilemmas with clients, supervisees, and students.* American Psychological Association Continuing Professional Education Pre-Convention Workshop. Chicago, IL.

Lamb, D. H., Anderson, S., Rapp, D., Rathnow, S., & Sesan, R. (1986). Perspectives on an internship: The passages of training directors during the internship year. *Professional Psychology: Research and Practice, 17,* 100–105.

Lamb, D. H., Baker, J., Jennings, M., & Yarris, E. (1982). Passages of an internship in professional psychology. *Professional Psychology, 13,* 661–669.

Lamb, D. H., & Catanzaro, S. J. (1998). Sexual and nonsexual boundary violations involving psychologists, clients, supervisees, and students: Implications for professional practice. *Professional Psychology: Research and Practice, 29,* 498–503.

Lamb, D. H., Catanzaro, S. J., & Moorman, A. S. (2003). Psychologists reflect on their sexual relationships with clients, supervisees, and students: Occurrence, impact, rationales, and collegial intervention. *Professional Psychology: Research and Practice, 34,* 102–107.

Lamb, D. H., Cochran, D. J., & Jackson, V. R. (1991). Training and organizational issues associated with identifying and responding to intern impairment. Professional impairment during the internship: Identification, due process, and remediation. *Professional Psychology: Research and Practice, 18,* 597–603.

Lamb, D. H., Roehlke, H., & Butler, A. (1986). Passages of psychologists: Career stages of internship directors. *Professional Psychology: Research and Practice, 17,* 158–160.

Lambert, M. J. (1982). *The effects of psychotherapy* (Vol. 2). New York: Human Sciences Library.

Lambert, M. J. (1983). Introduction to assessment of psychotherapy outcome: Historical perspective and current issues. In M. J. Lambert, E. R. Christiansen, & S. S. DeJulio (Eds.), *The assessment of psychotherapy outcome* (pp. 3–32). New York: Wiley.

Lambert, M. J., & Barley, D. E. (2001). Research summary on the therapeutic relationship and psychotherapy outcome. *Psychotherapy, 38,* 357–361.

Lambert, M. J., & Bergin, A. E. (1994). The effectiveness of psychotherapy. In A. E. Bergin & S. L. Garfield (Eds.), *Handbook of psychotherapy and behavior change* (4th ed., pp. 143–189). New York: Wiley.

Lambert, M. J., & Burlingame, G. M. (1996). *OQ-45*. Stevenson, MD: American Professional Credentialing Services, LLC.

Lambert, M. J., & Hawkins, E. J. (2001). Using information about patient progress in supervision: Are outcomes enhanced? *Australian Psychologist, 36*, 131–138.

Lambert, M. J., & Ogles, B. M. (1997). The effectiveness of psychotherapy supervision. In C. E. Watkins, Jr. (Ed.), *Handbook of psychotherapy supervision* (pp. 421–446). New York: Wiley.

Lambert, M. J., Whipple, J. L., Smart, D. W., Vermeersch, D. A., Nielsen, S. L., & Hawkins, E. J. (2001). The effects of providing therapists with feedback on patient progress during psychotherapy: Are outcomes enhanced? *Psychotherapy Research, 11*(1), 49–68.

Lambert, M. J., Whipple, J. L., Vermeersch, D. A., Smart, D. W., Hawkins, E. J., Nielsen, S. L., et al. (2002). Enhancing psychotherapy outcomes via providing feedback on client progress: A replication. *Clinical Psychology and Psychotherapy, 9*, 91–103.

Lanning, W. (1986). Development of the supervisor emphasis rating form. *Counselor Education and Supervision, 33*, 294–304.

Layman, M. J., & McNamara, R. (1997). Remediation for ethics violations: Focus on psychotherapists' sexual contact with clients. *Professional Psychology: Research and Practice, 28*, 281–292.

Lazarus, A. A., & Zur, O. (Eds.). (2002). *Dual relationships and psychotherapy*. New York: Springer.

Leach, D. C. (2002). Editorial: Competence is a habit. *Journal of the American Medical Association, 287*, 243–244.

Leddick, G. R., & Dye, H. A. (1987). Effective supervision as portrayed by trainee expectations and preferences. *Counselor Education and Supervision, 27*, 139–154.

Lee, R. M., Chalk, L., Conner, S. E., Kawasaki, N., Jannetti, A., LaRue, T., et al. (1999). The status of multicultural counseling training at counseling internship sites. *Journal of Multicultural Counseling and Development, 27*(2), 58–74.

Lefley, H. (1986). Mental health training across cultures. In P. Pedersen (Ed.), *Handbook of cross-cultural counseling and therapy* (pp. 256–266). Westport, CT: Greenwood Press.

Lehrman-Waterman, D., & Ladany, N. (2001). Development and validation of the evaluation process within supervision inventory. *Journal of Counseling Psychology, 48*, 168–177.

Leong, F. T. L., & Wagner, N. M. (1994). Cross-cultural counseling supervision: What do we know? What do we need to know? *Counselor Education and Supervision, 34*, 117–131.

Lerman, H., & Porter, N. (1990). The contribution of feminism to ethics in psychotherapy. In H. Lerman & N. Porter (Eds.) *Feminist ethics in psychotherapy* (pp. 5–13). New York: Springer Publishing Company.

Liddle, H. A., Becker, D., & Diamond, G. M. (1997). Family therapy supervision. In C. E. Watkins, Jr. (Ed.), *Handbook of psychotherapy supervision* (pp. 400–418). New York: Wiley.

Liddle, H. A., Breunlin, D. C., & Schwartz, R. C. (Eds.). (1988). *Handbook of family therapy training and supervision.* New York: Guilford Press.

Liddle, H. A., Davidson, G. S., & Barrett, M. J. (1988). Outcomes of live supervision: Trainee perspectives. In H. A. Liddle, D. C. Breunlin, & R. C. Schwartz (Eds.), *Handbook of family therapy training and supervision* (pp. 386–398). New York: Guilford Press.

Liese, B. S., & Beck, J. S. (1997). Cognitive therapy supervision. In C. E. Watkins, Jr. (Ed.), *Handbook of psychotherapy supervision* (pp. 114–133). New York: Wiley.

Lipovsky, Julie A. (1988). Internship year in clinical psychology training as a professional adolescence. *Professional Psychology: Research and Practice, 19,* 606–608.

Littrell, J. M., Lee-Borden, N., & Lorenz, J. (1979). A developmental framework for counseling supervision. *Counselor Education and Supervision, 19,* 129–136.

Lloyd, D. N., & Newbrough, J. R. (1966). Previous conferences on graduate education in psychology: A summary and review. In E. L. Hoch, A. O. Ross, & C. L. Winder (Eds.), *Professional preparation of clinical psychologists* (pp. 122–139). Washington, DC: American Psychological Association.

Lochner, B. T., & Melchert, T. P. (1997). Relationship of cognitive style and theoretical orientation to psychology interns' preferences for supervision. *Journal of Counseling Psychology, 44,* 256–260.

Loganbill, C., Hardy, E., & Delworth, U. (1982). Supervision: A conceptual model. *The Counseling Psychologist, 10,* 3–42.

London, P. (1964). *The modes and morals of psychotherapy.* New York: Holt, Rinehart and Winston.

Long, J. R. (2001). Goal agreement and early therapeutic change. *Psychotherapy, 38,* 219–232.

Lopez, S. J., Oehlert, M. E., & Moberly, R. L. (1996). Selection criteria for APA-accredited internship programs: A survey of training directors. *Professional Psychology: Research and Practice, 27,* 518–520.

Luborsky, L. (1994). Therapeutic alliances as predictors of psychotherapy outcomes: Factors explaining the predictive success. In A. O. Horvath & L. S. Greenberg, (Eds.), The *working alliance: Theory, research, and practice* (pp. 38–49). New York: Wiley.

Lynn, D. J., & Vaillant, G. E. (1998). Anonymity, neutrality, and confidentiality in the actual methods of Sigmund Freud: A review of 43 cases, 1907–1939. *American Journal of Psychiatry, 155*(2), 163–171.

Lyotard, J.-F. (1984). *The postmodern condition: A report on knowledge* (G. Bennington & B. Massumi, Trans.). Minneapolis, MN: University of Minnesota Press.

Magnuson, S., Wilcoxon, S. A., & Norem, K. (2000). A profile of lousy supervision: Experienced counselors' perspectives. *Counselor Education and Supervision, 39,* 189–202.

Mahalik, J. R., Worthington, R. L., & Crump. S. (1999). Influence of racial/ethnic membership and "therapist culture" on therapists' worldview. *Journal of Multicultural Counseling and Development, 27,* 2–17.

Mahrer, A. R. (1996). *The complete guide to experiential psychotherapy.* New York: Wiley.

Mahrer, A. R., & Boulet, D. B. (1997). The experiential model of on-the-job teaching. In C. E. Watkins, Jr. (Ed.), *Handbook of psychotherapy supervision* (pp. 164–183). New York: Wiley.

Makari, G. J. (1997). Current conceptions of neutrality and abstinence. *Journal of the American Psychoanalytic Association, 45,* 1231–1239.

Mannheim, C. I., Sancilio, M., Phipps-Yonas, S., Brunnquell, D., Somers, P., Farseth, G., et al. (2002). Ethical ambiguities in the practice of child clinical psychology. *Professional Psychology: Research and Practice, 33,* 24–29.

Marcus, H. E., & King, D. A. (2003). A survey of group psychotherapy training during predoctoral psychology internship. *Professional Psychology: Research and Practice, 34,* 203–209.

Marikis, D. A., Russell, R. K., & Dell, D. M. (1985). Effects of supervisor experience level on planning and in-session supervisor verbal behavior. *Journal of Counseling Psychology, 32,* 410–416.

Martin, D. J., Garske, J. P., & Davis, M. K. (2000). Relation of the therapeutic alliance with outcome and other variables: A meta-analytic review. *Journal of Consulting & Clinical Psychology, 68*(3), 438–450.

Martin, J. S., Goodyear, R. K., & Newton, F. B. (1987). Clinical supervision: An intensive case study. *Professional Psychology: Research and Practice, 18,* 225–235.

Mayfield, W. A., Kardash, C. M., & Kivlighan, D. M. (1999). Differences in experienced and novice counselors' knowledge structures about clients: Implications for case conceptualization. *Journal of Counseling Psychology, 46,* 504–514.

McCann, A. L., Babler, W. J., & Cohen, P. A. (1998). Lessons learned from the competency-based curriculum initiative at Baylor College of Dentistry. *Journal of Dental Education, 62,* 197–207.

McCarthy, P., DeBell, C., Kanuha, V., & McLeod, J. (1988). Myths of supervision: Identifying the gaps between theory and practice. *Counselor Education and Supervision, 28,* 22–28.

McCarthy, P., Kulakowski, D., & Kenfield, J. A. (1994). Clinical supervision practices of licensed psychologists. *Professional Psychology: Research and Practice, 25,* 177–181.

McCarthy, P., Sugden, S., Koker, M., Lamendola, F., Maurer, S., & Renninger, S. (1995). A practical guide to informed consent in clinical supervision. *Counselor Education and Supervision, 35*, 130–138.

McClelland, D. C. (1998). Identifying competencies with behavioral-event interviews. *Psychological Science, 9*, 331–339.

McConnaughy, E. A., Prochaska, J. O., & Velicer, W. F. (1983). Stages of change in psychotherapy: Measurement and sample profiles. *Psychotherapy: Theory, Research and Practice, 20*, 368–375.

McLaughlin, J. (1987). The play of transference: Some reflections on enactment in the psychoanalytic situation. *Journal of the American Psychoanalytic Association, 35*, 557–582.

McLaughlin, J. T. (1991). Clinical and theoretical aspects of enactment. *Journal of the American Psychoanalytic Association, 39*, 595–614.

McNamara, J. R. (1975). An assessment proposal for determining the competence of professional psychologists. *Professional Psychology, 6*(2), 135–139.

McNeill, B. W., Hom, K. L., & Perez, J. A. (1995). The training and supervisory needs of social/ethnic minority students. *Journal of Multicultural Counseling and Development, 23*, 246–258.

McNeill, B. W., Stoltenberg, C. D., & Romans, J. S. (1992). The Integrated Developmental Model of supervision: Scale development and validation procedures. *Professional Psychologist: Research and Practice, 23*, 504–508.

McNeill, B. W., & Worthen, V. (1989). The parallel process in psychotherapy supervision. *Professional Psychology: Research and Practice, 20*(5), 329–333.

McRoy, R. G., Freeman, E. M., Logan, S. L., & Blackmon, B. (1986). Cross-cultural field supervision: Implications for social work education. *Journal of Social Work Education, 22*, 50–56.

Meara, N. M., Schmidt, L. D., & Day, J. D. (1996). Principles and virtues: A foundation for ethical decisions, policies, and character. *The Counseling Psychologist, 24*, 4–77.

Mearns, J., & Allen, G. J. (1991). Graduate students' experiences in dealing with impaired peers, compared with faculty predictions: An exploratory study. *Ethics and Behavior, 1*, 191–202.

Meissner, W. (1998). Neutrality, abstinence, and the therapeutic alliance. *Journal of the American Psychoanalytic Association, 46*, 1089–1128.

Miller, C. D., & Oetting, E. R. (1966). Students react to supervision. *Counselor Education and Supervision. 6*(1), 73–74.

Miller, G. M., & Larrabee, M. J. (1995). Sexual intimacy in counselor education and supervision: A national survey. *Counselor Education & Supervision, 34*, 332–343.

Miller, L., & Twomey, J. E. (1999). A parallel without a process: A relational view of a supervisory experience. *Contemporary Psychoanalysis, 35*, 557–580.

Miller, M. (2002). The psychologist as defendant. In "Psychology in Litigation and Legislation," Presented at annual meeting of APA and reported by Eric Harris,

2002, Legal and ethical risk management in professional psychological practice: Sequence 1. APA Insurance Trust and California Psychological Association, Los Angeles.

Miller, R. K., & Van Rybroek, G. J. (1988). Internship letters of recommendation: Where are the other 90%? *Professional Psychology: Research and Practice*, *19*, 115–117.

Milne, D. L., & James, I. A. (2000). A systematic review of effective cognitive-behavioural supervision. *British Journal of Clinical Psychology*, *39*, 111–129.

Milne, D. L., & James, I. A. (2002). The observed impact of training on competence in clinical supervision. *British Journal of Clinical Psychology*, *41*, 55–72.

Milne, D. L., James, I. A., Keegan, D., & Dudley, M. (2002). Teacher's PETS: A new observational measure of experiential training interactions. *Clinical Psychology & Psychotherapy*, *9*, 187–199.

Milne, D. L., & Oliver, V. (2000). Flexible formats of clinical supervision: Description, evaluation and implementation. *Journal of Mental Health*, *9*, 291–304.

Mintz, L. B., Bartels, K. M., & Rideout, C. A. (1995). Training in counseling ethnic minorities and race-based availability of graduate school resources. *Professional Psychology: Research and Practice*, *26*, 316–321.

Mission Bay conference resolutions for professional psychology programs. (1987). In E. F. Bourg, R. J. Bent, J. E. Callan, N. F. Jones, J. McHolland, & G. Stricker (Eds.), *Standards and evaluation in the education and training of professional psychologists: Knowledge, attitudes, and skills* (pp. 25–29). Norman, OK: Transcript Press.

Mitnick, M. K. (2002). Internships and the law: Disability issues in internships and postdoctoral fellowships. *APPIC Newsletter*, *26*(3), 21.

Mohr, J. J. (2002). Heterosexual identity and the heterosexual therapist: An identity perspective on sexual orientation dynamics in psychotherapy. *The Counseling Psychologist*, *30*, 532–566.

Molinari, V., Karen, M., Jones, S., Zeiss, A., Cooley, S. G., Wray, L., et al., (2003). Recommendations about the knowledge and skills required of psychologists working with older adults. *Professional Psychology: Research and Practice*, *34*, 435–443.

Moline, M. E., Williams, G. T., & Austin, K. M. (1998). *Documenting psychotherapy*. Thousand Oaks, CA: Sage.

Montgomery, L. M., Cupit, B. E., & Wimberley, T. K. (1999). Complaints, malpractice, and risk management: Professional issues and personal experiences. *Professional Psychology: Research and Practice*, *30*, 402–410.

Moore, E. R. (1984). Competency-based training evaluation. *Training and Development Journal*, *38*(11), 92–94.

Morrison, A., O'Connor, L., & Williams, B. (1991). National Council of Schools of Professional Psychology core curriculum survey. In R. Peterson, R. J. McHolland, E. Bent, E. Davis-Russell, G. E. Edwall, K. Polite, et al. (Eds.), *The core curriculum in professional psychology* (pp. 49–55). Washington, DC: American Psychological Association.

Morrissey, J., & Tribe, R. (2001). Parallel process in supervision. *Counseling Psychology Quarterly, 14*(2), 103–110.

Mosher, P. W., & Squire, P. P. (2002). The ethical and legal implications of Jaffee v Redmond and the HIPAA medical privacy rule for psychotherapy and general psychiatry. *Psychiatric Clinics of North America, 25*, 575–584.

Moskowitz, S. A., & Rupert, P. A. (1983). Conflict resolution within the supervisory relationship. *Professional Psychology: Research and Practice, 14*, 632–641.

Mothersole, G. (1999). Parallel process: A review. *Clinical Supervisor, 18*(2), 107–121.

Muran, J. C., Segal, Z. V., Samstag, L. W., & Crawford, C. E. (1994). Patient pretreatment interpersonal problems and the therapeutic alliance in short-term cognitive therapy. *Journal of Consulting & Clinical Psychology, 62*(1), 185–190.

Muratori, M. C. (2001). Examining supervisor impairment from the counselor trainee's perspective. *Counselor Education and Supervision, 41*, 41–56.

Murphy, J. A., Rawlings, E. I., & Howe, S. R. (2002). A survey of clinical psychologists on treating lesbian, gay, and bisexual clients. *Professional Psychology: Research and Practice, 33*, 183–189.

Myers, H. F., Echemendia, R. J., & Trimble, J. E. (1991). The need for training ethnic minority psychologists. In H. F. Myers, P. Wohlford, L. P. Guzman, & R. J. Echemendia (Eds.), *Ethnic Minority Perspectives on Clinical Training and Services in Psychology* (pp. 3–11). Washington, DC: American Psychological Association.

Nathanson, D. L. (1992). *Shame and pride: Affect, sex and the birth of the self.* New York: Norton.

Natterson, J. (1991). *Beyond countertransference.* Northvale, NJ: Jason Aronson, Inc.

Neimeyer, R. A., & Mahoney, M. J. (Eds.). (1995). *Constructivism in psychotherapy.* Washington, DC: American Psychological Association.

Nelson, E. C., Batalden, P. B., & Ryer, J. C. (1998). *Clinical improvement guide.* Chicago: Joint Commission on Accreditation of Healthcare Organizations.

Nelson, G. L. (1978). Psychotherapy supervision from the trainee's point of view: A survey of preferences. *Professional Psychology, 9*, 539–550.

Nelson, M. L., & Friedlander, M. L. (2001). A close look at conflictual supervisory relationships: The trainee's perspective. *Journal of Counseling Psychology, 48*, 384–395.

Nelson, M. L., Gray, L. A., Friedlander, M. L., Ladany, N., & Walker, J. A. (2001). Toward relationship-centered supervision: Reply to Veach (2001) and Ellis (2001). *Journal of Counseling Psychology, 48*, 407–409.

Nelson, M. L., & Holloway, E. L. (1990). Relation of gender to power and involvement in supervision. *Journal of Counseling Psychology, 37*, 473–481.

Nerdrum, P., & Ronnestad, M. H. (2002). The trainees' perspective: A qualitative study of learning empathic communication in Norway. *The Counseling Psychologist, 30*, 609–629.

Neufeld, V. R. (1985). An introduction to measurement properties. In V. R. Neufeld & G. R. Norman (Eds.), *Assessing clinical competence* (pp. 39–50). New York: Springer Publishing Company.

Neufeldt, S. A. (1999a). Reflective processes in supervision. In E. Holloway & M. Carroll (Eds.), *Training counselling supervisors* (pp. 92–105). London: Sage.

Neufeldt, S. A. (1999b). *Supervision strategies for the first practicum* (2nd ed.). Alexandria, VA: American Counseling Association.

Neufeldt, S. A., Beutler, L. E., & Banchero, R. (1997). Research on supervisor variables in psychotherapy supervision. In C. E. Watkins, Jr. (Ed.), *Handbook of psychotherapy supervision* (pp. 508–524). New York: Wiley.

Neufeldt, S. A., Karno, M. P., & Nelson, M. L. (1996). A qualitative study of experts' conceptualization of supervisee reflectivity. *Journal of Counseling Psychology, 43*, 3–9.

Neville, H. A., Heppner, M. J., Louie, C. E., Thompson, C. E., Brooks, L., & Baker, C. E. (1996). The impact of multicultural training on white racial identity attitudes and therapy competencies. *Professional Psychology: Research and Practice, 27*, 83–89.

Newman, A. S. (1981). Ethical issues in the supervision of psychotherapy. *Professional Psychology: Research and Practice, 12*, 690–695.

Newman, J. L., & Scott, T. B. (1988). The construct problem in measuring counseling performance. *Counselor Education and Supervision, 28*, 71–79.

Nicolai, K. M., & Scott, N. A. (1994). Provision of confidentiality information and its relation to child abuse reporting. *Professional Psychology: Research and Practice, 25*, 154–160.

Nilsson, J. E., Berkel, L. A., Flores, L. Y., Love, K. M., Wendler, A. M., & Mecklenburg, E. C. (2003). An 11-year review of professional psychology: Research and practice content and sample analysis with an emphasis on diversity. *Professional Psychology: Research and Practice, 34*, 611–616.

Norcross, J. C., & Halgin, R. P. (1997). Integrative approaches to psychotherapy supervision. In C. E. Watkins, Jr. (Ed.), *Handbook of psychotherapy supervision* (pp. 203–222). New York: Wiley.

Norcross, J. C., Hedges, M., & Castle, P. H. (2002). Psychologists conducting psychotherapy in 2001: A study of the Division 29 membership. *Psychotherapy: Theory/Research/Practice, 39*(1), 97–102.

Norcross, J. C., Hedges, M., & Prochaska, J. O. (2002). The face of 2010: A Delphi poll on the future of psychotherapy. *Professional Psychology: Research & Practice, 33*, 316–322.

Norcross, J. C., & Stevenson, J. F. (1984). How shall we judge ourselves? Training evaluation in clinical psychology programs. *Professional Psychology: Research and Practice, 15*, 497–508.

Norcross, J. C., Stevenson, J. F., & Nash, J. M. (1986). Evaluation of internship training: Practices, problems, and prospects. *Professional Psychology: Research and Practice, 17*, 280–282.

Norman, G. R. (1985). Defining competence: A methodological review. In W. R. Neufeld & G. R. Norman (Eds.), *Assessing clinical competence* (pp. 15–35). New York: Springer Publishing Company.

Nwachuku, U. T., & Ivey, A. E. (1991). Culture-specific counseling: An alternative training model. *Journal of Counseling and Development, 70*, 106–111.

O'Donohue, W. (1989). The (even) bolder model: The clinical psychologist as metaphysician-scientist-practicitioner. *American Psychologist, 44*, 1460–1468.

Ogden, T. H. (1988). On the dialectical structure of experience: Some clinical and theoretical implications. *Contemporary Psychoanalysis, 24*, 17–45.

Ogden, T. H. (1994). The analytic third: working with intersubjective clinical facts. *International Journal of Psycho-analysis, 75*, 3–20.

Olk, M., & Friedlander, M. L. (1992). Trainees' experiences of role conflict and role ambiguity in supervisory relationships. *Journal of Counseling Psychology, 39*, 389–397.

Olkin, R. (2002). Could you hold the door for me? Including disability in diversity. *Cultural Diversity and Ethnic Minority Psychology, 8*(2), 130–137.

Olkin, R., & Gaughen, S. (1991). Evaluation and dismissal of students in master's level clinical programs: Legal parameters and survey results. *Counselor Education and Supervision, 30*(4), 276–288.

Omer, H. (1994). *Critical interventions in psychotherapy: From impasse to turning point.* NY: Norton.

Omer, H. (2000). Troubles in the therapeutic relationship: A pluralistic perspective. *Journal of Clinical Psychology/InSession: Psychotherapy in Practice, 56*(2), 201–210.

Orlinsky, D. E., Grawe, K., & Parks, B. K. (1994). Process and outcome in–psychotherapy—Noch einmal. In A. E. Bergin & S. L. Garfield (Eds.), *Handbook of psychotherapy and behavior change* (4th ed., pp. 270–376). New York: Wiley.

Osborne, C. J., & Davis, T. E. (1996). The supervision contract: Making it perfectly clear. *The Clinical Supervisor, 14*(2), 121–134.

Overholser, J. C., & Fine, M. A. (1990). Defining the boundaries of professional competence: Managing subtle cases of clinical incompetence. *Professional Psychology: Research and Practice, 21*, 462–469.

Patrick, K. D. (1989). Unique ethical dilemmas in counselor training. *Counselor Education and Supervision, 28*, 337–341.

Patterson, C. S. (1997). Client-centered supervision. In C. E. Watkins, Jr. (Ed.), *Handbook of psychotherapy supervision* (pp. 134–146). New York: Wiley.

Patton, M. J., & Kivlighan, D. M. J. (1997). Relevance of the supervisory alliance to the counseling alliance and to treatment adherence in counselor training. *Journal of Counseling Psychology, 44*, 108–111.

Pearlman, L., & MacIan, P. (1995). Vicarious traumatization: An empirical study of the effects of trauma work on trauma therapists. *Professional Psychology: Research and Practice, 26,* 558–565.

Peck v. The Counseling Service of Addison County, 499 A.2d 422 (Vt. 1985).

Pedersen, P. B. (2002). Ethics, competence, and other professional issues in culture-centered counseling. In P. B. Pedersen, J. G. Draguns, W. J. Lonner, & J. E. Trimble (Eds.), *Counseling across cultures* (2nd ed., pp. 3–27), Thousand Oaks: Sage.

Perris, C. (1994). Supervising cognitive psychotherapy and training supervisors. *Journal of Cognitive Psychotherapy, 8*(2), 83–103.

Peterson, D. R. (1991). Connection and disconnection of research and practice in the education of professional psychologists. *American Psychologist, 46,* 422–429.

Peterson, D. R. (2000). Scientist-practitioner or scientific practitioner. *American Psychologist, 55,* 252–253.

Peterson, D. R., & Bry, B. H. (1980). Dimensions of perceived competence in professional psychology. *Professional Psychology, 11*(6), 965–971.

Peterson, F. K. (1991). Issues of race and ethnicity in supervision: Emphasizing who you are, not what you know. In T. H. Peake & J. Ball (Eds.), *Psychotherapy training: Contextual and developmental influence in settings, stages, and mind sets* (pp. 15–31). New York: Haworth Press.

Peterson, R. L., McHolland, J. D., Bent, R. J., Davis-Russell, E., Edwall, G. E., Polite, K., et al. (Eds.). (1991). *The core curriculum in professional psychology.* Washington, DC: American Psychological Association.

Peterson, R. L., Peterson, D. R., Abrams, J. C., & Stricker, G. (1997). The National Council of Schools and Programs of Professional Psychology education model. *Professional Psychology: Research & Practice, 28,* 373–386.

Phillips, J. C. (2000). Training issues and considerations. In R. M. Perez, K. A. DeBord, & K. Bieschke (Eds.), *Handbook of counseling and psychotherapy with lesbian, gay, and bisexual clients* (pp. 337–358). Washington, DC: American Psychological Association.

Phillips, J. C., & Fischer, A. R. (1998). Graduate students' training experiences with lesbian, gay, and bisexual issues. *The Counseling Psychologist, 26,* 712–734.

Phinney, J. S. (1996). When we talk about American ethnic groups, what do we mean? *American Psychologist, 51,* 918–927.

Plante, T. G. (1995). Training child clinical predoctoral interns and postdoctoral fellows in ethics and professional issues: An experiential model. *Professional Psychology: Research and Practice, 26,* 616–619.

Poland, W. (1984). On the analyst's neutrality. *Journal of the American Psychoanalytic Association, 32,* 283–299.

Polanski, P. J. (2003). Spirituality in supervision. *Counseling & Values, 47,* 131–141.

Polite, K., & Bourg, E. (1991). Relationship competency. In R. Peterson (Ed.), *Core curriculum in professional psychology* (pp. 83–88). Washington, DC: American Psychological Association Press.

Polkinghorne, D. E. (1988). *Narrative knowing and the human sciences*. Albany, NY: State University of New York Press.

Ponterotto, J. G., Alexander, C. M., & Grieger, I. (1995). A multicultural competency checklist for counseling training programs. *Journal of Multicultural Counseling and Development, 23*, 11–20.

Ponterotto, J. G., & Casas, J. M. (1987). In search of multicultural competence within counselor education programs. *Journal of Counseling and Development, 65*, 430–434.

Ponterotto, J. G., Fuertes, J. N., & Chen, E. C. (2000). Models of multicultural counseling. In S. D. Brown, & R. W. Lent (Eds.), *Handbook of Counseling Psychology* (3rd ed., pp. 639–669). New York: Wiley.

Ponterotto, J. G., & Furlong, M. J. (1985). Evaluating counselor effectiveness: A critical review of rating scale instruments. *Journal of Counseling Psychology, 32*, 597–616.

Ponterotto, J. G., Gretchen, D., Utsey, S. O., Rieger, B. P., & Austin, R. (2002). A construct validity study of the Multicultural Counseling Awareness Scale (MCAS). *Journal of Multicultural Counseling and Development, 30*, 153–180.

Ponterotto, J. G., Rieger, B. P., Barrett, A., & Sparks, R. (1994). Assessing multicultural counseling competence: A review of instrumentation. *Journal of Counseling and Development, 72*, 316–322.

Pope, K. S. (1999). Dual relationships in psychotherapy. In D. N. Bersoff (Ed.), *Ethical conflicts in psychology* (2nd ed., pp. 231–234). Washington DC: American Psychological Association.

Pope, K. S., & Bajt, T. R. (1988). When laws and values conflict: A dilemma for psychologists. *American Psychologist, 43*, 828–829.

Pope, K. S., & Feldman-Summers, S. (1992). National survey of psychologists' sexual and physical abuse history and their evaluation of training and competence in these areas. *Professional Psychology: Research and Practice, 23*, 353–361.

Pope, K. S., Keith-Spiegel, P., & Tabachnick, B. G. (1986). Sexual attraction to clients: The human therapist and the (sometimes) inhuman training system. *American Psychologist, 41*, 147–158.

Pope, K. S., Levenson, H., & Schover, L. R. (1979). Sexual intimacy in psychology training: Results and implications of a national survey. *American Psychologist, 34*, 682–689.

Pope, K. S., Schover, L. R., & Levenson, H. (1980). Sexual behavior between clinical supervisors and trainees: Implications for professional standards. *Professional Psychology, 11*, 157–162.

Pope, K. S., Sonne, J. L., & Holroyd, J. (1993). *Sexual feelings in psychotherapy: Explorations for therapists and therapists in training*. Washington, DC: American Psychological Association.

Pope, K. S., & Tabachnick, B. G. (1993). Therapists' anger, hate, fear, and sexual feelings: National survey of therapist responses, client characteristics, critical events, formal complaints, and training. *Professional Psychology: Research and Practice, 24*, 142–152.

Pope, K. S., & Vasquez, M. J. T. (1998). *Ethics in psychotherapy and counseling*, (2nd ed.). San Francisco: Jossey-Bass.

Pope, K. S., & Vasquez, M. J. T. (1999). Ethics in psychotherapy and counseling: A practical guide for psychologists. In D. N. Bersoff (Ed.), *Ethical conflicts in psychology* (2nd ed., pp. 240–243). Washington DC: American Psychological Association.

Pope, K. S., & Vetter, V. A. (1992). Ethical dilemmas encountered by members of the American Psychological Association: A national survey. *American Psychologist, 47*, 397–411.

Pope-Davis, D. B., Liu, W. M., Toporek, R. L., & Brittan-Powell, C. S. (2001). What's missing from multicultural competency research: Review, introspection, and recommendations. *Cultural Diversity and Ethnic Minority Psychology, 7*(2), 121–138.

Pope-Davis, D. B., Reynolds, A. L., Dings, J. G., & Nielson, D. (1995). Examining multicultural counseling competencies of graduate students in psychology. *Professional Psychology: Research and Practice, 26*, 322–329.

Pope-Davis, D. B., Reynolds, A. L., Dings, J. G., & Ottavi, T. M. (1994). Multicultural competencies of doctoral interns at university counseling centers: An exploratory investigation. *Professional Psychology: Research and Practice, 25*, 466–470.

Pope-Davis, D. B., Toporek, R. L., Ortega-Villalobos, L., Ligiero, D. P., Brittan-Powell, C. S., Liu, W. M., et al. (2002). Client perspectives of multicultural counseling competence: A qualitative examination. *The Counseling Psychologist, 30*, 355–393.

Porter, N. (1985). New perspectives on therapy supervision. In L. B. Rosewater, & L. E. Walker (Eds.), *Handbook of feminist therapy: Women's issues in psychotherapy* (pp. 332–343). New York: Springer Publishing Company.

Porter, N. (1995). Therapist self-care: A proactive ethical approach. In E. J. Rave, & C. C. Larsen (Eds.). *Ethical decision making in therapy: Feminist perspectives* (pp. 247–266). New York: Guilford.

Porter, N., & Vasquez, M. (1997). Covision: Feminist supervision, process, and collaboration. In J. Worell & N. G. Johnson (Eds.), *Shaping the future of feminist psychology* (pp. 155–171). Washington, DC: American Psychological Association.

Powell, M., Leyden, G., & Osborne, E. (1990). A curriculum for training in supervision. *Educational and Child Psychology, 7*(3), 44–52.

Priest, R. (1994). Minority supervisor and majority supervisee: Another perspective of clinical reality. *Counselor Education and Supervision, 34*, 152–158.

Prilleltensky, I. (1997). Values, assumptions, and practices: Assessing the moral implications of psychological discourse and action. *American Psychologist, 52*, 517–535.

Procidano, M. E., Busch-Rossnagel, N. A., Reznikoof, M., & Geisinger, K. F. (1995). Responding to graduate students' professional deficiencies: A national survey. *Journal of Clinical Psychology, 51*, 426–433.

Proctor, B. (1997). Contracting in supervision. In C. Sills (Ed.), *Contracts in counselling* (pp. 191–206). London: Sage.

Prouty, A. (2001). Experiencing feminist family therapy supervision. *Journal of Feminist Family Therapy, 12*(4), 171–203.

Pulakos, J. (1994). Incidental encounters between therapists and clients: A client's perspective. *Professional Psychology: Research and Practice, 25*, 300–303.

Putney, M. W., Worthington, E. L., Jr., & McCullough, M. E. (1992). Effects of supervisor and supervisee theoretical orientation and supervisor–supervisee matching on interns' perceptions of supervision. *Journal of Counseling Psychology, 39*, 258–265.

Qualls, S. H., Segal, D. L., Norman, S., Niederehe, G., & Gallagher-Thompson, D. (2002). Psychologists in practice with older adults: Current patters, sources of training, and need for continuing education. *Professional Psychology: Research and Practice, 33*, 435–442.

Quintana, S. M., & Atkinson, D. R. (2002). A multicultural perspective on principles of empirically supported interventions. *Counseling Psychologist, 30*, 281–291.

Quintana, S. M., & Bernal, M. E. (1995). Ethnic minority training in counseling psychology: Comparisons with clinical psychology and proposed standards. *The Counseling Psychologist, 23*, 102–121.

Racker, H. (1953). A contribution to the problem of counter-transference. *International Journal of Psychoanalysis, 34*, 313–324.

Raimy, V. C. (1950). *Training in clinical psychology.* New York: Prentice Hall.

Ramos-Sanchez, L., Esnil, E., Goodwin, A., Riggs, S., Touster, L. O., Wright, L. K., et al. (2002). Negative supervisory events: Effects on supervision satisfaction and supervisory alliance. *Professional Psychology: Research and Practice, 33*, 197–202.

Ramsbottom-Lucier, M. T., Gillmore, G. M., Irby, D. M., & Ramsey, P. G. (1994). Evaluation of clinical teaching by general internal medicine faculty in outpatient and inpatient settings. *Academic Medicine, 69*(2), 152–154.

Range, L. M., Menyhert, A., Walsh, M. L., Hardin, K. N., Craddick, R., & Ellis, J. B. (1991). Letters of recommendation: Perspectives, recommendations, and ethics. Professional Psychology: Research and Practice, 22, 389–392.

Reichelt, S., & Skjerve, J. (2002). Correspondence between supervisors and trainees in their perception of supervision events. *Journal of Clinical Psychology, 58*, 759–772.

Renik, O. (1993). Analytic interaction: Conceptualizing technique in light of the analyst's irreducible subjectivity. *Psychoanalytic Quarterly, 62*, 553–571.

Renik, O. (1995). The ideal of the anonymous analyst and the problem of self-disclosure. *Psychoanalytic Quarterly, 64*, 466–495.

Renik, O. (1996). The perils of neutrality. *Psychoanalytic Quarterly, 65*, 495–517.

Renninger, S. M., Veach, P. M., & Bagdade, P. (2002). Psychologists' knowledge, opinions, and decision-making processes regarding child abuse and neglect reporting laws. *Professional Psychology: Research and Practice, 33*, 19–23.

Rest, J. R. (1984). Research on moral development: Implications for training counseling psychologists. *The Counseling Psychologist, 12*, 19–29.

Reynolds, A. L., & Hanjorgiris, W. F. (2000). Coming out: Lesbian, gay, and bisexual identity development. In R. M. Perez, K. A. Debord, & K. Bieschke (Eds.), *Handbook of counseling and psychotherapy with lesbian, gay, and bisexual clients* (pp. 35–55). Washington, DC: American Psychological Association.

Rhodes, R., Hill, C., Thompson, B., & Elliott, R. (1994). Client retrospective recall of resolved and unresolved misunderstanding events. *Counseling Psychologist, 41*, 473–483.

Richardson, T. Q., & Molinaro, K. L. (1996). White counselor awareness: A prerequisite for multicultural competence. *Journal of Counseling and Development, 74*, 238–242.

Ridley, C. R., Liddle, M. C., Hill, C. L., & Li, L. C. (2001). Ethical decision making in multicultural counseling. In J. G. Ponterotto, J. M. Casas, L. A. Suzuki, & C. M. Alexander (Eds.), *Handbook of multicultural counseling* (2nd ed., pp. 165–188). Thousand Oaks, CA: Sage.

Ridley, C. R., Mendoza, D. W., & Kanitz, B. E. (1994). Multicultural training: Reexamination, operationalization, and integration. *The Counseling Psychologist, 22*, 76–102.

Riva, M. T., & Cornish, J. A. E. (1995). Group supervision practices at psychology predoctoral internship programs: A national survey. *Professional Psychology: Research and Practice, 26*, 523–525.

Robiner, W. N., Fuhrman, M., & Ristvedt, S. (1993). Evaluation difficulties in supervising psychology interns. *The Clinical Psychologist, 46*(1), 3–13.

Robiner, W. N., Saltzman, S. R., Hoberman, H. M., & Schirvar, J. A. (1997). Psychology supervisors' training, experiences, supervisory evaluation and self-rated competence. *The Clinical Supervisor, 16*(1), 117–144.

Robiner, W. N., Saltzman, S. R., Hoberman, H. M., Semrud-Clikeman, M., & Schirvar, J. A. (1997). Psychology supervisors' bias in evaluations and letters of recommendation. *The Clinical Supervisor, 16*(2), 49–72.

Robinson, T. L. (1999). The intersections of dominant discourses across race, gender, and other identities. *Journal of Counseling and Development, 77*, 73–79.

Robinson, W. L., & Reid, P. T. (1985). Sexual intimacies in psychology revisited. *Professional Psychology: Research and Practice, 16*, 512–520.

Rock, M. H. (Ed.). (1997). *Psychodynamic supervision: Perspectives of the supervisor and the supervisee*. Northvale, NJ: Jason Aronson.

Rodenhauser, P. (1997). Psychotherapy supervision: Prerequisites and problems in the process. In C. E. Watkins, Jr. (Ed.), *Handbook of psychotherapy supervision* (pp. 527–548). New York: Wiley.

Rodenhauser, P., Rudisill, J. R., & Painter, A. F. (1989). Attributes conducive to learning in psychotherapy supervision. *American Journal of Psychotherapy, 43*(3), 368–377.

Rodolfa, E. R., Hall, T., Holms, V., Davena, A., Komatz, D., Antunez, M., et al. (1994). The management of sexual feelings in therapy. *Professional Psychology: Research and Practice, 25*, 168–172.

Rodolfa, E. R., Haynes, S., Kaplan, D., Chamberlain, M., Goh, M., Marquis, P., et al. (1998). Supervisory practices of psychologists psychologists—Does time since licensure matter? *The Clinical Supervisor, 17*(2), 177–183.

Rodolfa, E. R., Kitzrow, M., Vohra, S., & Wilson, B. (1990). Training interns to respond to sexual dilemmas. *Professional Psychology: Research and Practice, 21*, 313–315.

Rodolfa, E. R., Kraft, W. A., & Reilley, R. R. (1988). Stressors of professionals and trainees at APA-approved counseling and VA medical center internship sites. *Professional Psychology: Research and Practice, 26*, 396–400.

Roe, R. A. (2002). What makes a competent psychologist? *European Psychologist, 7*(3), 192–202.

Rogers, C. R. (1951). *Client-centered therapy.* Boston: Houghton Mifflin.

Rogers, C. R. (1957). The necessary and sufficient conditions of therapeutic personality change. *Journal of Consulting Psychology, 22*, 95–103.

Romans, J. S. C., Boswell, D. L., Carlozzi, A. F., & Ferguson, D. B. (1995). Training and supervision practices in clinical, counseling, and school psychology programs. *Professional Psychology: Research and Practice, 26*, 407–412.

Ronnestad, M. H., & Skovholt, T. M. (1993). Supervision of beginning and advanced graduate students of counseling and psychotherapy. *Journal of Counseling and Development, 71*, 396–405.

Rorty, R. (1991). *Objectivity, relativism, and truth.* New York: Cambridge University Press.

Rosenau, P. M. (1992). *Post-modernism and the social sciences.* Princeton, NJ: Princeton University Press.

Rosenbaum, M., & Ronen, T. (1998). Clinical supervision from the standpoint of cognitive–behavior therapy. *Psychotherapy: Theory, Research, Practice, Training, 35*(2), 220–230.

Rosenberg, J. I. (1999). Suicide prevention: An integrated training model using affective and action-based intervention. *Professional Psychology: Research and Practice, 30*, 83–87.

Rotholz, T., & Werk, A. (1984). Student supervision: An educational process. *Clinical Supervisor, 2*, 15–27.

Roughton, R. E. (1993). Useful aspects acting out: Repetition, enactment, actualization. *Journal of the American Psychoanalytic Association, 41*, 443–472.

Roysircar-Sodowsky, G., & Maestas, M. V. (2000). Acculturation, ethnic identity, and acculturative stress: Evidence and measurement. In R. H. Dana, (Ed.), *Handbook of cross-cultural and multicultural personality assessment* (pp. 131–172). Mahwah, NJ: Erlbaum.

Rupert, P., Kozlowski, N. F., Hoffman, L A., Daniels, D. D., & Piette, J. M. (1999). Practical and ethical issues in teaching psychological testing. *Professional Psychology: Research and Practice, 30,* 209–214.

Russell, R. K., & Petrie, T. (1994). Issues in training effective supervisors. *Applied and Preventative Psychology, 3,* 27–42.

Ryan, A. S., & Hendricks, C. O. (1989). Culture and communication: Supervising the Asian and Hispanic social worker. *Clinical Supervisor, 7*(1), 27–40.

Sabnani, H. B., Ponterotto, J. G., & Borodovsky, L. G. (1991). White racial identity development and cross-cultural counselor training: A stage model. *The Counseling Psychologist, 19,* 76–102.

Saccuzzo, D. P. (2002). Liability for failure to supervise adequately: Let the master beware. *The National Register of Health Service Providers in Psychology: The Psychologist's Legal Update, 13,* 1–14.

Safran, J. D. (1993a). Breaches in the therapeutic alliance: An arena for negotiating authentic relatedness. *Psychotherapy: Research, Theory, and Practice, 30,* 11–24.

Safran, J. D. (1993b). The therapeutic alliance as a transtheoretical phenomenon: Definitional and conceptual issues. *Journal of Psychotherapy Integration, 3,* 33–49.

Safran, J. D., & Muran, J. C. (1994). Toward a working alliance between research and practice. In P. F. Talley, H. H. Strupp, & S. F. Butler (Eds.), *Psychotherapy research and practice: Bridging the gap* (pp. 206–226). New York: Basic Books.

Safran, J. D., & Muran, J. C. (Eds.) (1995). The therapeutic alliance [Special issue]. *In Session: Psychotherapy in Practice, 1,* 1–2.

Safran, J. D., & Muran, J. C. (1996). The resolution of therapeutic of ruptures in the therapeutic alliance. *Journal of Consulting and Clinical Psychology, 64,* 447–458.

Safran, J. D., & Muran, J. C. (Eds.). (1998). *The therapeutic alliance in brief psychotherapy.* Washington, DC: American Psychological Association.

Safran, J. D., & Muran, J. C. (2000a). Introduction. *Journal of Clinical Psychology/ In Session: Psychotherapy in Practice, 56*(2), 159–161.

Safran, J. D., & Muran, J. C. (2000b). *Negotiating the therapeutic relationship.* New York: Guilford Press.

Safran, J. D., & Muran, J. C. (2000c). Resolving therapeutic alliance ruptures: Diversity and integration. *Journal of Clinical Psychology/In Session: Psychotherapy in Practice, 56*(2), 233–243.

Safran, J. D., Muran, J. C., & Samstag, L. W. (1994). Resolving therapeutic alliance ruptures: A task analytic investigation. In A. O. Horvath & L. S. Greenberg (Eds.), *The working alliance: Theory, research, and practice* (pp. 225–255). New York: Wiley.

Safran, J. D., Muran, J. C., Samstag, L. W., & Stevens, C. (2001). Repairing alliance ruptures. *Psychotherapy:Theory/Research/Practice/Training, 38*(4), 406–412.

Sala, F., & Dwight, S. A. (2002). Predicting executive performance with multirater surveys: Whom you ask makes a difference. *Consulting Psychology Journal: Practice and Research, 54*(3), 166–172.

Samuel, S. E., & Gorton, G. E. (1998). National survey of psychology internship directors regarding education for prevention of psychologist–patient sexual exploitation. *Professional Psychology: Research and Practice, 29,* 86–90.

Sandler, J. (1976). Countertransference and role responsiveness. *International Review of Psycho-analysis, 3,* 43–47.

Sansbury, D. L. (1982). Developmental supervision from a skills perspective. *Counseling Psychology, 10*(1), 53–57.

Santisteban, D. A., & Mitrani, V. B. (2003). The influence of acculturation processes on the family. In K. M. Chun, P. B. Organista, & G. Marin (Eds.), *Acculturation: Advances in Theory, Measurement, and Applied Research* (pp. 121–135). Washington, DC: American Psychological Association.

Scanlon, C. (2002). Group supervision of individual cases in the training of counselors and psychotherapists: Towards a group-analytic model? *British Journal of Psychotherapy, 19*(2), 219–233.

Schank, J. A., & Skovholt, T. M. (1997). Dual-relationship dilemmas of rural and small- community psychologists. *Professional Psychology: Research and Practice, 28,* 44–49.

Schneider, K., Bugental, J. F. T., & Pierson, J. F. (Eds.). (2001). *The handbook of humanistic psychology.* Thousand Oaks, CA: Sage.

Schön, D. A. (1983). *The reflective practitioner: How professionals think in action.* New York: Basic Books.

Schön, D. A. (1987). *Educating the reflective practitioner.* San Francisco: Jossey-Bass.

Schön, D. A. (1995). The new scholarship requires a new espistemology. *Change, 27*(6), 26–35.

Schulte, D. L., Skinner, T. A., & Claiborn, C. D. (2002). Religious and spiritual issues in counseling psychology training. *The Counseling Psychologist, 30,* 118–134.

Scofield, M. E., & Yoxtheimer, L. L. (1983). Psychometric issues in the assessment of clinical competencies. *Journal of Counseling Psychology, 30,* 413–420.

Scott, K. J., Ingram, K. M., Vitanza, S. A., & Smith, N. G. (2000). Training in supervision: A survey of current practices. *The Counseling Psychologist, 28,* 403–422.

Searles, H. F. (1955). The informational value of supervisor's emotional experience. *Psychiatry, 18,* 135–146.

Seligman, M. E. P. (2002). *Authentic happiness: Using the new positive psychology to realize your potential for lasting fulfillment.* New York: Free Press.

Sells, J., Goodyear, R., Lichtenberg, J., & Polkinghorne, D. (1997). Relationship of supervisor and trainee gender to in-session verbal behavior and ratings of trainee skills. *Journal of Counseling Psychology, 44*, 1–7.

Sexton, H. C., Hembre, K., & Kvarme, G. (1996). The interaction of the alliance and therapy microprocess: A sequential analysis. *Journal of Consulting and Clinical Psychology, 64*(3), 471–480.

Shafranske, E. P. (in press). Psychology of religion in clinical and counseling psychology. In R. Paloutzian & C. Park, (Eds.), *Handbook of the psychology of religion*. New York: Guilford Press.

Shafranske, E. P., & Falender, C. A. (2004). Addressing religious and spiritual issues in clinical supervision. Manuscript in preparation.

Shakow, D. (1976). What is clinical psychology? *American Psychologist, 31*, 553–560.

Shanfield, S. B., Hetherly, V. V., & Matthews, K. L. (2001). Excellent supervision: The residents' perspective. *Journal of Psychotherapy Practice and Research, 10*, 23–27.

Shanfield, S. B., Matthews, K. L., & Hetherly, V. (1993). What do excellent psychotherapy supervisors do? *American Journal of Psychiatry, 150*(7), 1081–1084.

Shanfield, S. B., Mohl, P. C., Matthews, K. L., & Hetherly, V. (1992). Quantitative assessment of the behavior of psychotherapy supervisors. *American Journal of Psychiatry, 149*, 352–357.

Shapiro, T. (1984). On neutrality. *Journal of the American Psychoanalytic Association, 32*(2), 269–282.

Sharkin, B. S., & Birky, I. (1992). Incidental encounters between therapists and their clients. *Professional Psychology: Research and Practice, 23*, 326–328.

Shaw, B. F., & Dodson, K. S. (1988). Competency judgments in the training and evaluation of psychotherapists. *Journal of Consulting and Clinical Psychology, 56*, 666–672.

Sherman, M. D., & Thelen, M. H. (1998). Distress and professional impairment among psychologists in clinical practice. *Professional Psychology: Research and Practice, 29*, 79–85.

Sherry, P. (1991). Ethical issues in the conduct of supervision. *The Counseling Psychologist, 19*, 566–584.

Sinclair, C., Simon, N. P., & Pettifor, J. L. (1996). The history of ethical codes and licensure. In L. J. Bass, S. T. DeMers, J. R. P. Ogloff, C. Peterson, J. L. Pettifor, R. P. Reaves, et al. (Eds.), *Professional conduct and discipline in psychology* (pp. 1–15). Washington, DC: American Psychological Association and Association of State and Provincial Psychology Boards.

Skorina, J., Bissell, L., & DeSoto, C. (1990). Alcoholic psychologists: Route to recovery. *Professional Psychology: Research and Practice, 21*, 248–251.

Slimp, P. A. O., & Burian, B. K. (1994). Multiple role relationships during internship: Consequences and recommendations. *Professional Psychology: Research and Practice, 25*, 39–45.

Slovenko, R. (1980). Legal issues in psychotherapy supervision. In A. K. Hess (Ed.), *Psychotherapy supervision: Theory, research and practice* (pp. 453–473). New York: Wiley.

Smith, D., & Fitzpatrick, M. (1995). Patient–therapist boundary issues: An integrative review of theory and research. *Professional Psychology: Research and Practice, 26*, 499–505.

Smith, T. S., McGuire, J. M., Abbott, D. W., & Blau, B. I. (1991). Clinical ethical decision making: An investigation of the rationales used to justify doing less than one believes one should. *Professional Psychology: Research and Practice, 22*, 235–239.

Snyder, C. R., Michael, S. T., & Cheavens, J. S. (1999). Hope as a psychotherapeutic foundation of common factors, placebos, and expectancies. In M. A. Hubble, B. L. Duncan, & S. D. Miller (Eds.), *The heart and soul of change: What works in therapy* (pp. 179–200). Washington, DC: American Psychological Association.

Sodowsky, G. R., Kuo-Jackson, P. Y., Richardson, M. F., & Corey, A. T. (1998). Correlates of self-reported multicultural competencies: Counselor multicultural social desirability, race, social inadequacy, locus of control, racial ideology, and multicultural training. *Journal of Counseling Psychology, 45*, 256–264.

Sodowsky, G. R., Kwan, K. L. K., & Pannu, R. (1995). Ethnic identity of Asians in the United States: Conceptualization and illustrations. In J. Ponterotto, M. Casas, L. Suzuki, & C. Alexander (Eds.), *Handbook of multicultural ounseling* (pp. 123–154). Newbury Park, CA: Sage.

Sodowsky, G. R., Taffe, R. C., Gutkin, T. B., & Wise, S. L. (1994). Development of the multicultural counseling inventory: A self-report measure of multicultural competencies. *Journal of Counseling Psychology, 41*, 137–148.

Sonne, J. L. (1999). Multiple relationships: Does the new ethics code answer the right questions. In D. N. Bersoff (Ed.), *Ethical conflicts in psychology* (pp. 227–230). Washington, DC: American Psychological Association.

Sperry, L., & Shafranske, E. (in press). *Spiritual-oriented psychotherapy: Contemporary approaches*. Washington, DC: American Psychological Association.

Stadler, H. A., Willing, K. L., Eberhage, M. G., & Ward, W. H. (1988). Impairment: Implications for the counseling profession. *Journal of Counseling and Development, 66*, 258–260.

Stedman, J. M., Neff, J. A., Donohoe, C. P., Kopel, K., & Hayes, J. R. (1995). Applicant characteristics of the most desirable internship training program. *Professional Psychology: Research and Practice, 26*, 396–400.

Stein, D. M., & Lambert, M. J. (1995). Graduate training in psychotherapy: Are therapy outcomes enhanced? *Journal of Counseling and Clinical Psychology, 63*, 182–196.

Steinhelber, J., Patterson, V., Cliffe, K., & LeGoullon, M. (1984). An investigation of some relationships between psychotherapy supervision and patient change. *Journal of Clinical Psychology, 40*, 1346–1352.

Sterba, R. (1934). The fate of the ego in analytic therapy. *International Journal of Psychoanalysis, 15*, 117–126.

Sterling, M., & Bugental, J. F. (1993). The meld experience in psychotherapy supervision. *Journal of Humanistic Psychology, 33*(2), 38–48.

Stevens, S. E., Hynan, M. T., & Allen, M. (2000). A meta-analysis of common factor and specific treatment effects across the outcome domains of the phase model of psychotherapy. *Clinical Psychology: Science & Practice, 7*(3), 273–290.

Stevens-Smith, P. (1995). Gender issues in counselor education: Current status and challenges. *Counselor Education and Supervision, 34*, 283–293.

Steward, R. J., Wright, D. J., Jackson, J. D., & Jo, H. I. (1998). The relationship between multicultural counseling training and the evaluation of culturally sensitive and culturally insensitive counselors. *Journal of Multicultural Counseling and Development, 26*, 205–217.

Stigall, T. T., Bourg, E. F., Bricklin, P. M., Kovacs, A. L., Larsen, K. G., Lorion, R. P., et al. (Eds.). (1990). *Report of the Joint Council on Professional Education in Psychology*. Baton Rouge, LA: Joint Council on Professional Education in Psychology.

Stolorow, R. D., Atwood, G. E., & Orange, D. M. (2002). *Worlds of experience: Interweaving philosophical and clinical dimensions in psychoanalysis*. New York: Basic Books.

Stoltenberg, C. D. (1981). Approaching supervision from a developmental perspective: The counselor complexity model. *Journal of Counseling Psychology, 28*, 59–65.

Stoltenberg, C. D., & Delworth, U. (1987). *Supervising counselors and therapists*. San Francisco: Jossey-Bass.

Stoltenberg, C. D., & McNeill, B. W. (1997). Clinical supervision from a developmental perspective: Research and practice. In C. E. Watkins, Jr. (Ed.), *Handbook of psychotherapy supervision* (pp. 184–202). New York: Wiley.

Stoltenberg, C. D., McNeill, B. W., & Crethar, H. C. (1994). Changes in supervision as counselors and therapists gain experience: A review. *Professional Psychology: Research and Practice, 25*, 416–449.

Stoltenberg, C. D., McNeill, B. W., & Delworth, U. (1998). *IDM Supervision: An integrated developmental model for supervising counselors and therapists*. San Francisco: Jossey-Bass.

Stone, G. L. (1980). Effects of experience on supervisor planning. *Journal of Counseling Psychology, 27*, 84–88.

Stone, G. L. (1997). Multiculturalism as a context for supervision. In D. B. Pope-Davis & H. L. K. Coleman (Eds.), *Multicultural counseling competencies: Assessment, education and anecdotal training* (pp. 263–289). Thousand Oaks, CA: Sage.

Storm, C. L., Todd, T. C., Sprenkle, D. H., & Morgan, M. M. (2001). Gaps between MFT supervision assumptions and common practice: Suggested best practices. *Journal of Marital and Family Therapy, 27*(2), 227–239.

Stout, C. E. (1987). The role of ethical standards in the supervision of psychotherapy. *The Clinical Supervisor, 5*(1), 89–97.

Stratford, R. (1994). A competency approach to educational psychology practice: The implications for quality. *Educational and Child Psychology, 11,* 21–28.

Stricker, G. (1990). Self-disclosure and psychotherapy. In G. Stricker & M. Fisher (Eds.), *Self-disclosure in the therapeutic relationship* (pp. 277–289). New York: Plenum Press.

Stricker, G., & Trierweiler, S. J. (1995). The local clinical scientist: A bridge between science and practice. *American Psychologist, 50,* 995–1002.

Stromberg, C. D., Haggarty, D. J., Leibenleft, R. F., McMillian, M. H., Mishkin, B., Rubin, B. L., et al. (1988). *The psychologists' legal handbook.* Washington, DC: Council for the National Register of Health Service Providers in Psychology.

Strupp, H. H. (1980). Success and failure in time-limited psychotherapy: Further evidence (Comprison 4). *Archives of General Psychiatry, 37,* 947–954.

Sue, D. W. (2001). Multidimensional facets of cultural competence. *The Counseling Psychologist, 29,* 790–821.

Sue, D. W., Arredondo, P., & McDavis, R. J. (1992). Multicultural counseling competencies and standards: A call to the profession. *Journal of Counseling and Development, 70,* 477–486.

Sue, D. W., Bernier, J. E., Durran, A., Feinberg, L., Pedersen, P., Smith, E. J., & Vasquez-Nuttall, E. (1982). Position paper: Cross-cultural counseling competencies. *The Counseling Psychologist, 10,* 45–52.

Sue, D. W., & Sue, D. (1990). *Counseling the culturally different: Theory and practice.* New York: Wiley.

Sue, S., Zane, N., & Young, K. (1994). Research on psychotherapy with culturally diverse populations. In A. E. Bergin & S. L. Garfield (Eds.), *Handbook of psychotherapy and behavior change* (4th ed., pp. 783–817). New York: Wiley.

Sullivan, H. S. (1954). *The psychiatric interview.* New York: Norton.

Sullivan, J. R., Ramirez, E., Rae, W. A., Razo, N. P., & George, C. A. (2002). Factors contributing to breaking confidentiality with adolescent clients: A survey of pediatric psychologists. *Professional Psychology: Research and Practice, 33,* 396–401.

Sumerall, S. W., Lopez, S. J., & Oehlert, M. E. (2000). *Competency-based education and training in psychology.* Springfield, IL: Charles C. Thomas.

Sutter, E., McPherson, R. H., & Geeseman, R. (2002). Contracting for supervision. *Professional Psychology: Research and Practice, 33,* 495–498.

Suzuki, L. A., McRae, M. B., & Short, E. L. (2001). The facets of cultural competence: Searching outside the box. *The Counseling Psychologist, 29,* 842–849.

Taibbi, R. (1995). *Clinical supervision.* Milwaukee, WI: Families International, Inc.

Takushi, R., & Uomoto, J. M. (2001). The clinical interview from a multicultural perspective. In L. A. Suzuki, J. G. Ponterotto, & P. J. Meller (Eds.). *Handbook* of multicultural assessment: Clinical, psychological, and educational applications, (2nd ed., pp. 47–66). San Francisco: Jossey-Bass.

Talbert, F. S., & Pipes, R. B. (1988). Informed consent for psychotherapy: Content analysis of selected forms. *Professional Psychology: Research and Practice*, 19, 131–132.

Talbot, N. L. (1995). Unearthing shame in the supervisory relationship. *American Journal of Psychotherapy*, 49(3), 338–349.

Talen, M. R., & Schindler, N. (1993). Goal-directed supervision plans: A model for trainee supervision and evaluation. *The Clinical Supervisor*, 11(2), 77–88.

Tarasoff v. Regents of the University of California, 13 Cal.3d 177, 529 P.2d 533 (1974), vacated, 17 Cal.3d 425, 551 P.2d 334 (1976).

Task Force on Promotion and Dissemination of Psychological Procedures. (1995). Training in and dissemination of empirically-validated psychological treatments. *The Clinical Psychologist*, 48(1), 3–23.

Taylor, C. (1989). *Sources of self: The making of the modern identity*. Cambridge, MA: Harvard University Press.

Taylor, L., & Adelman, H. S. (1995). Reframing the confidentiality dilemma to work in children's best interests. In D. N. Bersoff (Ed.), *Ethical conflicts in psychology* (pp. 198–201). Washington, DC: American Psychological Association.

Tedesco, J. F. (1982). Premature termination of psychology interns. *Professional Psychology:Research and Practice*, 13, 695–698.

Teitelbaum, S. H. (1990). Supertransference: The role of the supervisor's blind spots. *Psychoanalytic Psychology*, 7, 243–258.

Tepper, B. J. (2000). Consequences of abusive supervision. *Academy of Management Journal*, 43, 178–190.

Thompson, M. G. (1996). Freud's concept of neutrality. *Contemporary Psychoanalysis*, 32, 25–42.

Tipton, R. M. (1996). Education and training. In L. J. Bass, S. T. DeMers, J. R. P. Ogloff, C. Peterson, J. L. Pettifor, R. P. Reaves, et al. (Eds.), *Professional conduct and discipline in psychology* (pp. 17–37). Washington, DC: American Psychological Association and Association of State and Provincial Psychology Boards.

Tishler, C. L., Gordon, L B., & Landry-Meyer, L. (2000). Managing the violent patient: A guide for psychologists and other mental health professionals. *Professional Psychology: Research and Practice*, 31, 34–41.

Tjeltveit, A. C. (1986). The ethics of value conversion in psychotherapy: Appropriate and inappropriate therapist influence on client values. *Clinical Psychology Review*, 6, 515–537.

Tomlinson-Clarke, S. (2000). Assessing outcomes in a multicultural training course: A qualitative study. *Counseling Psychology Quarterly*, 13(2), 221–231.

Torres-Rivera, E., Phan, L. T., Maddux, C., Wilbur, M. P., & Garrett, M. T. (2001). Process versus content: Integrating personal awareness and counselling skills to meet the multicultural challenge of the twenty-first century. *Counselor Education and Supervision, 41,* 28.

Trimble, J. E. (1991). The mental health service and training needs of American Indians. In H. F. Myers, P. Wohlford, L. P. Guzman, & R. J. Echemendia (Eds.), *Ethnic minority perspectives on clinical training and services in psychology* (pp. 43–48). Washington, DC: American Psychological Association.

Trimble, J. E. (2003). Introduction: Social change and acculturation. In K. M. Chun, P. B. Organista, & G. Marin (Eds.), *Acculturation: Advances in theory, measurement, and applied research* (pp. 3–13). Washington, DC: American Psychological Association.

Tryon, G. S., & Winograd, G. (2002). Goal consensus and collaboration. In J. C. Norcross (Ed.), *Psychotherapy relationships that work* (pp. 106–122). New York: Oxford University Press.

Tyler, J. D., Sloan, L. L., & King, A. R. (2000). Psychotherapy supervision practices of academic faculty: A national survey. *Psychotherapy: Theory, Research, Practice, 17*(1), 98–101.

Tymchuk, A. J. (1981). Ethical decision making and psychological treatment. *Journal of Psychiatric Treatment and Evaluation, 3,* 507–513.

Tymchuk, A. J. (1986). Guidelines for ethical decision-making. *Canadian Psychology, 27,* 36–43.

Tymchuk, A. J., Drapkin, R., Major-Kingsley, S., Ackerman, A. B., Coffman, E. W., & Baum, M. S. (1995). Ethical decision making and psychologists' attitudes toward training in ethics. In D. N. Bersoff (Ed.), *Ethical conflicts in psychology* (pp. 94–98). Washington, DC: American Psychological Association.

Tyson, R., & Renik, O. (1986). Countertransference in theory and practice. *Journal of the American Psychoanalytic Association, 34,* 699–708.

Ulman, K. H. (2001). Unwitting exposure of the therapist. *Journal of Psychotherapy Practice Research, 10*(1), 14–22.

Urch, G. E. (1975). A philosophical perspective on competency-based education. In R. T. Utz & L. D. Leonard (Eds.), *The foundations of competency-based education* (pp. 30–47). Dubuque, IA: Kendall/Hunt Publishing.

U.S. Department of Education, National Center for Education Statistics. (2002). *Defining and assessing learning: Exploring competency-based initiatives,* NCES 2002–159, prepared by E. A. Jones and R. A. Voorhees, with K. Paulson, for the Council of the National Postsecondary Education Cooperative Working Group on Competency-Based Initiatives. Washington, DC: Author

U.S. Department of Health and Human Services. (1999). *Mental Health: A Report of the Surgeon General—Executive Summary.* Rockville, MD: U.S. Department of Health and Human Services, Substance Abuse and Mental Health Services Administration, Center for Mental Health Services, National Institutes of Health, National Institute of Mental Health.

U.S. Equal Employment Opportunity Commission. Executive Summary: Compliance Manual, Section 902, Definition of "Disability". Retrieved February 16, 2004, from http://www.eeoc./gov/policy/docs/902sum.html

Vacha-Haase, T. (1995). *Impaired graduate students in APA-accredited clinical, counseling, and school psychology programs.* Unpublished doctoral dissertation, Texas A&M University, College Station, Texas.

VandeCreek, L., & Knapp, S. (1993). *Tarasoff and beyond: Legal and clinical considerations in the treatment of life-endangering patients* (rev. ed.). Sarasota, FL: Professional Resource Press.

VandeCreek, L., & Knapp, S. (2001). *Tarasoff and beyond: Legal and clinical considerations in the treatment of life-endangering patients* (3rd ed.). Sarasota, FL: Professional Resource Press.

VanWagoner, S. L., Gelso, C. J., Hayes, J. A., & Diemer, R. A. (1991). Countertransference and the reputedly excellent therapist. *Psychotherapy, 28,* 411–421.

Vasquez, M. J. T. (1988). Counselor–client sexual contact: Implications for ethics training. *Journal of Counseling and Development, 67,* 238–241.

Vasquez, M. J. T. (1992). Psychologist as clinical supervisor: Promoting ethical practice. *Professional Psychology: Research and Practice, 23,* 196–202.

Veach, P. M. (2001). Conflict and counterproductivity in supervision—When relationships are less than ideal: Comment on Nelson and Friedlander (2001) and Gray et al. (2001). *Journal of Counseling Psychology, 48,* 396–400.

Vespia, K. M., Heckman-Stone, C., & Delworth, U. (2002). Describing and facilitating effective supervision behavior in counseling trainees. *Psychotherapy: Theory, Research, Practice, Training, 39*(1), 56–65.

Voorhees, A. B. (2001). Creating and implementing competency-based learning models. *New Directions for Institutional Research, 110,* 83–95.

Voorhees, R. A. (2001a). Competency-based learning models: A necessary future. *New Directions for Institutional Research, 110,* 5–13.

Voorhees, R. A. (Ed.). (2001b). Measuring what matters: Competency-based learning models in higher education. *New Directions for Institutional Research, 110,* 1–116.

Ward, L. G., Friedlander, M. L., Schoen, L. G., & Klein, J. G. (1985). Strategic self-presentation in supervision. *Journal of Counseling Psychology, 32,* 111–118.

Warech, M. A., Smither, J. W., Reilly, R. R., Millsap, R. E., & Reilly, S. P. (1998). Self-monitoring and 360-degree ratings. *Leadership Quarterly, 9*(4), 449–473.

Watkins, C. E., Jr. (1990). Development of the psychotherapy supervisor. *Psychotherapy, 27,* 553–560.

Watkins, C. E., Jr. (1990). The effects of counselor self-disclosure: A research review. *The Counseling Psychologist, 18,* 477–500.

Watkins, C. E., Jr. (1992). Reflections on the preparation of psychotherapy supervisors. *Journal of Clinical Psychology, 48,* 145–147.

Watkins, C. E., Jr. (1993). Development of the psychotherapy supervisor: Concepts, assumptions, and hypotheses of the supervisor complexity model. *American Journal of Psychotherapy, 47,* 58–74.

Watkins, C. E., Jr. (1995a). Psychotherapy supervision in the 1990's: Some observations and reflections. *American Journal of Psychotherapy, 49,* 568–581.

Watkins, C. E., Jr. (1995b). Psychotherapy supervisor and supervise: Developmental models and research nine years later. *Clinical Psychology Review, 15*(7), 647–680.

Watkins, C. E., Jr. (1997a). Defining psychotherapy supervision and understanding supervision functioning. In C. E. Watkins, Jr. (Ed.), *Handbook of psychotherapy supervision* (pp. 3–10). New York: Wiley.

Watkins, C. E., Jr. (Ed.). (1997b). *Handbook of psychotherapy supervision.* New York: Wiley.

Watkins, C. E., Jr. (1997c). The ineffective psychotherapy supervisor: Some reflections about bad behaviors, poor process, and offensive outcomes. *The Clinical Supervisor, 16*(1), 163–180.

Watkins, C. E., Jr. (1997d). Some concluding thoughts about psychotherapy supervision. In C. E. Watkins, Jr. (Ed.), *Handbook of psychotherapy supervision.* New York: Wiley.

Watson, J. C., & Greenberg, L. S. (2000). Alliance ruptures and repairs in experiential therapy. *Journal of Clinical Psychology/In Session: Psychotherapy in Practice, 56*(2), 175–186.

Weiss, B. J. (1991). Toward a competency-based core curriculum in professional psychology: A critical history. In R. Peterson (Ed.), *Core curriculum in professional psychology* (pp. 13–21). Washington, DC: American Psychological Association.

Weiss, J., Sampson, H., & Mount Zion Psychotherapy Research Group. (1986). *The psychoanalytic process.* New York: Guilford Press.

Weisz, J. R., & Weiss, B. (1991). Studying the "referability" of child clinical problems. *Journal of Consulting and Clinical Psychology, 59,* 266–273.

Welch, B. L. (2000). Preface. In Hedges, L. E., *Facing the challenge of liability in psychotherapy* (pp. xiv). Northvale, NJ: Jason Aronson.

Welfel, E. R. (1992). Psychologist as ethics educator: Successes, failures, and unanswered questions. *Professional Psychology: Research and Practice, 23,* 182–189.

Welfel, E. R. (1995). Psychologist as ethics educator: Successes, failures, and unanswered questions. In D. N. Bersoff (Ed.), *Ethical conflicts in psychology* (pp. 113–114). Washington, DC: American Psychological Association.

Wells, M. G., Burlingame, G. M., Lambert, M. J., Hoag, M. J., & Hope, C. A. (1996). Conceptualization and measurement of patient change during psychotherapy: Development of the outcome questionnaire and youth outcome questionnaire. *Psychotherapy: Theory, Research, Practice, Training, 33*(2), 275–283.

Werstlein, P. O., & Borders, L. D. (1997). Group process variables in group supervision. *Journal for Specialists in Group Work, 22,* 120–136.

Wester, S. R., & Vogel, D. L. (2002). Working with the masculine mystique: Male gender role conflict, counseling self-efficacy, and the training of male psychologists. *Professional Psychology: Research and Practice, 33,* 370–376.

Whaley, A. L. (2001). Cultural mistrust: An important psychological construct for diagnosis and treatment of African Americans. *Professional Psychology: Research and Practice, 32*, 555–562.

Whiston, S. C., & Emerson, S. (1989). Ethical implications for supervisors in counseling of trainees. *Counselor Education and Supervision, 28*, 319–325.

Williams, E. N., Judge, A. B., Hill, C. E., & Hoffman, M. A. (1997). Experiences of novice therapists in prepracticum: Trainees', clients', and supervisors' perceptions of therapists' personal reactions and management strategies. *Journal of Counseling Psychology. 44*, 390–399.

Williams, E. N., Polster, D., Grizzard, M. B., Rockenbaugh, J., & Judge, Ann B. (2003). What happens when therapists feel bored or anxious? A qualitative study of distracting self-awareness and therapists' management strategies. *Journal of Contemporary Psychotherapy, 33*(1), 5–18.

Williams, J. R., & Johnson, M. A. (2000). Self-supervisor agreement: The influence of feedback seeking on the relationship between self and supervisor ratings of performance. *Journal of Applied Social Psychology, 30*(2), 275–292.

Wise, P. S., Lowery, S., & Silverglade, L. (1989). Personal counseling for counselors in training: Guidelines for supervisors. *Counselor Education & Supervision, 28*(4), 326–336.

Wisnia, C. S., & Falender, C. (1999). Training in cultural competence. *APPIC Newsletter Journal of Training, 12*.

Wisnia, C. S., & Falender, C. A. (2004). Training in cultural competency. Manuscript in preparation.

Wong, L. C. J., & Wong, P. T. P. (2002). *What helps and what hinders in multicultural supervision: From the perspective of supervisors.* Paper presented at the convention of the American Psychological Association during the roundtable discussion "Hot Topics in Clinical Supervision and Training," Chicago, IL.

Wood, B. J., Klein, S., Cross, H., Lammers, C. J., & Elliott, J. K. (1985). Impaired practitioners: Psychologists' options about prevalence, and proposals for intervention. *Professional Psychology, 16*, 843–850.

Woods, P. J., & Ellis, A. (1997). Supervision in rational emotive behavior therapy. In C. E. Watkins, Jr. (Ed.), *Handbook of psychotherapy supervision* (pp. 101–113). New York: Wiley.

Woody, R. H. (1999). Domestic violations of confidentiality. *Professional Psychology: Research and Practice, 30*, 607–610.

Worthen, V. E., & Isakson, R. L. (2000). *Supervision Outcomes Survey.* Unpublished scale.

Worthen, V. E., & Isakson, R. L. (2002). *Using client outcome data in supervision.* Paper presented at the annual meeting of the American Psychological Association, Chicago, IL.

Worthen, V. E., & McNeill, B. W. (1996). A phenomenological investigation of "good" supervision events. *Journal of Counseling Psychology, 43*, 25–34.

Worthington, E. L. (1984a). Empirical investigations of supervision of counselors as they gain experience. *Journal of Counseling Psychology, 31*, 63–75.

Worthington, E. L. (1984b). Use of trait labels in counseling supervision by experienced and inexperienced supervisors. *Professional Psychology: Research and Practice, 15*, 457–461.

Worthington, E. L. (1987). Changes in supervision as counselors and supervisors gain experience: A review. *Professional Psychology: Research and Practice, 4*, 189–208.

Worthington, E. L., & Roehlke, H. J. (1979). Effective supervision as perceived by beginning counselors-in-training. *Journal of Counseling Psychology, 26*, 64–73.

Worthington, R. L., Mobley, M., Franks, R. P., Tan, J. A., & Andreas, J. (2000). Multicultural counseling competencies: Verbal content, counselor attributions, and social desirability. *Journal of Counseling Psychology, 47*, 460–468.

Worthington, R. L., Tan, J. A., & Poulin, K. (2002). Ethically questionable behaviors among supervisees: An exploratory investigation. *Ethics & Behavior, 12*, 323–351.

Wulf, J., & Nelson, M. L. (2000). Experienced psychologists' recollections of internship supervision and its contributions to their development. *The Clinical Supervisor, 19*(2), 123–145.

Yourman, D. B., & Farber, B. A. (1996). Nondisclosure and distortion in psychotherapy supervision. *Psychotherapy, 33*, 567–575.

Yutrzenka, B. A. (1995). Making a case for training in ethnic and cultural diversity in increasing treatment efficacy. *Journal of Consulting & Clinical Psychology, 63*(2), 197–206.

Zane, N., & Sue, S. (1991). Culturally responsive mental health services for Asian Americans: Treatment and training issues. In H. F. Myers, P. Wohlford, L. P. Guzman, & R. J. Echemendia (Eds.), *Ethnic minority perspectives on clinical training and services in psychology* (pp. 49–58). Washington, DC: American Psychological Association.

Zetzel, E. R. (1956). Current concepts of transference. *International Journal of Psychoanalysis, 37*, 369–376.

Zimmerman, T. S., & Haddock, S. A. (2001). The weave of gender and culture in the tapestry of a family therapy training program: Promoting social justice in the practice of family therapy. *Journal of Feminist Family Therapy, 12*(2–3), 1–31.

INDEX

335

program exit criteria as, 62–63
of psychologist
  defined, 39
  history and current conceptions
    of, 59–63
of supervisor, 72–74
  assessment of, 76
  core characteristics in, 74
  of novices, 74
  requirements for, 73
  supraordinate factors of, 73–74
  training for, 72–73
of supervisors, 149
technical, 80
of trainee, 67–75
  definition of, 67
  measurement of, 68
  self-assessment in, 69–70
  service population and, 71–72
in training and curricula
  evaluation of, 60
  guidelines for, 60–61
Confidentiality
  breach of
    by supervisees, 156
    by supervisors, 155
  dilemmas and breach of, 153
  "domestic violations" of, 164
  duty to warn and, 189
  informed consent and, 162
  limitations, 162, 163
  privilege and, 163
  in supervision, 163–164
  with minors, 162
Conflict resolution
  supervisors in, 48–49
  trainees in, 49
Consent
  informed (See Informed consent)
  in intern–supervisor sexual relation-
    ships, 171
Consultation
  in risk management, 194
  for trainee with problematic behav-
    ior, 219
Contract for supervision, 161
  description, 208–211
Countertransference
  characterization of, 82–83
  enactments in
    parallel process and, 84–85

intersubjectivity of relationships, 84
neutrality versus subjectivity and,
  83–84
as reactions to supervisees, 92
supervisees on, 86
in supervisee–supervisor relationship,
  103–104
in supervision, 85–88
  boundary between psychotherapy
    in, 87
  consultation for, 87–88
  exploration of, 87
supervisor
  benefits of, 109
  resolution of, 109
  sources of, 92–93
  therapeutic alliance and, 87,
    98–99
therapist, boundaries and, 113
treatment effects and, 85
Cultural competence, 52–53, 141
  enhancing, 146–149
  knowledge of and self-respect for
    one's own culture, 136
  negative incidents and, 52
  in supervision, 51, 52–53, 159
  supervisor deficiency in
    and diversity training, 119
Cultural provincialism, 120
Culture
  approach to in self and other,
    127–128
  aspects of, 127
  emic conception of, 116
  ethical decision making and, 181
  etic conception of, 116
  Falicov parameters of, 126–127
  fixed dimensions of, 126
  multidimensional approach to,
    125–126
  narrative of contexts in, 126
  parameters of
    forming membership in, 126
  race and, 120
  self-disclosure and, 51
  worldview in, 127

Developmental models of supervision
  empirical support and, 15–16
  integrated, 10–11, 12–13

Developmental models of supervision, *continued*
    Integrated Developmental Model, 10–13
    multicultural, 15
    in quality supervision, 42
    research in, 15
    shortcomings of, 15
    for supervisor, 11, 13–15, 74
Disability. *See also* Trainee with problematic behavior
    definition of, *215*
    individual with
        definition of, *133–134*
        training programs for psychologists, 134
Discrimination model of supervision, 17–18
    progression from clinician to supervisor in, 76
Dismissal
    criteria for, judicial precedents and, 219
    rates of, 218–219
    of trainee, 218
Diversity. *See also* Multicultural diversity
    appreciation of, 231
    APA on, *31–32, 33*
    education in, 117, 118
        barriers to, 120–121
    integration into training, 119–121
        barriers to, 119–121
        context change for, 121
    self-understanding and, 32
    within-group *vs.* between-group differences in, 120–121
Diversity competence, 31–33, 149
    aging and geriatric considerations in, 134
    barriers, 120
    definition of, 32–33, 115, 125
    emic parameters of, in training, 129–131
    enhancement of
        educational diversity experience in, 135
        general counseling competence in, 135–136
        personal experience in, 135
    interpersonal nonoppressive development model of

        adaptation in, 140
        exploration in, 141
        noncongruence in, 140–141
    minority identity development model in
        integration of White/Western values in, 139
    models of, 139–141
        limitations of, 141
    racial identity development in, 138
        as cognitive developmental continuum, 140
    training issues in disabilities, 133–134
    and treatment of mental illness, 33
    White racial identity development model in, 139
        vs. minority identity development model, 139–140
Documentation
    letters of recommendation as, 192–193
    retention of, 191–192
    by supervisor of supervisory work, *191*
Dual relationships, 153. *See also* Multiple and dual relationships
    decision-making model for
        internship, 179
        supervisor, 178
    in internship year, 167
Due process
    dismissal of trainee and, 218
    evaluation and, 214
    informed consent and, 161
    supervisee rights and, 159–160
Duty-to-warn, 188–190
    steps, 190

Emic factors
    examples of, 129
    in supervisor–supervisee interactions, 130
Emic parameters
    client–therapist factors in, 130
    in diversity competency training, 129–131
Emotion
    in ethics training, 181, 183–184
Epstein, R. M.
    on competency, 64

Multicultural competence, *continued*
    incorporation of diversity into supervisory process, 148
    "in-the-box/out-of-the-box" exercise in, 148
    maps in, 146, 147, 148
    progression in, 148–149
    through description of development of personal cultural identification, 148
    through enhancement of worldviews, 148
    in case conceptualization, 135
    minimal for practice, *123–124*
    religious/spiritual beliefs and values, 124
    self-awareness in
        dimensions of, 123, 137
Multicultural counseling training
    client–therapist interaction in
        emic factors in, 130
    developmental model of
        for supervisees, 137–138
    impact on White graduate level trainees, 136
    supervisor–supervisee interaction in
        emic factors in, 130–131
Multicultural diversity. *See also* Diversity
    education about in supervision, 117
    training in, 115
        current state of, 117–118
        deficiency in, 117–118
Multicultural supervision
    defined, *128*
Multicultural supervisory competence
    checklist for, 143, 249–252
    developmental stages in, 138
    program for, assessment of, 142–143
    steps toward, 142–145
    supervisee multicultural competency assessment in, 143–144
Multiple and dual relationships
    APA on, *164, 165–166*
    Association for Counselor Education and Supervision on, *164*
    boundary behaviors and, 166–167
    definition, 164
    during internship, 167
    dynamics of, 165

    feminist-therapy and, 166
    problem-solving models, 176–177
    sexual relationships and, 167–168

Outcomes
    of client evaluation, 202–203
    of supervision, 6–7

Parallel process
    of therapeutic and supervisory relationships, 84–85, 111–112
Patrick, K. D., *173–174*
Peck v. the Counseling Service of Addison County, 190
Peer supervision
    of supervisors, 229
Personal factors
    countertransference
        in psychotherapy, 82–85
        in supervision, 85–88
    self-disclosure, 88–92
    in supervision
        competencies in addressing, 92–93
        countertransferance, 85–88
    values, 81–82
Personal growth
    in supportive relationship, 40
Personalismo, 129
Practice improvement models
    supervision and, 228
Problematic behavior
    prevention of, 220–221
    remediation, 221–223
    in supervisors, 220
    in trainees, 215–220 (*See also* Trainee with problematic behavior)
Process-based models
    discrimination model, 17–18
    systems-based, 18–19
    usefulness of, 19
Process evaluation of teaching and supervision (PETS) instrument
    in competency-based supervision, 24, 26–27
Program evaluation, 225
Psychiatrist
    competency in, 64

Quality supervision
    supportive relationship in, 38–42

Race
    in clinical training and supervision,
        119, 146, 148
    culture and, 120, 136
    supervisor–supervisee relationship
        and, 142
Racial identity
    development, 138–142
    in multiculturally competent counsel-
        ing, 121, 124
Racial minorities
    acculturation and therapist roles
        with, 128
Rational-emotive therapy
    supervision and, 9–10
Reflective skills, 230, 232
Reflexive skills, 230
Religion
    in clinical training and supervision,
        119, 124, 127
Remediation
    Association for Counselor Education
        and Supervision guidelines for,
        221–222
    steps in, 222–223
    for trainee with problematic behav-
        ior, 220
Research
    on supervision, 38–42
Risk assessment, 190
Risk management, 193–194
Role conflict
    in supervision, 174, 265–267
Roles
    of supervisor, 151–152
        dual, *173–174*
        multiple, 165–167
Ruptures in alliance
    causes of, 101–102
    confrontation type, 105
    negative reactions and, 98–99
    stages in repair of, 105–109
        exploration of thoughts and feel-
            ings in, 106
        interpersonal dynamics in,
            106–107
        supervision role in, 107

transition of therapist in, 106
    withdrawal type, 105

Science
    practice and, 33–34
Self-assessment
    of competence, 75, 158
    competency and, 64
    by supervisee
        self–reflective, 29
    by supervisor, 76, 229
        metacognition and, 29
        of knowledge and skills, 257–
            263
Self-awareness
    cultural
        definition of, 122
Self-disclosure
    APA on, 173
    culture and, 51
    defined, 88
    dual relationship and, 173–174
    feminist-therapy and, 166
    framework for, 173
    guidelines regarding, 89
    in intake, 129
    intentional, 88–91
        countertransferance in, 89
        practice guidelines for, 89–90
        by therapist, 88–89
    levels of, 172–173
    nondisclosure and, 50–51
    by supervisee, 49–51, 91–92
    in supervision, 88
    by supervisor, 41, 49, 50
        impact of, 91
    unintentional, 91–92
Self-monitoring, 75–76
Setting
    "cultural competence" of, 129
Sexual attraction issues
    of client for supervisee, 170
    feelings of *vs.* acting out, 175
    sexual-boundary risk and, 170
    student understanding of, 168–169
    training in, 169–170
Sexual harassment
    of supervisees, 168, 170
Sexuality
    as continuum, 133

Sexual misconduct
client–therapist
prevention of, 170–171
feelings of sexual attraction and,
168–170
intern–supervisor, 171–172
prevalence of, 167–168
risk factors for, 170, 253–256
Sexual orientation
in clinical training and supervision,
120
in multicultural diversity training,
131–133
understanding of working models of,
133
Sexual relationships
APA on, *165*
malpractice and, 188
Shame
of supervisee
addressing of, 111
causes of, 110–11
hidden manifestations of, 111
Shuffer v. Trustees of California State University and Colleges, 219
Spiritual values, 119, 124, 127
Standard of care
malpractice suits and, 185, 186
Students
moral issues and, 152
Styles
of supervision, 41
Suicide/suicide attempt
frequency for trainee cases, 190
trainee preparation for, 190–191
Summative evaluation, 28, 80
Supervisee–client alliance. *See also* Therapeutic alliance
countertransferance in, 103–104
negative, 99–100
negative reaction to client in, 98–99
ruptures in, 100–109
causes of, 101–102
countertransferance in, 103–104
identification of causes for,
101–104
metacommunication in, 104–105
precipitation of, 102–103
shame and, 110
stages in repair of, 105–109
types of, 105

Supervisees
assessment of competency of, 67–71
in effective supervision, 43
disclosure, 49
nondisclosure, 50–51
preferred by supervisors, 42–43
role induction, 42, 161
on supervision, 40
Supervision
approaches to, 7–20
competency-based, 20–34 (*See also* Competency-based supervision)
developmental, 10–17
integrative, 232
process-based, 17–19
psychotherapy-based, 9–10
systems-based, 18–19
as a distinct competency area, 7
best characterization of, 56, 57
competence in, 5–6
contract, 161
critical incidents in, 48
defined, *3*
developmental models of, 10–17, 42
discrimination model of, 17–18, 76
distinguished from therapy,
174–175
goals in, 72
high-quality
factors in, 48–56
historical overview of, 8–9
integration of theory and practice
in, 228
master–apprentice model of, 8
negative, 109
analysis of, 42, 47–48
outcomes of, 6–7
pillars of, 3–4
preferred formats in, 54–56
group, 54, 55–56
individual case consultation, 54,
55
videotaped, 54, 55
vs. clinical practice, 227
present status of, 19–20
problematic
games in, 44–45
handling of, 45–46
process and outcomes of, 8–9
psychotherapy approaches to, 9–10

Transgender issues
in clinical training and supervision, 119–120
Turn exchange
in training, 129

U.S. Department of Health and Human Services
on diversity competency in treatment, 33

Values
modeling of, 31
in psychotherapy, 82

superordinate
appreciation of diversity, 31–33
ethical values-based practice, 31
integrity of supervisor-supervisee relationship, 30
science-informed practice, 33–34
Videotaping, 54, 55, 56, 57

Working alliance, 40–41, 237–241
supervisory styles and, 41
Worldview
awareness, 145
defined, 127
"Worst case thinking"
in risk management, 194

ABOUT THE AUTHORS

Carol Falender, PhD, is an adjunct professor at Pepperdine University and clinical professor in the Department of Psychology at the University of California, Los Angeles. Dr. Falender has been assistant director of training and then director of training for over 20 years at American Psychological Association (APA)-accredited community mental health programs. She spent 9 years as director of training, chief psychologist, and director of research at Saint John's Health Center. She has served as secretary of Division 37 (Child, Youth, and Family Services) of the APA, chair of the California Psychological Association Division of Education and Training, and has been a longstanding member of the Los Angeles County Psychological Association Ethics Committee. She received the Outstanding Supervisor of the Year award from the California Psychological Association, Division of Education and Training. She lectures widely and provides consultation on the topic of supervision, and she also contributes scholarship in this clinical specialty area.

Dr. Falender is a practicing clinician and clinical supervisor, with interests in assessment and treatment of children, adolescents, families, co-occurring disorders, ethics, diversity competency, juvenile corrections, interventions for children whose parent has been diagnosed with cancer, school consultation, and all aspects of supervision of psychology trainees.

Edward P. Shafranske, PhD, ABPP, is a professor of psychology, Charles and Harriet Luckman Distinguished Teaching Fellow (1997–2002), and director of the doctoral program in clinical psychology at Pepperdine University. A fellow of the American Psychological Association (APA), Dr. Shafranske has been the president of APA's Division 36 (Psychology of Religion), a member of the APA Council of Representatives, and the chair of the California Psychological Association Division of Education and Training. He served as editor of *Religion and the Clinical Practice of Psychology*, associate editor of the *Encyclopedia of Psychology* (APA, 2000), and coeditor of the forthcoming *Spiritually Oriented Psychotherapy* (APA).

A practicing clinician and clinical supervisor, his theoretical and research interests focus on integrative approaches to the psychotherapeutic process, competency-based supervision, religion and spirituality as clinical variables, and the contributions of neuroscience to psychological treatment. In addition to academic and research activities, Dr. Shafranske maintains a private practice in clinical psychology in Irvine, California.